Patrick Leigh Fermor

~~it~~ for several years; and, by the time ~~its time its first~~, its

                    was   new
scent ~~too gone~~ cold, ~~New travels and~~ projects ~~supervened~~

~~too~~ cropped up and the idea was abandoned for good.

            Or so I thought. Twenty years ~~rolled by and~~ until, only)
                                                rushed by
~~   ~~. ~~Then~~, a few years ago, the American

~~magazine~~

magazine Holiday asked me to write an article on the plea-

- sures of Walking. A short account of my pre-war trek,

I thought, accompanied by suitable reflections, might fit

the bill. I set to work, in London this time. But it was much
        long and
too ~~rambling~~ a theme for so small a compass, and the
attempt was damned from the start: compression and pruning, usual-
-ly so salutary, were mortal here. NO PARA.

                                                        almost
§ Meagre and plethoric by turns and lopped ~~almost beyond~~
into incomprehensibility ~~the~~ narrative grew slower with every pline
~~   sibility,~~
            and finally ~~stopped altogether on)~~
~~   ~~ the Hungarian approaches to Transylvania.
I (A dozen pages of
~~This~~ unnatural prose ~~   ~~
had frogmarched the story further /
~~dozen pages~~ than the entire distance covered by

The present book). ~~   ~~
~~   ~~
            spite of
But in ~~   ~~ these reverses, those old travels had come back
~~   ~~
to life in my mind and suddenly I was

Two manuscript pages from an early draft of an introduction to *A Time of Gifts*. Jock Murray would show these pages to anyone asking why the next book by Patrick Leigh Fermor was taking so long. *(Images courtesy of John Murray Collection)*

Patrick Leigh Fermor

An Adventure

ARTEMIS COOPER

JOHN MURRAY

First published in Great Britain in 2012 by John Murray (Publishers)
An Hachette UK Company

1

© Artemis Cooper 2012

The right of Artemis Cooper to be identified as the Author
of the Work has been asserted by her in accordance with the
Copyright, Designs and Patents Act 1988.

Maps drawn by Rodney Paull

A CIP catalogue record for this title
is available from the British Library

ISBN 978-0-7195-5449-0
Ebook ISBN 978-1-84854-670-7

Typeset in Bembo by Palimpsest Book Production Limited,
Falkirk, Stirlingshire

Printed and bound by Clays Ltd, St Ives plc

John Murray policy is to use papers that are natural, renewable and
recyclable products and made from wood grown in sustainable forests.
The logging and manufacturing processes are expected to conform to
the environmental regulations of the country of origin.

John Murray (Publishers)
338 Euston Road
London NW1 3BH

www.johnmurray.co.uk

For Adam and Nella
live well

Contents

Maps

A Note on Names

Patrick Leigh Fermor was always known as Paddy, except in Greece, where he was called Mihali. Leigh Fermor, or Fermor, would perhaps look more professional in a biography, but those names seem to rob him of that boyishness which was such a part of his nature. Some biographers use their subject's initials as a way of avoiding undue familiarity, but I find it looks so odd on the page when every other name is spelled out. Patrick? It is more formal, but in his case it was only ever used in his lifetime when joined with Leigh Fermor. So I am left with Paddy: the name I have called him since childhood, the name by which he was known by all the hundreds of people who knew and loved him: a friendly, cheerful name with a spring in its step.

As for place-names, wherever possible I have aimed to keep the spellings that he himself used. So in this book it is Rumania and not Romania, Euboea rather than Evvia, Calcutta rather than Kolkata, Constantinople rather than Istanbul.

A.C.
Lynsore Bottom, Canterbury
March 2012

I believe the power of observation in numbers of very young children to be quite wonderful for its closeness and accuracy. Indeed, I think that most grown men who are remarkable in this respect may . . . be said not to have lost the faculty, than to have acquired it; the rather, as I generally observe such men retain a certain freshness, and gentleness, and capacity of being pleased, which are also an inheritance they have preserved from their childhood.

Charles Dickens, David Copperfield, Chapter II

I

Neverland

The village of Weedon Bec in Northamptonshire was an unlikely setting for paradise, but for Patrick Leigh Fermor the years he spent there as a small child were among the happiest in his life. The people he lived with were not his family. While surrounding him with love and warmth, they imposed no constraints and made no demands. He was never scolded for being late for meals, or for coming home covered in mud and burrs. Until this idyll came to an abrupt end in the summer of 1919, all he had to do was get on with the exciting business of growing up.

The local children taught him how to run his hand up the dried stems of wild sorrel, and feel his palm swell with the kibbled seeds that he threw to the wind. They scrambled into half-used ricks and jumped; it was prickly but soft, so you sank into the sweet-smelling hay. They helped him clamber into the saddles of old apple trees, but soon he would be able to hoist himself into tall trees like the bigger boys. Then he would climb into the topmost branches, invisible, hidden by leaves, and no one would be able to find him. For now he hid in sheds and barns, and sometimes behind the big double doors leading into the yard of the Wheatsheaf, and people shouted, 'Paddy-Mike, where are you?' while he hugged himself because no one could see him, and no one knew where he was.

The grown-ups talked in low voices about the Germans and the war, which was going on a long time. No one liked the Germans but there were no Germans in Weedon – at least he didn't think there were. Once he found a big pile of earth and set to work digging and building, and one of the older ones said, 'You shouldn't do that!' – 'Why not?' – 'Because of the Germans.' – 'But you can't see any!' – 'No, you can't see them because they're so tiny!' He had no idea what they meant but he knew what Germans looked like: he had seen pictures of them in their funny helmets. He looked very hard, half-expecting to see miniature Germans in their pickelhaubes rising out of the earth.

He was not afraid of the Germans, but once he saw a steamroller the size of a house coming down the road. The driver looked so grim and fierce he was terrified. (The steamroller formed part of his childhood nightmares for years.) He ran as hard as he could till he found Margaret, and clung to her warm back and held on to her plaits as she brought him home, where Mummy Martin took him on her lap and gave him a hug. When she gave him bread and syrup, he turned the green and gold syrup tin round so he could see the picture of the lion and the bees. The lion looked asleep but in the bible story he was dead, that was why the bees were coming out of him.

George Edwin Martin and his wife Margaret lived at 42 High Street, Road Weedon, a small terraced house with a narrow garden at the back. They had three children. Their son Norman was ten in 1915, when Paddy-Mike came to live with them. Their daughter, also called Margaret, was eight. She helped her mother look after Paddy and her younger brother, Lewis, aged six. It was a big village, divided into three parts. The cottages and smallholdings of Upper Weedon were sunk in green fields. The church and village school were in Lower Weedon, whilst busiest of all was Road Weedon, which straddled the old turnpike between Northampton and Daventry. This was where the Martins lived, on the main road (now the A45), with shops and pubs on either side. Coal and beer were delivered to the Wheatsheaf and the Horseshoe in open lorries, while men on tricycles with creaking baskets delivered goods and groceries from Wilson's Stores and Adams the grocer. Sometimes you could see troops of soldiers marching past, and officers on gleaming horses, or the bus with its open top and its jangling bell – he always ran up to the top deck when the Martins went into Daventry.

Road Weedon was dominated by Weedon Barracks and the huge complex of the Royal Ordnance Depot. Set up for the storage of arms and ammunition during the Napoleonic wars far from possible landing sites on the coast, it had its own well-defended branch of the Grand Union Canal to secure safe delivery of its stores. Sometimes

Margaret would take Paddy-Mike to the barracks to watch the cavalrymen trotting and wheeling their horses round the great parade ground. It seems odd that the broad canal that divided Road Weedon from Lower Weedon does not feature in his memories, but no doubt Margaret was under strict orders to keep him away from it. Mr Martin, whom he was later to remember as a farmer, in fact worked at the Ordnance Depot as an engineer and served in the local fire brigade. He was huge and had a bristly moustache.

When the First World War ended in November 1918 Paddy-Mike was almost four, and Margaret almost twelve. They stood in the road and saw German prisoners in carts, on their way back to Germany – they wore rough grey uniforms with big red diamonds on their backs, so they would be easily identified if they tried to escape. Because the war had ended in winter, everyone decided to save the peace celebrations for the summer. It was going to be even better than Christmas, with a band and dancing, tea in a tent, and a huge bonfire with fireworks.

A few days before the peace celebrations, which were to take place on 18 June 1919, Paddy-Mike was washed and brushed and led into the parlour. There was a strange woman wearing the grandest clothes he had ever seen, and with her was a girl in a real sailor-suit, complete with a whistle attached to a thick white string. Mummy Martin said they were his real mother and his sister Vanessa, who was eight, and they had come from India. With them was a fluffy black dog with a squashed-in face and white feet like spats. He had never seen a lady so magnificently dressed and he was intrigued, but he remained wary of the yearning in her voice which seemed to claim him in some way. He bolted outside and ran and hid and they all chased after him calling, 'Paddy-Mike, where are you? Come back, Paddy!' while the dog with the white feet yapped hysterically. Reluctantly, he was persuaded back to the house where there was cake.

He looked at the lady's shoes which had a bumpy pattern on them and she said they were made of crocodile skin, which was interesting. He looked at the whistle on the girl's sailor-suit and she said he could blow it if he liked, so he did. The dog with the squashed face was called Sir Percy Spats S.T.A., which stood for Sweetest Thing in Asia. The smart lady went away, but the girl in the sailor-suit stayed.

3

Owing to bad weather, Weedon Bec's peace celebration bonfire had to be postponed till 21 June. A mountain of wood and straw and furze stood in the middle of a field between the canal and the railway, and at its summit were effigies of Kaiser Bill and 'Little Willie', the German Crown Prince, wearing captured German boots, and the Kaiser had a proper German helmet. First they all had tea in a tent, and in Paddy's memory, everyone lay about on the grass singing songs till it grew dark – though after three days of heavy rain the ground would have been sodden.

Before the bonfire was lit a man called Thatcher Brown seized a ladder and, despite protests from the spectators, scaled the pyre to relieve the effigies of their boots: 'Too good to waste,' he said.[1] Then at last the bonfire was set alight. Paddy was hoisted aloft so he could see better. The rising flames were accompanied by an explosion of firecrackers, and then everyone made a circle and danced around the blaze.

Fifty years later, relying on nothing but his memories, Paddy described the bonfire and its dramatic sequel in *A Time of Gifts*. From one moment to the next, people began screaming and calling for help. Margaret went to see what had happened. Then she hurried back, grabbed Paddy and dragged him away as fast as she could.

Margaret was very upset. 'When we got home,' he wrote, 'she rushed upstairs, undressed me and put me into her bed and slipped in, hugging me to her flannel nightdress, sobbing and shuddering and refusing to answer questions.'[2] According to Paddy, it was several days before she was willing to satisfy his curiosity. She said that one of the boys had been dancing around with a firework in his mouth. It had slipped down his throat, and he had died 'spitting stars'. There is no reference to this tragedy in the *Northamptonshire Chronicle*, nor is it mentioned in the Weedon Deanery Parish Magazine which described the celebrations in considerable detail. Was Paddy remembering another night and another bonfire, or did Margaret invent the story to cover up why she had been so upset?

The most likely reason for Margaret's distress was that she had realized what was about to happen. Paddy-Mike, to whom she had grown so attached and cared for so devotedly, was leaving them. Vanessa was his sister now; and when Mrs Fermor returned to

Weedon she would take her children back to London, and Margaret might never see Paddy-Mike again.

When the day of departure came he was sick with apprehension and misery, desperate at leaving Margaret and Mummy Martin. He was nauseated by the oily, sooty smell of the train that took him farther and farther away from Northamptonshire, stifled by the grimy maze of London from which he could never run away. Paddy was not yet five, and this was the second time he had been uprooted from one world and briskly repotted in another. Being a robust and cheerful child he adjusted to these upheavals, but he never felt as connected to his family as most children do. Like Peter Pan some part of Paddy refused to grow up, hankering for the Neverland from which he had been exiled.

Since his parents lived in India, Paddy liked to think that he had been conceived in Calcutta, Simla or Darjeeling. He was rather downcast to hear from his sister Vanessa that the most likely venue for this important event was the seaside town of Bournemouth on the south coast, where the Fermors came to spend a few weeks in the spring and summer of 1914.

As a member of the Indian Civil Service, Paddy's father Lewis Fermor was granted six weeks' leave in England every three years, and Lewis used his furlough to pursue his passion for botany and natural history. Leaving his wife and four-year-old daughter to enjoy the delights of Bournemouth, Lewis took long walks inland to collect wild flowers, or searched the Eocene-age strata of Bournemouth Cliffs for plant fossils. When the family were together, Dr and Mrs Fermor made an odd pair – he tall and scholarly, she short and high-spirited. The dissimilarities in their characters were just as marked. 'You could not imagine two people more different in taste, outlook, and temperament,' said Paddy of his parents. 'What *were* they doing in each other's company?'

That question can only be answered by retracing their story. Lewis Leigh Fermor was born in September 1880 in Peckham, south London. (He was called 'Leigh' not because it was a family name, but after one of his father's closest friends.) He was the eldest son of Lewis Fermor, who worked as a clerk in the London Joint Stock

Bank, and Maria James, a woman of intelligence and determination. She schooled Lewis herself till he was seven, by which time he could not only read and write but was showing considerable skill in mathematics.

He won a scholarship to Wilson's Grammar School in Camberwell, and decided to try for a scholarship to the Royal College of Science. He was told by his tutor at Wilson's that this would only be achievable if, on top of his schoolwork, he put in an extra four hours a day for two years. This punishing workload was most arduous in the summer, when the evenings were long and he could hear the sounds of his five siblings – Ethel, Bertram, Aline, Frank and Gerald – playing in the garden below his window.

One reason why Lewis worked so hard was that he was determined not to let life get the better of him. His father's misfortunes had started when he was obliged to retire from the bank as a result of chronic writer's cramp. Not having served the time required to gain a pension, he was given a gratuity. With this he set up a sign-writing business, but it never prospered and eventually closed.

Young Lewis won a national scholarship to the Royal College of Science in 1898, and having completed his studies in the Royal School of Mines he was appointed Assistant Superintendent in the Geological Survey of India. He set out on the long journey to Calcutta in October 1902, and this was to be his base for the rest of his working life. Compared to the enormous efforts he had made over the past years, his duties in India must have seemed leisurely. There were long months in the field, mapping the stratification of rocks and mineral deposits and inspecting mines, but he had time enough to prepare for his BSc (1907) and DSc (1909). In the early days he also kept a diary, in which he writes matter-of-factly about the hunts laid on by local maharajahs, various clashes with porters and uncooperative villagers, and the musicians and dancers who appeared out of nowhere to entertain the camp. The diary is also dotted with descriptions of flowers, birds, animals and insects. His air of lean austerity was complemented by a tall figure, fine features, and deep-set brown eyes. Despite his dedication to work, Lewis enjoyed society. He was a keen racegoer, and the elegance of his dancing was noticed at the balls given by the ladies of Calcutta.

Paddy's mother was Muriel Æileen Ambler, the daughter of Charles Taaffe Ambler, founder and owner of Ambler's Slate & Stone Co. Ltd, of Dharhara near the town of Monghyr, some two hundred and fifty miles to the north-west of Calcutta. It may be that Lewis first made a connection with the Amblers through professional channels: in 1904, the Geological Survey had tested Charles Ambler's slate and found it to be unusually strong, breaking at a pressure of three tons per square inch.

Charles's first wife died in 1884, and within the year he had married Amy Webber, an artistically talented woman less than half his age. They had two children: Huart, commonly known as Artie, who was born in 1886, and Muriel Æileen, Paddy's mother, who was born in 1890. Like most children of the empire, Artie and Æileen were largely brought up in England. But they were not left in the hands of sadistic aunts or Dickensian boarding schools; their mother Amy spent long stretches of time with her children in Dulwich, a prosperous suburb of south-east London, where they were raised and educated. Artie attended Dulwich College, while Æileen was educated by her mother and a succession of governesses at home.

Education done, the family returned to India. The Amblers had built a villa a few miles from Dharhara, at a place called Bassowni: a high-ceilinged house with a vaulted roof and a wide veranda. Artie took up work in the family business, while Æileen and her mother began the task of finding her a husband. This meant abandoning Charles and Artie in Dharhara while Amy and Æileen based themselves in Calcutta. The city not only provided an active social life and suitable young men, but also portrait commissions for Amy.

In a family that appreciated the arts, Æileen was a keen reader and a good pianist, with a broad repertoire of songs. In company she sparkled a little too brightly, talked and laughed rather more loudly than was considered proper. Her tendency to set off on long rides at dawn, unchaperoned, also raised a few eyebrows. The only release for her energy and emotional extravagance was the stage, and she was happiest when surrounded by the trappings and excitement of amateur theatrical life. It was unthinkable that a young woman from her background should become a professional actress; but there was drama in her movements, in the rich mass of wavy auburn hair that she was so proud of, and the large untidy scrawl of her letters written in purple ink.

Æileen was one of those people who feel a need to reinvent themselves from time to time, and she had used a bewildering variety of names. As a girl she signed herself 'Avrille' or 'Mixed Pickles' when writing to her parents, while they and her husband most often referred to her as Muriel. She signed herself 'Muriel' too, though in later years this name was consigned to oblivion because Paddy hated it. She also used Æileen, though she liked her intimates to call her Pat or Fudge. As for surnames, two were definitely better than one. Though her parents always addressed each other on their envelopes as Mr and Mrs Charles Ambler, Æileen referred to her family as the Taaffe Amblers.

The Amblers believed themselves to be descendants of Sir John Taaffe of Ballymote, County Sligo (d. 1641), whose descendants served as chancellors, diplomats and cavalrymen in Austria and became Counts of the Holy Roman Empire. Gaps in the genealogical record mean that these dashing figures cannot be linked with any certainty to James Ambler, Charles's father, a builder born in County Cork in the first half of the nineteenth century. But when Æileen (and later Paddy) referred to their Irish ancestry, this is what they meant. On Lewis's side, things were more prosaic. Since the eighteenth century the Fermors of Kent and Sussex (the name is a variant of 'farmer') had been yeomen, brewers and builders, whose descendants would gradually join the professional classes as the century progressed.

Æileen Ambler and Lewis Fermor probably met in 1907, and became engaged soon after. She always called him 'Peter' though his middle name was Leigh, and it was she who hitched the Leigh on to Fermor.

In the first flush of love Æileen was willing to overlook Lewis Fermor's lack of connections, and their mutual attraction must have seemed very natural – she so vivacious and artistic, he so focused and ambitious. As for her parents, the match must have looked promising enough, as long as the young couple did not rush into marriage. Neither party was rich and they had no expectations, but in a few years Fermor would surely be able to provide a comfortable life for their daughter.

In early 1909 Lewis was in his late twenties, and his career had reached a critical point. He had been publishing papers in geological journals since 1904, and much of this research was now supporting his monumental memoir on *The Manganese-ore Deposits of India* which, along with maps, diagrams and photographs, ran to over 1,200 pages. No wonder that the eighteen-year-old Æileen felt rather sidelined, as he prepared the most important publication of his professional life for the press.

Realizing that her demands would always come a long way behind those of her future husband's work, Æileen told Lewis that she would not marry him after all. 'Perhaps it's just as well,' wrote Charles Ambler's daughter-in-law Ruth, 'as it was to have been a very long engagement.'[3] But they were reunited, and married in St Paul's Cathedral, Calcutta, on 12 October 1909.

Until she met Lewis Fermor the most important man in Æileen's life had been her brother Artie, whom she revered as a paragon among men. A great winner of prizes at school, he settled down to work in the family business with commendable zeal. He was a volunteer in two local regiments, and according to Æileen he would vanish into the jungle for days at a time armed only with a kukri. He was also an enthusiastic sportsman: the only surviving family photograph shows him standing nonchalantly over a dead leopard.

Æileen and Lewis had been married seven months when they heard that Artie had collapsed with a high fever at the slate works. He was taken to the Jamalpur hospital, where the only way they could reduce his temperature was by packing him in ice; but as soon as the ice was removed his temperature soared back to 107 degrees. He died on 19 May 1910, aged twenty-four.

The loss of Artie was a crippling blow for his parents. Æileen too had idolized her brother, but her life was moving on, as Lewis wrote to his mother-in-law in July:

> [Æileen] has now become resigned to the facts and is becoming merry once more, for two reasons: firstly, because she thinks Artie would not like her to grieve too much: and so she constantly tells that Artie used to love doing this, or didn't like that, in tones almost as joyful as if he were still with us. Secondly, my Loved One is rejoicing in the fact that she is going to replace Artie with another, the fruit of our love, Mother, and we hope that this will be a consolation . . .[4]

The 'consolation' was their first child, born in Calcutta on 17 February 1911. She was named Vanessa Opal, for Lewis liked the idea of his children bearing the names of semi-precious stones.

Soon the baby was joining her parents on long trips upcountry. They travelled with a team of cooks, drivers, servants and bearers, plus mules, oxen or camels depending on the terrain, and lived in tented camps the size of a small village. The tents for the family were large and well appointed, with carpets and furniture. Æileen even had her own travelling 'cottage piano', and cherished a romantic image of herself playing Rimsky-Korsakov's 'Chanson Hindoue' in the sunset, looking out towards the campfires while her husband wrote up his notes. Yet rain and wind could make camp life miserable, whilst the minor complaints that bedevilled everyone's health could turn swiftly into life-threatening illnesses.

It was with relief that they returned to Europe in the spring of 1914, though a distinct malaise hung in the air. Those astute enough to see the fragility of the European status quo were seriously alarmed, yet most newspapers were more interested in reassuring the public than in tracing the political fault lines as they split asunder. But on 28 June, Franz Ferdinand Archduke of Austria was assassinated in Sarajevo, and events began to accelerate at a bewildering speed. Germany declared war on France the following month, and Britain declared war on Germany on 4 August, the day that German troops marched into Belgium.

As a member of the Indian Civil Service, Lewis was in a reserved occupation and was soon called back to India. But Æileen, pregnant again, decided to stay on in England with Vanessa and await the birth of her second child.

Patrick Michael Leigh Fermor (not Jasper or Garnet, thanks to his father's absence) was born on 11 February 1915, at 20 Endsleigh Gardens, in the district of St Pancras, London. The house belonged to a Miss Mary Hadland, who had rooms to rent. Perhaps Æileen chose Endsleigh Gardens because it was not far from the Three Arts Club in Marylebone Road, to which she belonged; perhaps Miss Hadland was already a friend. Yet it is strange that she did not lodge with members of her own family, or even with Lewis's relations in Camberwell. (Paddy had a strong suspicion that his mother did not get on with his father's relations, and that the feeling was mutual.) Paddy was christened that spring in the village of Coldharbour, near Dorking in Surrey.

Æileen realized that the longer she stayed in England, the harder it would be to return to India. The first Zeppelin raids on Yarmouth and King's Lynn had taken place in January 1915, a month before Paddy was born, and in May, London itself came under attack. The raids were not very effective considering the effort and investment that had gone into the development of the new flying weapon; nonetheless the Zeppelin gave rise to a lot of public anxiety, and the country had no means of combating this terrifying new form of warfare. Æileen had originally planned to take both children back to India, but the sinking in May of the *Lusitania* by a German submarine convinced her that passenger vessels were no longer safe. She could not risk losing both her children. Instead she resolved to return to Calcutta with Vanessa, leaving her infant son in England. Thus it came about that, when almost a year old, Paddy-Mike was settled in Northamptonshire with George and Margaret Martin.

Paddy himself, though endowed with a prodigious curiosity, never asked his mother how she came to know the Martins. He said it had never occurred to him to ask, and perhaps some of the golden bloom that dusted his changeling childhood would have worn off had he known the answer. It remains a mystery still, though a clue might lie in Mrs Martin's maiden name of Hadland: a name she shared with Mary Hadland, the owner of the house in Endsleigh Gardens where Paddy was born.

His memories of Weedon became greener and more rural as they receded into the past. The Royal Ordnance Stores faded, as did the parade ground and the shops, the pubs and traffic of the High Street. What was left was 'a background of barns, ricks and teazles, clouded with spinneys and the undulation of ridge and furrow . . . I spent these important years, which are said to be such formative ones, more or less as a small farmer's child run wild: they have left a memory of complete and unalloyed bliss.'[5]

Paddy's misery at leaving Weedon did not last long, for Æileen laid on a series of treats and outings designed to make his new world as delightful as possible. There was also a trip to Rowe's, the fashionable children's outfitter in Bond Street. A stuffed pony stood in the shop, on which children being fitted for jodhpurs would be asked to mount. Paddy came out with several boxes of new clothes including, to his great satisfaction, his own sailor-suit, with HMS *Indomitable* emblazoned in gold letters on the cap ribbon.

No. 3 Primrose Hill Studios, where Æileen had installed her family, seemed palatial after Weedon; they were so close to the zoo that at night one could hear the lions roaring. The house was on two storeys, reached through a gateway rather like a cloister, and the nursery was equipped with toys from India: brass figures of elephants and camels on wheels, and painted clay figures of maharajas and maharanis, merchants and shopkeepers, dancers and musicians. One of their neighbours was the illustrator Arthur Rackham, whom Æileen had persuaded to paint one of the doors on the ground floor. He sketched in a huge tree with Peter Pan sleeping in a bird's nest, and among the roots a number of carousing mice toasting each other in acorn cups.

Paddy was about six when for the first time he met his father, then home on leave. He longed to show off in front of this impossibly tall and remote figure, but Vanessa had a great deal more to show. She had been reading since the age of four, whilst her brother was still struggling with his letters. He found this shameful and, to camouflage his slowness, he would memorize long passages of text which could then be reeled off by heart: an early exercise which must have strengthened his extraordinary memory.

From the moment he mastered reading (an edition of Robin Hood stories unlocked the code) there was no turning back. Soon he was on to *Puck of Pook's Hill*, *Rewards and Fairies*, and – a book that was to sow the seeds of his passion for Greece – Charles Kingsley's *Heroes*. 'Till it was light enough to read, furious dawn-watches ushered in days flat on hearth-rugs or grass, in ricks or up trees, which ended in stifling torchlit hours under the bedclothes.' Thus he gobbled up *Treasure Island*, *Kidnapped*, *Black Beauty*, *Wet Magic*, *Lamb's Tales from Shakespeare*, *Three Men in a Boat*, and *The Forest Lovers* by Maurice Hewlett – a romantic love story full of knights and ladies and enchantments. His lust for books was much encouraged by Æileen, who also loved reading aloud. She could do any number of different accents which brought books to life, especially Dickens and Shakespeare. Since Æileen was reading for Vanessa as well some books were inevitably a little beyond Paddy, but he was more than willing to listen. He was also an enthusiastic singer, and as Æileen played the piano, he picked up her huge collection of traditional and music-hall songs.

'Book-ownership was the next step,' wrote Paddy. 'To assuage a mania for Scott, I was given four Collins pocket Waverley novels every birthday and Christmas and my father sent sumptuous works about animals or botany from India, wrapped in palm leaves and sewn with a thousand stitches by Thacker & Spink in Calcutta or Simla.'[6]

Æileen was a great believer in looking smart and presentable: she wore well-tailored jackets and skirts, and an eyeglass on the end of a black string which Paddy thought very dashing. Unquestionably a snob and a terrific name-dropper, she thought that her family was nobler and more romantic than the Fermors. Some of this rubbed off on Paddy whose recklessness and wild imagination she associated with her own Anglo-Irish genes. Whenever Paddy looked serious or glum Æileen would say, 'You look just like your father.'

Living with Paddy must have been like living with a very boisterous puppy, despite the hours he spent reading. No wonder Æileen was often angry and exasperated – though his sister Vanessa felt that their mother's punishments were sometimes unnecessarily severe. It was not so much the spanking with the back of a hairbrush that hurt: it was the way she could be so loving and friendly one minute, and then icily cold and unapproachable the next. Sometimes she would turn her back and refuse to acknowledge his existence – not for a few minutes, but for hours at a time. Vanessa remembered him, even at the age of ten, being made to sit on the front step, again for several hours, with a bib around his neck.

But whatever her faults, Æileen was the most inspiring and amusing figure in his life. She wrote plays and always dreamed that one day one of them might be staged, but it never happened. Paddy had a look at some of them after her death, and admitted that 'they weren't up to much.' She had a knack of making things fun or memorable, and he described her as 'a mine of disinformation, but the sort of thing that made you more interested in a character rather than less'.[7]

She told him, for example, that Mary Queen of Scots had such white skin and such a slender neck that people said they could see the red wine going down her throat as she drank.

Æileen's parents left India after the war and retired to Brighton, and occasionally she would take the children down to see them. Only once did Paddy meet his paternal grandparents, when his father took him and Vanessa to lunch with them at the East India United Service Club in London. Æileen was not there. Both she and Lewis had decided to lead more or less separate lives, although appearances were maintained for the few weeks that he was back on leave. She never returned to India again after the First World War.

In the early 1920s, Æileen had taken the Vicarage Cottage in Dodford: a tiny hamlet at the bottom of a wooded valley, some two miles west of Weedon where Paddy had lived with the Martins. A broad brook ran beside its only street, ending in a ford at one end of the village; while at the other end stood a pub called the Swan, more commonly known as the Dirty Duck, where visiting friends stayed since the cottage was so tiny. This was where Æileen and her children spent most Christmases and holidays until 1930. Since she remained in touch with the Martins, Paddy must have met them from time to time, and he remembered going to see *The Four Horsemen of the Apocalypse* with Margaret, a film that came out in 1921. But the spell was broken, and no further memories remained of Mummy and Daddy Martin.

After a few terms at a school called Gordon Hall, just the other side of Regent's Park from Primrose Hill, Paddy and Vanessa were sent to an establishment in West Byfleet, Surrey, called The Gables. But despite an early taste for English and history, Paddy was not an easy child to handle. On one level he wanted to do well and impress people; but a sense of mischief was never far below the surface, ready to overturn his efforts at conformity in an instant. Describing himself in *A Time of Gifts*, he wrote that since he was 'Harmless in appearance . . . and of a refreshingly unconstricted address, I would earn excellent opinions at first. But . . . soon . . . those short-lived virtues must have seemed a cruel Fauntleroy veneer, cynically assumed to mask the Charles Addams fiend that lurked beneath.'[8]

His first proper school was St Piran's, a preparatory school for boys near Maidenhead. Lewis Fermor chose it because, unlike most prep schools of that date, it gave priority to scientific subjects and its pupils went on to schools such as Oundle and Haileybury, which were known for producing scientists and engineers. The trouble was that, unlike Lewis, Paddy had never been inspired by the sciences and was spectacularly bad at them, whilst Latin, history and English, at which he excelled, were accorded little value at St Piran's. Paddy was miserable, and detested the team games that were considered so vital to the formation of young Englishmen. He described St Piran's as 'all cricket pads and snake belts', and he particularly hated the headmaster, Major Bryant, 'who beat us all quite a lot'.[9]

One small incident from his days at St Piran's is worth mentioning because it shows how willing Paddy was to romanticize people, to give them a story which immediately cloaked them in a subtle glamour. There were whispers running around school that Anthony West, a boy who was one of Paddy's few friends, was *a bastard*. Paddy had no idea that Anthony West was the illegitimate child of H. G. Wells and Rebecca West, but he was very impressed. To his Shakespeare-tinted imagination, the fact that West was a bastard meant that he was almost certainly of Royal Blood.

Fermor was in constant trouble for being absent-minded, noisy, a show-off, answering back, losing his kit, along with all the other schoolboy transgressions that Major Bryant raised to the level of cardinal sins. Although he failed to beat some discipline into his pupil, he did instil a new and darker streak of aggressive frustration, and a dull conviction in Paddy that he could never do anything right. After about a year the headmaster's patience snapped and Paddy was sent home in disgrace in early 1924.

Lewis and Æileen were so worried by reports of Paddy's behaviour at St Piran's that they decided to consult a specialist. The first was the genial Sir Henry Head, who had at one point been consulted by Virginia Woolf. Sir Henry must have found nothing wrong with the boy, for the Fermors then consulted a Dr Crichton-Miller. He had heavy spectacles and his manner was a good deal drier than Sir Henry's, but he did have a solution: there was an experimental school for difficult children at Walsham Hall, Walsham-le-Willows, Suffolk. Perhaps Paddy might do better there.

In the spring of 1924 Lewis Fermor was back on leave. The family travelled to the Swiss ski resort of Zweisimmen near Gstaad, which Æileen and Lewis had discovered early on in their marriage. They always stayed at the Terminus Hotel, which had a lot of regular English visitors who enjoyed not only skiing but bobsleighing and skating. But as Paddy grew older he liked to slope off with the village boys, whose daredevil sport was ski-jumping. The jumps were never more than about three feet high, but you were in the air for a few glorious seconds, and Paddy was overjoyed when he won second prize in their contest, which consisted of two oranges wrapped in a pair of ski-socks. Æileen did not approve of the village boys; nor did all the guests at the Terminus Hotel measure up to her standards. Her manner in the dining rooms and lobbies depended very much on who she was talking to. She could be loftily mono-syllabic, or very chatty and gregarious – particularly in the evenings, when she and her coterie got together for fancy-dress or dancing parties. Paddy particularly enjoyed doing the Charleston, which was at the height of its craze in the mid-twenties.

After ten days or so Æileen and Vanessa went back to England, where Vanessa had to return to school at Malvern Abbey. Since Paddy's term at Walsham Hall was not due to begin for another week he stayed on with his father, who was to attend a conference of geologists in Milan.

This was the first time that Lewis and his nine-year-old son had been alone together. They went round a great many churches and art galleries, and in Baveno, on the west side of Lake Maggiore, they stayed in a hotel with an abandoned music room where Paddy made a lot of noise on an electric organ.

In the train between Baveno and Lake Como, Lewis demonstrated the new knife he had just bought. He told Paddy he would peel an apple without breaking the long spiral of skin, which he did; but when he tossed the peel out of the window, he accidentally let go of the knife as well. Paddy collapsed into fits of laughter, which he prolonged with ever more raucous guffaws when he saw how much it annoyed his father. Lewis finally lost patience and banished him to the next carriage. It was very hot and in an attempt to open the window Paddy pulled the communication cord, with dramatic results.

They made an expedition into the Dolomites to collect plants and geological specimens. Lewis was an imposing figure in his plus-fours and Norfolk jacket, but this attire was topped off with an item that made his son writhe with mortification: 'a vast semi-circular cap, I think originally destined for Tibetan travel, like a bisected pumpkin of fur armed with a peak and with fur-lined ear-flaps that were joined (when not tied under the chin which was worse still) by a disturbing bow on the summit.'[10] Slung over one shoulder on a strap of webbing was his vasculum, a flat oval tin lined with moss in which he would carefully place the flowers he collected. (He never travelled without his flower presses.) Stuck in his belt was a geological hammer, used to strike off chunks of rock to observe their stratification and check for fossils with a pocket lens. The large arrow marked on the hammer meant it was Government Property, and Lewis told Paddy that only convicts or members of the civil service could be seen with tools marked in this way. Paddy was acutely embarrassed by the arrow. He turned the hammer round on his father's belt to hide it, in case people should think his father was a convict. Lewis must have enjoyed his young son's intelligence and curiosity, when he was not misbehaving; it was sad for both that they were never to be so close again.

Paddy's new school, Walsham Hall, was run by Major Faithfull (discreetly referred to as Major Truthful in *A Time of Gifts*). He was a pioneer of the wilder shores of education, and looked the part with messianic eyes and a shock of grey hair. The staff were bohemian: the men in hairy tweed jackets and knitted ties, the women in beads and homespun skirts.

The thirty-odd children who made up the school ranged from the emotionally damaged to the intractably wayward, with a sprinkling of children who would now be diagnosed as dyslexic or dyspraxic. Both boys and girls wore brown jerkins and sandals, with skirts or breeches. Lessons were very haphazard; there was also what Paddy described as 'a lot of lying down and doing free association while Major Faithfull took notes. I used to invent all sorts of things for him.'[11] Most bewildering of all were the country dancing and eurhythmics, in which both staff and pupils participated in the nude. 'Nimbly and gravely, keeping time to a cottage piano and a recorder, we sped through the figures of Gathering Peascods, Sellinger's Round, Picking-up Sticks and Old Mole.'[12]

For all its oddness Paddy enjoyed Walsham Hall, because the pupils were allowed to do more or less as they pleased. Armed with bows and arrows made of raspberry canes and dressed in hoods of Lincoln green, Paddy and his Merrie Men turned the nearby woods into their own Sherwood Forest. Not all pupils held the school in such affection. Years later Deryck Winbolt-Lewis wrote to Paddy with memories of Walsham Hall which he called 'a crazy establishment', and where he remembered Paddy as 'a rebel but never a bully'. The letter continues: 'Instead of Scouts, Faithfull had to have another crackpot association called Woodcraft and one summer we went to camp at Ringwood where we were duly starved. With others . . . I pinched bags of crisps from the stores, and when we went to the beach we ate raw mussels from the rocks with conspicuously unpleasant results.'[13]

The one school that did not order Paddy's expulsion, Walsham Hall was too unorthodox to last. Æileen herself had never approved of it and might have been among those who wanted the school shut down. She had heard a rumour that Major Faithfull was in the habit of bathing the older girls, and towelling them dry himself.

Persuading Major Bryant that Paddy was a reformed character, the Fermors succeeded in reinstating him at St Piran's. Paddy tried to keep the Fauntleroy veneer in place, but it proved impossible and before long he was expelled for the second time, and had to make the humiliating journey home accompanied by a master. His parents' dismay and disappointment, and his own inability to do what was expected of him, reduced Paddy to near despair. Compared to his father's academic progress, his own school career had been an unqualified failure.

By now, Æileen and Lewis were contemplating divorce. Lewis needed a wife who was quieter and less demanding than she would ever be, while she could not live with a man who paid her so little attention. It was bad enough that all Lewis's energies were focused on his work; but Æileen also suspected him of indulging in a string of casual affairs in Calcutta – as she revealed in a letter to her mother in Brighton.

[Lewis] having made the most solemn oaths to me has quite cheerfully broke them all – you can never guess just quite what a blighter and a mongrel that man is – he even astonishes me – and I thought I knew him pretty thoroughly . . . there is one thing I regret and that is that I didn't leave him straight away the first time I longed to – which was three days after my wedding day. He is impossible.

Geoffrey Clarke is home and has taken me dining and dancing once or twice which has saved my life – at the Savoy the other evening we ran into Mrs Strettell that was – she was divorced you know and is now Mrs Dane – she looked so well and young and happy.[14]

The mention of how well Mrs Dane looked was evidently a way of preparing her mother for the worst. Lewis and Æileen were divorced in May 1925.

The problem of Paddy's schooling was finally solved by sending him to a tutorial establishment at Downs Lodge near Sutton, in Surrey. It was run by a couple called Gilbert and Phyllis Scott-Malden – both descended from long lines of prep-school masters – who would take in six or seven boys at a time to prepare them for the Common Entrance exam. Paddy was very happy here, and the only surviving letter from his childhood was written from Sutton. It is not dated but presumably he was eleven or twelve when he wrote it, and the spelling has not been corrected.

Dear Mummy, I hope you are getting on alright. We went to Cheam church, and had a topping sermon, preached by Mr Berkeley, who always preaches good sermons. The day before yesterday a lot of new furniture arrived from Windlesham. They are topping. We have got a topping old oak chest, which is carved, just such a one as old Samuel Pepys hid in. Also there is a ripping role-top desk for Mr Malden, when you role the top up, it looks [?sounds] like a switchback railway at a fair. Last and best, there is a fine old cupboard, probably as old as James the first. It has got a lovely circular shelf supported by a pillar. It has got cable carving along the front. There are two brass lions-heads on the doors to open them by. The lions have both got brass rings in their mouths. We have christened both after their masters, one S. Jerome, and the other is called Androcles. There are two carved dragons on the top. The whole thing looks topping because we have polished it up. it's fine. Love from Paddy[15]

Paddy was as happy at Downs Lodge as he had been miserable at St Piran's. He was welcomed into the easy warmth of the Scott-Maldens' family life, and he got on well with their three sons, particularly David (who became a pilot during the war and, eventually, an Air Vice-Marshal). There was a lot of reading aloud and acting in the evenings, and in the summer the boys built a tree house in a huge old walnut tree. It had a tin roof, and for his last summer term Paddy was allowed to sleep in it.

They also let him pursue what he referred to as his budding religious mania. The Scott-Maldens were not particularly religious, but Paddy – as the letter above indicates – took a deep interest in religion at this stage. Catholicism and the Latin mass exerted a strong appeal, as did the candles and bells, incense and statues of the Roman tradition. Paddy never converted, but he identified himself as 'R.C.' on official forms until the end of the war. His religious feelings seemed to subside after that.

Paddy remembered the Scott-Maldens as the two best teachers he ever had. Instead of being constantly checked as a know-all who knew nothing worth knowing, his enthusiasms for religion, history, languages, drawing and poetry were fostered and encouraged, as was his reading. Paddy applied himself assiduously to his Latin and French, yet to his disappointment he was not allowed to start Greek because his maths were still so bad. In fact so poor was his grasp of this subject that he was obliged to take his Common Entrance a year late, at the age of fourteen; but he passed.

Lewis Fermor still hoped he would go to Oundle, which Paddy thought sounded very gloomy, whilst his mother pined for Eton or Winchester, which were out of the question. With his relatively poor Common Entrance marks no first-division public school would have considered Paddy, unless there had been a strong family link, and Lewis Fermor – scholarship boy that he was – did not have such connections. In the end, his parents decided to send him to the King's School, Canterbury. King's was not particularly distinguished at the time; but it was the oldest school in England, counted Christopher Marlowe and Walter Pater among its old boys, and lay in the shadow of an ancient cathedral where a saint had met his martyrdom. As far as Paddy was concerned, no school had better credentials.

2

The Plan

In the centuries that followed its foundation by Henry VIII, the King's School had attracted few rich patrons to increase its prosperity, and in the years after the First World War it was very down-at-heel. The headmaster, Algernon Latter, believed that tradition was sacrosanct and kept the school firmly in the nineteenth century. The late Canon Ingram Hill, an old King's boy who joined a year or two before Paddy, described the school then as 'very, very tough – just like *Tom Brown's Schooldays*'.[1] The buildings were shamefully threadbare and run-down, the dormitories still lit by gas, and the school was so desperate for pupils that it would take any boy who applied. It was rare for King's, Canterbury, to get any student into Oxford or Cambridge; most followed their fathers into whatever the family business happened to be.

By the time Paddy joined the school for the summer term of 1929, things were looking up. The school governors had recently appointed a new headmaster, Norman Birley, who was to pull King's out of the doldrums. One of the first changes he made was to divide the school into two houses. School House, which had been in existence for generations, was now joined by the Grange. Birley also curbed the worst excesses of bullying, and made it known that any suspicion of homosexuality was enough to merit instant expulsion.

Paddy was assigned to the Grange, whose housemaster was Alec Macdonald. Canon Hill described him as '*very* Cambridge – he always had a hat in one hand, umbrella in the other. He was highly civilized, and had a passion for music.' He spoke beautiful German, had translated *Winnie the Pooh* into French, and had slightly staring eyes which some boys found alarming. Alec Macdonald would have regular musical get-togethers at which he would play classical records on the gramophone, which would then be discussed over tea. It was rumoured that he voted Labour, which was considered very peculiar for someone so obviously a gentleman; and Paddy admired his thoughtfulness and humanity.

> Once, when his class was translating a short story by Maupassant, a boy mistranslated *un accent populaire*. 'No,' Macdonald said, 'it's not exactly a *popular* accent, but an uneducated one.' – 'What,' someone else said, 'a common one, Sir, a street-cad's accent?' – 'Exactly,' Macdonald said lightly, 'just the sort of accent we'd all have if we lived a hundred yards from here.' There was an uncomfortable silence, and we all felt we had been unmasked as the horrible little middle-class snobs that we were.[2]

Canon Hill remembered that Paddy's arrival had had an immediate impact on the school. He spoke in elaborate sentences, a mode of speech quite unlike the monosyllabic schoolboy slang of his contemporaries. He would launch into blank verse or Shakespearean dialogue at the drop of a hat, and recited poetry by the yard. Hill remembers once coming back from games and hearing someone singing 'Ye Watchers and Ye Holy Ones', an unusual choice from the English Hymnal. Intrigued, he followed the sound and found Fermor dancing about in the showers, stark naked, singing 'Alleluia! Alleluia!' at the top of his lungs, all by himself. With his ebullience and charm Paddy soon collected a band of hangers-on, many of whom were just interested to see what he would do next.

All went well at first. Paddy gained good marks in French, German, Latin, history and geography, and the fact that he was hopeless at maths and science was accepted with equanimity. Given that he could box above his weight and rowed in the Junior Fours, one might have expected Paddy to have had some success in sport, but he was never going to be a team player. Having chosen rowing rather than cricket, he spent summer afternoons smoking cigarettes with the aesthetes of King's, reading Gibbon and Michael Arlen by the banks of the Stour.

'I wrote and read with intensity, sang, debated, drew and painted; scored minor successes at acting, stage-managing and in painting and designing scenery . . .'[3] This last was for a production of *Androcles and the Lion*, in which Paddy did all the above and took the eponymous role. He gave talks on Walter Pater and Dante Gabriel Rossetti to the school's literary society (known as the Walpole Society), and won the Divinity Prize twice. Religion still exerted a powerful attraction. He claims that it went hand in hand with his passion for history, art, architecture, music and poetry: religion gave a depth and colour to all these things.

One of Paddy's contemporaries at Canterbury was Alan Watts, who was even then turning himself into an expert on Japanese art and Zen Buddhism. 'And I shall not forget', wrote Watts in his autobiography, 'the awed and almost respectful way in which Patrick Leigh Fermor said to me, "Do you really mean that you have renounced belief in the Father, Son and Holy Ghost?"'[4] Watts and Paddy enjoyed each other's company. Long bicycle rides through narrow country lanes took them to the churches of Patrixbourne and Barfreston, and 'when utterly oppressed by the social system of the school, we would sneak off to Canterbury Cathedral – which, because of its colossal sanctity, could never be made out of bounds . . .'[5]

Paddy always maintained a scrupulous loyalty to his mother, but the way she veered between possessive love and complete neglect for weeks at a time was enough to destabilize anyone. She did not always want him back in the holidays. Once or twice he had been farmed out to Fermor relations, but had so hated the experience that he refused to go back. Now it was more often the Scott-Maldens who took him in. He also spent some weeks at Fredville Park, near Nonington in Kent, where his hosts were the Misses Hardy – or as he knew them, Aunt Mary and Aunt Maud – who took in young lodgers from King's if they were not going home. Paddy was particularly fond of the handsome Aunt Maud. She lent him a pony whenever he wanted to ride, and he went hunting on a couple of occasions with the West Street Harriers.

He saw less and less of his sister Vanessa, who was now a young woman of twenty. She was spending much of her time in India, keeping house in Calcutta for her father whom, curiously, Paddy never went to visit. The voyage was so long that it was scarcely worthwhile undertaking in the course of a school vacation. Moreover, though the wish was there, two things held him back. He was acutely aware of being a disappointment to his father, and of their being ill-at-ease together; he knew also that it would displease Æileen, who saw him as *her* son. It was one thing for Vanessa to spend months with Lewis in India, but not Paddy.

Æileen had given up the house in Primrose Hill, and was now living on the south side of Piccadilly, close to the Circus, at the top of No. 213. The flat consisted of one huge room, an Aladdin's cave full of the exotic furniture that had stood in Primrose Hill. On the few occasions that Paddy spent the night there, he slept in a tiny box room. As he fell asleep he could see the faint pulse of light from a huge neon cocktail shaker, which poured a drink over and over again with the words 'GORDON'S GIN THE HEART OF A GOOD COCKTAIL'.[6]

At Canterbury, Paddy was at last allowed to take up Greek. He plunged in with enthusiasm; but his Greek grammar was soon 'smothered with scrawled and inky processions of centaurs, always bearded like Navy Cut bluejackets and often wearing bowler-hats and smoking cherry-wood pipes'.[7] Apart from Homer, Greek at this stage did not have the hold on him that Latin did. When describing his 'private anthology' in *A Time of Gifts* – those passages and poems he had absorbed with joy or deliberately chosen to learn – the Latin far outweighs the Greek. Besides, at this stage he had his own poetry to write.

'Verse, imitative and bad but published in school magazines nevertheless, poured out like ectoplasm,' wrote Paddy.[8] He also wrote short stories which, like his contributions to the Walpole Society, were read aloud, usually to small groups of boys gathered in the housemaster's study. Alec Macdonald was impressed. 'There you are!' he said. 'You're going to be a writer.'[9] Paddy was gratified, because he too was beginning to think along those lines. His first appearances in print, to be found in the school magazine *The Cantuarian*, are under the pen-name 'Scriptor'.

'All Saints' is a story about one of the King's School's most distinguished old boys, the physician and scholar Thomas Linacre, whose ghost appears to the narrator in utterances such as 'Right merry days were those i'faith'. Those volumes of Scott, plus the historical romances he read as a child, had left their stain.[10]

His next contribution, 'Phoebe', was a glutinous confection liberally sprinkled with classical figures seemingly designed to impress the masters.[11] 'To Thea', on the other hand, with its roses and ruby lips and a final commitment to play Romeo to her Juliet, sounds as if it was written to dazzle a real girl.[12] Paddy already had form for pressing poems into the hands of girls he was keen on, and even if the poetry did not improve his chances it could always be recycled for *The Cantuarian*.

In December 1930, he translated Horace's Ode 1.9, 'To Thaliarchus'.* Years later, this poem was to prompt a moment of sympathy, when a kidnapped German general and the young English major who had captured him realized they had more in common than they thought. He was introduced to the poems of Horace by his Latin master, Nathaniel Gosse, who was delighted with his enthusiasm for the poet and encouraged his efforts at translation. On seeing it again seventy years later, Paddy pronounced it '*terrible*. The whole point of Horace is tautness and concentration, and perfection, whereas my version is a metrically sloppy, falsely rhyming, roly-poly pudding.'[13] The poem that most clearly points the way to the author Paddy would become was entitled 'The Raiding Song of the Vandals', and was based on a poem by James Elroy Flecker, 'The War Song of the Saracens'.

> In the market we throng, and our steeds are laded with loot underneath us
> Through the carnage we ride, and the massacred townsfolk we trample beneath us;
> The houses blaze round us, the timbers cave in where the firetongues have found them,
> And crash as the sparks shower skywards, the flames flicker madly around them.[14]

His intoxication with the thundering rhythm and tongue-tripping alliteration make the poem hard work. As he matured he learned to use these tools to astonishing effect, but he never lost his taste for the richness of words and the verbal acrobatics they could perform.

---

* See Appendix III, page 396.

The first time Paddy met a real poet was when the young John Betjeman came to lecture at King's, though at that time he was not yet a celebrity and he had come to talk about architecture, not poetry. Paddy remembered the occasion sixty-five years later, when he gave the address at the unveiling of a memorial to Betjeman in Poets' Corner at Westminster Abbey, on 11 November 1996.

> His discourse was light, spontaneous, urgent and convincing, and it began with a eulogy of the spare and uncluttered lines of the Parthenon and this led on, astonishingly as it may sound today, to a eulogy of the spare, uncluttered lines of the modern architecture of Le Corbusier and the Bauhaus School – the year was 1931 – and then the merits of ferro-concrete and the simplicity of tubular steel furniture were rapturously extolled . . . Wonderful jokes welled up in improvised asides and when, as if by mistake . . . a slide of Mickey Mouse playing a ukulele dropped on the screen for a split second, it brought the house down. We reeled away in a state of gaseous exhilaration and the result would have been the same, whatever his theme.

The sort of myths that float around schools tended to settle on Paddy. It was said that someone heard Fermor creeping out of the dorm in the middle of the night, and decided to follow him. Lighting his way with a torch and unaware that he was being shadowed, he made his way to the gym, which had a very high ceiling spanned by a great beam, hung with climbing ropes. Hidden in the shadows, the boy watched with mounting alarm as Fermor shinned up one of the ropes, clambered on to the beam and walked from one end to the other. Having completed this feat, he came down the rope and made his way back to the dormitory.

He was making good use of his time at King's, although the energy he put into learning and reading was matched by less edifying habits. If anyone was caught hanging around the betting shops, smoking cigarettes, clambering over the roof or getting into fights, it was probably Fermor; and his sins were compounded by a fearless swagger and total disregard for punishment. He was suspended at one point, and taken back to his mother at 213 Piccadilly.

Paddy explained his increasingly wild behaviour as 'A bookish attempt to coerce life into a closer resemblance to literature', encouraged by 'a hangover from early anarchy: translating ideas as fast as I could into deeds overrode every thought of punishment or danger.'[15] The prefects and monitors thought he was mad, and even Paddy found his antics inexplicable. His housemaster's much-quoted penultimate report reads, 'He is a dangerous mixture of sophistication and recklessness which makes one anxious about his influence on other boys.'[16]

Æileen took him skiing that year in the Bernese Oberland, where he was suddenly taken ill. The doctors said he had 'strained his heart', for which the only cure was an extended rest.[17] He was not allowed back to school for several weeks, and when he returned the summer term was well under way. All sports were forbidden, so Paddy was left with a glorious windfall of idle hours in which to polish his daredevil reputation.

At that time some of the senior boys were swooning over a new discovery – the exceptionally pretty daughter of Mr E. J. Lemar, a greengrocer with premises in Dover Street. As soon as Paddy heard about Nellie Lemar he sought her out, and found that she embodied his ideal of feminine beauty, formed by the long-haired goose girls and princesses in Andrew Lang's Coloured Fairy Books. His visits to Nellie did not pass unnoticed, for in the school uniform of black coat, striped trousers and a speckled straw boater, Paddy was a conspicuous figure in Dover Street – which was in any case out of bounds. He was caught red-handed: 'holding Nellie's hand, that is to say, which is about as far as this suit was ever pressed'.[18]

The purity of Paddy's intentions cut no ice with his housemaster Alec Macdonald, for whom this particular escapade was the last straw. He was sent to see the headmaster, Mr Birley, who saw the incident as a good opportunity to get rid of a troublesome pupil. Paddy's reaction was one of utter dejection. He had been thrown out of schools before, but this was the first time he had really minded: the King's School had stirred his imagination, and he had felt happy and fulfilled there. Moreover, his expulsion came before he had sat the School Certificate. Paddy was no longer a child, he lacked all formal qualifications, and in a few years' time he would be expected to earn his own living.

Æileen was dismayed by this turn of events, but Paddy knew that she had always taken a lenient view of his wildness: 'I think her own rather headstrong and turbulent career as a girl charitably tempered exasperation with a secret sympathy, however much it had to be repressed for decorum's sake.'[19]

How the news was received by Lewis Fermor in Calcutta is not hard to imagine. The dream of Paddy going into any branch of the sciences had died long ago, and neither he nor his son had any idea of how he was going to make a living. In terms of practical help, there was very little Lewis could do. He had spent all his working life in India, and had few contacts outside the scientific community.

The solution to the Paddy problem was the army, and at first Paddy welcomed the idea. He had strength, energy and confidence, lively spirits and courage (the acceptable face of recklessness). Why should he not make a good soldier? And indeed, the British had a long tradition of soldier poets and writers, from Sir Philip Sidney through to Robert Graves and Siegfried Sassoon. But before he could be considered by the Royal Military College at Sandhurst, he had to pass his School Certificate.

He was sent to a crammer in London where he studied for the London Certificate, which was acknowledged by Sandhurst but did not require such a high standard in mathematics. The crammer was run by Denys Prideaux, and most of his students expected to join the army. Now that Æileen was living once more in the village of Coldharbour near Dorking, Paddy lodged with Mr and Mrs Prideaux, first in Queensberry Terrace, then in Lancaster Gate.

In the summer of 1932 he took the London Certificate and passed, even in maths; but Sandhurst did not accept cadets till they had turned eighteen, which in his case was over six months away. With the exams done, he entered a period of intense reading, 'and read more books than I have ever crammed into a similar stretch of time', he wrote in *A Time of Gifts*.[20] His great enthusiasms at this period were for the works of Aldous Huxley, Evelyn Waugh and Norman Douglas: Douglas's *Old Calabria*, published in 1915, he always considered the greatest travel book ever written. In French he read Rabelais, Ronsard and Baudelaire, but was particularly drawn to the fifteenth-century poet François Villon. Villon's dark, exalted poetry – particularly 'La Ballade des Pendus' – exerted a powerful attraction, and he translated a number of Villon's rondeaux and ballades.

And literature was not the only thing that absorbed him. Hours were spent wandering round the National Gallery and that treasure-house of visual history, the National Portrait Gallery. He also became familiar with the monuments, churches, museums and pubs of London.

He was introduced to Mrs Minka Bax, wife of the writer Clifford Bax, who lived in Addison Road off Kensington High Street. Mrs Bax held an informal literary salon, where young men and women talked about books, plays, aesthetics and the meaning of art. Paddy enjoyed these afternoons, but found her guests rather too earnest and high-minded.

He had more fun with a group of 'fellow crammers' pups', mostly a little older than Paddy but like him destined for the army. In *A Time of Gifts* they are described as 'wide-eyed, pink-cheeked and innocent boys with tidy hair; cornets and ensigns in the larva phase'.[21] It is rare for Paddy to be ungenerous to old friends in his writing, particularly ones from whom he has taken a certain amount of hospitality; yet at this time he himself was going through a 'larva phase' of which he was to be slightly ashamed a few months later. His new friends admired his dash on a horse, and laughed like hyenas when he dived into a lake in full evening dress (remembering only on re-emerging that he was in borrowed tails). They had him to stay for weekends, in the company of people who read little more than the sporting pages and treated books with suspicion – but Paddy didn't mind. He enjoyed the boisterous company, the balls and hunts and point-to-points; while his young hosts knew that however wild Fermor might be, he could be trusted to look presentable in front of their relations.

The grace and panache of fine clothes were a lifelong pleasure for Paddy, whose books describe the dress of both men and women in meticulous detail. Clothes were also an important component of his historical memory. He used to say that while he could never remember dates on a page, he had only to see a painting of a prince or cardinal and he could date it by the costume to within fifty years. Now that he was moving in a crowd of young blades who defined themselves by their tailoring, he easily persuaded himself that the boots, bowler hat, double-breasted waistcoat, hacking jacket and riding breeches he ordered were not just essential kit but an investment. He overspent wildly on his allowance of thirty shillings a week, and the bills poured in. Lewis was alerted. First expulsion, now debts. As a father he knew he had been almost totally absent, but like Paddy's masters he probably blamed Æileen. Her over-romantic imagination, her disdain for the mundane and the practical, not to mention her insistence on smart (that is, expensive) turnout, had a lot to answer for. Lewis took care of the most urgent demands and, in a couple of blistering letters from India, told Paddy that he was responsible for the rest. Some of the bills remained unpaid for years.

Yet the debts had revealed a stark truth. Life for a junior officer, based at Aldershot or Tidworth for months on end in peacetime, would be impossible to sustain on army pay alone, and Paddy had no private income. Among his fellow cadets he would be irresistibly drawn to the fast and dangerous set, who would be far richer than himself and secure in the knowledge that money and connections would ease their way out of boredom and trouble. Paddy had no such advantages, and he knew it.

It was in the spring and summer of 1933 that Paddy began to frequent the bar of the Cavendish Hotel in Jermyn Street, to which he was first introduced by one of his fellow crammers at Prideaux's. Under its famous Edwardian owner Rosa Lewis, the Cavendish was closer in spirit to an old-fashioned and rather raffish club than a hotel. The young men favoured by Mrs Lewis in those inter-war years enjoyed generous credit, often settled by her slippery accounting. She knew exactly which of her older and richer clients could be relied on not to examine their bills too closely.

Rosa Lewis took a shine to Paddy, whom she always called 'Young Feemur', or sometimes 'Young Fermoy'. With Rosa gripping his arm like a vice and her two pekingese panting behind, Paddy would occasionally escort her on her routine inspection of the shops along Piccadilly and St James's. She enjoyed picking delicacies off the counters in Fortnum & Mason, daring the assistants to challenge her. Mrs Lewis thought that Evelyn Waugh's description of her as Mrs Crump in *Vile Bodies* did not do her justice. 'If I get my 'ands on that Mr Woo-aagh,' she told Paddy, her false teeth rattling ominously, 'I'll cut 'is winkle orff!'[22]

Since the mid-1920s, the Cavendish had been the haunt of that group of resolutely decadent youth whom the *Daily Mail* had dubbed 'The Bright Young People'. Although they had phases of preferring the Café Royal they never abandoned the Cavendish altogether, and it was from his visits there that Paddy came to know Brian Howard, Jennifer Fry, Elizabeth Pelly, Eddie Gathorne-Hardy, Alistair Graham and Mark Ogilvie-Grant. By 1933, when Paddy fell into their orbit, the wild parties that had so scandalized the nation were over and the revellers were almost a decade older; but they were still dedicated to pleasure, still set against all that was pompous and stuffy, still resolutely refusing to take themselves seriously. They also loved conversation, and drinking late into the night. To Paddy they were godlike, irresistible, and exactly like their alter egos in *Vile Bodies*. They spoke an elaborate language that contrived to be both donnish, shocking and rather camp, and assumed you knew who they meant when they talked so easily of William Walton or Eric Satie, of the Futurists or Man Ray or Picasso. Art, music and literature were forces of change and liberation, and so was socialism: 'The Left Wing opinions that I occasionally heard were uttered in such a way that they seemed a part merely, and a minor part, of a more general emancipation.'[23]

More seductive than their light-hearted socialism was their disdain for all things English: for among these new friends, 'it was an article of faith that every manifestation of English life or thought or art was slightly provincial and a crashing bore.'[24] Paddy found that these sentiments suited him very well, since the tedium of England and English life provided a convenient excuse for his feelings of inadequacy, claustrophobia and boredom: 'all of a sudden, everything attractive or exciting seemed to be foreign.'[25]

Paddy described slipping into this bohemian world, so different from that of the larval officers, as going through the looking glass. Before this passage, he had always been suppressing some part of himself: the boisterous part was stifled when he went to tea with Mrs Clifford Bax, the bookish part when he was among his army friends. Now he had found a group of people who accepted both the bookish and the boisterous in him, and saw nothing odd in cultivating both.

He lost his virginity to Elizabeth Pelly, one of the wildest of those partygoers whose antics had filled the papers in the mid-1920s. Now divorced from her husband Denis, her hopes of marrying a friend called John Ludovic Ford (known as Ludy) were waning. But it does seem strange that her trysts with Paddy ('a few secret afternoons', he called them) should have taken place in Ford's house in Cheyne Row.

His new friends enjoyed seeing themselves reflected in the way he copied their tastes and mannerisms, laughed at the fact that he had been thrown out of school and were pleased that he had given up the idea of going to Sandhurst – '"The Army! I should hope *not* indeed. The very idea!"'[26] Paddy was treated with a fair degree of indulgence, and they paid for more of his drinks than they might have done had he been older. '"Where's that rather noisy boy got to? We may as well take him too."'[27] They took him to the Café Royal, and later in the evening to nightclubs such as the Nuthouse, the Boogie-Woogie and (raunchiest of all) Smoky Joe's. He thought it was in Smoky Joe's that he met the writer Robert Byron, whose works *The Station* (1928) and *The Byzantine Achievement* (1929) argued that Byzantine art was as good as anything produced in the classical period. The meeting was a disappointment because Byron was too drunk to make much sense; and though they met again some years later, it was only as fellow guests at drinks parties.

Another great haunt of literary and unconventional London in the early thirties was the Gargoyle Club, founded in 1925 by the wealthy aristocrat and partygoer, David Tennant. Its main L-shaped room took its inspiration from Byzantium: the coffered ceiling was covered in gold leaf, while the walls were a mosaic of mirrored tiles (an idea suggested by Henri Matisse, who was immediately made an honorary member).

The Gargoyle attracted an eclectic mix of social celebrities, artists, writers, actors, musicians, journalists and publishers, which was given a raffish tone by a sprinkling of the younger Guinnesses and Tennants, Wyndhams and Trees. A photograph of hard-core Gargoylers taken in the late 1930s included the then gossip columnist Patrick Balfour, better known as the historian Lord Kinross, the composer Constant Lambert, the artist Dick Wyndham and the writer Cyril Connolly – all of whom were to become Paddy's friends in the late forties and fifties.

In the summer of 1933, Paddy moved out of Mr and Mrs Prideaux's and into 28 Market Street in Shepherd Market, where several friends already had rooms. His parents would have preferred him to stay under a tutor's eye, and they refused to increase his allowance; but he was determined to move, even though it would mean that he would have to live on a pound a week.

His parents had not been told that he had given up the idea of Sandhurst, though perhaps they were beginning to realize it. Given his interest, not to mention talent, in history and languages and literature, one wonders whether Denys Prideaux ever tried to persuade him or his parents to let him try for university. But it would have been a struggle to get him accepted, and doubtful whether he would have lasted the course. He was on the other side of the looking glass by now.

He vaguely hoped that once on his own, some glorious opportunity would reveal itself. He might get one or two more pieces published. Some influential critic might notice his work, and set him on the road to a prosperous future. He tried to look at his restricted allowance as a blessing in disguise: since he could not afford to go out, he would have to work at his writing.

Paddy could not remember what he was trying to write, except to say that it was probably poetry; however, little was written because the house became the scene of wild and continuous parties. Time and time again, their long-suffering landlady, Miss Beatrice Stewart, would hammer on the doors trying to silence their din. Nor could he remember the names of his Shepherd Market friends. Alcohol may have had a lot to do with it, and perhaps the lodgers came and went as lodgers do. Even so, it says something about the selectiveness of his memory: in turning the spotlight on the romantic figure of his landlady Miss Stewart, he leaves his fellow lodgers as ill-defined shadows. The most he could say was that, like him, they were living on small independent allowances.

Miss Stewart had been an artist's model, who had sat for Sargent, Augustus John and J. J. Shannon among others. By the time Paddy knew her, she had lost a leg in a car accident; but her greatest claim to fame was to have been the model for the statue of Peace that dominates Adrian Jones's great bronze quadriga mounted on top of the Wellington Arch at Hyde Park Corner. 'I can never pass the top of Constitution Hill', wrote Paddy, 'without thinking of her and gazing up at the winged and wreath-bearing goddess sailing across the sky.'[28]

Another reason why he was not writing much was that he was trying to make some money. In a pub called the Running Horse in Davies Street, he was introduced to a man who sold silk stockings. He ran a team of well-spoken, middle-class youths like Paddy who would take his wares to the ladies of the London suburbs, and sell them door to door. The young salesmen were encouraged to scan the telephone directory for names and addresses in a chosen area so that, when they came to a particular house and the door was answered by a maid, they could ask whether Mrs Richardson or Mrs Jones was at home; and, if asked to come in, they then had the opportunity to lay out and describe their stockings in glowing terms.

For a few weeks he sold stockings to the ladies of Richmond, Chiswick and Ealing, and though he hated it he was successful in turning a profit. One evening at the Running Horse, the boss singled him out as a star salesman and asked him to give the other members of the team a few tips. According to Paddy, he pulled a stocking over his hand and described its properties as if it were a condom – which had the team howling with laughter, and his boss purple in the face with rage. He was sacked immediately.

It is strange that this story does not appear in *A Time of Gifts*. When asked why, his reply was that Esmond Romilly had written a very funny passage about selling stockings door to door, and he did not want to repeat it.[29] Yet it seems more likely that Paddy preferred to forget this rather shabby moment in his life. It did not sit comfortably with the innocent, enthusiastic and bookish image of his young self.

Paddy was aware that he was 'slowly and enjoyably disintegrating in a miniature Rake's Progress'.[30] For most of the night, he could drink himself into a genial euphoria; but in the chill hours between one party and the next, he grew ever more restless and depressed.

For most of his life he was susceptible to emotional extremes, and bouts of depression triggered by the feeling that he seemed unable to measure up to people's expectations. He was not yet nineteen, but the doors of opportunity seemed to be closing rather than opening before him. His academic career had been a disaster; the combination of tedium and temptation meant that he was unlikely to succeed in the army; nor could he see himself in an office from nine till five. By now his parents had realized that he had turned against a military career, and their disappointment increased his sense of inadequacy. In a moment of despair, his father had even suggested that he might consider becoming a chartered accountant.

He was struck by 'a sudden loathing of London. Everything suddenly seeming unbearable, loathsome, trivial, restless, shoddy . . . Detestation, suddenly, of parties. Contempt for everyone, starting and finishing with myself. Everything jarred, hurt, discouraged. Felt all faculties dispersed, whatever was worthwhile stifled, all that was worst taking over . . . Atmosphere of dead-beat, hungover idleness.'[31]

The answer, he wrote, came suddenly one rainy evening. To leave England and travel would solve all problems. Sandhurst and the army would be indefinitely postponed. On his pound a week allowance he would walk from west to east across Europe, sleeping in barns and hayricks, eating bread and cheese, living like a wandering scholar or pilgrim, keeping company with tramps and vagabonds, peasants and gypsies. At last he would have something to write about. His goal would be the city which, in 1930, had officially changed its name to Istanbul, although Paddy never called it anything but Constantinople.

To walk from the Hook of Holland to Constantinople. His ambition was contained in a single sentence, that sounded like a drumroll ending in a clash of cymbals. The words became a spell, an amulet, which swept all doubts aside. His real goal was Greece, but there is no doubt which sounded better. To walk from the Hook of Holland to Athens keeps you firmly in Europe, but to walk from Holland to Constantinople takes you to the very gates of Asia. It crosses cultural as well as geographical boundaries, and to the romantic imagination it sounds a good deal farther.

Once the Plan had taken form, it had to be put in place. Mr

Prideaux was told about it, and not unnaturally expressed grave misgivings; at the same time it was better than frittering his time away in Shepherd Market, and might give him some experience of the world. Mr Prideaux undertook to write to Lewis in Calcutta – although Paddy was almost certain that his father would take a dim view of the plan, however Mr Prideaux presented it.

Apart from his pound a week, which the loyal Mr Prideaux agreed to post in monthly packets to various consulates along the way, the young man needed some money to launch himself on the journey. In *A Time of Gifts* he says he borrowed some money from the father of a friend, 'partly to buy equipment and partly to have something in hand when I set out'.[32] His generous patron was the father of Graham Cook, an old school friend, whose family Paddy often visited in Hampstead. Fascinated by the quest, Mr Cook had asked Paddy how he was going to manage. Paddy, of course, had no idea beyond his four pounds a month, but Mr Cook came to the rescue: 'Here you are, my boy, here's twenty pounds and good luck to you.'[33]

Another gift was to prove even more valuable since it grew like a capital sum. It was the gift of a friend of Miss Stewart's, Mrs Sandwith, who might have been Paddy's fairy godmother. Hearing of his plan, Mrs Sandwith wrote two or three letters of introduction for him to present to friends of hers in Germany. Paddy had no idea, as he put them in his pocket, what a profound and far-reaching effect they would have on his passage through Europe, and indeed his whole life.

The next step was to convince his mother, who was at that time staying with his newly-married sister in Gloucestershire. It had been a bad year for Æileen: although she had been divorced from Lewis for eight years, the news that he had married a Miss Frances Mary Case underlined both her loneliness and her diminished status as a divorcee. (A further humiliation came two years later when Lewis was knighted, and his second wife became Lady Fermor.) When Paddy announced that he was about to take off on a walk across Europe that winter, she felt another lifeline breaking. Yet part of her wanted to be persuaded: she loved the adventurer in him, which marked him so firmly as her son rather than his father's.

Paddy himself had no doubts, no moments of wondering whether he was making a terrible mistake – though everyone he talked to tried to persuade him, if not to drop his great plan, to postpone it. After all, it was mid-winter: why not stay for Christmas and then go in the spring? But he understood the importance of the moment: if he did not leave while still in the grip of excitement and enthusiasm, something else would intervene and he would end up not going at all. He bought a ticket for passage to Holland on a Dutch steamer, the *Stadthouder Willem*, that was to leave Tower Bridge on the afternoon of Saturday 9 December 1933.

Most of the clothes he bought for the journey were from Millet's army surplus store in the Strand. The most important item were his hobnailed boots, which he says were comfortable from the first day and lasted him the whole journey. He also had a soft sleeveless leather jacket with pockets, in which he kept passport and money. His everyday trousers were comfortable riding breeches, the rest of his legs being protected by puttees – long bandages made of stiff wool which were wound round the sock and up to the knee, where they were tucked in with a bit of tape ('though in cavalry regiments', he observed, 'you started at the knee and worked your way down').[34] He also bought an army greatcoat (stiff and heavy, but it did duty as a bedroll and blanket) and a sleeping bag, which he lost almost at once and never bothered to replace.

The rest of his pack consisted of drawing blocks, notebooks, an aluminium cylinder full of pencils, and three books: a small English–German dictionary, *The Oxford Book of English Verse*, and the first volume of Loeb's Horace. The last was a present from Æileen, who had asked Paddy what he would like. On the flyleaf of the book she wrote out a translation of a short poem by Petronius: it is one of the three verses that open *A Time of Gifts*.

> Leave thy home, O youth, and seek out alien shores . . . Yield not to misfortune: the far-off Danube shall know thee, the cold North-wind and the untroubled kingdom of Canopus and the men who gaze on the new birth of Phoebus or upon his setting . . .

Lewis Fermor was informed of Paddy's plans in a letter sent just before he left England, so that he would be well on his way by the time it arrived in Calcutta. In the event, Lewis took the news better than might have been expected: 'Perhaps he felt that they were the beginning of the dissolution of our remote link which in fact it turned out to be.'[35] Mark Ogilvie-Grant inspected his kit, and pronounced himself satisfied with everything except the flimsy canvas rucksack. Ogilvie-Grant said he would lend Paddy his own rucksack, which was supported by a metal frame and therefore more comfortable. This was the very pack that Ogilvie-Grant had taken round Mount Athos in 1927, in company with David Talbot Rice and Robert Byron – a journey that Byron had turned into *The Station*, the book that Paddy always claimed had inspired his resolve not to stop at Constantinople, but to plunge on into Greece.*

On the morning of 9 December, Paddy woke with a hangover – the result of a farewell party the night before. He went first to Cliveden Place to pick up the famous rucksack, and then bought a tall walking stick of ash in Sloane Square. From there he walked to Petty France to pick up his new passport.

His ate his last lunch in London with Miss Stewart, in company with three friends: Geoffrey Gaunt, Tony Hall, and a girl called Priscilla Wickham. It was raining hard. They accompanied him by taxi to Tower Bridge, and briefly wished him well on the steps leading down to Irongate Wharf; there was not a moment to lose, for the *Stadthouder Willem* was making ready to leave. Paddy hurried over the gangway, clutching his stick and his rucksack, and waved from the deck at his friends who were shouting their last goodbyes from the top of Tower Bridge. Then, with a rattle of anchor chain and a blast from her siren, the *Stadthouder Willem* pushed out into the Thames.

---

* However, his reactions on reading *The Station* on Mount Athos (see pages 97–8) seem to imply that he had not read it until then.

3

'Zu Fuss nach Konstantinopel'

Rocking on the dark sea between England and mainland Europe, Paddy could not sleep – 'it seemed too important a night.'[1] It was as if he were sloughing off the skin of his old self, rank with academic failure and family disappointment, to reveal a new one glowing with hope and excitement. To separate the new self from the old, he took a new name: for the next sixteen months he called himself by his middle name, Michael.

He reached Rotterdam just before dawn, and after an early breakfast strode off through the snow. It fell so thickly that his bare head was soon white with it, but he was in such a state of exalted energy that he did not care. He spent his first night in Dordrecht, some twenty kilometres south of Rotterdam. Having fallen asleep at the table after his supper in a waterfront bar, he was guided upstairs to a little room where he fell asleep under a huge quilt. Payment was accepted for his meal, but none for the lodging: 'This was the first marvellous instance of a kindness and hospitality that was to occur again and again on these travels.'[2]

He walked through the Netherlands in five days, marvelling at how much the landscape mirrored the paintings of Cuyp and Ruysdael, the interiors giving life-size glimpses into the worlds of Hoogstraten and Jan Steen. The river Waal gave way to the Rhine, churches became Catholic. After spending his last night in the Netherlands over a blacksmith's shop in Nijmegen, he walked over the border into Germany on 15 December 1933.

Hitler had dominated the country since the end of January 1933, and had invested himself with supreme power in March. His cult was raised to the status of a religion, and the idea of a nation arising was all-pervasive. 'If you listen to the wireless in Germany today,'

The Walk, 1933–4:
From Rotterdam to the Iron Gates

International frontiers shown are pre-Second World War

POLAND

Prague

CZECHOSLOVAKIA

hlarn-
bbs-
ding
nz
Dürnstein
Pottenbrunn
Vienna
Kövecses
Eigendorf
Bratislava • Nové Zámky
Karva •
Melk
Esztergom
Persenbeug
Budapest •
ochscharten

RIA

HUNGARY

Cegled
Szolnok

Körösladány •
Vesztö
Békéscsaba •
O'Kígíos •
Doboz
Ötvenes
Ineu (Borosjenö) •
Konop Zám •
Kápolnás •
Guraszáda

Tomeşti •
Caransebeş

Danube

YUGOSLAVIA

Orşova •
The Iron
Gates
Turnu
Severin

Ada Kaleh

RUMANIA

Mureş

the journalist Gareth Jones reported at the time, 'you will hear in the intervals four notes being played time and again, and you find it is the tune, "People to Arms!", which is being drummed into the ears and minds of listeners.'[3]

Soon after his arrival in the town of Goch, Paddy watched a parade of the local unit of stormtroopers (*Sturmabteilung*, or SA). Sure enough, they sang 'Volk, ans Gewehr!', keeping time to the thumping rhythm with their boots as they marched into the town square where they were addressed by their commander. Paddy's German was not good enough to catch it all, but 'the rasp of his utterance, even robbed of its meaning, struck a chill'.[4] Later that evening he saw a group of SA men singing in a tavern. At first they were raucously noisy, but later on 'the thumping died away as the singing became softer and harmonies and descants began to weave more complex patterns . . . And the charm made it impossible, at that moment, to connect the singers with organized bullying and the smashing of Jewish shop windows and nocturnal bonfires of books.'[5] Ubiquitous symbol of the new order was the 'Heil Hitler' salute, which provided a contemporary version of the pickelhaube'd, goose-stepping cartoon German of his inter-war childhood. 'People meeting in the street would become performing seals for a second. This exchange, soon to become very familiar, seemed extremely odd for the first few days, as though the place were full of slightly sinister boy scouts . . . The utterances sounded as though centuries of custom lay behind them, not a mere eleven months.'[6]

There had also been a dramatic swing in political opinion. In some 'lost Rhineland town', he had met a group of factory workers coming off their shift in a local bar and one of them offered him a place to spend the night. To Paddy's surprise, his room was a Nazi shrine, complete with banners and photographs of Hitler – though the year before, his friend admitted, he had been a die-hard Communist. 'I used to punch the heads of anyone singing the *Horst Wessel Lied*! It was all the *Red Flag* and the *International* then . . . We used to beat the hell out of the Nazis, and they beat the hell out of us . . .'[7]

His conversion to Nazism, he said, had been very sudden; but he also claimed the same for everyone he worked with. Paddy could scarcely believe it: had so many people really changed from being Communists to Nazis, almost overnight? 'Millions! I tell you, I was astonished how easily they all changed sides!'[8] For those who thought about it seriously, it cannot have been an easy decision; but if you wanted to survive and work, all signs of Bolshevism had to be concealed.

For all Hitler's confident promises before coming to power, it was still a time of great economic hardship and unemployment. In a Franciscan workhouse in Düsseldorf, Paddy met a Saxon from Brunswick who had failed to find any jobs in Duisburg, Essen, Düsseldorf, and the whole of the Ruhr valley. Probably most of the men in the workhouse that night were in a similar situation, wandering from one place to another trying to find a day's work.

In Cologne he bought Goethe's *Faust* and Schlegel & Tieck's translation of *Hamlet*. He also spent his first night in a German house, and had his first bath since leaving London. The following day he took a lift with a string of barges carrying cement, crewed by Uli and Peter, two men with whom Paddy had got spectacularly drunk in a waterfront bar. They welcomed him on board, and fed him with fried potatoes and speck – cold lumps of fat that struck him as the nastiest thing he had ever eaten – while Uli did his Hitler impression. Rolling upstream by barge was an ideal way to watch the changing landscape, as the Rhine became ever more mountainous and dramatic, with castles perched on crags reflected in the water, as the line of barges slid past Bad Godesberg, Andernach and Ehrenbreitstein.

He jumped ashore at Coblenz and spent Christmas Eve singing carols round a Christmas tree in a friendly *Gasthof* in Bingen. Christmas Day might have been rather lonely, but at some inn or other (he could not remember where) he was drawn into another family gathering which went on carousing into the night. It must have been quite a party, for he 'lost' several days between Christmas and New Year: all that remained were scattered visual fragments of Oppenheim, Worms and Mannheim. In Heidelberg he again struck lucky at an inn called the Red Ox. The owners, Herr and Frau Spengel, treated him as their guest and insisted that he stay with them for the following day, which was New Year's Eve.

Paddy came across kindness and generosity wherever he went,

despite the harshness of the times. It had something to do with the word 'student', written in his passport and which he used to describe himself. The word was evocative of the wandering scholars who had been a feature of European life since the twelfth century, as they walked from one university town or monastery to the next in pursuit of knowledge. With his rucksack and his notebook he looked and felt the part, but what made him so immediately engaging to people was that he shone with joy. Until he left home, his desire to live with an intensity that seemed only to exist in books had always got him into trouble. Now there was no one to tell him what to do, no one even to know where he was – a thought that gave him a rush of pleasure every time it occurred to him. This sense of freedom was so intoxicating that he described himself as living in a state of almost constant euphoria and well-being. He was becoming fitter and stronger by the day. At night he fell asleep 'in a coma of happiness',[9] although he wished he were awake all the time: 'Living in a yeasty ferment of excitement I grudged every second of sleep. All I saw, heard, smelt, touched and tasted or read was brand new. The intake, total and continuous, was crowding in to bursting point.'[10]

Happiness, excitement, youth, good looks, eagerness to please and an open heart: Paddy had them all. The combination was irresistible, and people responded to it with warmth and delight. The Spengels' student son, Fritz, took him round Heidelberg the next day while Paddy pumped him for details about the drinking and duelling rituals that lent such dark glamour to German student life. Back at the inn, sitting with Fritz in the early stages of the New Year's Eve festivities, he was brought up against darkness of a different sort. 'So? Ein Engländer?'[11] A fair-haired young Nazi came up to the table where he and Fritz were sitting together. England, he said through gritted teeth, had stolen Germany's colonies, stopped her from having a proper army or a fleet, and was run by Jews. Fritz was embarrassed and apologetic. 'You see what it's like,' he said.[12]

Although he was walking through Germany at one of the most significant moments in its modern history, Paddy's head was full of the romance of Germany's past. 'If only I had had less of a medieval passion, more of a political sense,' he admitted in a notebook entry thirty years later, 'I would have drunk in, sought out so much more.'[13] He had spent very little time thinking about political ideas. At home he had absorbed the middle-class conservatism of his mother, and his ancient school in its rural backwater had given him no reason to question it. At the bar of the Cavendish, socialism was considered radical and exciting, but held little aesthetic appeal for his imagination.

Yet despite his political myopia, what he saw of Nazism in those few weeks of 1933 was enough to fill him with abhorrence. Beyond the venomous young man in Heidelberg, Paddy does not identify the Nazis he talked to. There may have been anything between two to a dozen such conversations, in cafés and bars, beer halls or wine-cellars. The only thing they had in common was that Paddy always came off worst.

The Nazis he spoke to were very interested in talking to an Englishman. So, what did he think of National Socialism? Here he was on solid ground, even though he could not move far off it. He said he had three objections: the use of concentration camps, the burning of books, and hatred of the Jews. For the keen Nazi, the first two objections were easily dealt with. The camps held only a few Jews and Communists, whose fates were dismissed with a shrug. As for the books, that's what seditious literature deserved. And how could he be so blind to the threat posed by the Jews? Their aim was nothing less than world domination, to be achieved by a devilish combination of Bolshevism and unfettered capitalism.

Even Paddy could see the contradiction here, but as he put it:

> [this] illogical sequence of ideas had to be presented in a kind of logical disguise. Each step must be marked with a didactic blow of the forefinger on the table, each idea defined and put in a small labelled box, agreed to – '*Nicht wahr?*' – A nod. '*Also!*' – before moving to the next . . . I had not a chance of winning in any of these colloquies, I could only stonewall. There was always some handy slogan of Hitler's to deal with everything one said; '*Der Führer sagt*' they would begin, or sometimes, with bold familiarity, '*Der Adolf sagt*' . . .[14]

This inability to get through the fortress of Nazi ideology was echoed by another student travelling in Germany at this time. Daniel Guérin was a young Communist far more skilled in political debate than Paddy, who recalled his experiences in a book entitled *La Peste brune*. 'My impression is that this is an absolutely closed world with which no contact is possible. What's the use of talking? What we have to say would no longer be understood.'[15]

Paddy felt most exposed when the subject of the Oxford Union debate came up. Almost a year before, the Union had passed a motion that it would 'under no circumstances fight for King and Country', a pronouncement that had sent shock waves throughout Europe. The vote reflected an angry disillusionment with the politicians and generals who had led thousands of young men to their deaths in the Great War, coupled with the determination that a war on that scale should never be allowed to happen again. Paddy described it as an act of defiance against the older generation, *pour épater les bourgeois*. He even suggested that it might have been a sort of joke. To young Nazis, for whom the words *Koenig und Vaterland* sounded inspiring rather than faintly embarrassing, the idea that the motion might have been 'a sort of joke' was baffling: but it pleased them to think that British youth was in the final stages of intellectual and moral degeneracy.

One of the letters written by Mrs Sandwith had secured Paddy two very happy evenings with Dr Arnold, the mayor of Bruchsal, who lived in one of the most beautiful baroque palaces in Germany. Paddy had never seen such architecture before, and he was dazzled by its glittering beauty on a snowy morning. Two days later he was in Stuttgart where, in a café, he met two music students called Liselotte and Annie. Annie's parents were away, and since it was pouring with rain they took pity on him and asked him back to the flat. There followed two happy days of high jinks, lubricated by Annie's father's best wine. He insisted that the interlude was perfectly innocent, apart from a cuddle on the sofa with Annie. Did Liselotte exist, one wonders? Paddy has been known to insert a fictitious third figure to protect a girl's reputation; but when the question was raised in this case, he indignantly denied it. There were definitely two girls in Stuttgart.

Leaving the city, he set off in a south-easterly direction. The road passed through a country of pasture and ploughland, broken by dense woods of conifer – the outermost edges of the Black Forest, which lay to the south-west.

It was at Ulm, the highest navigable point of the Danube, that he had his first sight of the great river. He climbed into the cathedral belfry to admire the view. The Danube lay below him, and far away to the south he could see the Alps, shining in the early morning sun.

As he travelled on, he began to see the contrasts between the Rhine and the Danube. The Rhine had been far busier, and seemed to carry a great deal more freight; while sometimes he might walk for hours within sight of the Danube without seeing any traffic at all. Yet on both rivers, there was hardly a hill or a promontory that was not topped with a castle or a church.

A flash of illumination came at Augsburg, with what he called the Landsknecht formula. He had been looking for something that expressed the character and feeling of a pre-Baroque German town, the Teutonic link between the medieval and the Renaissance; and he found it in the figure of the Landsknechts at the time of Maximilian I, with their floppy hats and ostrich feathers, their slashed doublets and beribboned hose. He had first seen them in a book in Stuttgart, but it was in Augsburg cathedral that the idea suddenly fell into place. 'Once I had got hold of the Landsknecht formula – mediaeval solidity adorned with a jungle of inorganic Renaissance detail – there was no holding me! It came into play wherever I looked.' And he did look, at every decorative detail that came his way. 'Taking their cue – subconsciously, perhaps – from those soldiers, the masons and smiths and joiners must have conspired together; everything that could fork, ramify, coil, flutter, fold back or thread through itself, suddenly sprang to action.'[16] It is obvious that he could never have written a virtuoso passage like this at the age of eighteen. But he came up with the idea then, and years later could still recapture the joy of its discovery and the fun he had with it.

Four fresh pound notes were waiting for him in Munich. He went to the youth hostel and dumped his rucksack and stick on one of the long line of empty beds. At that moment, a pimply young man came in and sat down as though to start up a conversation, but

Paddy was impatient to get to the *Hofbräuhaus*, and so he clattered back downstairs again and out into the street, leaving the rucksack on his bed.

He did not like Munich. The wind swirled down vast avenues, the architecture was impersonal and pompous, and the Stormtroopers and SS were much in evidence. Eventually he found the *Hofbräuhaus*, where a Brownshirt was being sick on the stairs. In *A Time of Gifts*, there follows a vision of hell: from the vastly fat and glistening burghers and their wives stuffing themselves with gargantuan helpings of meat and sausage, to the great vaulted hall where the serious drinking happened. As he downed one elephantine mug after another and watched people beside him flop unconscious into puddles of beer, the great hall seemed to sink into the murky depths of the Rhine.

He woke the next day on a sofa, with a dreadful hangover. He had passed out in a drunken stupor, but the kind carpenter who had been sitting next to him took him home in a handcart full of turned chair legs. He felt terrible, but worse was to come. Back at the youth hostel, he found that his rucksack had been stolen by the pimply youth who had sat next to him. Paddy had lost everything: the talismanic rucksack, his passport with four brand new pound notes in it and, most painful of all, the notebook and sketches that had recorded the journey so far.

He had visions of a humiliating deportation back to England, but the British Consul, Mr D. St Clair Gainer, was kinder than he had expected. The following day he was given a fresh passport, and 'His Majesty's Government will lend you a fiver. Send it back some time when you're less broke.'[17] (He sent it back from Constantinople, almost a year later.)

A few days before this shattering loss, he had sent off another of Mrs Sandwith's letters, to Baron Rheinhard von Liphart-Ratshoff. Originally from Estonia, the family had settled in Gräfeling, just outside Munich. Paddy spent five days with them, during which time the Baron's sons did much to replace what had been stolen in the youth hostel. They gave him an old rucksack and warm clothes, while the Baron wrote letters to several of his friends, urging them to do what they could for this curious and amusing young man. Best of all was the Baron's parting present. It was a small, mid-seventeenth-century volume of Horace's Odes and Epodes, gilt-edged with engraved illustrations, and bound in green leather. He loved and treasured this book and kept it safe, till a Stuka raid in 1941 sent it to the bottom of the Gulf of Argolis.

Well rested and freshly kitted out, he set off across Bavaria. Here the countryside was still steeped in tradition, and Paddy was far more at ease. It was a fairy-tale winter. As he crunched through frozen puddles and waded through thick, silent snow, he memorized Hamlet's soliloquy in German. Cottages like cuckoo clocks nestled in drifts of snow, branches bent down with it, creating scenes as from a medieval Book of Hours where, in his persona as a wandering scholar, he felt particularly at home. The only people he met were woodcutters, who offered him swigs of schnapps. He was given shelter in barns and farmhouses and, if the burgomaster was around, he often received a free night's lodging at the inn and breakfast at the expense of the parish. The custom of hospitality to travelling journeymen and students still prevailed in Germany and Austria, and Paddy took advantage of it. In town and country, the unexpected kindness and generosity he met called into question the anti-German jingoism he had grown up with.

Bavarian inns also had their photos of Hitler on the wall, but politics was not such a regular topic of conversation. Here he sensed a different mood, one less in thrall to Nazi propaganda. He described it as a 'bewildered acquiescence' that would sometimes descend into pessimism, distrust and foreboding when nobody else was in earshot. There were pitfalls, he realized, in setting up this oversimplified, town-versus-country picture of German politics, but he found it hard to resist. In towns he was confronted by a political ideology that forced people to take sides. In the country he found it easier to surround himself with the beautiful, illusory continuum of history, which connected him to a past that made no demands.

Another thing that kept his imagination alive and ugly reality at bay was singing, which always lifted his spirits; poetry also would be recited for hours as he walked along. His need for poetry and song had been awoken early by his mother's voice, whilst he had been obliged to learn poems by heart at school: an occupation he enjoyed more often than not. This intake had been more than doubled 'as it always is among people who need poetry, by a private anthology, both of those automatically absorbed and of poems consciously chosen and memorized as though one were stocking up for a desert island or for a stretch of solitary'.

The list of poetry he had committed to memory in *A Time of Gifts* covers almost three pages, and he does not include songs, which are too numerous to mention. He knew all the schoolboy favourites – Rolleston's translation of 'The Dead of Clonmacnois', 'The Burial of Sir John Moore' by Charles Wolfe, Macaulay's 'Horatius'; long passages from *A Midsummer Night's Dream*, most of the choruses from *Henry V*, and many of Shakespeare's sonnets; most of Keats's Odes, stretches of Spenser and Marlowe, 'the usual pieces' of Tennyson, Browning and Coleridge, lots of Rossetti for whom he had a passion, and Kipling. That is not to include the French, Latin and (admittedly not much) Greek poetry he knew. When asked whether the list was, perhaps, remembered with advantages, Paddy admitted that the one poet he felt uneasy at mentioning was John Quarles, who had only a single poem in *The Oxford Book of English Verse*.

He still referred to it all as 'a give-away collection . . . a mixture of a rather dog-eared romanticism with heroics and rough stuff, with traces of religious mania, temporarily in abeyance, Pre-Raphaelite languor and Wardour Street mediaevalism; slightly corrected – or, at any rate, altered – by a streak of coarseness and a bias towards low life'.[18] But the reader cannot help feeling he was rather proud of it, too. It is almost inconceivable that anyone of eighteen today should have absorbed so much verse, in English, French, Latin and a little Greek – five languages, indeed, if one includes the bits of *Hamlet, Prinz von Dänemark* and *Faust* that were being sucked into that prodigious memory. Among poetry lovers of his generation such command would not have been thought so unusual, except that it contained so little modern poetry. He was certainly familiar with Rupert Brooke, Wilfred Owen and the poets of the First World War, and Yeats and T. S. Eliot were not unknown; but their preoccupations were not his, for Paddy had no need of poetry that tried to make sense of the twentieth century. His poetry was for inspiration, company, a story, and to pass the time as he marched along.

★

By now he had been walking for over a month, and was learning how to survive on the road. Provided he reached some sort of human settlement by nightfall, he could usually rely on his charm and people's generosity to provide shelter and hospitality, which he would gratefully accept. Before leaving London, he had imagined himself curling up in barns and apple lofts, with the occasional bed in an inn or farmhouse. But that was about to change, for in Munich he had effectively been given two passports.

One replaced the real passport he had lost. The other, provided by the letters written by Baron Liphart-Ratshoff to his friends, opened up an unexpected world of schlosses and country houses, taking Paddy into a landed, aristocratic milieu that he would otherwise have been unlikely to penetrate. 'From then on, in the hall of many a baroque or medieval schloss, many a green-clad butler with bone buttons was to summon many a bewildered Graf and many a puzzled Baronin to deal with the affable and snow-covered tramp fidgeting about under the antlers in a pool of melting snow . . .'[19]

The recipient of the Baron's first letter, Graf Arco-Valley, had been away at the time of Paddy's visit but he had been given a good meal by the Graf's agent. After a night in a cowshed, he made his way to the house of Count and Countess Botho Coreth at Hochscharten, south-west of Linz. The Count's visiting card proclaimed him to be 'K. und K.' (that is Kaiserlich und Königlich, Imperial and Royal) Chamberlain of the Austro-Hungarian Empire. Well aware that the Austro-Hungarian empire had been swept away by the First World War, and that new nations and political tensions were rising from the rubble, Paddy was still more interested in what survived. The fragile old Count was a magnificent example, with his memories of Edwardian house parties at Chatsworth and Dunrobin.

Paddy was always happy to talk to anyone, but there was something about an ancient lineage that he found irresistible. While he never showed more than a passing interest in his own family tree, he was stirred by the idea that there were people who could follow their ancestors back, as if by a hand rope, into the distant past – and if they had arms and mottoes, mantled helmets and shields, titles and quarterings, so much the better. 'Only candidates with sixteen or thirty-two quarterings, I learnt later, were eligible for the symbolic gold key that court chamberlains wore on the back of their full-dress uniforms.'[20] 'I learnt later' is one of those phrases, so colloquial that it glides past as if in conversation, that Paddy uses to underline the fact that he was only eighteen and barely out of school when embarking on his journey. The phrase also makes it clear that he felt he was learning as he wrote, as he relived the walk and looked things up as they occurred to him.

Salzburg had been filled with people carrying skis on their shoulders, about to take to the slopes or relaxing in cafés on their return. The sight of them had made him feel sad and left out; but entering a café in Linz a little later, he was lucky. The young couple who owned it put him up for two nights in their flat, lent him some boots, and took him skiing.

He thought he would like to spend his nineteenth birthday in comfort, so the day before he telephoned Count and Countess Trautmannsdorff at Pottenbrunn, some fifty kilometres west of Vienna. The line was very bad when he rang, but the Gräfin said they would be glad to see him at Pottenbrunn about teatime. When he turned up they were kind, but slightly puzzled; and as they talked about Baron Liphart and his family, it dawned on him that they had no idea who he was: sure enough, it emerged that the Baron's letter had never arrived.

Paddy was mortified. The Trautmannsdorffs persuaded him to stay the night, but he insisted that he had to take a train to Vienna by noon the following day to meet a friend. Had he been allowed to walk out of the house he could have continued to Vienna on foot, but their chauffeur was summoned to take him to the station. The humiliation was compounded when, in the presence of the bemused chauffeur, he realized that he didn't have the money for the train he had never intended to take. In fact he had no money at all, but for the batch of four one-pound notes that would be awaiting him in Vienna. He often thought of the Trautmannsdorffs who, like so many people he met on this journey, never survived the war. When they heard the news of the German surrender, they thought it was all over; but within half an hour an SS truck appeared at the house: the men marched in, and the Count and Countess were shot dead in cold blood.

So much for birthday comforts. It was raining heavily, his boots were leaking and he was hungry – all good enough reasons to hitch a lift in the back of a truck, where he found a girl called Trudi taking some eggs and a drake in a basket to her aunt. It was still raining when Paddy and Trudi were dropped off, and together they squelched through the outer suburbs of Vienna. The atmosphere was dark and tense: they had to pass barbed-wire checkpoints manned by soldiers with rifles, and in the distance they could hear the ominous booming of guns and mortar fire. Trudi bade him goodbye and he went on alone, heading for the *Heilsarmee*, the Salvation Army hostel.

Paddy liked to think that, if he looked in the right way, he could still see Europe as the Congress of Vienna had left it: a sort of eternal, cultural Europe that lay untouched behind its cities, factories and railway lines; a continent where peasant life was dictated by the round of the seasons and the feasts of the Church, where strange costumes were worn as real clothes and not donned for the tourist trade, where passing from a beer-drinking region to a wine-drinking region was like passing an invisible frontier. Yet the Great War and the peace conference that followed had wrought changes so profound and far-reaching that Europe had already altered beyond recognition. Nowhere was this more true than in Vienna. Once the heart of a great empire, it was now the capital of a country that felt so reduced that the Austrian writer Stefan Zweig described it as 'a mutilated stump which bled from every vein'.[21]

The cold, starving years of the early twenties, accompanied by unemployment and rampant inflation, had concentrated the Austrian working class round the banner of the Social Democratic Party which was large and well organized. It was feared not only by the government, but by the *Heimwehr* – traditionalist, Catholic, anti-Communist militias formed in the aftermath of the war, whose present leader was the young Prince Starhemberg.

On 12 February 1934 in Linz, members of the *Heimwehr* broke into the Social Democrat Party headquarters looking for weapons. Riots began, spread to the capital, and fighting went on for three days, with government forces deploying artillery in the working-class areas of the city. Over a hundred civilians, including women and children, were killed, and over three hundred wounded.[22] It was a key moment in Austria's move to the far right, which culminated in the *Anschluss* four years later. By the time Paddy arrived on the night of the 14th the upheaval was almost over, although pockets of resistance continued in the Simmering and Floridsdorf areas for another two days.

He was to spend the next few weeks in Vienna and, in retrospect, blamed himself for not having realized what was going on. 'Looking back,' he wrote in 1963, 'I am *maddened* by not having seen, written, looked, heard – but it's no good pretending.'[23] He has been accused of deliberately turning away from the crisis. Yet even Stefan Zweig, living in Vienna at the time, had to admit that he had no idea what was happening that February.[24]

He spent a week in the Salvation Army hostel in Vienna, where he found someone as innocent of politics as himself. His new friend was a tall, gentle Friesian Islander who had taught himself English from the works of Shakespeare. It was Paddy who gave him the romantic name of Konrad, but more probably it was Peter, the name he has in 'A Youthful Journey'. As they talked, Paddy made a sketch of Peter. The sketch does not survive, but doubtless it shared the defining characteristics of all his portraits, which he dismissed as more of a 'half-taught knack' than a talent. Everyone he drew (usually in three-quarter face) looked poetic and fine-boned, their clear eyes fixed on distant horizons of limitless possibilities. Peter was delighted with the result. And when it turned out that there was no money waiting at the British Consulate, Peter suggested they might earn some by selling portraits door to door.

At first rather shy, Paddy was soon peddling his portraits 'with nerves of brass' at a schilling a time, and in doing so he collected a series of little vignettes of the people who invited him into their apartments and posed for him. Once again, the details are remembered with extraordinary clarity – though, of course, the magpie mind adds details freely. One of his sitters is 'a genial old gentleman from Bosnia, probably of Islamized Bogomil descent, Dr Murad Aslanovic Bey'. He admitted that the paperweight he describes in the old man's room, a memento of the First K.u.K. Bosniak Infantry Regiment, was actually something he saw many years later in an antique shop in Salonika – 'but it fitted so perfectly,' as he put it.[25]

Peter selected the apartments that Paddy would approach, suggested a price in line with the prosperity of the neighbourhood, and provided praise and company when he re-emerged with some schillings. Although Paddy had been giving him half the takings (most of which went on food and wine), Peter insisted on giving them back; but at the end of their time together, Paddy managed to give him one of the pound notes that had finally arrived from England. This was to launch Peter on a new career as a saccharine smuggler. They had one last celebratory dinner together, spent the evening talking and reading Shakespeare, and parted the following day.

Peter's departure left Paddy feeling lonely and broke. Without a partner to steel his nerves the urge to make money by pencil portraits withered away, yet he only had three pounds to last him the rest of the month. He also had a letter from his father, the first he had received since the journey began. He carried it round for a while, steeling himself to open it, and when he finally did, the contents came as a huge relief. Lewis had taken things better than expected and, best of all, had included a birthday cheque for five pounds.

Paddy spent a further two weeks in Vienna. His base was a large flat belonging to a woman called Robin Forbes-Robertson Hale, who kept open house 'for a small Bohemian half-native, half-expatriate set that suited me ideally'.[26] One member of this set was Basset Parry-Jones who taught English at the Konsularakademie, which had trained candidates for the imperial diplomatic service. It was thanks to the elegant and rather sardonic Parry-Jones that Paddy was allowed to consult the academy's library, where he spent hours calculating his mileage with dividers over a map ('I never tired of this') and 'mugging up' the next leg of his journey across Hungary and Rumania. Parry-Jones had another bond with Paddy: neither of them liked going to sleep. Together they prowled the bars and cabarets that masked the dark side of Vienna – the opposite of the assiduous, scholar-gypsy sightseeing that he did during the day.*

---

* Four years later, in March 1938, Parry-Jones did a notable service for one of his students, a young Jew called George Weidenfeld. Following the *Anschluss*, life for the oppressed and harassed Jews of Vienna had become very frightening. Weidenfeld's father had been arrested, all the family assets frozen, and George needed to get out of Austria. With every consulate in Vienna besieged by Jews

Another person Paddy met was Baron Einer von der Heydte, a young German in his mid-twenties who was a colleague of Parry-Jones' at the Konsularakademie. Paddy describes him as 'quiet, thoughtful and amusing',[27] and no supporter of the Nazis. Einer came vividly to mind again in May 1941, when Paddy was a junior officer in the Intelligence Corps attached to a brigade headquarters in Crete trying to defend the island in the face of a massive airborne German invasion. A captured enemy document, revealing the entire German order of battle, was passed to him for translation. One of the *Fallschirmjäger* battalions was led by Captain Einer von der Heydte.

Paddy was astonished to find he had spent three weeks in the Austrian capital, utterly absorbed. He had found a group of congenial friends, explored the city thoroughly, and had enjoyed what seemed to be a cheerful, end of carnival atmosphere. If he had not noticed the vein of sadness running through the city at the time, he did not overlook it when he came to write the book. 'Later, when I read about this period in Vienna, I was struck by the melancholy which seems to have impressed the writers so strongly. It owed less to the prevailing political uncertainty than to the fallen fortunes of the old imperial city.'[28]

in the same desperate situation, Parry-Jones ensured that Weidenfeld was accorded an interview with a British passport officer, who grudgingly allowed him a three-month transit visa to England. See George Weidenfeld, *Remembering My Good Friends* (HarperCollins, 1995), p.76.

4

An Enchanted Summer

Paddy crossed the frontier into Czechoslovakia at Bratislava, and immediately contacted Hans Ziegler, another friend from Vienna. He already had an invitation: 'Come and stay on your way to Hungary and cheer me up,' Hans had urged, 'I get so bored there.'[1] Hans went to Vienna as often as he could, though he was obliged to spend most of his time in Bratislava where he managed a branch of his family's bank. Known in previous centuries as Pressburg, or Pozony if you were Hungarian, Bratislava had been one of the most important cities in Hungarian history. Now it was a shadow of its former self and people sighed, 'You should have seen it before the war.'

Born out of the ashes of the Austro-Hungarian empire, Czechoslovakia had a broad industrial base and a promising future. At the same time, its borders contained a range of ethnic groups. Czechs and Slovaks, Magyars and Germans all vied for power, territory and autonomy, and these internal tensions did not bode well for the new nation's stability. The Zieglers had been Czechoslovaks only since 1918 when the country was created, and they were not overjoyed by the loss of prestige that came with their new nationality. Under the old empire they had been German-speaking Bohemians, part of the ruling Austrian élite – a 'sahib' class among the Czechs, whose language they seldom spoke. The family's bank was based in Prague and they had a country property at Loyovitz, but Vienna was still the social and cultural centre of their world.

However lacklustre the city seemed to its inhabitants, Paddy found it utterly absorbing. He sat in cafés observing the first signs of another culture, in this case, the Slav world: 'the moulding of a window, the cut of a beard, overheard syllables, the unfamiliar shape of a horse or hat, the taste of a new drink, the occasional unfamiliar lettering . . .

the accumulating fragments were beginning to cohere like the pieces of a jigsaw puzzle.'[2] He watched the dark gypsies in their brilliantly coloured clothes, and the Talmudic students, pale and waxy from their years of study. He was especially intrigued by the prostitutes whose booths lined the narrow lanes that crept up the hill towards the Schlossberg – 'a Jacob's ladder tilted between the rooftops and the sky, crowded with shuffling ghosts and with angels long fallen and moulting'.[3]

Hans Ziegler proposed a quick trip to Prague before Paddy moved on to Hungary, saying it would be a shame if he plunged eastwards without seeing the old capital of Bohemia. Paddy could not afford such a jaunt but Hans insisted on paying, saying they would stay with his parents. Paddy acquiesced, and they arrived to find Prague under a blanket of snow. He was warmly received by Hans's parents, Ernst and Alice Ziegler, and especially his older and younger brothers, Heinz and Paul. Heinz, the eldest of the three, was professor of political theory at the Charles University of Prague, while Paul was still a student.

Over the next few days as he explored Prague with Hans, the city revealed itself as 'the summing-up of all I had gazed at since stepping ashore in Holland',[4] its cultural influences far wider than just the Teutonic world. He developed this idea over several pages in A Time of Gifts, describing the city's astonishing architectural variety, the tiers of tombstones in its Jewish cemetery, its taste for arcane knowledge, and the burden of its history at the heart of the dynastic and religious turbulence of Mitteleuropa.

He spent his last evening in Prague in the library of Heinz Ziegler's flat, trying to resolve one of his current obsessions: whether Shakespeare had been right when he gave Bohemia a coast in The Winter's Tale. Heinz came to the rescue, with a fact that seemed to vindicate his faith in the Bard's geography: Bohemia had indeed had a coastline but only for thirteen years (1260–73), under Ottokar II. Paddy was jubilant, and everyone celebrated his success. Only later did he discover that Shakespeare had based the play on a story set in Sicily, which he casually changed to Bohemia: 'It was total defeat.'[5] That night, he and Hans were on their way back to Bratislava.

The Zieglers were among the many thousands of families ripped apart by the events of the next few years. Appalled by the rise of Nazism all three brothers moved to England in the late 1930s, whilst Hitler's designs on Austria and then Czechoslovakia transformed them from reluctant Czechs into fervent nationalists. During the war Hans joined the RAF, served in North Africa and Italy, and had a child (the literary agent Toby Eady) with Lady Swinfen, later the novelist Mary Wesley. He was killed in action in early May 1944. Hans settled in the United States, while Paul, the youngest, became a Benedictine monk at Quarr Abbey on the Isle of Wight.

Whilst Paddy did see Hans and Paul Ziegler again after the war, their parents had refused to leave Prague after the German invasion of 1938. Since Ernst was of Jewish descent the bank was seized, Loyovitz plundered. In 1942 the couple were sent to Theresienstadt, some miles outside Prague, which the Nazis presented as a sort of model holding camp for Jews. When Ernst died six months later, Alice was deported to Auschwitz where she died in December 1943.

From Bratislava, Paddy's most logical route would have been to cross the Danube and strike south into Hungary. Instead he headed north-east, to visit a man he had briefly met and heard much about. This was Baron Philip Schey v. Koromla, more commonly known as Pips Schey. The Baron was spending the winter on his estate at Kövecses, near the village of Soporna on the river Váh, south of Sered. The young man was shown into a library so crammed with books in English, French and German that the panelling could scarcely be seen. His host was sitting in a big armchair, reading Proust.

Paddy felt instantly at ease with Baron Schey: he spoke faultless English, was formidably well read, and had been intimate with pre-war high society in courts and castles from London to Vienna. Never having had a glittering career, he nonetheless possessed a fund of knowledge and anecdotes that his young friend never tired of. He had two daughters by his first wife and was celebrated for being a man of unusual charm.

The days that Paddy spent at Kövecses were of huge significance. At a time when younger men were expected to treat their elders with marked deference, Pips Schey was the first older man he had ever met who treated him naturally, as an equal: a gift that he described as 'a sort of informal investiture with the *toga virilis*'.[6]

Reflecting on the visit in his diary, Paddy wrote: 'I am just living in a pre-war world, and I really think that we get on so well that Baron Schey has been as keen for me to stay as I have been myself. These long walks are wonderful, and we talk about every possible thing, and there are frequently the easy silences of perfect company.'[7]

Schey, who was about the same age as Lewis Fermor, became an idealized father-figure to Paddy, whose own hard-working father cannot be blamed for wishing his son would develop a more serious attitude to life. But Pips Schey, the cultivated bibliophile, a man of considerable experience if not great achievements, could see Paddy's extraordinary gifts and appreciate them.

When Paddy felt the time had come to leave, his host presented him with a little edition of Friedrich Hölderlin's poetry, some cigars and tobacco, and a fine series of large-scale, pre-war Austrian staff maps reprinted by Freytag & Berndt in Vienna. He then walked with Paddy as far as the village of Kissujfalu, and bade him goodbye. Paddy never saw Pips Schey again, though they corresponded a little. Schey left his homeland for ever at the time of the *Anschluss*. With his second wife he settled in Ascona, on the western shore of Lake Maggiore, and died in Normandy in 1957.

Paddy left Pips Schey on 28 March. In the coffee house in Nové Zámky where he spent the night he was approached by a prostitute called Mancsi; a man who played the violin urged him to have nothing to do with her. But on hearing that Paddy was heading for Budapest, he urged him to visit the Maison Frieda where every man could be 'a cavalier' in safety, for five pengoes. 'This sort of advice has been very frequent, ever since the polyglot beckonings from the windows of the Schlossberg, and the head waiter at the Astoria asking Hans and I which of the ladies we would like.'[8]

The following night he spent in a little village called Köbölkut, where a Jewish baker, seeing him looking lost, suggested he spend the night in his bakery; the baker helped him make up a bed of straw and blankets on the floor. He spent the next morning talking and smoking with his host, who insisted he stay to lunch. Reaching the bank of the Danube at the village of Karva, he followed the river eastwards into a remote landscape of watermeadows, populated by waterfowl and reverberating to a million croaking frogs. Early evening by now, it was balmy as summer, without a breath of wind, and Paddy suddenly realized with a surge of excitement that he was about to spend his first night in the open. He made his bed three yards from the river in a hollow among the willows, and watched the moon and stars until he fell asleep.

He was rudely awakened in the middle of the night by two frontier guards shining a lantern in his face. They hauled him off at gunpoint to a hut where they tipped his rucksack on to the floor and went through it, item by item. He could speak no Hungarian, so there was no means of explaining himself until a third guard appeared, who spoke German. It turned out that the other two suspected Paddy of being a celebrated saccharine smuggler, despite the fact that the latter was well over fifty. They all had a good laugh and a smoke and then the guards made Paddy comfortable in a stable, although he would rather have spent the rest of the night outside.

Walking through southern Slovakia towards the Hungarian border, Paddy had begun to get some inkling of the ethnic tensions in this part of the world. They were not new, many being based on historical grudges that had been perpetuated for generations. He had met a group of Hungarians who bitterly resented the fact that their country's ancient borders had shrunk, and that their children were being forced to learn Czech in school.

The following day, Paddy crossed the Danube into Hungary via the great bridge which took him from Parkan in Slovakia to the cathedral city of Esztergom. He stood for some time on the bridge, and his recollection of that moment marks the end of *A Time of Gifts*: 'I found it impossible to tear myself from my station and plunge into Hungary. I feel the same disability now: a momentary reluctance to lay hands on this particular fragment of the future; not out of fear but because, within arm's reach and still intact, this future seemed, and still seems, so full of promised marvels.'[9] It was Easter Saturday, 31 March 1934. The evening drew in as the bells pealed, summoning the citizens to mass.

The Burgomaster, to whom Paddy had a letter of introduction, put him under the care of a group of men all dressed in the magnificent furred and brocaded court tunics of Hungarian noblemen. 'Best of all', Paddy wrote excitedly in his diary, 'were the curved sabres they wore, more like scimitars, with eastern silver hilts, the scabbard covered with black velvet and the silverwork all along studded with gems.'[10] (The amiable, stork-loving, monocled figure whom Paddy describes in *A Time of Gifts* is an amalgam of them all.) By staying close to this group he enjoyed a ringside view of the Easter ceremony and the procession that followed it, during which the cardinal-archbishop walked through the candle-lit streets just behind the sacred monstrance under its golden canopy.

Before the war, most of Hungary had belonged to a handful of great families whose wealth was the product of their enormous estates. When not enjoying the pleasures of country life, these families were totally assimilated into fashionable Europe. Sons were educated in England, daughters finished in Switzerland, and they were just as much at home in Paris and Vienna as they were in cosmopolitan Budapest. This Magyar oligarchy kept a firm grip on power, even though non-Magyars (Rumanians, Slovaks, Croats and Jews) made up more than half the population. At the same time, the contrast between the landowners' way of life and that of the peasants was immense. Although serfdom had been abolished in the mid-nineteenth century, the Hungarian peasantry were among the poorest and least emancipated in Europe.

Part of the Austro-Hungarian empire, Hungary had been on the German side in the war and had had to pay the price. Its borders began to shrink in October 1918, when Croatia unilaterally joined the new Yugoslavia. In 1919, the Rumanians and Czechs invaded – the Rumanians at one point occupying much of the country and looting Budapest. The Allies called everyone to order, but Hungary was the loser. The Czechs united with Slovakia, formerly northern Hungary, while the Rumanians took Transylvania.

The dominant political figure in Hungary between the wars was the Regent, Admiral Horthy. (Hungary was still a monarchy, though there was no king.) Horthy suppressed the short-lived Communist government of Belá Kún in 1919, and the early years of his regency saw limited attempts at land reform; but Horthy was fundamentally conservative, as were those surrounding him. Political power remained where it always had been: in the hands of the great families, the Church, and the financial and industrial oligarchy surrounding the Regent.

As for the peasants, their lot had not changed much. Paddy's walk to Budapest took him through the woods and meadows of the Pilis Hills, and one evening he joined a couple of swineherds in their reed-thatched hut. They had no language in common, and had no idea what he meant when he described himself as 'Angol'; but when he produced a bottle of *barack*, their faces lit up. It was an infallible way of making friends, particularly when combined with Paddy's appetite for words. His attempts to communicate, by sign language and pointing, touched and amused his hosts who often descended into helpless laughter.

Bálint and Géza, as Paddy called his companions, may not have known where England was, but they knew what had happened to Hungary, and how those changes had affected themselves and their families. Yet what excited Paddy was that, as swineherds, they were living a life and dressed in clothes that would have been recognizable in the Bronze Age. 'They were cloaked in rough white woollen stuff as hard as frieze. In lieu of goads or crooks, they nursed tapering shafts of wood polished with long handling and topped with small axe-heads.' On their feet were moccasins he had seen before, on Slovaks in Bratislava:

> pale canoes of raw cowhide turning up at the tips and threaded all round with thongs which were then lashed round their padded shanks till half-way up the calf of the leg; inside, meanwhile, snuggly swaddled in layers of white felt, their feet were wintering it out . . . The firelight made them look like contemporaries of Domesday Book and we ought to have been passing a drinking-horn from hand to hand instead of my anachronistic bottle.[11]

The contrast between this evening in the forest and the ten days he spent in Budapest could not have been greater. A letter from Tibor v. Thuróczy, one of the 'breezy Hungarian squires' he had met in Bratislava, opened a series of hospitable doors, the first being that of Baron and Baroness Berg (Tibor and Berta). The Baron had done wartime service as a captain in a regiment of horse artillery; he and his family lived in an eighteenth-century house among the winding lanes of the citadel of Buda, next to Trinity Square. They gave Paddy the use of a large room, lent him some evening clothes, and secured an invitation for him to attend a dance given by friends nearby.

There he met a girl called Annamaria Miskolczy, who was studying history of art: more doors opened, invitations multiplied; suddenly Paddy was swept up into a new crowd of 'dashing, resplendent and beautiful new friends'. There was a restaurant called the Cuckoo where gypsies played, and a spectacular nightclub called the Arizona with a revolving dance floor. 'Who paid for all this?' asked Paddy. 'Certainly not me – even a gesture towards helping was jovially brushed aside as though it were not worth the waste of words.'[12]

Through the Trautmannsdorffs at Pottenbrunn (where he had spent his uneasy nineteenth birthday) he met the ex-prime minister Count Paul Teleki, who must have been one of the most interesting men in Budapest. Paddy listened to him 'talking about old Turkey, the Levant and Africa, of his travels as a geologist, of his share in the leadership of the counter-revolution against Belá Kún, and his time as Prime Minister'.[13]

In *Between the Woods and the Water*, the next passage takes Paddy on horseback across the Great Hungarian Plain – the *Alföld*, in Magyar. The ride begins in mid-April, and the horse is provided by a shadowy member of the Szapáry family whom he had never met. Described as a very fine creature, it shared many of its rider's characteristics: 'Malek's alert and good-tempered ears, his tireless and untiring gait and the well-being he radiated, meant that we infected each other's mood . . .'[14]

They set off south-east, in the direction of the Rumanian frontier, spending the first night encamped with a band of gypsies. Sharing some food, he and the group laughed together at the words of Rumanian and Hindi which Paddy tried out in an effort to grasp some of their language. Yet lying awake with Malek hobbled close by, he could not believe he had been so foolish as to bring such a valuable beast among people renowned as the most skilful horse thieves in the world. But Malek was still there next morning, and soon they were on their way again. Strung out on the road were ox- and horse-drawn carts, straggling bands of gypsies, a few cars. The landscape of the plain was one of immense pastures dotted with herds of sheep and straight-horned cattle, occasional woods alive with birds, and farms where women in bright embroidered clothes spun wool on a distaff. Fields stretching out across the limitless steppe were watered by wells, whose counterbalanced poles looked like 'derelict siege engines'. At a friendly farmhouse Paddy watches himself thinking: 'I'm drinking this glass of milk on a chestnut horse on the Great Hungarian Plain.'[15]

In fact, Paddy walked the first part of the Alföld. It was only when he reached Körösladány, a hundred and twenty miles east of Budapest, that riding became more frequent. And since he was still on the Alföld, which spills into western Rumania, the claim was hardly a fabrication. Later, when asked precisely where and by whom he had been lent the horse, he admitted to having smudged the facts a little: 'I did ride a fair amount, so I decided to put myself on horseback for a bit. I felt the reader might be getting bored of me just plodding along . . . *You won't let on, will you?*'[16]

This is just one instance of the interplay of Paddy's memory and his imagination. It is hardly surprising that in the act of transposing one part of the journey to another, different memories of being on horseback in Hungary were grafted on to his earliest impressions of the Alföld. This is what novelists do every day. But since Paddy was making a novel of his life – and his readership would expect the story to be true – he was also creating a new memory, shaped and coloured by his imagination, so perfect in every detail that he could say: 'When I was riding across the Alföld', meaning most of it, without a trace of self-consciousness.

The next few weeks mark a kind of hiatus in the journey, a sunlit upland of ease during which he spent every night in comfortable country houses. His hosts were a series of inter-related Hungarian landowners, who passed him on to each other like an enjoyable and rather unusual parcel. He did not even have to walk: they usually lent him a horse.

He stayed with the Merans, at single-storeyed Körösladány: a long, ochre-coloured eighteenth-century house with rounded baroque pediments. There he spent an idyllic afternoon under the trees, within sight of the river Körös, with Countess Ilona in white linen dress dispensing tea to Paddy and her family and friends. They had a good library, where Paddy read everything he could find about the Alföld. The children, Hansi and Marcsi, remembered him reading and writing at a Biedermeier table while their lessons went on next door.

Travelling south-east, his next stop was Vesztö with the wistful, bird-loving Count Lajos Wenckheim. The Count's current preoccupation was a pair of great bustards, and he was waiting for their clipped wings to grow again before releasing them into the wild. He it was who gave Paddy a new stick, carved with leaves and the arms of Hungary.

The next stop was Doboz, with Lajos's cousin Lászlo and his plump English wife. They were appalled at the idea of him going into Rumania. '"It's a terrible place . . . They'll take everything you've got, and" – voices sank collusively here – "whole valleys are riddled with VD, oh do beware!"'[17] His hostess ran upstairs, and returned with a lady's miniature pistol with a mother-of-pearl handle, and a box of small-bore ammunition. Paddy was intrigued by their warnings, but not particularly alarmed; the more he travelled in the Balkans, the more he found that every country was deeply suspicious of the morals and intentions of its neighbours.

His next halt was a spectacularly ornamented nineteenth-century house, O'Kígyós, near the town of Békéscsaba. Here lived Count Józsi Wenckheim, Lászlo's elder brother, and his wife Denise. Paddy had met them in Budapest, and he was expected. 'You are just what we need!' cried the Count. 'Come along!' – which was how Paddy found himself playing four-a-side bicycle polo in the courtyard, with real polo sticks cut down to size. 'The game was quick, reckless and full of collisions, but there was nothing to match the joy of hitting the ball properly: it made a loud smack and gave one a tempting glimmer of what the real thing might be like.'[18] He was amazed that all the windows on the front of the house were intact.

Paddy had been told that the Rumanians would not allow anyone to cross their frontier on foot, so he spent his last day in Hungary walking towards a station and a train that would take him across the Rumanian border. It was almost the end of April. After the difficulties of Magyar, that sheer cliff of a language on which even Paddy failed to find much of a foothold, it was a great relief to be back in the familiar territory of a Romance language: a place where words sprang easily from Latin roots, where man was *om* and woman was *femeie*, and great skeins of words were instantly recognizable.

★

Transylvania, 'the place beyond the woods', once formed part of the Roman province of Dacia. It is a natural fortress, a high plateau surrounded by mountains, the highest of these rising to the south and east. The mountains are riddled with streams and natural springs, and secret lakes lie hidden among the crags. On the plateau, crops and fruit grow in abundance while cattle, buffalo and horses grow sleek on rich pasture. Below ground, salt has been mined here since Roman times, and Transylvania holds the richest gold mines in Europe. It is a place full of stories and superstitions, ably exploited by Bram Stoker, Anthony Hope and their host of followers. Even its name sounds enchanted, not quite real: Dervla Murphy called it 'a one-word poem'.[19]

Paddy crossed the frontier into Rumania on 27 April, continuing his country-house progress. His hosts, mostly friends and relations of the people with whom he had just been staying, were not Rumanian but Hungarian. Transylvania had belonged to Hungary until the peace treaties of 1920, and had been ceded to Rumania because the majority of the population were Rumanian peasants. For the Hungarian landowners whose families had lived in Transylvania for centuries, it was like an amputation: a loss they could never get used to. Post-war agrarian reforms had broken up many of the old estates and redistributed them among the peasants. The Hungarians did not blame the peasants: it was the administration they hated, the bureaucrats above all.

His first stop was the house of Baron Tibor Solymosy, who lived near Borosjenö (now Ineu), north of Arad, in a house 'pillared and Palladian like the Haymarket Theatre in a sea of vineyards'.[20] His bachelor host, another former horse-gunner, lived with a charming ex-mistress, a Pole called Ria Bielek. She was an inspiration to Paddy, who describes her with an affection that implies rather more than it reveals. Unlike the easy-going Tibor, Ria was a reader. She lent Paddy several French books, and seems to have encouraged his long hours in the library, stocked with works in Hungarian and German. He made no progress with Hungarian – even a song he loved, about a swallow sweeping low over a field, refused to stick in his memory. But he did improve his German over the days in Borosjenö, and with Ria's help, read Thomas Mann's *Tod in Venedig* over a couple of weeks.

The next house was Tövicseghāza, 'a sort of hacienda among huge trees', home of Jaš and Clara Jelensky. Jaš was full of eccentric ideas on every subject from agriculture to economics, and enjoyed exploring the wilder reaches of speculative science, while Clara was a brilliant horsewoman with wild hair that seldom saw a comb (a detail noted by the fastidious Paddy). Then, with the von Kintzig family at Ötvenes, he remembered 'woodland paper chases and fireworks after dinner'.[21] Almost everyone mentioned in *Between the Woods and the Water* was swept up into the war and the long disaster of Communism; but at Ötvenes, the whole family perished after the war in a fire.

He moved on to Kápolnás to stay with Count Jenö Teleki, first cousin of ex-prime minister Paul Teleki whom Paddy had met in Budapest. Count Jenö was a celebrated entomologist who had made a particular study of the moths of the Far East, a passion which (it was said) kept two insect-collectors permanently employed. His English was peppered with phrases such as 'I hae me doots' and 'I'll dree my own weird', legacy of a Scottish nanny.[22] While he unpacked and classified his specimens at a desk in his library, Paddy read historical novels by Maurus Jókai celebrating the heroes and legends of Hungarian history. But the Count's wife was Rumanian, and it was through the couple's occasionally prickly exchanges that he began to understand how deep the national rivalry ran.

As time went on and Paddy made more and more Rumanian friends, he began to hear about the handover of Transylvania from the other side. Ever since the boundaries of the modern nation-state had come into existence, Rumanians had always made up the majority of the population. As far as they were concerned, justice had finally been done. Paddy's position was based on his feelings of loyalty and friendship – and he hated to betray anyone's feelings – so when he came to write about it, having friends on both sides, he was diplomatic. 'I am the only person I know', he wrote, 'who has feelings of equal warmth for both these embattled claimants.'[23] These tensions had little impact on him at the time, and did not seem to affect what he saw as the easy relations his Hungarian hosts had with the Rumanian peasants who still worked for them.

It was also this summer, in the hours spent in country-house libraries, that Paddy began his first explorations into what would be a lifetime's passion: the early history of languages and peoples as they drifted across a frontierless, uncharted Europe, and but for the Romans, unchronicled. He inquired into the Cunans and the Petchenegs, the Magyars and Vlachs, and began to tease out the claims and counterclaims of their descendants, the modern-day Hungarians and Rumanians. He brooded on the thousand-year gap between the withdrawal of the Romans from Transylvania in 271 AD, and the next recorded mention of the Vlach people in Transylvania in the eleventh century: that there was no trace of them for a millennium was probably the result of the Mongol invasions, which destroyed everything in their path. Words too were nomads, migrating from one language and grafting themselves on to another. Strings of words moved down rivers or valleys, while different dialects grew up on opposite banks or adjacent hillsides. Invaders came burning and plundering, tribes crossed and criss-crossed the land with their flocks, bringing more verbal cross-fertilization; and everything he read was used to build up the three-dimensional panorama of Europe he was acquiring, both in memory and imagination.

He was beginning to feel rather guilty about accepting so much hospitality for so long, from people whom he often met for the first time when he appeared on their doorstep. If in some ways this life chimed with his idea of the wandering scholar, it also seemed like a luxurious interlude of protracted sponging. For his hosts, there was nothing unusual in having people to stay for days or even weeks at a time. Food was locally produced, the servants lived on the estate, and thus one extra guest was no great strain on the household – though Paddy was perhaps more inconvenient than some. He burnt holes in the sheets with his cigarettes, drank a lot, and the clothes and books he borrowed were left lying about, to be soaked with rain or slept on by dogs. Perhaps people did sometimes wonder when he was going to leave. Yet whatever his faults, he had one gift so enchanting that it made up for all his shortcomings. He was genuinely fascinated by his hosts, and wanted to hear everything they could tell him about their families, their history and their way of life.

The greatest blessing a guest can bring to his host is the right kind of curiosity, and it bubbled out of Paddy like a natural spring. At this age, everything he came across was worth knowing – 'I was un-boreable, like an unsinkable battleship,' he wrote.[24] Above all,

Paddy did not see the people he stayed with as casual acquaintances or meal tickets; to him they were true friends, people he thought of and cared about. In years to come, as he travelled between Rumania and London by train in the late thirties, he would spin out the journey to stop off and visit them. No wonder he could remember them so vividly several decades after that enchanted summer.

One has also to imagine the impact of Paddy on an old count from eastern Europe, barely able to live off his much-diminished lands and keep the roof on a house stocked with paintings and furniture that harked back to better days. His children might take a certain pride in their ancient lineage, but they had also made it clear that the world had moved on and they planned to move with it. Then a scruffy young Englishman with a rucksack turns up on the doorstep, recommended by a friend. He is polite, cheerful, and he cannot hear enough about the family history. He pores over the books and albums in the library, and asks a thousand questions about the princely rulers, dynastic marriages, wars and revolts and waves of migration that shaped this part of the world. He wants to hear about the family portraits too, and begs the Count to remember the songs the peasants used to sing when he was a child. Instead of feeling like a useless fragment of a broken empire, the Count is transformed. This young Englishman has made him realize that he is part of living history, a link in an unbroken chain going back to Charlemagne and beyond.

Paddy was just as good at getting on with the younger generation, welcoming every suggestion. Whether they wanted to ski, ride, swim, sing, hunt or play tennis, whether they wanted to go to a nightclub in town or dance at a village wedding, whether they were going to visit a distant cousin in a legendary castle or an old aunt round the corner, he was ready and eager to join in. No wonder they urged him to stay a few more days, and he was easily persuaded. Not just his interest and enthusiasm engaged them. In Paddy's company everyone felt livelier, funnier and more entertaining, and the gift never deserted him. Decades later one of his oldest friends remarked, 'Wouldn't it be lovely if Paddy came in pill-form, so you could take one whenever you felt depressed.'[25]

For the last and longest of Paddy's Transylvanian sojourns, he was a guest of Elemér von Klobusitzky ('István' in *Between the Woods and the Water*) whom he had met with the Telekis at Kápolnás. Elemér had run away from home to join a Hussar regiment during the war, fought against the Communist regime of Belá Kún, and escaped from one of the execution squads organized by Számuely, Belá Kún's terror man. He joined the counter-revolution at Szeged, and Paddy hints that he may have been involved in the 'White Terror' that followed the downfall of the Communists. Yet the fact that he was able to live in Hungary after the war, under his own name, implies that he was not involved in any atrocities. He was a brilliant rider, a crack shot, and a skilful 'cocktail pianist' who could thump out the latest tunes with brio.

Elemér was then in his thirties, looking after his family's shrinking estate at Guraszáda. He, his sister Ilona and his elderly parents lived in an ancient house that looked to Paddy like 'a mixture of manor house, monastery and farmstead' overlooking the river Maros. Elemér missed the musketeerish life he had led, but at the same time he was deeply committed to maintaining what remained of the fields and forests that his family had held since the mid-nineteenth century. He unleashed his considerable energies in riding and hunting, and like Paddy, he was always reluctant to go to bed: it was more fun to sit out on the terrace, drinking and rolling cigarettes and talking through the night.

Hungarian passion burst into Paddy's life a week or two after his arrival in Transylvania. A party of Elemér's friends met for a picnic of crayfish, which they gathered in abundance from under the rocks and waterweeds of a fast-running stream high up in the mountains. There were about a dozen crayfish-catchers, of whom the most active was a vivacious, dark-haired Serbian woman in a red dress called Xenia Csernovits. She was married to a Hungarian, Mihaly Betheg, and lived in Budapest; but that summer, feeling profoundly depressed and miserable, she had come to spend some time on her own at her childhood home which lay three miles upstream from Elemér's house, near the village of Zám.*

They made love in the woods that afternoon, after the crayfish feast. After dinner at Elemér's she sang lieder by Schubert, Wolf and

---

* In *Between the Woods and the Water,* Zám was Paddy's first stop in Transylvania. There he mentions Xenia by name, but later she is disguised as 'Angéla'.

Richard Strauss in what Paddy called 'a slight, clear, ravishing voice'. He begged her to sing again and again. Paddy was in love: 'It was one of those rare times, remembered with wonder ever after, when fortune, which so often besets these paths with hopeless hazards, suddenly and gratuitously relents and all seems leagued in a benevolent conspiracy.' She was alone in her house, and an amused Elemér was happy to oblige whenever Paddy asked him for the loan of a horse at odd hours after dark. He learnt

> where to tie up a horse without attracting attention, which track to follow without alerting a dog, where to tread on tiptoe past the cottage where two old servants lived, and which French window would be ajar . . . The moon seemed to fill the whole silent house and when our own voices stopped we could hear frogs from a nearby pool, a few crickets and an occasional owl's hoot. A stream sounded from the thickest of the woods and the branches were full of undeserved nightingales.[26]

Paddy went over this passage several times. 'Those passages dealing with sentiment can be jolly tricky,' he confided years later to his publisher, 'half caddish, half milksop. I must get it absolutely right.'[27] They did not see each other much in daylight, for Xenia had to be careful.

One passage in *Between the Woods and the Water* often leaves readers wondering what exactly happened. Returning from a lunch with neighbours, Paddy and Elemér were so hot that they unsaddled their horses, stripped off and dived into the water. They had swum a fair way downstream when they were surprised by two laughing peasant girls, who threatened to find their clothes and run off. Elemér shouted back that he and Paddy would come out and catch them. '"You wouldn't dare," came the answer. "Not like that, naked as frogs."'[28] After a few more taunts, Paddy and Elemér scrambled out of the river and gave chase, hopping over the stubbly fields in bare feet in pursuit. The girls squealed with delight and threw sheaves of wheat at them, and brandished sickles — but not very seriously. Paddy and Elemér caught up with them, and soon all four were frolicking about in a hayrick. Then, all passion spent, they fell asleep. Elemér woke with a start some hours later, remembering there was company coming to dinner, and it was a rush to get back to Guraszáda in time. According to Paddy there was nothing half-hearted, nor interrupted, about the sex they enjoyed that afternoon; but were Rumanian peasant girls really so spontaneous and easy-going? It was accepted at that time, so a Hungarian friend of Paddy's has commented, that female house servants and migrant harvest-workers were, if asked, expected to oblige young gentlemen of the estate.[29]

Xenia would soon have to return to Budapest; and when the lovers had no more than a few days left together, Elemér came to the rescue. He borrowed a car, and he and Paddy met Xenia at a discreet rendezvous and headed north. In *Between the Woods and the Water* Paddy describes the drive through Alba Iulia, Turda, and Cluj, where they came down to breakfast to hear that Chancellor Dollfuss had been assassinated.*

Or perhaps not. 'Paddy told me the whole drive through Transylvania was invented,' said Rudolf Fischer; 'what is more, inspired by and based on a book I had given him.'[30] Fischer also suggested the pseudonym Angéla, though in old age Xenia was quite happy to let it be known that Paddy had been her lover. Xenia wrote to Paddy after reading *Between the Woods and the Water* in Hungarian – translated by her nephew, Miklós Vajda. She told Paddy she had worked in a textile factory for twenty-six years. She had also been arraigned for murder, having in a fit of rage killed a woman with whom she shared a flat in post-war Budapest. 'My black hair is now white. I am seventy-six years old. I am homesick . . . your book brought me home.'[31]

Elemér tried to persuade him to stay on, tempting him with the delights of the hunting season: chamois, stags and – if he stayed on for the winter – bears. Yet Paddy felt he had already lingered at Guraszáda too long. Feeling very lonely for the first time in weeks he walked on towards Tomeşti, where he was expected by Herr Robert v. Winckler – a tall, thin, scholarly man, living alone with his books on the edge of a forest. Paddy was not long in his company, but it made a lasting impression. Winckler was the main ingredient in the composite portrait of the Polymath in *A Time of Gifts*.†

* Dollfuss was assassinated by the Nazis in Vienna on 25 July 1934.
† The Polymath is a vehicle for a series of digressions on such subjects as the Knight of Ybbs, the movement of early tribes, the titles of the Holy Roman

By now it was high summer. For two days Paddy scrambled through valleys and foothills, heading south–west towards Caransebeş to avoid the main road to Lugoj. He missed the company of Xenia and Elemér, but being on the march again brought solace, and he was pleased to find that his strength and endurance returned quickly after the weeks of soft living.

In *Between the Woods and the Water*, Paddy extended and elaborated the bare facts of his south-easterly walk through the forests and canyons of the southern Carpathians. Time and place are blurred, new scenes are added. Line breaks become mysterious: sometimes they signal a change of tone, sometimes they seem to indicate a shift in time. The result is a passage that, over several pages, recreates with astonishing intensity the feeling of being alone in the mountains: the sense of release, of time expanding, all cords cut, and a height-ened awareness of the natural world.

He kept to the west of the main mass of the mountains, trying not to lose height, guided by the position of the sun, and his watch and compass. Paddy saw no one for two days and nights in the wilderness – rising with the dawn, wrapping himself in his greatcoat at sundown, and sleeping fitfully through the cold night with a million stars for company. He carried plenty of food and drank from the streams, which harboured clumps of watercress. Early one morning he stumbled upon a huge golden eagle, preening its feathers on a ledge overlooking a ravine in the mountains. He watched it a long time before it spread its enormous wings and launched into the void.

At some point in his walk across the Carpathians he spent the night in a wooden house with a tin roof that belonged to the Jewish manager of a timber company. This burly man was dressed in working clothes but his brother the Rabbi, who had come on a visit with his two sons, wore long black robes, while the boys had corkscrew curls. Speaking Yiddish among themselves, they talked to Paddy in German: of Hitler and Israel, about Jewry in England, and he per-suaded them to recite from the scriptures in Hebrew. At the same time, he was aware that an unbridgeable gulf lay between them.

Empire or the variety of fish in the Danube. By putting these into the mouth of an enthusiastic teacher, Paddy allows his older self into the story to instruct his younger self.

The two young bespectacled Talmudic students were already dedicated to a lifetime of rigorous study: 'Their pale faces, in the
lamplight, looked as though they had never been out of a shuttered
room.' They in turn could not imagine why anyone would want to
walk across Europe, out of interest and just for fun: it was a *'goyim
naches'* – a goyish fancy, an outlandish idea, which made no sense to
a practical, God-fearing Jew.[32]

He spent a few days near Băile Herculane, the Baths of Hercules,
in the last friendly house on the north side of the Danube that belonged
to Heinz Schramm. No one he had met over the course of the summer
had ever set foot in Bulgaria, and they thought he was mad. Bulgaria,
as everyone knew, had been under Ottoman rule for longer than any
other country in Europe, and was a rough and backward place. Paddy
was keen to move on, but reluctant to leave too: the days of castles,
libraries, good wine and hot baths were almost over. It was three or
four days before he said goodbye, and set off southwards.

For several miles of its length the Danube forms a spectacular
natural frontier between Rumania and Serbia as the great river,
swollen by thousands of streams pouring off the mountains, is forced
through a steep and jagged gorge. Only the most skilful pilots could
navigate the currents and eddies created by the Danube as it roared
through this narrow defile, the most dangerous point being the
Kazan, or Cauldron, west of Orşova.

There was one other place Paddy wanted to explore before plunging
into Bulgaria: Ada Kaleh, an island four kilometres long by a kilometre
wide, some three miles downstream from Orşova. The majority of
its inhabitants were Turkish: its name in Turkish meaning 'island
fortress', it was a tiny fragment of the Ottoman empire that had
somehow survived with its language, religion and customs intact. In
a little coffee shop he was welcomed by old men in fezzes, who
touched their heart, lips and brow in welcome. He wandered in the
maze of cobbled lanes where whitewashed houses were adorned with
wooden balconies and vine-covered trellis, tobacco leaves were hung
out to dry 'like kippers', and veiled women carried firewood and fed
their chickens. He heard the call of the muezzin, watched the men
at prayer. It was his first glimpse into an Islamic world.

5

Bulgaria to Mount Athos

Paddy entered Bulgaria on 14 August, and felt he had crossed a cultural divide.* To the north lay a Romanized, western culture that looked towards Paris and Vienna; while on the south bank, the town of Lom was part of the Balkans, the Orthodox and Ottoman east. The speed with which it had happened was both exciting and disturbing, and the evidence was everywhere: 'in the domes and minarets and the smoky tang of kebabs cooking on spits, in the jutting wooden houses and the Byzantine allegiance of the churches, in the black cylindrical hats, the flowing habits, the long hair and beards of the priests, and in the Cyrillic alphabet on the shop fronts which gave a fleeting impression of Russia.' There were no women in the streets, only men. 'Rough-hewn and tough, shod and swaddled in the same cowhide footgear as the Rumanians, they padded the dusty cobbles like bears.'[1]

He began walking south towards Sofia. Soon he was in the huge, rolling, ochre-coloured folds of the Stara Planina, otherwise known as the Great Balkan range, which marches right across the country from Serbia to the Black Sea. Over the four-day trek he joined a caravan of peasants with their bullock wagons; they invited him to spend the night beside their campfire, and took

---

* In following Paddy's trans-European odyssey so far, I have relied mainly on the manuscript of *A Time of Gifts*, its published edition, and *Between the Woods and the Water*. But once Paddy crossed the Danube into Bulgaria, those works are left behind. The following chapter is assembled from interviews with Paddy and two other sources, which have also been quoted earlier. They are described in more detail in Appendix I, p.390. The first is his only surviving diary, a thick green exercise book which he bought in Bratislava in March 1934. The other is 'A Youthful Journey', written in 1963–4 and discussed in Chapter 18, which covers the events of the final third of the walk.

him as far as Petrochan. Beyond Petrochan the road unfurled 'like a gypsy's ribbon'.[2] He listened to a herdsman playing his flute, and the tinkling bells of the flocks of black and white sheep and goats.

After spending his first night in Sofia in a verminous lodging house, he got in touch with Rachel Floyd, an English girl he had met on the steamer to Lom. Paddy was immediately scooped up by her hosts, the British Consul Boyd Tollinton and his wife Judith, and was surprised to find what comfort he took in being among his own countrymen again. He spent five or six days with the Tollintons, through whom he met several of the French, British and Americans living and working in Sofia. He also went exploring with Rachel, bought a dagger and a fur kalpak, began reading Lawrence's *Revolt in the Desert* and the poems of Rilke, and played cricket with Boyd Tollinton: 'I made five. Out middle stump, amazing incongruousness of scene, diversity of nations. Bulgarian onlookers realizing that it is true that the English are not quite right in the head.'[3]

On 27 August he left Sofia and headed south towards the great monastery of Rila. 'Wore my fur kalpak, braid sash and dagger for the first time. Effect excellent.'[4]

The monastery of Rila is set deep in the mountains of the Rilska Planina, which were steeper and more dramatic than the undulating Balkan range he had crossed on his way to Sofia. A hard day's climb took him over the watershed into a burning wilderness of boulders and dried-up torrent beds; then a broad valley descended in a series of huge steps, tarns appeared among the rocks, deciduous trees overtook the conifers, a trail appeared, and he reached Rila at dusk. The effort was worth it. The monastery, which had been sacked and vandalized several times over the centuries, looked heavily fortified from the outside, with a forbidding perimeter wall and a fourteenth-century keep that rose above the shining silver domes of the church. Inside, was an inner courtyard 'the size of half Trafalgar Square . . . half orthodox, half madrassa'.[5] Surrounding the courtyard were three tiers of arcaded galleries, adorned with loggias and open stairwells.

It was night by the time he arrived. He made his way to a little

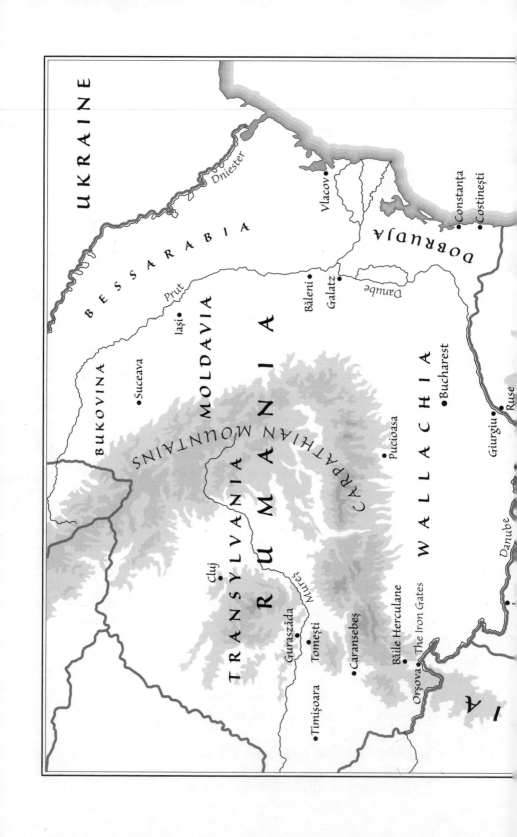

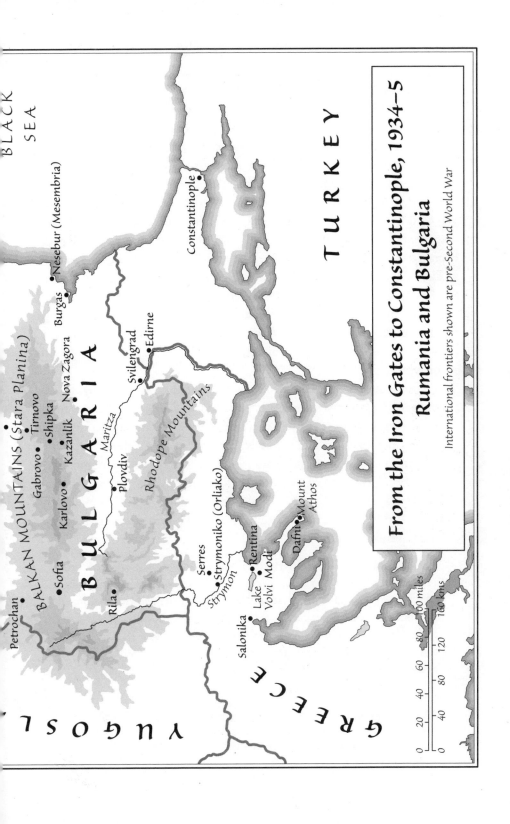

From the Iron Gates to Constantinople, 1934–5
Rumania and Bulgaria

International frontiers shown are pre-Second World War

BLACK SEA

TURKEY

Constantinople

Nesebur (Mesembria)

Burgas

Edirne

Svilengrad

Nova Zagora

Shipka

Kazanlik

Tirnovo

Gabrovo

BALKAN MOUNTAINS (Stara Planina)

Karlovo

Sofia

Petrochan

Rila

B U L G A R I A

Plovdiv

Maritza

Rhodope Mountains

Serres

Strymoniko (Orliako)

Strymon

Rentina

Lake Volvi

Modi

Dafni

Mount Athos

Salonika

G R E E C E

Y U G O S L

miles

0   20   40   60   80   100 miles

0   40   80   120   160 kms

*khan** outside the walls of the monastery, where a party was in full swing: the Abbot was celebrating the arrival of a friend who had studied with him in St Petersburg. There was much singing and drinking, and Paddy spent the night in a big dormitory on a hard wooden bed. Over the next few days, the monastery courtyards filled with pilgrims coming to celebrate the feast of St Ivan Rilski, founder of the monastery and patron saint of Bulgaria.

Paddy walked in the mountains to avoid the crowds, and on his return to the monastery two days later he met, among a group of students, a beautiful girl called Penka Krachanova, though Paddy preferred to call her Nadejda. They walked in the mountains, sat and talked and sang, with the monastery laid out beneath them. They spent the evening together, and all of the following day. 'Lay in each other's arms talking desultorily. Walked home in the sunset. One of the happiest days of my life,' he wrote in his diary.[6] She lived in Plovdiv, and he promised to look her up when he passed through.

Returning to the Tollintons in Sofia, Paddy found a Byzantine congress in progress. Among the scholars was Thomas Whittemore, best remembered for his work in uncovering the mosaics of Haghia Sophia in Constantinople. Paddy met him first in the smart Café Bulgaria one evening, and before long they were deep in conversation about Byzantium, especially the monasteries of Athos, the Meteora and Anatolia. Over the next few days, Whittemore introduced Paddy to two other eminent scholars: Steven Runciman and Roger Hinks.

> They were impeccable in Panama hats and suits of cream-coloured Athenian raw silk and their bi-coloured shoes were beautifully blancoed and polished. Both were in their early thirties and they belonged much more to the deck of an Edith Wharton yacht or to the cypress-walk of a *palazzo* in Henry James than to this hot little Balkan capital. We met several times; their conversation was dazzlingly erudite and comic; then the end of the conference scattered them again.[7]

---

* A Balkan word for caravanserai: it can be anything from a large open courtyard with galleries to a more modest enclosure where travellers and their animals can stay. Stalls selling food, wine and groceries are often found nearby.

Steven Runciman also remembered meeting Paddy in Sofia – 'a very bright, very grubby young man', he recalled.[8]

Leaving Sofia Paddy set off south-east, across the plain that had once swarmed with invading armies. The Ottoman occupation of Bulgaria 'started before the Wars of the Roses, and ended after the Franco-Prussian War', wrote Paddy. It left desolation: 'Everything is still impoverished and haphazard, and history in smithereens.'[9] He spent the night in a Turkish khan, where families camped and cooked beside their mules and donkeys, and followed the river Maritza to Plovdiv – once known as Philippopolis: a city named after Alexander the Great's father, Philip of Macedon.

There he looked up Penka, the girl met at Rila. She lived with her grandfather in a house with an inner courtyard, in which grew a pomegranate tree. Paddy was presented to her frail grandfather, a Greek from Constantinople who spoke perfect French – Paddy remembered her kissing his hands in greeting.[10] In 'A Youthful Journey', he spends happy hours with Penka in an airy room with divans around the walls at the top of the house. Here they dressed up in antique clothes from a huge chest, staged mock sword-fights, and he drew her portrait wearing Turkish clothes and smoking a chibouk. In his diary, there is nothing like such detail – though he does mention spending an afternoon at her house, 'drowsy and amorous, she's a grand girl'.[11] He described her as his twin since they were born within a day of each other, and she gave him 'all the fun and the lightness and ease that one had been missing since the banks of the Maros'[12] – since his time with Xenia, that is. She also gave him a heavy silver medal bearing an image of St George, or possibly St Dimitri, slaying a dragon. He wore it on a leather bootlace round his neck, and lost it swimming in the Bay of Artemis by Lemonodassos two or three years later.*

Paddy spent five days in Plovdiv. He recalled the metal-workers, saddle-makers, wool-carders and tobacco-sorters whose workshops lined the cobbled alleys. He saw Turks, the first since Ada Kaleh, and Pomaks: Bulgarians who had converted to Islam. Listening hard, he caught at the languages that flowed all around him: Greek, Turkish,

* See page 2 of first plate section.

Armenian, Romany, and – from the Sephardic Jewish quarter – Ladino, a form of fifteenth-century Castilian Spanish.

He decided to leave on 24 September. 'Rather sentimental tonight,' he wrote in his diary, 'as I have decided to quit tomorrow.'[13] Years later, he was not so emotionally brisk.

> The whole itinerary was a chain of minor valedictions . . . But when, through some natural affinity . . . these encounters plunged deeper and spread their quick roots of friendship, affection, passion, love – even if it were no more than the unavowed electrical flicker of its possibility – these farewells became shattering deracinations; as they had been in Transylvania and as they were now. *Voilà l'herbe qu'on fauche*, in the words of Banville that I had been listening to so recently, *et le laurier qu'on coupe.*[14]

The Turkish border was now only about a hundred and forty kilometres away, if Paddy had followed the Maritza valley south-east from Plovdiv. But he did not want to leave Bulgaria without seeing the Byzantine treasures that lay in and around the ancient city of Tirnovo, a hundred and fifty kilometres to the north. From there he planned to return to Rumania, visit as yet unseen Bucharest, and eventually make his way down the Black Sea coast to Constantinople. It would add several hundred miles to the journey but Paddy was in no hurry; travelling had become a way of life.

Karlovo was far more Turkish than Bulgarian, both in its inhabitants and its architecture. He saw a Turkish wedding procession – 'Flute, bagpipes, tambourine . . . bride unveiled . . . Flowers stuck on cheek, kissing the elders' hand. Sweets. Scrabble. Caught one.' In a mosque, he attended prayers for the first time: 'obeisances, standing, squatting, touching floor with foreheads . . . watched it all, fascinated.'[15]

He walked north-eastwards, following the line of the Stara Planina mountains that rose abruptly from the plain. His destination was the monastery that had been built on the Shipka Pass, where he arrived long after dark after an exhausting walk. The monastery looked magical in the moonlight, but he was not allowed in. There was no choice but to curl up in his coat under an oak tree. He woke 'feeling like death, cold and still, aching in every joint, with a coating of dew on my clothes'.[16]

Walking down the hill to the hospital part of the monastery, he took breakfast with a group of people who, from their shirts, boots and peaked caps, he saw to be Russian refugees. One of them, a Captain Yanoff, though dressed in rags, was educated, well travelled, and spoke both English and French: he gave Paddy a detailed account of the Battle of Shipka Pass, in which the Russians and Bulgarians defeated the Turks in 1877–8.

The way to Kazanlik lay south-east through a walnut forest, where a band of gypsies were beating the branches with poles to release the nuts. Their children swarmed round Paddy, whining and begging till he waved his stick and swore at them in English, 'which shut them up like a box'.[17] He had often passed bands of gypsies as he travelled through eastern Europe, and their brazen mockery made him feel uncomfortable. Near Esztergom, gypsy boys had tried to sell him bunches of dead weasels, stoats and rats, which they had chased out of their holes with buckets of water. Pips Schey told him that when they buried a dead horse on the farm at Kövecses, the gypsies would dig it up for meat. The authorities hated them for they refused conscription and census alike, but they were highly skilled musicians. 'The songs they play', wrote Paddy, 'are wild and intoxicating . . . and some of the airs . . . are so melancholy and touching that it is hard to keep the tears from one's eyes when hearing them.'[18]

Kazanlik, the centre of the rose-oil industry, was a sad little town where Paddy had an introduction to Mr Barnaby Crane. This faded Englishman had come from Lancashire in his youth to work in the textile trade, and had married a Bulgarian girl. He did not miss England, and told Paddy he would 'breathe his last in Bulgaria',[19] which Paddy – prone to bouts of severe homesickness – found very depressing. But Mr Crane treated him to a good dinner, and gave him 250 levas after breakfast the following morning. Paddy accepted it gratefully, as he was almost out of money.

He made his way back to the Shipka monastery and from there set off northwards, along the old Turkish way that climbed up the mountain to the pass itself. Soon the monastery's glinting domes were out of sight; and as he climbed, the folds of the mountains rolled out below him covered with golden beeches. Further up, a mist gathered till he could hardly see, and soon came ominous rolls of thunder. The rain fell in torrents, and for three quarters of an hour he stumbled on, soaked to the skin, till he came upon a little khan. Inside were the owner, and four or five whiskery shepherds in fur kalpaks.

The owner made him take off his wet things and set them to dry before the stove; and sitting him down in pyjamas and a sheepskin overcoat, the kind man gave him a drink of hot brandy and water, followed by a plate of boiled mutton and potatoes. Paddy spent the rest of the evening 'yarning with the peasants, the rain beating on the windows and the wind rattling them and the thunder crashing outside . . . I won't ever forget it; it was one of the jolliest evenings I have ever spent.'[20]

In Gabrovo he looked up another compatriot: a young English woman in her twenties called Mrs Pojarlieff, married to a Bulgarian. Paddy stayed the night with her and her husband, who played the violin, and they gave him some books – Shaw's *Androcles and the Lion* and *Pygmalion*, and Balzac's *Contes drolatiques*; but the whole visit was tinged with sadness, for it was obvious that Mrs Pojarlieff was very ill.

Tirnovo, the old capital of the Bulgarian tsars, is built in a series of steps on the edge of a spectacular canyon, at the bottom of which roars the river Yantra. It was already dark when Paddy reached it, on the evening of 4 October. He found a little khan full of peasants who had come to town for market day. The owner spoke German, and told Paddy he could sleep there. In the morning he explored the tangled network of busy streets and steps. 'Moccasins, scarlet sashes and sheepskin hats crowded the steps and intermingled with flocks, donkeys and mules, climbing and descending the steep thoroughfare like the traffic of Jacob's ladder.'[21]

The man who owned the khan also had a grocer's shop; and his son, whose name was Georgi Gatschev, decided to take the young Englishman under his wing. This was lucky, for Paddy was down to his last few pence and there was nothing waiting for him at the post office. Georgi taught Paddy some Bulgarian songs, and Paddy taught him some English and German ones in return.

On 9 October, while he was still anxiously awaiting the arrival of money from England, Tirnovo erupted into a fierce celebration on hearing the news that Alexander I of Yugoslavia had just been assassinated by a Bulgarian nationalist. The Bulgarians had a particular loathing of the Greeks and Serbs, who had gained territory at their expense at the end of the Balkan wars. To punish Bulgaria for joining the wrong side, the peace treaties of 1919 decreed that the province of Macedonia be divided between Greece and the newly-formed Yugoslavia. It was a bitter loss, which the Bulgarians now felt had been avenged.

Paddy noted the assassination in his diary, but wrote almost nothing at the time about the reactions of those around him. But years later he described how the town went wild. In a restaurant he visited that evening everyone was jubilant, laughing and hugging each other and calling for more wine and slivo as they sung 'Shumi Maritza', the Bulgarian national anthem. 'The tinkle of a thrown slivo glass on the dance floor evoked a cheer. Soon they were whizzing and smashing all over it . . .'[22] People got to their feet and, throwing their arms round each other's shoulders, began to dance, grinding the smashed glass under their heels while the band tried to keep up. Georgi joined a particularly rowdy set, who were pulling the table-cloths off the laid tables, while – to the manager's dismay – another group threw an entire table, fully laden, over the railing and into the ravine.

Paddy did not elaborate further on the festivities, having come across a German traveller with an English mother called Hans Franheim, with whom he found he had several friends in common. Paddy and Hans spent the next few days together, visiting the Preobazhensky monastery, a Turkish cemetery, a mosque, and wandering about the town. They took their meals together, went drinking and dancing – sometimes joined by Georgi, sometimes not. For Paddy, the company of the well-read, cultivated Hans was a relief from that of Georgi and his boisterous circle.

This put Georgi into a very irritable mood, as did Paddy's plan of leaving Tirnovo and heading north for Bucharest. All Rumanians were cheats, liars and thieves, and the very fact that Paddy wanted to visit them was a betrayal, Georgi said. Paddy tried to tell him that politics were of little interest to him: he wanted to know what people were like, to learn about their history and what they ate and wore and sang. Georgi refused to understand. In his world-view there was no room for innocent bystanders, and if Paddy was Georgi's friend, then he should feel like a Bulgarian. A slight chill settled over his last few days in Tirnovo, and not only from Georgi: his friends, too, seemed to be giving Paddy the cold shoulder. Georgi said it was because they thought he was a spy. Paddy scoffed at the idea, and Georgi evidently thought better of it too. Paddy promised to visit him in Varna on his return from Bucharest.

He left Tirnovo on 15 October, heading north for Rustchuk (now Ruse), on the Bulgarian side of the Danube. His allowance had still not arrived, but Georgi lent him three hundred levas that Paddy promised to pay back. At Trambes there was a fair, after which he fell in step with a man with a dancing bear. That night, after much carousing and dancing to gypsy music in a tavern, Paddy and the bear-owner were told they could sleep on the balcony. His companion slept with his arms round the bear, 'which snorted and grunted all night'.[23]

Arriving in Rustchuk, he made his way with pounding heart to the post office where, to his intense relief, money and letters were waiting. After sending the money he owed Georgi, Paddy sat down in a café with a pile of newspapers and read all about the assassination of King Alexander. He crossed the Danube into Rumania on 23 October, and the following evening, he was in Bucharest.

'Bucharest amazing town,' wrote Paddy in his diary, 'almost like London or Paris, not like Sofia . . . Wandered around ages, soaking it in. Lights, cars, everything. *Lovely* town.'[24] He also noticed the horse-drawn cabs, driven by stout figures in long blue caftans with tiny eyes, soft skin and a strangely high-pitched voice. He later discovered they were Russian and belonged to the Skopzi, a religious sect spread across Bessarabia and southern Russia. The adult males, having married and sired one or two children, castrated themselves to achieve a closer union with God.

Thanks to Tibor and Bertha Berg, Elemér von Klobusitzky, Count and Countess Jenö Teleki and others, Paddy arrived in Bucharest well armed with telephone numbers and letters of introduction. Among the first people to scoop him up were Count Ambrose

O'Kelly and his wife Elena Filipescu. He spent the weekend with them in their villa in the mountain resort of Sinaia, where King Carol had a summer palace bristling with towers and finials. Everyone spoke French, and Paddy was enchanted by the sophistication and beauty of the women.

He had been invited to stay with Josias ('Joey') von Rantzau, a German diplomat whom he had met in Transylvania. His new lodgings were close to perfection: Josias begged him to help himself to drinks, cigarettes and cigars – 'We get them practically free' – while his flat was filled with books on Rumania and various encyclopedias. Josias's Rumanian mistress, Marcelle Catargi, came from a great boyar family; and together they introduced Paddy to the cream of Bucharest society. Evenings passed in a whirl of cocktail parties, dinner parties and nightclubs, and often ended with late-night talking sessions with his host over a bottle of brandy. Rantzau once asked Paddy: 'Do you believe in the phrase, *my country right or wrong?*'[25] He was deeply troubled by the rise of Nazism.

The Nazis did not cast much of a shadow over Paddy's glamorous life with the beau-monde of Bucharest, nor the flirtation he was enjoying with a woman called Angy Dancos: 'Sweet Rumanian type – *enormous* eyes, long lashes, very red mouth, perfect figure, very chic Parisian.' Paddy did not like her husband: 'think he suspects I've designs on his wife (he's right, too).'[26] Angy was part of what Paddy saw as Bucharest's bohemian circle, while Josias's mistress, Marcelle Catargi, belonged to the society set.

Staying with Josias Rantzau opened several diplomatic doors. Paddy lunched and dined not only at the German Legation with Rantzau, but also at the Polish Legation, and the British Legation with the minister Michael Palairet (who was later Ambassador in Athens). There were shooting parties and visits to the opera, and he became great friends with Constantine Soutzo and Nico Chrissoveloni, with whom he got drunk and went 'on the prowl'. It is surprising that he had any time for books at all, but he mentions reading Harold Nicolson's *Some People*, R. W. Seton-Watson's *History of the Roumanians*, and a play: Noël Coward's *The Vortex*.

Although Paddy had the knack of rising to the top of any society he found himself in, the smart, French-speaking Bucharestis seemed particularly susceptible to his charm. He found them equally engaging, for reserve and self-control are not overrated virtues in Rumania. The fury of their quarrels, the ease of their wit and laughter, the exaggeration of their gestures, their deep respect for art, books and ideas, their love of gossip and their happy-go-lucky attitude to sex, all made him feel he could never tire of their company. They did not seem to mind his shabby clothes, nor the fact that he could not pay for anything.

The only thing to which Paddy objected, though it was just as bad in Hungary, was their anti-Semitism. To Hungarians and Rumanians, a dislike of Jews was seen not as a prejudice but as a natural response. Paddy's friends could not understand why their resentment of the Jews made him so unhappy (though he expresses this unhappiness in his later writing more than in the diary written at the time). They gave him anti-Jewish books to read such as *The Protocols of the Elders of Zion*, whilst one Hungarian showed him a copy of the *Semi-Gotha*, as though its contents represented the cast-iron truth. Designed as a companion to the Almanach de Gotha which lists the aristocratic families of Europe, the *Semi-Gotha*'s purpose was to illustrate the deliberate infiltration of those bloodlines by the Jews as part of their scheme to dominate the world. Paddy tried to protest, but a grateful guest is always at a disadvantage. Looking baffled and sad, he would drop the subject long before the argument became angry.

Paddy left Bucharest by train early on 14 November, re-entered Bulgaria and arrived at Varna on the Black Sea late that night. Varna he described as 'a depressing place in winter, like all sea-side towns'.[27] His friend Georgi from Tirnovo was delighted to see him again, their last disagreement quite forgotten, and they went out to celebrate with a crowd of friends.

Georgi offered Paddy the use of his digs for as long as he liked, and arranged for credit at the local restaurant – Bucharest had taken quite a toll on his funds. Judith Tollinton had also put him in touch with the British Consul in Varna and his wife, Frank and Eva Baker. The hospitable Bakers invited him to lunch, lent him a pile of books and told him to visit whenever he liked. He borrowed T. E. Lawrence's *Revolt in the Desert*, which he had not yet finished, Peter Fleming's *One's Company* and Richard Oke's novel *Frolic Wind*.

Paddy came back to Georgi's digs late one evening from a party at the Bakers'. Being very drunk he made a lot of noise coming in, and Georgi flew into a temper. Though he knew Georgi's brooding nature, knew he could uncoil and lash out at the slightest provocation, Paddy found the situation so absurd he started to laugh. At that point Georgi 'seized my dagger off the table and went for me, grazing my shoulder. Luckily I got him down. Then he was filled with remorse, and begged my pardon again and again . . . It was my fault really, though I was surprised about the dagger.'[28]

Georgi's action puzzled him. The two of them had parted at the beginning of the evening on good terms; there had been no rivalry over the *studentkas* (female students) whom Georgi was in love with. Had he said something stupid and tactless? Had he outstayed his welcome? Georgi assured him that he had done no such thing; he would not hear of him moving out. So they went out to lunch, got drunk and put the incident behind them. But Paddy held to the idea that Georgi's rage had been provoked by some unpardonable thing that he had said or done, yet it seems more likely that Georgi was jealous of the time Paddy was spending with his smart consular friends.

It was 1 December. Paddy had hoped to take a boat to the coastal town of Burgas but, not finding one, he prepared to walk down the coast instead. Determined to give him a good send-off, Georgi and twelve of his friends decided to accompany him. They walked along the rocky coast till sunset, when Georgi's companions lit torches and sang through the woods. 'We arrived at Fisherman's hut, drank all evening, played peasant instruments, sang. *Gaida, gadulka, caval, kazakduk, ratchiza, horo, kütchek.** Grand firelight, read, peasant Bulgaria. Slept in a pile of fishing nets.'[29]

At no point in his original account did he walk down this stretch of coast alone, nor did he lose his footing and find himself floundering among freezing rock-pools after dark. But this evening in the fisherman's hut, with another incident that took place on Mount Athos a few weeks later,† were combined into one astonishing

---

* *Gaida*, bagpipes: *gadulka*, a stringed instrument played with a bow: *caval*, flute. I cannot identify *kazakduk* and *ratchiza*, but *horo* and *kütchek* are dances – the last being a burlesque belly-dance.

† See pages 95–6.

description. Later published in *Holiday* magazine as *A Balkan Welcome*, it describes how Paddy – half-frozen, bleeding and exhausted – stumbles into a cave occupied by some Bulgarian shepherds and a few Greek fishermen. Decades later, when he came to tell the tale to Ben Downing in the *Paris Review* in 2003, the two separate incidents had fused together to become one memory: 'Slogging on south, I lost my way after dark, fell into the sea, and waded soaked into a glimmering cave full of shepherds and fishermen – Bulgars and Greeks – for a strange night of dancing and song. It was like a flickering firelight scene out of Salvator Rosa.'[30]

The following morning, the company walked on. The path took them first across a country of entrenched headlands which gave way to marshland at the mouth of a river, where a man with a muzzle-loader was shooting duck. They walked upstream for a while, seeing wild boar and some shepherds. Most of Georgi's friends decided to return home that afternoon, except for Cerno, who stayed on with Georgi. Long after dark the three companions reached a grim Turkish village, where they were allowed to sleep in the morgue.

On the evening of 3 December they reached the peak above the bay of Nesebur, or Mesembria – Paddy preferred the old name. As they walked along the man-made isthmus into the ancient town, they watched a school of dolphins leaping out at sea. The following day Paddy walked around Mesembria, looking at its wealth of Byzantine churches and 'wishing I knew more about them';[31] he noted their names and made a map of their positions in the back of his diary. After one long last drinking session, Georgi and Cerno took a boat back to Varna and Paddy was alone. It took him a day to reach Burgas, which he did on 5 December.

Following a pattern that was becoming familiar, Paddy immediately looked up the British Consul. The Consul in Burgas was Tony Kendall, and as he advanced to shake hands with Paddy, he was conscious of an overpowering smell: his guest had been eating *pastrouma*, a dried meat heavily flavoured with garlic and herbs. But thanks to warm recommendations from the Tollintons and the Bakers, Paddy again found himself being asked to stay. Tony and Mila Kendall were as hospitable and gregarious as he had hoped, and as well as introducing Paddy to their local circle of friends, Tony

Kendall took him boar shooting. On 12 December Paddy began to feel unwell, and within two days he was seriously ill: 'Sweating till my pyjamas and the sheets were sodden rags, my teeth chattering and my temperature high.'[32] He had caught malaria – a disease that was, and still is, common round the Black Sea.

Once he had begun to feel better, Tony Kendall gave him Foreign Office reports to read which 'set me wise about the Balkans a good deal'; and in the *Encyclopaedia Britannica*, he read up on 'Bulgaria, Hungary, Rumania, Yugoslavia, Greece and Albania . . . Learnt lots that I ought to have known before.'[33] Through the Kendalls he met people, both Bulgarian and English, who spoke of the Balkan wars, the Macedonian question, the political tensions of the region. He wrote long letters: to his mother, to Elemér von Klobusitzky at Gurászáda. His next batch of pound notes arrived on 23 December, and the Kendalls invited him to stay on for Christmas. He was still weak from his recent bout of malaria and, though a relatively mild attack, its repercussions may well have affected him over the coming weeks.

Paddy resumed his journey after Christmas. He had hoped to take a boat south down the coast, but finding none, he went by train. This involved a long loop westwards to Nova Zagora, and after a night in the station buffet reading Edgar Wallace, he caught a train at six the following morning to Svilengrad. The train was full of soldiers, as was the next train he was obliged to take to reach Constantinople.

The whole region was a sensitive demilitarized zone, supervised by an international commission headed by Turkey. There was no question of his being allowed to walk the last few miles of his epic journey, and to judge by the tone of Paddy's diary, this does not seem to have upset him at the time. But in later years, as the journey began to take on an artistic shape and significance in the story of his life, he seemed to mind it more. 'I chafed bitterly', he later wrote, 'as we chugged across the rough Thracian plain.'[34]

After a year and twenty-one days, having passed through seven countries and walked hundreds of miles, Paddy reached Constantinople in the early hours of 31 December 1935. He found a cheap hotel in the Taksim district called the Bensur, rambled round the back streets of the city, and in the Vienna café he made friends with a Greek woman called Maria Passo. With her he drank the New Year in, joining crowds of revellers as they sang in the streets. Then he went back to the hotel and slept. He did not wake up till the early evening at which point, thinking it was dawn, he rolled over and slept for another twelve hours – 'so New Year's Day 1935 will always be a blank for me.'

The town seemed to him vibrantly alive and 'full of a hundred sounds'. Yet for all its exoticism, Istanbul had died twice. The first time was in 1453, when eleven hundred years of Byzantine civilization fell to the Turkish conqueror, Mehmet II. What remained of Constantinople was absorbed into its new incarnation, Istanbul: the name being a corruption of a Greek phrase meaning 'to the city'. As the Ottoman empire disintegrated, so did its centre. In 1923, Kemal Atatürk gave Istanbul the *coup de grâce* by moving the capital to Ankara, and the old city was left to crumble under the weight of its history.

Over the next few days he ate at an Armenian restaurant, where the proprietor told him hair-raising stories of the Turkish persecutions; a German restaurant, where he enjoyed talking German to the eccentric proprietor; and a Jewish restaurant, where Spanioli Jews played the guitar and sang in Ladino. The only Turk he visited was Djerhat Pasha, a general to whom he had been given a letter of introduction by Count Teleki. The Pasha had a bristling moustache, 'very English country gent – he spoke good French (and looked as if he might have massacred a few Armenians in his day).'[35] Although Paddy had been offered a cup of coffee, nothing could pass the general's lips till sundown for it was Ramadan.

On 5 January, Paddy went to visit the Greek Consul, Dimitri Capsalis, and his wife Hélène, who were friends of Marcelle Catargi, Josias von Rantzau's mistress. The consuls of eastern Europe seem to have had a particular weakness for Paddy. His magic worked yet again, and they happily swept him into their orbit. They took him to the bazaar and on walks round the city, introduced him to their friends, and best of all, put him in touch with the Ecumenical Patriarch, spiritual head of the Greek Orthodox Church, who in turn gave Paddy a letter of introduction to the Holy Synod of Mount Athos.

Yet Paddy was in a strange mood, brooding on that sense of anti-climax and taking stock that the end of a journey brings. He wrote nothing in his diary between 11 and 24 January. He also never looked up the Byzantist Thomas Whittemore, though in his diary he had written, 'Promise of rendezvous in Constantinople.'[36] Looking back, Paddy thought it rather odd too. 'I knew so *little* about Constantinople,' he admitted. 'I really needed a teacher, and [Whittemore] would have been perfect . . . I can't think why I didn't.'[37]

On 24 January 1935, Paddy took a third-class ticket on a boat that picked its way round the northern coast of the Aegean to Salonika. The boat was a shambles, 'with enormous banks of coal in the passages, and peasants lying in their blankets in despondent groups everywhere . . .' Third class meant travelling, sleeping and eating on deck. Paddy was told by one of the officers that, as a foreigner and therefore a guest, he could move up to second class for which he was very grateful. Here he lay on a cushioned bench reading *Don Juan*, which he described as 'grand stuff, though no poetry'[38] – a verdict soon overturned.

He was the only person on board to disembark at the little port of Dafni, on the western coast of Mount Athos, on the morning of 25 January. It was cold and snowy, the whole peninsula wrapped in the deep silence of winter. Spending the first night at Xeropotamos, he then walked eastwards over the spine of the peninsula to the little capital of Karyes. While there is nothing odd about a monastery being celibate, it was in Dafni and Karyes, filled with ordinary workmen, craftsmen and shopkeepers, that the lack of women struck him most forcibly.

Tradition has it that the exclusively masculine character of the Holy Mountain was commanded by the Panaghia, the All-Holy Virgin. When the ship on which she had set out from Jerusalem was washed up on this spit of land, she declared it holy ground, dedicated to her: no other woman should set foot on it. The first holy men on Athos were hermits and ascetics, but by the early Middle Ages several monasteries had been established on the Mountain. The monks planted beans and onions, fish were plentiful, and they were supplied with wool and milk by the Vlach shepherds who were allowed on the peninsula to graze their flocks. Then, in the late eleventh century, word got out that the shepherds were also supplying their wives and daughters. From Constantinople, a scandalized Patriarch ordered the monasteries to be purged. The shepherds were banished, only male animals were permitted, while some of the most fertile land in Greece lies buried beneath dense woodland.

As soon as he had received his laissez-passer from the Holy Synod at the Chapter of the Monasteries at Karyes, Paddy set off for the nearby monastery of Koutloumousiou whose walls he could see not far down the hill. It is a small monastery but the room he was put up in was remarkably luxurious, with tapestry cushions on the divan and rich curtains. They lit the stove, made up the bed, laid the table – and here Paddy was faced with the first of those monotonous plates of beans in oil that are the staple fare of every visitor to the Mountain. 'Of this I could hardly eat a mouthful . . . so I ate lots of bread and sugar, and several oranges. Not wishing to offend the monks I wrapped most of it up in paper, and clandestinely disposed of it later.'[39]

He felt very alone. 'Later I could hear the deep plainsong chants and strange Orthodox antiphony and, with the last streaks of daylight fading behind the Byzantine cupolas and red and white masonry of the chapel, I felt suddenly terribly sad . . . At such times I nearly always remember England, and London and the hooting of cars in Piccadilly, or the soft English countryside, which becomes so blessed in memory . . .'[40] He devoted much time adding to his small store of Greek, and the monks did what they could to help; but being in a monastery was not the same as being in a village. A monk's work is to pray. Paddy attended a few of the lengthy periods of service and liturgy that punctuated life on the Holy Mountain, but when he saw his hosts file into church to begin their devotions, he knew he would be alone for several hours. The advantage was that he was able to spend far more time writing.

On 27 January he reached the eastern coast and the monastery of Iviron, where he joined the monks for vespers. 'To me there is something absolutely mystical, sinister and disturbing about the

Orthodox liturgy,' he wrote.[41] Yet there was nothing sinister about the jolly supper he enjoyed with the monks in the kitchen, with Greek traders, lots of wine and peasant songs – a party that carried on in Paddy's guest room afterwards.

He spent two days at Stavronikita, and one at the Pantocrator. Then, after a lunch of oily vegetables which he barely touched, he set off for Vatopedi. The way lay uphill, but he missed a turn and the path became more and more overgrown. He was obliged to go downhill, and on a slope so precipitous that he had to cling to stones and branches to stop himself falling. Slithering down as best he could he ended up on the rocky shoreline, in a landslide of pebbles and boulders. For some time he made his way on hands and feet, scrambling from one boulder to the next by the sea's edge, hoping to come across a path going back up; but when he met a solid over-hanging wall of rock, it was obvious he could go no further.

He found a place where the black cliff seemed a little less steep, and tried to climb up; but the slope grew steeper, and he lost his footing. 'I slipped on a bit of wet rock and skidded down the last 20 yards or so, getting bumped and bruised and battered, my wrist deeply cut, and finally ending up in a foot of water, where the tide had come in, soaking one leg to the waist.'[42] He tied up his wrist, made his way back to the place where he thought he had gone wrong, and set off with fresh hope. When this way too became impassable, he determined to make his way back to Pantocrator. By now it was raining, and the light was beginning to fail. He was cold, hungry, and a strap on his rucksack had broken.

Again and again the paths he hacked out through the thickets led back to the sea. 'Then my guts seemed to drain right out of me and a fit of panic came, thoughts of passing the night there, without food in the rain . . .' He began to yell for help, at six-second inter-vals, but no one heard. Then he gave up. He found himself praying, though expecting little response since he only ever prayed when in trouble. On the other hand it was God's mountain, 'so I felt he had some sort of responsibility'.[43]

There remained one thicket to try, which involved crawling on his belly under some fallen yew trees, and then – 'the thrill of relief was scarcely bearable' – in the light of a match he saw the pathway winding up in front of him. 'Getting my rucksack I started running uphill, shouting and singing at the top of my voice, anything, as an outlet. If I'd had my revolver with me I'd have emptied it into the air . . . however I stabbed savagely at the bushes and trees, sinking my dagger into them with wild shouts. A stranger meeting me then would have thought I was a dangerous lunatic.'[44]

He came upon another monastery: not, he says, the Pantocrator (which is at sea level) but one of the smaller ones up in the hills. Paddy hammered on the door and shouted, again and again; but the doors and walls were thick, and his voice was drowned out by the wind and the rain. A little further down the hill he saw a hut and knocked at the door. It was opened by a black bearded woodsman, who immediately invited him in. He and his three companions drew Paddy to the fire, gave him a glass of raki and a cup of hot coffee; they pulled off his wet puttees, squelching boots and sodden clothes, wrapped him in rough blankets and gave him sweet tea and a bowl of food. Then one of the men took down a Turkish *baglama*: a beautifully carved and inlaid instrument with a small deep bowl and long handle, with three or four wire strings plucked with a plectrum. 'It has a queer note, and the tunes played on it are oriental ones, with a scale of about five notes, melancholy, monotonous and insistent but not without charm . . . The other woodsmen joined in that strange, wailing chant, clapping their hands together, and tossing their heads about like dogs baying [in] the full moon.'[45]

The next morning everything was covered in snow. His host took him to the monastery, where he was lent a horse and given detailed descriptions of the path to Vatopedi. He knew it would be an insult to offer money to the woodsman to repay his kindness; instead, Paddy gave him the Bulgarian dagger (the one Georgi had tried to kill him with). The woodsman was delighted, 'though loath to deprive me of such a beautiful weapon'.[46]

Paddy's horse scrambled through thick snow to a crossroads, and in the absence of signposts, he found two Macedonians who told him he had missed the turn to Vatopedi some four kilometres back. Eventually he reached it: a great agglomeration of fortified walls, towers and belfries the size of a small village. Vatopedi is one of the richest of all the monasteries, its huge church containing what Robert

Byron described as the finest interior on the Mountain. Every inch is covered in frescoes, while behind the altar lies one of the most celebrated and miraculous icons of the Virgin. He was taken to see the library, with its priceless collection of Greek manuscripts and Byzantine psalters. He also saw the cook's cat, which could do somersaults.

From Vatopedi he went on to the Great Lavra, which boasted the largest and oldest library on Mount Athos. At the monastery of Grigoriou, Paddy was slightly embarrassed by one monk who insisted on holding his hand and pressing it affectionately. 'This is the first time I have had the slight inkling on Mount Athos that abnormality exists, though, in a permanently celibate community, it is obvious that it must.'[47] From there he climbed to the vertiginous monastery of Simopetra. Standing on the balcony outside his room 'brought one's chest into one's mouth, as there was a complete drop of several hundred feet, onto the jagged rocks and boulders below'.[48] Or, as he put it when repolishing his Athos diary years later: 'Once there, on a shuddering balcony in the eye of the wind, one was afloat above the whole Aegean.'[49]

In Dafni Paddy wrote and posted some letters, then walked on to St Panteleimon, also known as Russiko. It was 11 February, his twentieth birthday. 'Woke up this morning, the weight of my 20 years heavy upon me, wondering how many people at home were wishing me many happy returns, and whether the waves of their well-wishing would make contact with my mental apparatus.'[50] At Russiko he had been told to look out for a remarkable monk called Father Basil, who could speak English, German and French as well as Greek. Paddy found him inspiring. 'I had an unusually strong desire to be at my best in his presence, and suffered agonies when I said anything that jarred against [his] quiet conversation . . . His society was delightful to me, famished after an uninterrupted stretch of peasant company for some of the subtler shades of human inter-course than saying I come from London, and giving the number of inhabitants . . .'[51]

A little later he was taken to visit the library, where he was allowed to borrow a copy of Robert Byron's *The Station*. 'It's a splendid book,' he wrote in his diary. 'I roared with laughter, making the cloisters echo with solitary mirth . . . The description of [Father] Basil under the name of Father Valentine is a masterpiece.'[52] That evening was the vigil of the feast celebrating SS. Basil, Gregory and John Chrysostom. Paddy listened to the litany weaving its unearthly complexities for hours in a semi-trance, and watching the ceremony as it unfolded in a leisurely way around various parts of the church. The gale was still blowing, and finally Father Basil persuaded him to go to bed. 'It has been a wonderful day and I couldn't have wished for anything better for my birthday. Just a year ago I was in Schloss Pottenbrunn, in upper Austria . . .'[53]

One of the last monasteries he visited was Esphigmenou, where he met Father Belisarios. Although he had spent many years in America and worked for a bookie in San Francisco, Father Belisarios was now preoccupied with the iniquities of Freemasons, Catholics, and the degenerate state of humanity in general. '"They may be having a good time now", he growled, "but God'll see to 'em, God'll fix them fellers up OK."'[54]

Paddy never imagined he would be so sad at leaving Mount Athos. He had been deeply touched by the kindness of the monks, and had lived for over a month in a place unlike anywhere else on earth. All that day he walked through the forests of pine trees, never out of sight of the sea. It was not until he saw a group of little girls playing in the sun that he knew he had left the Holy Mountain.

6

Balasha

One of the letters Paddy posted from Dafni was to Peter Stathatos, a friend of Dimitri and Helene Capsalis with whom he hoped to stay when he left Mount Athos. Stathatos had an estate at Modi, about fifty miles north west of Mount Athos by the shores of Lake Volvi. Paddy found he was expected. When on 22 February he arrived at Rentina, just short of Modi, his host's Russian groom appeared, with a horse for Paddy to ride the last few miles.

Peter Stathatos had been brought up in Rumania, and was a keen horseman. The Stathatos estate at Modi included stables and a stud farm where horses were bred for sale to the army, so there was no shortage of mounts. Paddy rode around the lake, took part in the reed-cutting, and sat up late talking and drinking with his companionable host. After a few days, Stathatos announced that he had to go and help stamp out a revolution. Republican Venizelist elements in the army had staged a coup and, as a loyal officer who favoured a return of the monarchy, he had been called to rejoin his regiment at Salonika.

From 1910 till his death in 1936, Greek public life was dominated by the figure of Eleftherios Venizelos, whose outstanding political skill was combined with a charm few could resist. A Cretan by birth, he had taken Greece into the First World War on the Allied side, against the express wishes of the King who was pro-German. After the war the King went into exile, and as maps were redrawn in 1919, Venizelos was rewarded: Greece was enlarged to include great swathes of Epirus and Thrace. His policies were broadly republican, irredentist, and pro-Western, while his opponents were those who favoured a constitutional monarchy.

The struggle between the monarchists and Venizelists divided

Greek politics for decades, splitting the army, the judiciary and most of the professions. Both sides operated within a system of patronage that had taken root under Ottoman rule, whereby a man's status depended on how useful he could be to those above him, and the favours he could distribute to those below. The result was that when the king and his party were in power, the Venizelists were removed from every position of importance; when the Venizelists were trium-phant, the monarchists were purged. (Paddy was familiar with this system: every time there was a change of government in Athens, he said, the post office in Kardamyli changed hands.)[1]

Greece had been a republic since 1924 when King George II had been sent into exile, but Venizelos, now seventy, and his party were weakening. His last government was defeated by the Populists, the royalist party, in March. Their leader Tsaldaris accepted the republic, but many in his party talked of reinstating the King, and the repub-licans felt increasingly under threat.

In early 1935 the republican officers in the Greek army and navy laid plans for a full-scale revolt, which was doomed from the start. Venizelos urged the ringleaders not to act unless the Populist govern-ment announced its intention to bring back the King, but on 1 March they went ahead anyway. One ship, the *Averoff*, mutinied and many of the army's republican elements rose up in revolt. In northern Greece, the dividing line between the Venizelist rebels and those loyal to the government was the river Strymon, some fifty miles north-east of Salonika.

As Peter Stathatos made preparations to join his regiment, Paddy asked whether he might come along too, as an observer. Stathatos did not know if this was permissible, but they would go to Salonika together and find out. The commander of his regiment had no objection, but felt that Paddy should clear it with the British Consul. When Paddy put the matter to him, the British Consul was outraged at the very idea. 'What the bloody hell do you think you're playing at?' he shouted at Paddy. 'Nobody wants you, so stop being a nuisance and bugger off!' He came back rather crestfallen, but Stathatos was encouraging. He told Paddy to go back to Modi, ask the groom to give him a horse, and then return.

That was Paddy's version of events. But in the Stathatos family,

three generations of whom were Paddy's friends, the story takes a
different turn. Once the British Consul had given a firm refusal,
Stathatos felt he had done all he could to indulge Paddy's desire to
play soldiers and told him to go back to Modi. With the greatest
reluctance, Paddy obeyed, but once back at Modi, his thirst for
adventure got the better of him. He 'borrowed' a horse called Palikari
(the brave, the gallant) from the stables, and rode back as fast as he
could towards the action.[2]

Following the coast road to the mouth of the river Strymon he
headed north, along the western bank. He was rather disappointed
not to see a single soldier; and thinking that things might be more
interesting on the eastern bank, which was supposedly held by the
Venizelists, he urged Palikari into the river. Paddy had never forded
a river on horseback before. The horse was reluctant, but after a
couple of good kicks he stepped gingerly into the water. Suddenly
Paddy was in waist deep, with nothing but the horse's head and
neck sticking out in front. Looking behind he could see the top of
its rump and, to his surprise, the tail spread out in a great fan on
the surface of the water. Then he felt the horse beginning to turn
round in the current, and feared they might both be swept away.
They managed to return to the west bank, and Palikari turned to
look at Paddy with an aggrieved expression, 'like an indignant
chessman'.[3]

That night was spent in an Armenian village halfway up the river,
and in the morning some cavalrymen appeared, who immediately
arrested him as a spy. They took him to Orliako (Strymoniko), where
luckily Paddy managed to contact Peter Stathatos who could vouch
for him. Stathatos evidently did not have the heart to send Paddy
back to Modi a second time, so told him he could tag along if he
kept out of trouble.

A certain amount of fighting was going on, with the royalist
troops firing from along the edge of the river, and the rebels
responding from the eastern bank. It was a rather desultory engagement in Paddy's view, but local civilians were nonetheless leaving
with all their belongings to get out of harm's way. The following
day, Paddy joined a friendly sergeant and rode up to view the battle
for the bridge at Orliako. Tying Palikari to a tree trunk, he climbed

the tree and settled himself in an unoccupied stork's nest. By five in the afternoon, the enemy were in full retreat and he clambered down. A bullock cart passed by, in which lay a man badly wounded and another one dead – his first sight of the reality rather than the romance of war. A Greek officer approached him, accompanied by the British Consul. The Consul hissed at Paddy through clenched teeth, but there was nothing more he could do.

By now the royalist cavalry squadrons were forming up, with no sign of the rebels on the other side of the bridge. Paddy quickly joined the rear. The order came to draw sabres as they all trotted over, breaking into a canter as they reached the eastern bank – there was nobody there, but the troops were not going to be robbed of their moment of celebration. As the bugles sounded, they pulled out their carbines and let them off, sometimes shooting at birds perched on the telegraph wires. Paddy followed them all the way to Serres.

For him the crossing of the Orliako bridge had been a moment of wild exhilaration, and the closest thing he would ever get to taking part in a cavalry charge. But as revolutions go, this one was a flop. Signals were ignored, orders disobeyed, and such was the chaos that everyone waited to see what their colleagues would do before committing themselves. The revolt fizzled out in two weeks, leaving a handful of casualties. Venizelos went into exile, and died in Paris in 1936, while the winning royalist faction purged the army of most of its republican elements.

Paddy was riding eastwards with 'a friendly squadron of light cavalry'[4] when a group of strange, conical huts caught his eye on the left-hand side of the road. Having seen several similar encampments both in Bulgaria and when walking to Modi, he knew these huts to be the dwellings of the Sarakatsans, aristocrats among the many tribes of Greek nomads. 'Ordinary Greek villagers approve of their Greekness, envy their freedom, admire the primeval sternness of their regimen, and despise their primitive ways – "they never wash", they say, "from the day they are born till the day of their death."'[5]

Now he rode into a *stani* of some fifty huts, 'alive with bleating and barking and bells'. Looking like Benedictine monks in their thick black cloaks, the men were aloof and suspicious at first. Though he could barely understand their dialect, one of the leaders seemed to be asking Paddy what had been happening – perhaps more to find out about him rather than about the situation. 'Anyway, eagerly or ironically, they listened to my stumbling, gesticulating, half-ancient and half-modern onomatopoeia-laced pantomime of the tidings.' Invited to stay, he spent the night in one of their huts filled with the 'pungent aroma of milk, curds, goats' hair, tobacco and woodsmoke',[6] and shared their meal of black bread broken into hot milk, their coffee and hand-rolled cigarettes.

Instead of returning the horse to its stables in Modi, he now set off into the Rhodope mountains to explore eastern Macedonia and Thrace, an area inhabited by people who spoke more Bulgarian than Greek. Palikari 'carried me over . . . more than five hundred miles by the time we got back to his stable a month later'.[7] It seems extraordinary that he should have been allowed to keep the horse so long. But Peter Stathatos's grandson wrote that 'If my grandfather had been convinced that Paddy was as capable of looking after a horse as he was at riding one, he would probably not have raised any objection.'[8]

Paddy always regretted giving up the knight's-eye view he had from a horse. Local buses were far less romantic, but a good way to cover the hundred and fifty miles south to his next objective. These were the monasteries of the Meteora, perched on huge cylinders of volcanic rock that soared hundreds of feet into the clouds. First to colonize this unearthly landscape had been hermits, around whom, by the fourteenth century, churches and cloisters had begun to cluster. Once housing hundreds of monks, the monasteries were now at the end of a long decline. Paddy stayed at St Barlaam's, where the bed in the little guest room was far more comfortable than the hard pallets and flea-infested khans of the Rhodope mountains. No longer a great hive humming with prayer, the monastery was an echoing emptiness maintained by three monks: Father Christopher the abbot, Father Bessarion the deacon, and another ancient monk who tapped his way into the church with a stick.

In Kalabaka, the little town lying at the end of the long path at the foot of the Meteora, he met Hans Dyckhoff, from Coblenz, and his wife Tatiana, who were to become good friends. Hans was based in Athens where he worked for a German company, but he was also a keen Byzantinist.

Paddy arrived in the capital at the beginning of May 1935. To the excitement of reaching Athens was added the anticipation of finding letters from home, and four more pound notes. After spending a night with the Dyckhoffs he hurried to the British Consulate, and there met a young man called John Waterlow. That two young Englishmen should meet in the British Consulate in Athens is not so remarkable; but John Waterlow happened to be the son of the Ambassador, Sir Sydney Waterlow, and after a convivial drink, John Waterlow found himself inviting Paddy to spend a few days at the Embassy.

Sir Sydney Waterlow was an intelligent and cultivated man but quite immune, if not allergic, to Paddy's high spirits and exotic conversation. Although Paddy took care to gloss over much of his brief stint as an unofficial 'observer' with the Greek army at Strymoniko, Sir Sydney thought all his talk of Sarakatsans and Kutsovlachs, of riding through Macedonia and Thrace and scaling the dizzy heights of the Meteora was little more than showing off. 'You seem bloody pleased with yourself, don't you?' he growled.[9]

Only two or three days after arriving at the Embassy Paddy was approached by John Waterlow, looking terribly embarrassed. 'I'm so sorry,' he said, 'but you will have to leave.' Paddy was never told why, but no doubt reports from the British Consul in Salonika had something to do with it: Sir Sydney had discovered that he was a troublemaker as well as a show-off.

However, during those few days at the Embassy Paddy had met a young, Oxford-educated Greek diplomat called Aleko Matsas. Funny and urbane, with a taste for books and poetry, Matsas found Paddy engaging company. One evening, when Aleko was entertaining a few friends on his roof terrace, a slim woman with dark dramatic looks walked in. Her name was Princess Balasha Cantacuzene, and she had just come from a party at the British Embassy. 'I liked you immediately,' she wrote to Paddy over thirty years later. 'You were so fresh and enthusiastic, so full of colour and so clean – I shall never forget that impact of fresh air.'[10]

★

Balasha Cantacuzene belonged to one of the great dynasties of eastern Europe. There were Cantacuzenes in Greece, Rumania and Bessarabia, and they had governed Moldavia and Wallachia as *voivodes*.* The family had produced soldiers and poets, ministers and diplomats, and possibly (though the line cannot be traced with certainty) an Emperor of Byzantium. Balasha's great-grandfather, Alexander Cantacuzene, had fought in the Greek War of Independence and taken the surrender of the Turks at Monemvasia, while his brother had died at the Battle of Borodino.

No wonder Paddy fell in love. She was sixteen years older than he (in later years, he would gallantly reduce this figure to twelve) and far more sophisticated, with a flowing physical grace. Like his, her imagination was drawn to a romanticized past. Her talk was playful and lively, enriched by much reading. She had studied painting, and had developed a serious interest in culture in reaction to the superficial tastes of her *mondaine* mother. To each the other came as a revelation. She was touched by Paddy's youth, and saw that his erratic brilliance was in need of some polish – though she refused to call him Michael, the name he had used since leaving London. She preferred Paddy, so Paddy he became once again.

The eldest daughter of Prince Léon Cantacuzene and his wife, Princess Anna Vacaresco, Balasha and her younger sister Hélène (always known as Pomme) were brought up speaking French, English and Rumanian. They had a house in Bucharest and an estate in Moldavia, the northernmost of the two principalities that originally made up Rumania.

In 1924 she had married a Spanish diplomat, Francisco Amat y Torres, known as Paco, who served for three years as third secretary in Bucharest. They were *en poste* together in Warsaw, Spain, Belgrade and, latterly, Athens. Balasha had turned a blind eye to Paco's infidelities but in Athens he fell seriously in love with Clothilde, the American wife of the British diplomat Bill Bentinck (Victor Frederick William Cavendish-Bentinck, later 9th Duke of Portland). They started an affair, and – about a year before she met Paddy – Paco

* *Voivode*: an eastern European term for an official administrator, who governs an area on behalf of its ruler; in this case, the Ottoman sultan.

had left Balasha for Clothilde. His next posting was to Buenos Aires, and Balasha never saw him again.

Balasha stayed on in Athens. She found a small pink cake of a house on Tripod Street near the Plaka, described by Paddy as 'half a minute from the Choragic Monument of Lysicrates, where Byron had first taken lodgings in the now-vanished Capuchin Monastery'. From there, he says, 'a sleeper-out on the balustraded roof could gaze straight up the cliff of the Acropolis at the stars'.[11] It is typical of Paddy that although he writes of his unnamed painter-hostess as 'more than a friend', he banishes himself to the roof alone.

Neither he nor Balasha had much money, and leading a glamorous life in Athens was expensive. After two or three weeks on Tripod Street they began to look for somewhere more secluded to spend the summer, and to get away from the heat and dust of the capital. Hans Dyckhoff, Paddy's friend from the Meteora, told them of a watermill at Lemonodassos, 'the lemon grove', south-east of the little town of Galatas which looked across a narrow channel to the island of Poros. The mill, a working water-mill built to irrigate the groves of orange and lemon trees that grew around the house and over the hillside, was maintained by Spiro and Marina Lazaros, who lived downstairs with their eight children. The airy upstairs room was let out to lodgers.

The room contained three old brass beds, while just beyond it the torrent that drove the mill came thundering down into the pool: 'so you had only to step out', said Paddy, 'and you were in a glorious cold shower.'[12] It had no telephone and no electric light, and Marina fed her guests on a diet consisting mainly of eggs: four each, for breakfast, lunch and dinner. Her eldest children, Kosta and Katrina, were about twelve or thirteen, while the youngest was still in its cradle, slung in a walnut tree and soothed by the sound of the water. The water driven by the mill was directed into a network of little channels, tended by a group of men who would gather in the evening to drink and sing on the terrace, which served as a café.

Paddy and Balasha spent the mornings painting and writing. Balasha worked on a portrait of Paddy,* whilst he wrote about people

---

* See page 3 of first plate section.

and places he had seen in Greece, borrowing books on Greek history, ethnography and folklore from Aleko Matsas and the British School in Athens with a view to writing a book about Greece himself. After a swim and a long siesta they would walk down to the little town of Galatas, along a rocky path that wound its way through pine and myrtle, fig and olive trees. Here they would sit at little iron tables under the plane trees, drinking and talking as they gazed out over the water to the monastery on the island.

On one of their occasional visits to Athens, Paddy and Balasha stayed with Constantine ('Tanti') Rodocanachi and his Rumanian wife Margèle, who were particularly attached to Balasha since she had introduced them. Born in Egypt and educated in England, Rodocanachi was a veteran of the Graeco-Turkish and Balkan wars, as well as the Great War. He had made and lost fortunes, served in the diplomatic corps, and when he retired he devoted himself to writing. His first novel *Ulysse fils d'Ulysse*, was loosely based on the life of the arms dealer and financier Basil Zaharoff.

Rodocanachi gave Paddy a copy of the book in French. He hoped to publish it in America and England, but needed a translator. Paddy leapt at the chance to translate it, and Rodocanachi's terms were generous. If the book were published in English, Rodocanachi was prepared to give him a third of his royalties.

He and Balasha were living the life of Daphnis and Chloe, but a spectacular summer storm heralded a chill wind that whipped up the clouds and blew through their thin clothes. Not even Lemonodassos would be idyllic in winter. Rather than return to Athens, Balasha suggested that they go to Rumania and spend the winter at Băleni, her family home, close to the Bessarabian border.

They went by sea to Constanţa, by train to Galatz, and then (by which time the train had dwindled to a very rustic conveyance) to a tiny station where they were met by an old Polish coachman called Pan Stanislas. It took them another hour to reach Băleni.

The long, low manor house was one storey high with thick whitewashed walls and green shutters; one visitor described it as looking 'like a sunken ship'.[13] Outbuildings and stables, barns and cow byres were built around a courtyard full of deliriously barking dogs. On one side, the house looked on to a village of white cottages with thatched roofs, their windows and doors outlined in a thick band of brightly coloured paint. The peasants wore black and white homespun clothes and felt hats, and almost all the women spun from a distaff when not engaged in other work; the men drove high carts pulled by pale oxen. To the other side, the house looked over a vast undulating plain, which was brown and windswept when Paddy and Balasha arrived. Soon the winter winds would drive the snow into impenetrable drifts that came up to the windowsills.

They were ushered into the house by Balasha's sister Pomme, who had run the estate with her husband, Constantin Donici, since the death of her parents. It had been in a sorry state when they took it over, since the old Prince was more of a gambler than a land-owner. Pomme and Constantin had thrown all their energy into Băleni, and Constantin also acted as agent for his neighbour, Prince Zuzev.

Constantin's grandfather had been a celebrated Moldavian writer and translator of Pushkin, but he himself was a practical, easy-going man who didn't have much thirst for literature. He was attractive to women and had taken part in two or three duels in his youth – always as the challenged party. But he had now settled down to life as a country gentleman, and his greatest pleasure was hunting. Pomme too was a countrywoman, and a bee-keeper. She and Constantin had a daughter just into her teens called Ina, whom Paddy thought resembled Millais' Ophelia.

> Plaster flaked from the columns and pediments, and indoors, room opened into room in vistas of Louis Philippe and Second Empire furniture. Benevolent or wicked voivodes gazed from the walls in half-Byzantine, half-Slavonic panoplies of fur hats, aigrettes, furred robes and pearls. There would be a Western relation or two with powdered hair, Boyar descendants with epaulettes and sabres, some touching girls in crinolines holding flowers and pigeons . . .

He also remembered 'glass cases with the lumpy seals of parchments, the family's two-headed eagle, tall china stoves, the prisms of chan-deliers, stags' antlers, the glass eye of a huge bear's pelt from the Carpathians, and thousands of books in several languages'.[14]

Everything was rather run-down and shabby. The Cantacuzene

estates had been much diminished by land reforms after the Great War, and at the time Paddy arrived in Rumania, the country was still in the grip of economic stagnation caused by the great depression. Though there was never much cash, Constantin managed the land well. There was still something to be made from the sale of grain and cattle, but the day-to-day economy depended largely on barter and payment in kind, and feudal customs still persisted: one visitor to Băleni recalled that when Balasha went out on the estate, peasants would go down on one knee and kiss her hand. In such a society there was no shortage of servants and retainers; their wages amounted to little more than board and lodging, but working in the big house held a certain prestige.

Niculina, with her white coif, came in with a spill every evening to light the shaded kerosene lamps with hummingbird swiftness. She was in love with one of the woodsmen, Mihai Pintili. There was Ionitza the cook, Ifrim Podubniak the slightly sozzled butler, Ivan the Russian plumber, and Mustafa from the Dobrudja. Paddy particularly enjoyed talking to the old Polish coachman, Pan Stanislas. 'He had done his military service in the 2nd Schwartzenberg Dragoons when Galicia was still Austrian, and he seemed to know all the novels of Sienkiewicz by heart.'[15] It is hardly surprising that Paddy remembered them all so well, for Băleni was where he spent much of the next four years. The Cantacuzenes, who welcomed him so warmly, almost began to take the place of his family.

Paddy's relations with his mother had been reduced to a frozen silence as a result of Æileen's jealousy of Balasha, which erupted with the unexpected force of a genie from a bottle. Little realizing what he was doing, Paddy had written his mother a letter to tell her about Balasha and how wonderful she was. He looked forward eagerly to her reply, and an envelope duly arrived addressed in his mother's hand. Inside he found nothing but his original letter, torn to shreds. 'It created a chasm between us for many years,' he said. 'In fact, I don't think it was ever quite right between us after that.'[16]

In February 1936, still at Băleni, Paddy turned twenty-one and received an unexpected windfall – a godfather he had never met, Sir Henry Hubert Hayden who had been Director of the Geological Survey of India between 1910 and 1921, had made him a gift of

£300. This was a considerable sum of money, and he hoped to make it last as long as possible.

Paddy spent all of 1936 at Băleni, translating Tanti's book in the octagonal library, and reading, mostly in French: Mallarmé, Apollinaire, Gide and, for the first time in its entirety, *A la recherche du temps perdu*. He also read Tolstoy and Turgenev in French translation, while *Les Enfants terribles*, *Le Grand Meaulnes* and *L'Aiglon* were read aloud in the evenings. His Rumanian improved, and with Balasha's help, he translated the hauntingly beautiful Rumanian folk poem, 'Mioritza'.

He rode almost every day, though Balasha had lost her nerve after a bad fall. He begged her to try again. She did, riding side-saddle which made her feel more secure, 'but she didn't really enjoy it,' said Paddy sadly. 'She only rode to please me.'[17] Dressed in long sheepskin coats and hats, they went for long rides under white skies, coming back at dusk. Then tea was served from a samovar, accompanied by a raisin bread called *cozonac*.

As the weather grew warmer the snows retreated, the brown plain turned green.

> A shepherd called Petru played a long wooden flute. Ifrim the butler's father carved me a three-stringed *rebeck* out of a walnut tree, blown down in a storm; Anton, an accomplished violinist with a kicked-in face, played and sang when called upon, backed by half a dozen fellow-gipsies settled in the village. There was a crone there who knew how to cast spells and break them by incantations; another, by magic, could deliver whole villages from rats. After sheep-shearing, these would all gather in a barn to spin the wool – hilarious days with a lot of food, drink, singing, story-telling . . . I got to know everyone for miles: hardy men in sheepskin jerkins and conical fleece hats and women in coifs. I felt half-Moldavian by adoption and tried to pick up their dialect and turns of phrase.[18]

With a cousin of Balasha's, Alexander Mourouzi, who lived a few hours away in a neo-Palladian house called Golásei, Paddy explored the Danube delta. They set off to Galatz by train, then took a steamer up the northernmost arm of the river to the town of Vlacov: 'a maze of willow-shaded canals and the huts of White Russian fishermen who, every few hours, landed an enormous sturgeon from which huge slimy troves of caviare were untimely ripped.'[19] They found a boatman called Nicolai who, like most of the Russians of the delta, belonged to a sect known as the Lipoveni.

When the reformed or Nikonian Orthodox Church was established in Russia in the seventeenth century, the 'old believers' were branded as heretics, to be persecuted and hounded out of the country. The Old Religion splintered into many sects, one of which was the self-mutilating Skopzi, who traditionally drove the horse-drawn cabs in Rumanian towns and whom Paddy had seen in Bucharest. The Lipoveni were another: the men had long hair and beards, and spoke a curious dialect of their own.

Nicolai's boat was a *lotka*, a long, black, steeply prowed and masted craft, manoeuvred with a long pole. For two weeks Paddy and Alexander Mourouzi wove their way among the meandering channels and lagoons of the delta, thick with feathery reeds twenty foot high, alive with fish and water fowl, and heavily infested with mosquitoes. The birds seemed quite fearless, 'scarcely moving as the prow of our *lotka* forged through their floating tribes. They swarmed and settled on the masts and on the bulwarks, and looked at us with curious or brazen scrutiny . . . Cranes and herons fished among the weeds, and swans drifted by in flotillas and every now and then a pink cirrus of flamingos would loom over overhead through the manifold wheeling phalanxes of geese and ducks.'[20]

Later in the summer, Paddy and Balasha travelled in Bukovina and Bessarabia. Bessarabia (now the Republic of Moldova) is a long triangle of land between the rivers Prut and Dniester going all the way down to the Black Sea. It had been ceded to Russia in 1812; but in 1918 it had declared its independence and united with Rumania. The Bukovina, northern Moldavia, had been ceded to Austria in the eighteenth century. Ukrainians, Poles, Hungarians, Jews and Germans had settled there, but Rumanian speakers were still in the majority.

In Bukovina they visited the churches and painted monasteries around Suceava; while in Bessarabia they stayed with General Volodya Cantacuzin, who lived on a huge estate among rolling hills. He lent them horses and they rode about the countryside, visiting friends and relatives of Balasha's. Somewhere else, Paddy could not remember where, there was a great banquet under the trees. Yet for all their warmth, laughter and hospitality, the people here were living under a shadow. Soviet Russia had never accepted that Bessarabia was part of Rumania, and was bent on claiming it for the Ukraine.

It was a terrifying prospect, for everyone knew what had happened in 1932 and the years that followed. The farmers and peasants of the Ukraine had been subjected to the forced collectivization of their fields and farms, which had led to man-made famines accompanied by cruelty on an unimaginable scale. People died in their millions, while their orphaned children were either abandoned, shot, or locked into camps where they starved to death. Communism had never exerted any pull on Paddy, any more than Fascism. Both were ready to destroy everything he loved about European civilization in order to build their aggressively utilitarian, industrial superstates. Yet it was the experience of living with the Cantacuzenes on the eastern edge of Rumania and the visit to Bessarabia that, in his own words, 'inoculated me against Communism'.[21]

Paddy had kept in regular touch with Tanti Rodocanachi during the translation of *Ulysse fils d'Ulysse*, and once completed it found an English publisher. William Heinemann would be bringing out the book, now called *No Innocent Abroad*, in 1937. He and Balasha therefore decided to go to England. Neither of them had much money, but Paddy hoped to pick up some work on the back of the novel's publication. Balasha would try and sell her paintings of Rumania and, perhaps, secure some portrait commissions.

When Paddy had left England that rainy night in December 1933, he was escaping: from his parents' disappointed expectations and his own hopeless, idle, easily distracted, unemployable self. He returned three years later, having travelled more than most people then did in a lifetime, with the knowledge that all he really wanted to do was write. He also knew that he possessed an exceptional gift for companionship and entertaining people. The magic did not always work; there were plenty of people who found him an insufferable show-off. But when it did work, he found he could lift people's hearts and spirits, and enchant both men and women. This was all

Above: Lewis Leigh Fermor at his desk in Calcutta; (*right*) Æileen Leigh Fermor on her wedding day

'What were they doing in each other's company?'

Paddy's elder sister Vanessa in India

Vanessa's sketch of Paddy, aged five or six, done when she was nine or ten

Paddy

Above left: Paddy at the King's School, Canterbury (*back row, centre*): 'a dangerous mixture of recklessness and sophistication'
Above right: Paddy's second passport photo, taken in Munich, January 1934

Above: Paddy at Rila Monastery, August 1934, probably taken by Penka Krachanova
Right: Greece, 1935: Paddy is wearing the silver medal Penka gave him in Plovdiv, in September 1934

Left: Balasha at work on a portrait of Paddy,
Lemonodassos, 1935
Above: Băleni, Moldavia. The corner portrait is
of George Cantacuzene, who took the Turkish
surrender of Monemvasia during the Greek War of
Independence

Above: Paddy at Băleni with Pan Stanislas,
the coachman

Right: Balasha at Băleni, *c.*1946. On the back she
has written, 'They do not want us, our education or
our culture any more'

Left: Guy Branch in the Danube delta, summer 1937. He died in the Battle of Britain, September 1940

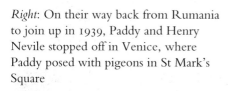

Right: On their way back from Rumania to join up in 1939, Paddy and Henry Nevile stopped off in Venice, where Paddy posed with pigeons in St Mark's Square

Above: Denise Menasce, Paddy's girlfriend in Cairo, 1943
Above right: Major Patrick Leigh Fermor, DSO, at the end of the war

Above: Paddy, known as Mihali, looking very Greek with a moustache
Right: General Angelo Carta, whose escape from Crete after the Italian surrender in 1943 prompted Paddy to think of kidnapping a German general

Left: Father John Alevizakis of Alones. His son Siphi was taken and tortured by the Germans
Below: Manoli Paterakis and Paddy, in Manoli's village of Koustoyerako after the war

Right: Billy Moss and Paddy in German uniform. It was just as well that the abduction took place after dark. Billy is wearing puttees, which had not been worn in the German army since before the First World War

Below: George Tyrakis, Antoni Papaleonidas and Manoli Paterakis, all great examples of Greek *leventeia*: defined by Paddy as high spirits, humour, quickness of mind and action, charm, the love of living dangerously and a readiness for anything

Above: A break on the slopes of Mount Ida. The strain is showing on General Kreipe's face, while Paddy seems almost embarrassed at having to put him through such an ordeal

Right: The General, with his arm in a sling, is received in Egypt by Brigadier Barker–Benfield of SOE

Below: Paddy's sketch of George Psychoundakis, author of *The Cretan Runner*

Left: George Katsimbalis, George Seferis and Paddy, at the Platanos taverna in the Plaka, Athens, 1946

Left: Summer 1946: Paddy on his lecture tour for the British Council, talking about the abduction of General Kreipe. Note how he has decorated his map of Crete on the blackboard with a galleon, a zephyr and a sea-serpent

Right: The reunion of General Kreipe with his abductors, 1972. Left to right: George Tyrakis, Manoli Paterakis, Paddy, General Kreipe and Frau Kreipe

very well, but surely his scholar-gypsy life must come to an end sooner or later. The time had come to take a grip.

Paddy, Balasha and Pomme arrived in London in January 1937, a month after the abdication of King Edward VIII. They stayed with Guy Branch, a friend of Balasha's who was living with his widowed mother and his younger sister Biddy in Pembroke Square. Guy lent them his studio at the bottom of the garden, but in time Paddy and Balasha found a flat of their own at 9 Earl's Walk, off the Earl's Court Road.

Without much enthusiasm Paddy set about finding a job that would earn some money, while still giving him time to write and translate. He enrolled as a tutor with the educational consultants Gabbitas & Thring, but after a few sessions with a sullen child whose mother sat in on all the lessons, he decided that tutoring was not for him. His next job was reading German film scripts for Twentieth Century-Fox. Here too he proved unsatisfactory, since Paddy's German was not quite good enough to judge whether a script was good or bad.

The most congenial work he found was on the *World Review*, a right-wing political monthly featuring articles from the international press, created by the journalist and later MP Vernon Bartlett. Paddy acted as sub-editor and general dogsbody to Kathleen Outhwaite, who ran the magazine from an office in Chandos Street. He may have been responsible for one or two of the short, unsigned reviews in the book section, but only one was printed under his name. It discussed a book called *Count Your Dead – They are Alive!*, a polemic which was also an urgent warning against the perils of totalitarianism by the author and painter Wyndham Lewis. It was while he was working for the *World Review* that Paddy met Kim Philby, who was an occasional contributor (Paddy noticed the leather patches on the elbows of his tweed jacket, a sartorial feature he had never seen before).

For many of Paddy's generation, the years 1936 to 1938 were dominated by the Spanish Civil War, but he felt no urge to rush to the aid of the Spanish Republic. The left-wing intellectuals who campaigned passionately on its behalf were not only sympathetic to Communism, but also thought it inevitable. Paddy had been too well inoculated by his years in eastern Europe to trust the Left's position, which presented the civil war as a definitive choice between good and evil. 'Are you for or against the legal government of Republican Spain?' was the challenge. 'Are you for or against Franco and Fascism?'[22] But Paddy did not move in left-wing circles, except at literary cocktail parties. At one of these he locked horns in a furious debate with the publisher John Lehmann, a Communist sympathizer who supported the Spanish Republic to the hilt. What the row was about specifically, Paddy could not remember; but unforgivable things were said, and they never spoke to one another again.

He had never liked political intellectuals, preferring the friends he was introduced to by Balasha and Guy. Paddy met Robert Byron again with Mark Ogilvie-Grant. Another friend from this time was Lady Bridget Parsons whose blonde beauty attracted the sort of men she despised, though she never lacked friends. Her brother Michael Rosse had a Gothic castle in Ireland called Birr, where Paddy became a regular visitor after the war. He also saw a lot of John Chichester, whose sister, Lady Prudence Pelham, married Guy Branch in 1939. When he had to look presentable, Paddy borrowed clothes from Guy, while Balasha wore clothes lent by her friend, the designer Victor Stiebel.

Through Balasha he met three people who were to weave in and out of his life from then on. The first was Costa Achillopoulos, a polyglot Greek photographer who lived at the hub of an infinite number of interconnecting worlds. Small and lithe, he had pale green eyes made even more startling by a dark complexion, and hair that had turned snow-white in his twenties. His family was from Tsangarada on the flanks of Mount Pelion, but his grandfather had made his fortune in Egypt. Costa had been brought up in Switzerland, and was equally at home in Bucharest, Athens, Paris or London. Bisexual and a great traveller, he never married but shared a house with the Rumanian Princess Anne-Marie Callimachi, a cousin of Balasha's whose non-stop chatter Balasha found exasperating, though she was very attached to Costa.

At a lunch given by Costa and Anne-Marie in April 1937, Paddy met a couple who were to play an even greater part in his life

– Georgia and Sacheverell Sitwell. Georgia (née Doble) was Canadian, with high spirits, a generous smile and a very low voice. One of the reasons Sachie loved her was that she represented an escape from the aesthetic hothouse that he had created with his siblings Edith and Osbert. The days of *Façade* were long gone, but Sacheverell Sitwell had made a name for himself as an art historian. His works on the long-neglected Italian and German Baroque had opened the eyes of a generation to the painting and architecture of the seventeenth century. He had the same sort of magpie mind as Paddy, darting from one subject to the next, and each amused and stimulated the other. The meeting had been arranged so that Sachie could question Paddy and Pomme (Balasha was not at this particular lunch) about Rumania. It was the start of Paddy's long friendship with Georgia and Sachie, and many happy weekends at Weston Hall, the Sitwells' Jacobean house in Northamptonshire.

Every once in a while Paddy went to see his mother, who was still living in Coldharbour near Dorking. Following the episode of the torn-up letter he had decided never to discuss his love-life with her again, nor had Æileen shown any wish to talk about Balasha. This gave a certain artificiality to their meetings, yet there was still much to talk about. Paddy was planning at some point to write up his journey, and Æileen was able to give him all the letters he had written to her over those years.

Balasha did join him when he visited his sister Vanessa, now living in Gloucestershire. She had married an accountant, Jack Kerr Fenton, and had two children with him: Francesca, born in 1934, and Miles, born two years later. It was not a happy marriage. Jack was an obsessive perfectionist, which must have been an asset in his professional life. But he had no time for his children whom he found messy and demanding, and he made Vanessa's life miserable. Paddy knew she was unhappy and hated his brother-in-law. The feeling was mutual. The final straw came when Paddy flung himself down on a new mushroom-coloured sofa, on which Balasha had left a tube of emerald-green paint.[23]

As spring of 1937 turned into summer they began to miss the mill at Lemonodassos, and after visiting friends in France, a boat from Marseilles took them to Greece. One day, a week or so after their arrival at the mill, three figures approached along the path. One was Aleko Matsas, and with him was 'a slim, long-legged woman in a green top, green shorts, sandals and dark glasses, and a tall rather willowy chap of my age' (Paddy was then twenty-two) 'in rust-coloured sailcloth trousers'.[24]

The woman was Lady Idina Wallace. Orginally De la Warr (she was the sister of Buck, who nearly swept Balasha off her feet during her London season), she first married Euan Wallace. When she abandoned him she was obliged to abandon her two infant sons, and she was soon notorious for being a serial divorcee. In the summer of 1937 she was on husband number four, but her companion was her son David Wallace, whom she had not seen since childhood. 'They stayed with us ten days including a *three-day* peasant feast at the mill . . . She was [then going to] Prague to meet "somebody I'm a bit potty about, I'm afraid, a sea-dog called Ponsonby".'[25]

Although *No Innocent Abroad* did not make Paddy much money in England, it was a great success in America. Published in January 1938 as *Forever Ulysses*, it became a Book of the Month Club choice, translating into sales which earned Paddy the princely sum of £800 – more money than he had ever had in his life. Encouraged by this success he set to work again on hammering his trans-European walk into a book. The letters to his mother would be invaluable at filling in the gaps in the journal, but Paddy was reluctant even to look at them. Also, he was uneasy at the thought of how much the letters might diverge from or muddy his memory. With the aid of his passport he established the chronology, but the work 'wasn't coming easily. The words wouldn't flow . . . I couldn't get them to sound right.'[26]

A glimpse of Balasha is found in two long, undated letters of 1937 or 1938, written in a mixture of English and French, that she wrote to her cousin Prince Serge Cantacuzene-Speransky. The bulk of these letters are about Cantacuzene ancestors, and the jigsaw puzzle of their combined family tree. It seems that Paddy, who is described as 'very expert in genealogy', was instrumental in helping to put the information together. She touches on her life in London. In Paris, people were interested in her portraits of Rumanian peasants and gypsies, while in London, one was expected to paint people who are 'in the news'. But she could not find any commissions, so had to rely on 'Cheap journalism, advertising, selling one's name to Pond's Cold Cream, painting surrealist portraits that look like an earthquake on a pedestal; all that means money.'[27]

Before returning to Rumania in late spring of 1938 they decided to leave some of their belongings behind in England, including a great many papers to do with Paddy's trans-European walk. They packed up two large trunks, one of which was an elaborately carved and painted Rumanian marriage chest. These were left with the Baroness d'Erlanger, who had a house in Mayfair. Catherine d'Erlanger, wife of the Anglo-French financier Emile d'Erlanger, was one of those hostesses who threw gorgeously extravagant parties in the mid-1920s. She was also a painter, and had painted Paddy's portrait. Lady d'Erlanger told him that the trunks would be no trouble at all, and they could stay in her house for as long as he cared to leave them there.

That August, Guy Branch's sister Biddy came out to Băleni. Biddy was in her late teens, and it was the first time she had been away from home. The account she wrote at the time was that of someone plunged into a very adult world, whose conversation and way of life she could never have imagined.

She remembered Balasha's red lips and strongly arched eyebrows, her simple clothes. To Biddy she seemed much older than the puppyish Paddy, whom she treated with a rather maternal affection: 'Oh Paddy, do stop it', or 'Paddy, you're talking too much again' – admonitions which Paddy would accept with good-tempered humility. At the same time, conversation was the centre of their lives:

> How [Balasha and Hélène and Paddy] could talk! . . . [They] argued and discussed and pleaded, their voices moving in and out, each speech a recital yet a part of the pattern, a creation, seemingly tireless, endless. An afternoon, an evening would pass, and the voices would go on. Talking was not a luxury, or a duty, it was a work of art to be practised seriously. Constantine was different: ever practical, he dismissed subjects quickly with definite views.

Within the household they had a verb for Paddy's linguistic enthusiasms – 'to cumber', used to describe his penchant for interminable conversations of the kind that left everyone else standing about. Once he and his interlocutor had finally parted Paddy would turn to the company, enlarging on the man's fascinating dialect and turns of phrase: that was the cue to say 'You're cumbering again!' Biddy remembered him 'in the summer house, writing, the floor littered with sheets of paper, his writing as voluble as his talk'.[28]

Their world had little time left, as the prospect of war darkened the horizon. 'I cannot fear anything for myself,' Balasha wrote to her cousin Serge, 'but I fear for the young people whom I love and about whom I'll wait for news . . . It is so much better to be a man in time of war. For us, it's once again the hospitals and the waiting.' Only a hand-written '1938' in the margin gives the date, so it is impossible to tell whether she wrote in March when the *Anschluss* was declared, or late September following the Munich agreement, or October when Hitler occupied the Bohemian Sudetenland. 'All Europe seems mad,' she continued, 'and I'm no longer the age when I can think of war as a magnificent adventure.'[29]

That winter, Paddy had a new literary project. He had met the French writer Paul Morand, who was married to the Rumanian Princess Hélène Soutzo. Morand had had a recent success with his book *Isabeau de Bavière, femme de Charles VI*, part of a series entitled *Reines de France*. Morand presents Isabeau's ill-starred life in a series of dramatic tableaux. 'It's a brilliant book, very colourful and exciting,' wrote Paddy.[30] During his last winter in Moldavia, he translated the book into English. Years later, when Paddy tried to get John Murray to publish his version of *Isabeau de Bavière*, Murray's reader gave a not very enthusiastic response. Even the successful passages reminded him of 'an MGM swashbuckling costume epic'.[31]

In an Introduction to Matyla Ghyka's book, *The World Mine Oyster*, Paddy describes the last day of peace. Ghyka was a naval officer turned diplomat, a gentle and erudite polymath with thick, bristling eyebrows who had been educated in France. He was one of the party at Băleni on a day in the late summer of 1939, when they set off for the woods to pick mushrooms. The mushroom wood lay about ten miles away, and their little cavalcade of horses and an old open carriage clattered through sunlit fields and vineyards. Having gathered mushrooms till all the baskets were full, they enjoyed a long and leisurely picnic before making their way home. The day was heavy with enchantment, and an aching beauty. 'The track followed the crest of a high ridge with the dales of Moldavia flowing away on either hand. We were moving through illimitable sweeps of still air.'[32] The passage is a love song and an elegy to the Rumania that was about to vanish for ever.

In the dark years following the war and the descent of the Iron Curtain, the people Paddy had known in Rumania were thrown to the winds. Constantine Soutzo escaped and made a new life in Canada; his mother too escaped, crawling under the wire of the Hungarian frontier. The architect George Cantacuzene and his wife Elizabeth said goodbye to each other in 1940, when she took his children to England. It was the last time they saw each other.

Stories of families being torn apart became all too familiar, and Paddy came to see his time at Băleni as another paradise from which he – and they too, a few years later – had been exiled. Living with the Cantacuzenes in Rumania had granted Paddy several of the opportunities afforded by a university education. He had been given four more years of freedom from the necessity of earning a living. Although he had no scholarly framework or discipline in which to marshal it, he had learnt Rumanian, studied its history, and read as much as he could in that language and French. Above all, Balasha and the Cantacuzenes had given him a sense of family: a set of people among whom he felt he belonged and was understood.

7

An Intelligence Officer

Balasha was in her car listening to the radio when she heard the news that England had declared war on Germany, and in that moment she knew her time with Paddy was over. He did not want to leave her, but he was so keen to get back to London and join up that he started making arrangements at once. Her friends asked why he was in such a hurry to go to war, could he not wait a week or two? Yet as Balasha wrote to him years later, she understood and made no attempt to hold him back: 'your heart and soul were straining for it.'[1]

With Henry Nevile, a friend who had been staying in Bucharest, Paddy made his way back to England by train, hoping to enlist in the Irish Guards. Being 'of Irish descent' was very much part of the romantic persona he had created for himself, and his desire to serve in the Irish Guards was a way of claiming that Irishness. What he really coveted, Paddy maintained, was the uniform, with its Star Saltire of St Patrick emblazoned on the cap badge and its buttons in groups of four. 'I had read somewhere that the average life of an infantry officer in the First World War was eight weeks, and I had no reason to think that the odds would be much better in the Second. So I thought I might as well die in a nice uniform.'[2]

The five regiments of the Brigade of Guards had a cachet in the British army that few other regiments came close to. It was the army's equivalent of Oxford or Cambridge, and its officers were drawn from the social élite of the country. Normally, entry into any Guards regiment would be a matter of family connection or the right school. Paddy had neither, but he did have contacts.

Sir Alec Hardinge had been private secretary to three kings and was now serving George VI. His wife Helen was very fond of Paddy and had had him to stay at Windsor Castle, where they had an apartment in the Winchester Tower. Sir Alec, who had been a major in the Grenadier Guards, had a word with Lieutenant Colonel the Honourable Thomas Vesey, Colonel Commandant of the Irish Guards. It was fixed. Paddy was accepted as a cadet and earmarked for a commission in his chosen regiment once his preliminary training was over.

On 14 November, Paddy was ordered to make his way to the Guards Depot in Caterham, and submit to a regime that came as a severe shock to his system. He was physically tough, but he now found himself in a place where his charm cut no ice and the pressure to conform was remorseless: like going back to school, only more brutal. The men slept thirty to a room, and whether they were square-bashing or doing rifle drill, on fatigues or undergoing inspections, they were constantly being bawled out at close range by red-faced men bristling with anger, loathing and projectile spit. The slightest mistake was savagely punished, and Paddy's absent-minded bookishness (not to mention his 'trying to be funny') was guaranteed to raise the hackles of the sergeant majors. Yet there were compensations: here he met lifelong friends such as the genealogist Iain Moncreiffe, Anthony Holland, Michael Scott and Adrian Pryce-Jones.

That December, Paddy caught scabies, and on the 16th he was diagnosed with rheumatism in the back.[3] In hospital for five days, he was discharged just before Christmas, which he was looking forward to spending with the Sitwells at Weston. He apologized in advance for the fact that he would be looking pretty wrung out (he still had scabies on his chin). 'I'm glad you warned me,' Georgia said, when he arrived.[4]

Christmas was enjoyable, but Paddy was still not feeling well. On 8 January, he was admitted to Redhill County Hospital, complaining of headache, 'pain in the waist' and a cough. He was diagnosed with influenza which by the following day had become pneumonia; the crisis nearly killed him. His mother and sister were summoned, and at one moment things looked so bad that a priest was sent for too. A male nurse at the hospital later recalled Paddy, in his delirium, begging whoever was near him to tell a princess from Bucharest.[5]

Biddy Branch, who had been with Paddy and Balasha at Băleni

and was now Mrs Tom Hubbard, went to visit him on 12 January 1940. 'He was ghastly-looking – pale parchment skin stretched tight over his bones, eyes huge, dark as I never remembered . . .' He talked of the past few weeks of training. 'Two months of hell he must have had at his Guards Depot,' wrote Biddy, '. . . drudgery, heart-breaking drudgery. He spoke softly but so bitterly. Full of hate – brutality, intrigue, "every sort of punishment but the cat".'[6]

Two weeks later he was feeling much better. On 1 February 1940 he wrote a long letter, accompanied by some carefully drawn cartoons, to Adrian Pryce-Jones. There is no mention of the horrors of training, though he was evidently pleased by all the attention he was receiving from nurses and visitors. He was also anxious about his immediate future, and felt bitterly frustrated at the consequences of having been ill for so long. 'My fate is positively tragic . . . as I have missed over five weeks training . . . the authorities are regretfully obliged to *backsquad* me.' This meant that while Pryce-Jones and the rest of Paddy's friends were beginning their officer training at Sandhurst, Paddy was condemned to more weeks of square-bashing at the hated depot. 'Isn't this wretched? I am more vexed and disappointed than I can say . . .' This delay also weakened his chances of a commission in the Irish Guards, for they only had so many places and competition was stiff.

The most exciting moment of his convalescence at Redhill was when he received a surprise visit from Anne-Marie Callimachi and Costa. Anne-Marie was dressed in black satin and sparkling with diamonds, while Costa was wearing an emerald green polo-neck sweater and a coat with a huge astrakhan collar. They had arrived by taxi with a lot of luggage stamped with princely coronets, which made a deep impression – 'the hospital hasn't recovered yet, and my glamour-value among the nurses is at fever-pitch.'[7]

On release from hospital in early February, Paddy went to stay with his sister Vanessa. He had high hopes of joining the Karelian campaign, in which the Finns were fighting off a Soviet invasion. He had heard about a unit that was going to support the Finns and he was keen to join, but was still too weak; Finland was then forced to concede to Russia's demands. The Intelligence Corps, on the other hand, were very interested in the fact that Paddy spoke French,

German, Rumanian and Greek, and with the situation in the Balkans developing fast they offered him a commission. If he took it, he would be spared any more training at the Guards Depot, but he still clung to the hope of a commission in the Irish Guards.

He had an interview with the regiment's commander. There was no opening for him in the Irish Guards at present, Lieutenant Colonel Vesey told him; indeed, he might have to wait for months before the opportunity arose. Although most regiments at this time were desperate for young officers, Vesey was in no hurry to commission this particular cadet: one of Paddy's reports had described his progress as 'below average'. The Intelligence Corps, on the other hand, were offering immediate employment and the opportunity to return to Greece.

The Intelligence Corps uniform was not very romantic, and he disliked the cap badge – a pansy resting on its laurels, as it was disparagingly known. But the lure of Greece was strong, and financially he could not afford to wait for a place in the Irish Guards. Paddy began his officer training in the Corps in early May, stationed at the 168th Officer Cadet Training Unit at Ramillies Barracks, Aldershot. Here he learned how to keep records of enemy movements, how to read and make maps, and how to assemble and coordinate intelligence. There was also much to absorb about the formation of the German army, and he tried to learn the Gothic *deutsche Schrift*. One of his fellow trainees was Laurens van der Post. Years later, on a television show with Paddy, van der Post recalled the moment they heard about the fall of France. The news left everyone shocked and aghast, van der Post recounted, except for Paddy 'who was writing a poem about a fish pond in the Carpathians, and he didn't really take it in until he had finished the poem'. Slightly embarrassed, Paddy added, 'Well, I was pretty smitten after that.'[8]

Soon Free French soldiers who wanted to continue fighting began to appear at Ramillies Barracks, and word went round that the Corps was looking for people who would be willing to be parachuted into occupied France. Paddy volunteered, and was rather offended when they rejected him. He spoke the language fluently and was widely read in French literature: why was he passed over? That the selectors were looking for quiet, inconspicuous people seems not to have crossed his mind. His training finished on 12 August. The final, prophetic remarks on Paddy's report were written by his commanding officer, Lieutenant Colonel R. C. Bingham: 'Quite useless as a regimental officer,' he wrote, 'but in other capacities will serve the army well.'[9] Paddy himself had very mixed feelings about his future. 'I looked forward to my new life with interest and misgiving. It was rather like going to a new school.'[10]

Second Lieutenant Fermor was ordered to proceed to the Intelligence Training Centre in Matlock, Derbyshire, where he was to take two month-long courses: one on war intelligence, and another on interrogation. The training centre, filled with polyglot officers, was housed in Smelton's Hydro – 'a castellated, bleak and blacked-out Victorian pile perched high above the rushing Derwent'.[11] His initial reaction to the place was 'Bedlam in a *Morte d'Arthur* setting',[12] made more depressing by the fact that all the windows were blacked out; but there were compensations. One of the perks of being an officer was that Paddy now had a batman, Geoffrey Olivier – 'my first soldier-servant. It was peculiar to think that I would probably never shine a button or spit and polish a toe-cap again.'[13]

The war intelligence course was hard work. Lectures were interspersed by long spells 'scrambling over the Derbyshire hills . . . making out strategical and technical plans for advancing to, holding, or withdrawing from various features, holding improvised conferences . . . which invariably ended with the Major saying: "Now Leigh Fermor . . . What information have we about the enemy in the sector 22314567 to 4678?"'[14]

In between one course and the next, there was a week's break which Paddy spent in blitz-torn London. He saw three fires blazing in Piccadilly, while in Berkeley Square, 'the blaze of an explosion revealed two sides of that sentimental quadrangle in a disordered wreckage of wood and stone. Only one thing remained standing. Perched three stories high on a tottering pinnacle was a white marble privy, glowing shyly in this unaccustomed radiance.'[15]

Thanks to the services of anti-Nazi and Jewish volunteers, much of the interrogation course was conducted in German. One of the secrets of a good interrogation, he learned, was to conduct it while the prisoner had an empty stomach and a full bladder. With friends such as Gerry Wellesley and Osbert Sitwell at Renishaw close by, the high point of this happy time came when someone decided to organize a ball. One of the instructors, Henry Howard, brought over a spectacular couple from nearby Chatsworth: a tall young ensign in the Coldstream Guards, and an incredibly beautiful girl. He was Andrew Cavendish, who in 1950 was to become the 11th Duke of Devonshire; while she was Deborah Mitford, whose sister Diana and her husband, Sir Oswald Mosley, were in prison as pro-Nazi sympathizers. 'Funny, Howard bringing that Mitford girl,' said someone when they had gone. 'After all, this *is* meant to be the Intelligence Training Centre, and there *is* a war on.'[16]

Another of the Matlock instructors was Stanley Casson, 'donnish, witty and slightly disreputable',[17] a Greek scholar and archaeologist who had had a lot to do with the British School of Archaeology in Athens. Casson, who always spoke to Paddy in Greek, was one of the moving spirits of what was to become the Greek Military Mission.

The Italians had invaded Greece on 28 October 1940, and Paddy followed their rapid advance with anxiety. When the Greek army began to turn the Italian tide a few weeks later, 'It was joy and agony mixed', as he put it:[18] joy that Greece was acquitting herself so well, agony because he was not there. Stanley Casson went to London, and soon after Paddy was told to join Casson's Greek Military Mission.

Paddy reported to the War Office. Ordered to sail from Glasgow the following day, he was instructed to pick up two service revolvers before catching the train – one for himself, and one for another member of the mission, C. M. ('Monty') Woodhouse. He spent that evening in Bruton Mews with Eileen and Matyla Ghyka. Also there was the sad figure of Prue Branch: Guy had been shot down in the Battle of Britain that August, and his family had had to wait for months before his death was confirmed. Prue noticed the service revolvers that Paddy had in his pocket; they had no holsters, since Paddy had been unable to produce the separate forms required. 'I wish I could have one of those,' she said.[19]

Monty Woodhouse was a Greek scholar with an austere cast of mind, who admitted that he was slow to appreciate Paddy's qualities. 'I first saw him on the platform at Glasgow, with an Irish Guards [*sic*] cap pulled so low over his eyes he had to lean over backwards to look at you.'[20] The bone of contention between them was Greece. Woodhouse, who had a double first in Classics from Oxford and had studied in Athens, was an academic. Paddy, on the other hand, had lived among the Greeks, meeting Vlachs and Sarakatsans, soldiers, monks and shepherds. As Paddy put it, 'This was always the real root of the friction, a constant jealous, unarmed struggle as to who had the greater proprietory rights to Greece.'[21]

At Gibraltar, they were transferred to the cruiser HMS *Ajax*, and went on to Alexandria where he saw Aleko Matsas. Then, on the final stretch to Athens, they stopped at Suda Bay in Crete to refuel. The ship would not leave for another three hours, so Paddy suggested to Woodhouse that they visit the island's western capital, Chania. After a few rounds of coffee and *sikoudia* (a spirit made from mulberries) in the waterfront bars, they found it was getting late. A soldier of the Black Watch gave them a ride back to Suda in a truck full of oranges. Very drunk, he lost control of the truck and it overturned, sending an avalanche of oranges bouncing into the dust.

Woodhouse and the driver were unhurt but Paddy, who had been thrown out of the back with the oranges, was covered in blood from a gash to the head. Woodhouse was obliged to rejoin the ship without him, while Paddy was taken to a doctor in Halepa who insisted on his staying a night or two since the wound was serious. This was Paddy's first time among Cretans, and he claimed an instant empathy: 'they were like the Greeks, only more so.'[22]

The failure of the Venizelist coup of 1935 had paved the way for the return of King George II, and a period of royalist dominance. The King wanted to reunite the country, but all political energy was focused on power struggles in Athens, while the poverty and hardship afflicting the rest of the country was ignored. The only people who seemed to care were the Communists. When the prime minister Konstantinos Demertzis died of a heart attack in April 1936, King George appointed General Ioannis Metaxas to succeed him. Over the coming months, widespread industrial unrest and major electoral gains by the Communists alarmed the King, the army and the prime minister. Metaxas established a state of emergency, followed on 4

August by a dictatorship. He dissolved parliament, banned all political parties including the Communists, and muzzled the press. Greece does not like dictators, but Metaxas had one moment of glory. It was said that his rejection of the arrogant Italian ultimatum of October 1940 was couched in a single defiant word, *No* – and *Oxi* Day is still celebrated every year in Greece.

The Italian invasion of Greece was an ill-conceived shambles, but it united the Greeks in a way the politicians never could. Thousands of young men volunteered immediately, and were sent on their way to the front in the mountains of Epirus through cheering crowds waving flags and flowers. The role of the British Military Mission was to offer advice on mountain warfare. The Greeks had considerable experience of this, but tended to treat it as a series of guerrilla engagements. Michael Forrester, who was to become one of the most celebrated leaders of Cretan irregulars, described it as 'like one of the Balkan wars with somewhat updated weapons'.[23]

In Athens Paddy found a room at the Hotel Grande Bretagne, most of which had been requisitioned by the Greek government as its General Headquarters. He was still supposed to be resting, but he could never resist the gravitational pull of the bright lights and threw himself happily into a round of parties. One evening found him at the Argentina nightclub, where the heroic-looking bandage round his head produced a great many pats on the back and free drinks. The next drink was offered by 'a tall, interesting-looking man in a Greek artillery captain's uniform'.[24] The captain asked where he had been wounded, and was very amused when he heard that Paddy had merely been overturned in a truck full of oranges. 'Splendid, but not so loud! You're only getting the drinks because they think you've been fighting alongside us against the Italians!'[25] The Greek captain turned out to be George Katsimbalis: a patron of poets, editor, translator, and Olympic-class raconteur. Katsimbalis was a hugely influential figure in modern Greek letters, and the hero of Henry Miller's *The Colossus of Maroussi*.

It was a curious moment to be in Athens because, while Greece was at war with Italy, it was not yet at war with Germany, so there was still a German military mission. Paddy was in uniform in the bar at Zonar's when he saw his old friend Hans Dyckhoff. They greeted each other, slightly bewildered; but once the greetings were over, Paddy said, 'We can't really go on, you know, until after this war is over.'[26]

The Italian advance into Greece collapsed in November, and soon the Greeks were pushing them back into Albania. The weather turned bitterly cold. In thin coats and tattered boots, the Greek troops – including the Cretan 5th Division – were ill-equipped to deal with sub-zero temperatures in the wind and snow that lashed the mountains. Greek optimism began to falter and the front stabilized at Koritza, where Paddy was sent to report on the situation.

Arriving in a big car with a driver, followed by a wireless truck, he was billeted in a hotel where he was the only guest, and attached to the headquarters of the Greek III Army Corps whose chief was General Giorgios Tsolakoglou: a stiff, formal man who later surrendered his army to the invading Germans and led the puppet government put in place by the invaders. For the moment, however, the Germans were still beyond Greek borders and there was very little to do. Paddy joined up with two old friends from Athens: Nico Baltazzi Mavrocordato, a cavalry officer who had a job on the staff, and Nicky Melas, the town commandant. 'We roared around in the car I'd been given like the three Musketeers.'[27]

Another friend he met then was Panayiotis Canellopoulos, a professor of sociology at the University of Athens who later became prime minister. Appalled by the Metaxas dictatorship, Canellopoulos had refused to accept a commission in the army and was serving as a private soldier. He was also a fine poet, and published a literary journal called *Achris*. Paddy contributed an article to the journal about Lemonodassos, which Canellopoulos translated: thus becoming one of Paddy's earliest translators and publishers.

Soon after Christmas, Paddy and Canellopoulos went by car to visit Pogrodetz, the northernmost point of the front. Conditions were bleak, with random firing muffled by the snow; but at least the troops here had enough to eat, and morale was good. With Nicky Melas, Paddy explored southern Albania, visiting Agrilokastro (Gjirokastër) and Lescovic, and going as far as Tepeleni. The Albanians seemed more suspicious than friendly, rarely responding to their greetings and watching warily till they were out of sight.

Metaxas died of throat cancer at the end of January 1941, and within days the artificial unity he had forced on Greek political life began to split along the usual royalist-republican fault line. In late February, the British committed themselves to sending an expeditionary force to Greece, but it was far smaller and weaker than the Greeks had expected. Known as W Force, it was made up of the New Zealand Division, the 1st British Armoured Brigade and the 6th Australian Division, all under the command of Lieutenant General Sir Henry ('Jumbo') Maitland Wilson.

On 1 March Bulgaria joined the Tripartite Pact, making them part of the Axis with Germany, Italy and Japan. The Germans crossed the Danube and began massing on the Bulgarian border with Greece. Three weeks later under heavy pressure from Hitler, the regent of Yugoslavia, Prince Paul, also signed the Tripartite Pact. The Yugoslavs were outraged, and the German Ambassador was booed and spat at in the streets. They paid heavily for their defiance: on 6 April the Germans launched their double invasion of Greece and Yugoslavia, and Belgrade was smashed by Luftwaffe bombers.

The Greek commander-in-chief, General Alexandros Papagos, had always counted on the Yugoslavs for help in the event of a German invasion, but the Yugoslavs were fighting for survival and the Greeks had only W Force for support. The Germans broke through to capture Salonika on 9 April, and a few days later they were streaming in from Yugoslavia, through the Monastir Gap.

Paddy, who had returned to Athens from the Greek-Albanian border, was now ordered north towards Kozani. His orders were to keep in touch with British units, act as liaison to the Greeks, and report on the build-up of German troops. His superior was a man called Peter Smith-Dorrien, 'who was great fun and a bit of a bounder'.[28]

In an effort to hold up the German advance, the commander of 1st Armoured Brigade, Brigadier Harold 'Rollie' Charrington, had tanks stationed across the road at Ptolemais just north of Kozani. A troop of the Northumberland Hussars were providing support with anti-tank guns mounted on the back of lorries. Paddy and Smith-Dorrien drove to Kozani and from there Paddy started to walk northwards, to talk to the Allied troops who were already pulling back across the fields.

One man he stopped to talk to was a Northumberland Hussar with an Afghan coat to the ground. 'The Germans will be here soon,' he said. Seeing a huge anti–aircraft gun in a nearby field that looked as if it was going to be abandoned, Paddy asked: 'Shouldn't we take that, rather than let it be captured?' The Hussar agreed and they managed to find a truck to help, though it took a long time to dismantle the gun and load it into the truck. When all was done they exchanged names. His new friend was called Brown-Swinburne, who was related to the poet – which gave Paddy almost as much satisfaction as saving the gun from the Germans.[29]

The enemy advance was unstoppable. At one moment Paddy was told to stand by a crossroads, to point the way to tattered and exhausted Greek troops who were retreating from Albania. A bridge had been blown up behind them, and he attracted a certain amount of suspicion. Was he a spy? Had he been responsible for blowing up the bridge? Why wasn't there a Greek officer to supervise the retreat?

Back in Kozani, Paddy was outraged to see that a white flag had been put up. The townspeople told him that the priest had ordered this sign of surrender: Paddy insisted it be taken down. He had no authority beyond pointing out that 'I'm an ally, and the Germans aren't here yet!'[30] Two or three defiant voices agreed with him, and the townsfolk reluctantly removed the flag.

On his return to Athens, Paddy was told to take charge of the *Aghia Varvara*, a caique formerly converted into a yacht and now fitted with Lewis guns. Orders were to stand by and evacuate General Maitland Wilson and his entourage, together with Prince Peter or any other members of the Greek royal family who might need help. Prince Peter, a grandson of King George I, was an anthropologist who had made a study of Tibet, and he and Paddy had become friends in Athens.

On 25 April, Paddy left Athens in a truck full of supplies which included a wireless set. Athens itself was a city on the edge of its nerves. Refugees from the north were bombarded with demands for the latest news: where were the Germans, when would they arrive? Panic buying had already stripped everything from the shops, and the banks were besieged with everyone desperate for news. Most of the roads going west towards Corinth and the Peloponnese were packed with army trucks, and cars and carts filled with people.

Fewer people were heading east where the *Aghia Varvara* was moored at Sunium, dominated by the great temple to Poseidon. They set off just after dark in the yacht, skippered by Captain Mihali Mystos and about six crew. Their destination was Myli, on the other side of the Gulf of Nauplia, where they were to rendezvous with the General, Prince Peter, and Peter Smith-Dorrien. The constant threat of Stuka activity meant that they could move only under cover of night. In the darkness they could see ships burning in the harbours.

They reached Myli after nightfall. Mile upon mile of army vehicles revealed a whole army in retreat. Paddy finally made contact with Smith-Dorrien, who had driven down from Athens with General Wilson and Prince Peter. They had crossed the bridge over the Corinth Canal just in time – the Germans seized it a few hours later. By now it was past midnight. With the German Stukas giving them no peace by day, they would not be able to leave till the following evening.

As it turned out, the *Aghia Varvara* was not needed by Prince Peter, or by the General or his entourage. A flying boat came to collect the General at about 8.30 p.m., although all his luggage and one of his ADCs, Lieutenant Philip Scott, went on board the boat. By the time they had picked up a few more servicemen, the number of passengers had risen to fourteen. It was by now 1.30 a.m. on 27 April. Smith-Dorrien dug out some bottles of champagne he had managed to rescue, and he, Paddy and Philip Scott drank them as the *Aghia Varvara* weighed anchor.

Their revised orders were to sail southward down the eastern edge of the Laconian peninsula, and help with the general retreat. The yacht reached Leonidion at dawn. It was a wild part of the coast, linked by a ravine to its village in the hills, and inhabited by the Tzakonians who spoke an ancient Doric dialect. Knowing they were in for several hours of unremitting assault from enemy planes, they unloaded the wireless set and the cases of money they were carrying, and concealed themselves among the rocks. The village of Leonidion endured a savage machine-gun attack and the little harbour was bombed. Rounds of tracer bullets put the radio set out of action, and in the early afternoon an aerial torpedo scored a direct hit on the boat. In the clear water, they could see the *Aghia Varvara* resting on the bottom of the sea.

Despite the fact that the area was bombed and machine-gunned for the rest of the afternoon, there were no casualties. But Paddy was dismayed to find that he had left his *Odes of Horace* on board the sunken caique. Losing the little green leather-bound volume, given to him by Baron Liphart-Ratshoff eight years before in Munich, felt like losing a talisman.

There now followed three days of profound frustration. The caique they managed to commandeer was missing a vital part; all they could find to replace it was a rowing boat, at which point the Greek crew thought it best to go home – though Captain Mystos stayed with the party, and Smith-Dorrien was grateful that he did: 'without [his] help, I am quite convinced we should not be here today.'[31]

They set off in the rowing boat just before midnight, and arrived at Kiparissi early on the morning of 29 April. Once again Smith-Dorrien and Paddy set off to the village to find a caique. The one they bought for an exorbitant sum also had engine trouble, and by the time it was repaired at Velanidion, they had been joined by eleven stranded New Zealanders, five Australians, and three Greeks determined to continue the fight from Crete.

On the evening of 1 May they set sail again, and by the following day they were struggling in gale-force winds and a heavy swell. When the engine failed, they turned back to the island of Antikythera. Smith-Dorrien and Paddy walked to the village of Potamos, where they found a magnificent boat which had been taken at pistol-point by a Greek infantry captain. He already had about a hundred men on board, but he agreed to take their whole party – now over thirty strong – as far as Crete. There was little food or water to go round; but they managed to reach Kastelli Kissamo, on the north coast of the island, on 4 May.

The following day, Smith-Dorrien drew up his report. 'I should like specially to mention the excellent work done by Leigh Fermor and Scott in their respective spheres,' he wrote, 'and it would be difficult to imagine how we would have got on without the persuasive powers and linguistic ability of the former in obtaining both food and transport.'[32]

Paddy made his way to the British Headquarters in a quarry outside Chania, which consisted of a tent containing Brigadier Brumskill and a skeleton staff. There was nothing for him to do, so he spent some idle days with Michael Forrester relaxing at Prince Peter's villa in Galatas.

Around mid-May, Paddy was posted to headquarters at Heraklion as a junior intelligence officer, Greek speaker and general dogsbody to Brigadier B. H. Chappel, of 14th Infantry Brigade. Heraklion HQ, sited between the town and the aerodrome to the east, was in a deep cave in a quarry, well concealed from enemy planes. Here Paddy was to meet some of the legendary figures of the war in the Mediterranean. Mike Cumberlege was the first man he had ever seen who sported a gold earring. Born amphibious, as he described himself, Cumberlege had trained in the navy and been recruited for secret operations. He was now captain of the caique *Dolphin*, which had been armed and refitted in Haifa for clandestine missions. Among his crew was a Greek scholar, Professor Nicholas Hammond, formerly a young don at Cambridge, an expert on Epirus and Albania. Recruited into military intelligence, Hammond now specialized in explosives.

Cumberlege and Hammond had been working closely with another remarkable figure, John Pendlebury. Pendlebury was an archaeologist, who had been simultaneously Curator of Knossos in Crete, and Director of Excavations at Tel El Amarna in Egypt. At the outbreak of war he had joined Military Intelligence, and – with the rank of captain – he was laying the foundations of Cretan resistance, with the help of the most powerful clan chieftains of central Crete. These were Manoli Bandouvas, Petrakogeorgis, and Antonis Grigorakis, also known as Satanas. Speaking fluent Cretan, dressed in a shepherd's cloak and armed with his swordstick, Pendlebury would stride into the mountains for days or weeks at a time. It was a delicate and difficult job, setting up chains of command and opening lines of communication among mountain men who had been feuding and rustling each other's sheep for generations. Pendlebury won their respect and affection, and they liked the way he left his glass eye (the result of a childhood accident with a pen) prominently on his desk when he was not at home.

Brigadier Chappel's 14th Infantry Brigade consisted of 4,000 Australian, British and Greek troops, deployed to defend the Heraklion sector. The 3rd and 7th Greek regiments, three battalions strong but short of arms and ammunition, were concentrated in and around the west of the city. The airfield, five miles to the east, was guarded by the 2nd battalion of the Black Watch. The area in between these two positions was covered by the York and Lancaster regiment, an Australian battalion, and the 2nd battalion of Leicesters.

For the Cretans, it was a tragedy that the battle for their island would be fought without the support of the 5th Cretan Division, which had gone to fight the Italians in November 1940 and many of whose units were still stranded on the Albanian front. Those who had tried to get back home were often frustrated by petty officialdom, which insisted that vessels commandeered by W Force were exclusively for the use of British and Dominion personnel.

The German invasion, expected for weeks, finally came on the morning of 20 May. Its main objectives were the airfields of Maleme in the west, Rethymno and Heraklion. The Germans needed to secure at least one of them so that reinforcements could be flown in by Junkers 52 transport aircraft. Just after breakfast, the first waves of paratroopers and gliders were sighted just beyond Maleme and south-west of Chania. The sheer scale of the airborne invasion, the astonishing sight of thousands of paratroopers descending in wave after wave, took everyone by surprise. Despite sustaining huge casualties, the enemy succeeded in maintaining their hold on the airfield at Maleme.

The news of the invasion at Maleme and south-west of Chania only reached Brigadier Chappel at two-thirty that afternoon, and at four there was an exceptionally heavy bombardment. An hour and a half later the alarm for a parachute attack was sounded. Paddy was stationed in the operations room, in a house only a few minutes away from their quarry-based headquarters. Here Group Captain Trumbull, armed with headphones and a cue, was moving more and more little model planes (which represented whole aircraft units) on a flat map of Crete. 'We'll probably be able to see them now,' said Trumbull. He and Paddy went out on to the roof, and sure enough the sky was black and throbbing with the noise of Ju 52s. 'Yes, here they are,' said Trumbull calmly.[33]

Pouring out of the planes, the paratroopers began their descent. The Allied troops had been ordered to aim at their feet as they came down, and many were shot before they even reached the ground. Some, dropping further inland, became entangled in olive trees and were shot or knifed there by Cretan civilians. The Germans, sticklers for the rules of engagement, were profoundly shocked to find their paratroops attacked by old men, women and children, armed with anything they could find. They had overlooked the island's long tradition of resistance to the Turk, and in the face of such a dramatic invasion, the Cretans acted instinctively. The force landing on and around the airfield was virtually wiped out. But another battalion, dropping closer to the city walls of Heraklion, collected itself and prepared to attack the town next day. Its men were desperately thirsty, but Cretan irregulars had staked out almost all the likely water sources.

On 21 May, the battalion of German paratroopers tasked to take the city divided into two groups. One was to attack the Chania Gate to the west, while the other was to tackle the northern gate and the seafront. The fighting round the Chania Gate was particularly intense, and among the defenders were John Pendlebury and Satanas. Any Germans who got through found themselves in fierce guerrilla combat in the narrow streets. Some managed to get as far as the quayside after dark. Nick Hammond and Mike Cumberlege sailed into Heraklion that evening on the *Dolphin*. When they came under fire and saw the swastika flying over the power station, they assumed the town was already in German hands. They slipped out quietly, thinking there was little more they could do in Heraklion.

But the Germans were not yet in control. In the late afternoon, a shortage of ammunition had obliged them to fall back to the ridge they had occupied the night before. Soon after their retreat, Pendlebury decided the time had come to call the guerrilla bands – or *andartes*, as they were known in Greek – into action. He left Heraklion by the Chania Gate, in a car with a driver. They had not gone far when Pendlebury was seriously injured by enemy fire. At first he was brought to a house where a German doctor dressed his wounds; but the following morning he was taken outside, leaned against a wall and shot.

Over the days that followed, Paddy said that going through Heraklion was 'desperately sad'.[34] He remembered an old man, lying dead on the ground as though he were resting. Beyond the city wall, dead bodies rotted among the flowers. Their stomachs had swollen in the warm weather, making it look as though they were on all fours. The wrecks of charred, shot-down planes scarred the olive groves. One day he walked out with some Greek soldiers, who came across three wounded Germans and shot them all. 'We always do that,' one of them said. 'It's the best thing for them.'[35]

The German assaults on both Rethymno and Heraklion had been effectively contained, if not defeated; but in the west, General Kurt Student's paratroopers had secured Maleme airfield, despite such initially heavy losses that the whole invasion had nearly been called off. With Maleme secured, Student was able to fly in the 5th Mountain Division. Major General Bernard Freyberg VC, commander of the Allied troops in Crete (known as 'Creforce'), concluded that the battle was lost and decided to withdraw.

On 25 May Heraklion suffered intense bombing, resulting in appalling destruction and loss of life. Yet as far as holding the sector was concerned, the Allied troops had grounds for optimism. They had captured a considerable amount of enemy supplies and felt there was every possibility of holding out till help arrived. Had they been in radio contact with Creforce Headquarters in the west, their morale might not have been so high, but they knew nothing of the disaster unfolding there.

The order to evacuate was given on 27 May. In the western part of the island British, New Zealand and Australian troops, bitter and exhausted, began their long walk over the White Mountains to the south coast. To the east, news of the catastrophe finally came through on 28 May. As Brigadier Chappel broke the news to his officers early that morning, they could scarcely believe it.

A squadron of the Royal Navy was going to take all Allied troops in the Heraklion sector off the island that night, leaving the Cretans to face their enemy alone. The Cretans took the news without complaint or recrimination. The andarte leader Satanas, who had fought with Pendlebury at the Chania Gate, came to see Brigadier Chappel that evening, as his staff were busy burning documents and preparing to leave. Paddy translated his words: '"My son," he said, placing his hand on the Brigadier's shoulder, "we know you are going away tonight. Never mind! You will come back when the right time comes. But leave us as many of your guns as you can, to carry on the fight till then." Deeply moved, the Brigadier told us to hand over all the arms we could collect.'[36]

The evacuation began just before midnight. Long queues of men lined up in silence along the mole, from where they were ferried by destroyers to two waiting cruisers, the *Dido* and the *Orion*. Paddy spotted one particularly diminutive soldier under a tin hat, who proved to be a woman escaping with her lover; he made no attempt to stop her. When the cruisers were loaded, the destroyers went back to pick up those who were left, including Chappel and his staff. By 2.45 a.m. on 29 May, almost three and a half thousand men had been safely embarked.

Stepping aboard the destroyer was like stepping into another world. Paddy found himself dazzled by the crisp white uniforms, the soup and tea and sandwiches. But the illusion of being whisked away from the dirt and horror of war did not last long. One of the ships in the squadron broke down irreversibly, and it took a long time for the passengers and crew to be taken off and the ship scuttled. By then it was nearly daylight. The squadron was supposed to be out of range of German aircraft by dawn; the delay had made them sitting ducks.

Waves of bombers attacked the squadron for six hours. The *Orion* received two direct hits that went through three levels of decks crowded with men. The damage was terrible: two hundred and sixty men were killed, and slightly more injured. Paddy was not in the part of the ship that was hit, and had been told to stay below. He went on deck anyway, just after a bomb had hit the front gun turret. Curious debris, including several boxing gloves and a banjo, were strewn about all over the place. There were also two dead sailors, one horribly mangled. Once out of enemy range and heading for

Alexandria, a funeral service was held for the dead. The bodies were dropped into the sea, followed by what looked like a series of parcels: the remains of those who had been blown to bits.

The evacuations of Allied personnel from Crete had been unable to round up all the servicemen on the island, and their number was increased by those who managed to escape from German POW camps. Over a thousand hungry, exhausted, leaderless men were wandering over the mountains, trying to survive and keep out of German hands. Their only hope was to make for the south coast, the most likely place for the navy to attempt further evacuations.

The kindness and generosity with which the Cretans looked after Allied stragglers was remarkable, especially since they were putting their own lives at risk by doing so. And as they fed and sheltered these ragged men, passing them from one village to the next on their way south, so the networks of the future resistance movement were born, strengthened and tested. One of those evacuated at that time was a young barrister serving in the RASC, Jack Smith-Hughes. He had been taken prisoner, escaped, and while on the run he had encountered a Cretan officer. Colonel Papadakis told him that the Cretan resistance had been established and was in need of support.

Once in Egypt, Smith-Hughes volunteered to return and help organize the resistance. He was sent back into Crete in October 1941, with a radio operator called Ralph Stockbridge from the Inter-Services Liaison Department (ISLD, a cover name for MI6). This was the first British mission to the Cretan resistance. Their orders were 'to feel out the country and see who had influence', and establish what might usefully be done.[37]

Paddy spent a few days in barracks in Alexandria before moving to Cairo, where he found himself a room at the Continental Hotel. The Continental was neither as smart nor as expensive as Shepheard's next door, but it was in the heart of the city. To those coming from a battle zone, life in wartime Cairo seemed unreal. As one observer put it, 'You are right in the middle of the "Darling belt". You arrive there from the material and emotional austerity of England' (or Crete, for that matter), 'and before you know where you are your two hundred most intimate friends are dining with you by candle-light at small tables in a garden.'[38]

The small candle-lit tables might have been at the Auberge des Pyramides, one of the smartest restaurant-nightclubs in Cairo; or in the extensive grounds of the Gezira Club, the heart of British life, enclosed by its own racetrack. In the jasmine-scented garden of Groppi's, pashas in tarbooshes and their Levantine mistresses sipped coffee and ate ices. After dinner in any number of restaurants, the nightclubs beckoned: the Kit Cat Club and the Deck Club were on boats moored at the riverside, while at Madame Badia's one could enjoy a good band, the best belly-dancers, and a cabaret that included comic Nazis.

At the top end of society, the rich and educated mixed freely. At any party one might find Muslim Toussouns, Sadiks and Abouds as well as members of the extended Egyptian royal family, happily gossiping with Jewish friends bearing the names of Cattaui, Harari or Menasce, or making plans with Coptic friends called Wissa or Wahba, Ghali or Khayatt. They all spoke English and French, but one could hear several other languages as well, as they gossiped over lunch at the Fleurant, the St James or the P'tit Coin de France. These hospitable people welcomed the sudden influx of British officers, both those on leave from the front in the Western Desert and those in desk jobs, who were known as 'The Gabardine Swine' or 'Groppi's Horse'.

As the war progressed, more women appeared: clerks, secretaries and cypherenes, as well as FANYs and WAAFS, ambulance drivers and nurses. For them, the glamour and excitement of wartime Cairo was unforgettable. Everyone was young, and involved in the vital work of winning the war – and as women, their company was much in demand. If you fell into bed with your date at the end of the evening, there was no one to disapprove. In fact there was something noble and generous about it, since he might be dead in a week.

Everywhere there were men in a bewildering array of caps and tunics: South Africans, Australians, New Zealanders, Scots and Sikhs, Free French and Poles. To test the alertness of the troops, Field Security put two men into German uniform: they wandered about all day without being challenged once. To the disgust of troops from the Dominions, officers and men were strictly segregated. Only officers could enter the better cafés, restaurants and nightclubs, while the other ranks drank beer and ate chips at places like the Café Bar Old England, Cosy Corner or Home Sweet Home. Here they were accosted by boys selling naughty magazines with names like *Zip*, *Laffs* and *Saucy Snips*, while others sang out, 'Hey, Mister! You want my sister? Very nice, very clean, all pink inside like Queen Victoria.' For more innocent diversions, the ladies of the British community started the Tipperary Club, where tea and toast could be consumed to the sound of the Forces Network wireless; and Music for All, which put on concerts.

One of the first people Paddy met up with was his old friend Costa Achillopoulos, who was now in the sky-blue *képi* of a Free French lieutenant. Costa had been asked to take some photographs of his cousin, Marie Riaz, and asked Paddy to come along – guessing, no doubt, how much his company would amuse her. Marie was then married to a rich Cairene sugar magnate called Mamduh Riaz Bey. Blessed with a strong bohemian streak, she took to Paddy at once and he was soon a familiar figure at her parties, picnics and expeditions into the desert.

Through Marie Riaz he met Sir Walter and Lady Smart, who were to become important figures in his life. Smartie, as he was known, was the Oriental Councillor at the British Embassy, a diplomat and scholar of distinction. Such mandarins could be daunting, but Smartie was engagingly modest and funny, the very antithesis of stuffy. His first marriage had ended in divorce, which in those days meant that he would never reach ambassadorial rank. His second wife was Amy Nimr, a painter. They lived in a house full of beautiful things on the island of Zamalek, and entertained an eclectic mixture of Greek, Egyptian and British writers and intellectuals in their shady garden. Lawrence Durrell was a frequent visitor, as was Paddy, who often borrowed books from their library.

One party led to another. At the house of Bernard and Inez Burrows in Boulaq Dacrour, Inez's Thursday nights were often graced by King Farouk, who would bring along a case of champagne. The Princess Shevekiar gave spectacular dinners in elaborate Ottoman style: guests were welcomed by girls in flowing gauze spreading rose petals at their feet, and the courses at dinner seemed to go on for ever. There were not many unmarried Muslim girls in evidence, but the cosmopolitan Jewish, Coptic and Greek families did not keep their daughters so rigorously confined. Paddy saw a great deal of Denise Menasce, who came from a grand Sephardic Jewish family which had been granted an imperial title by the Emperor Franz Josef.

At the Anglo-Egyptian Union he encountered the writers and poets in exile who contributed to *Personal Landscape*, the most influential literary magazine to come out of the war. Among them were its pacifist founder Robin Fedden (with whom Paddy often travelled in later years), Durrell, and the poets Terence Tiller and Bernard Spencer. Paddy hoped that he might be published too, and submitted one or two poems, but they were politely rejected. When asked why, Paddy replied: 'I think my stuff was a bit too *fin de siècle* for them.'[39] His old friend Dimitri Capsalis, whom he had met in Constantinople, was now the Greek Ambassador, while Aleko Matsas was consul in Alexandria.

After a brief stint at a boring job in the Canal Zone, Paddy returned to Cairo in July where things suddenly became more interesting. He was summoned to Rustum Buildings, known to every Cairene taxi driver as 'Secret Building', from where covert operations were controlled. Here he was inducted into what became known as the Special Operations Executive, although in those days it lurked behind a smokescreen of different names, of which perhaps the best-known were MO4 and Force 133. Paddy was interviewed by an unknown colonel whose language was so veiled and elliptical that he had no idea what was being said, nor how he should respond. But his pay was raised, and he was told he would soon receive his orders.

He was to join a unit known as ME 102, probably at the suggestion of Monty Woodhouse. The unit was a training camp for people who wanted to continue the fight by joining resistance units that had been formed across occupied Europe. Paddy went to Palestine in September 1941 to join ME 102, established in a spacious house on the slopes of Mount Carmel overlooking the town of Haifa. They called the house Narkover, after the imaginary school invented by J. B. Morton ('Beachcomber') where the pupils were taught forgery, gambling, theft and arson. From his only surviving notebook of the time, the place seems aptly named: it is peppered with remarks such as 'Demolitions were new to all except the fishermen and sailors, and as usual aroused great interest',[40] or 'The Molotov cocktail lecture and practical went off successfully.'[41] The students also learnt map-reading and report-writing, how to handle boats, wireless sets and small arms. They came from a wide range of nationalities, including Yugoslavs and Kurds.

Among the Cretan Greeks, Paddy met two men who were to be among his closest wartime companions: George Tyrakis and Manoli Paterakis, both of whom were later key figures in the Kreipe Operation. Paddy was probably more useful as a Greek speaker than as a weapons expert. Most of his students had been handling guns since childhood and had an instinctive grasp of how they were put together, whereas their instructor had to spend hours in the armoury, mugging up how to dismantle and reassemble guns with the aid of an instruction manual.

Paddy went to Jerusalem for the New Year 1942, where a number of friends from Cairo had gathered. Roaring about on a motorcycle, he took the opportunity to visit all the holy places round the Sea of Galilee. At the Hotel Saint-Georges in Beirut he ran into Costa again, and that night the energy and skill of Costa's dancing brought the hotel ballroom to a standstill.[42] Costa explained that this was probably his last opportunity to dance, for he had only joined the Free French in order to get himself to the Middle East. Now he was transferring to the Greek army, in which dancing was forbidden for as long as the homeland was occupied.

8

Crete and General Carta

Paddy left Narkover for Cairo in April 1942, and soon after that new orders came through: in the next few weeks he would join the handful of SOE officers sent into occupied Crete, to work with the Cretan resistance. He would be in Crete, out of uniform, living in the open, in constant danger. This was the opportunity he had been waiting for.

Although the airborne invasion of Crete in May 1941 had been an impressive demonstration of German might, they had paid a high price for it and the island had now to be held at all costs. In 1941 the Commander of Fortress Crete was General Alexander Andrae, whose headquarters were at the capital, Chania, at the western end of the island. (In autumn 1942, he was replaced by General Bruno Bräuer.) Under him was a divisional commander with headquarters at Archanes, in the central section south of Heraklion. The eastern part of Crete was flatter than the mountainous central and western sections, and was occupied by the Italians. It does not play a part in this story until the Italian surrender, in September 1943.

The number of Axis forces rose and fell throughout the occupation, 'according to the fortunes of the North African campaign, the situation on the eastern front, or the perceived threat of invasion: it ranged from around 75,000 in 1943, to just over 10,000 at the time of surrender in 1945.'[1] The local population numbered some 400,000, spread across an island about a hundred and sixty miles long.

In the months leading up to his death, John Pendlebury had been developing contacts with the *kapetans* in central Crete (known to the British as 'Pendlebury's Thugs'). These powerful clan leaders had to be treated with care, but the effort was worth it because they could mobilize hundreds of men who knew how to survive and move across the mountains by day or night.

The three most important kapetans were Antoni Grigorakis, known as Satanas, who had approached Brigadier Chappel for guns at the time of the British evacuation. Petrakogeorgis was the most pro-British of the guerrilla leaders, and also the easiest to work with; he had run a successful olive-oil and food business before the war, so was given the code-name 'Selfridge'. The third guerrilla leader was Manoli Bandouvas, a wealthy shepherd whose vast flocks suggested his code-name, 'Bo-Peep'; although he had a huge following, working with him was complicated by the fact that he liked playing people off against each another. All the kapetans and their men were dependent on the villages in their territory for news and supplies, but some villages were more involved in the resistance than others.

Monty Woodhouse had arrived to take charge of SOE activities on Crete in November 1941. As well as coordinating the evacuation of stragglers, his orders were to explore the possibility of a Cretan guerrilla uprising, which would be unleashed only in the event of an Allied invasion of the island. These orders reflected the optimistic mood prevailing in Cairo at the time: the Afrika Korps, which had raced across North Africa that spring, was now limping to a halt at the end of dangerously attenuated supply lines.

Woodhouse set about his task with energy, but everything conspired against him. The activities of the Royal Navy and the large numbers of stragglers still to be rescued brought German attention to the two main evacuation points, Tsoutsouros and Treis Ekklisies, until it became too dangerous to use them. Then in early 1942 the Germans began the reinforcement of Crete, which was to be used as a supply centre for warships, planes and troop-carriers on their way to Libya. Many more troops now patrolled the south coast and the construction of a new airfield began. The village of Tymbaki was evacuated and destroyed, and men and boys from the surrounding area were forced into labour gangs to level and prepare the ground.

Cretan faith in the Allies reached a low ebb. Many had thought that the arrival of SOE officers on the island meant that their liberation was imminent, but now there were rumours that the officers were secretly planning to abandon the island altogether. At the same

Crete

AEGEAN SEA

LIBYAN SEA

time, the enemy's strength encouraged the recruitment of a number of Cretan spies, who helped to expose and kill members of the local resistance. The kapetans lay low, being too vulnerable to move about much in the existing climate. Monty Woodhouse left Crete in April 1942, stating in his final report that once the remaining Allied stragglers had been evacuated, there was nothing else that SOE could do – especially since there was, for the moment, no hope of combining an invasion of the island with a guerrilla uprising.

Jack Smith-Hughes, who with Ralph Stockbridge had made the first tentative contacts with the Cretan resistance after the German invasion, had returned to Cairo to run SOE's Cretan Desk. In mid-December 1941 he appointed a young officer, Alexander Fielding, to take charge of the western end of the island. Slim, dark and fine-boned, with a hawkish face and fiery temper, Fielding looked the part of a Cretan shepherd more than most of his compatriots. Commonly known as Xan, he had been running a bar in Cyprus when war broke out. He spoke good Greek and was not afraid of fighting, but he so dreaded the prospect of regimental life that a year had gone by before he joined the Cyprus Regiment as an Intelligence Officer. The job Smith-Hughes now offered him seemed to include an unusual degree of independence: 'Do you have any personal objection to committing murder?' was one of his more surprising questions.[2]

Fielding reached the island in January 1942 and soon made contact with Ralph Stockbridge, who for some months had been manning the radio set hidden in the isolated house of Colonel Papadakis. Papadakis's influence did not stretch far beyond the Chania region, but he had declared himself Leader of the Cretan Supreme Liberation Committee. Though more interested in establishing his own personal power base than in harassing the German war effort, he had recruited some remarkable men into the resistance, whom Xan put to good use.

One of these was George Psychoundakis, a young shepherd from a poor family in Asi Gonia. At a time when few men in rural Crete were literate, George – who had had no more than elementary schooling – had a passion for reading, writing and poetry; Xan Fielding described him as 'the most naturally wise and instinctively knowledgeable Cretan I ever met'.[3] He had been part of the relay of guides and runners who took Allied servicemen down to the monastery of Preveli, from where the first large-scale evacuations took place under Commander Francis Poole in the summer of 1941.

With George Psychoundakis as his guide, Xan worked closely with Papadakis's secretary, a young lawyer called Andreas Polentas, and the Vandoulakis family of Vaphes. This family had helped so many Allied servicemen that their two houses were known as the British Consulate. Xan appointed a guerrilla leader for each province in the area, made contact with the Cretans best placed to report on German activity, and organized networks of runners with code-words to take their information to the wireless station.

Monty Woodhouse was replaced by Tom Dunbabin, an Oxford-educated archaeologist, Fellow of All Souls and one of the most important Greek scholars of his day. He spoke Cretan like a native, and although taller and broader than most Cretans, like them he sported a fine moustache. In his threadbare Cretan clothes, Tom Dunbabin reminded Fielding of 'a successful local sheep-thief'.[4] Dunbabin's first task was to round up what was left of the stragglers, most of whom were evacuated in the coming months.

The Germans increased pressure on the resistance with raids on mountain villages, and arrests made all the more terrifying for being undertaken by huge numbers of men. The kapetans responded by executing six informers in May, but this led to the immediate killing of fourteen patriots. In June, the first of what became an annual sabotage operation was undertaken by the Special Boat Service. One team destroyed five aircraft at Kastelli while another Free French team, under Captain the Earl Jellicoe, destroyed eighteen planes and a number of vehicles at Heraklion airfield. The following day fifty hostages, including the ex-mayor of Heraklion and the ex-governor general, were shot by the Germans.

Such a brutal show of strength threw the Cretans into a state of shock and panic, and many questioned whether there was anything to be gained from heroic resistance. But the instinct to strike back at the oppressors was as strong as ever and, in the hope of launching a general uprising, the kapetans urged SOE to give them more support. Tom Dunbabin explained that the moment was not yet ripe, but they insisted on being taken to Egypt in order to put their case to GHQ Cairo. Dunbabin agreed with reluctance and, on the night of 23 June, Bandouvas, Petrakogeorgis and their families, together with Satanas who was gravely ill with cancer, were assembled on a beach near Trypiti, awaiting the caique *Porcupine*, which was bringing Paddy for his first spell of duty in occupied Crete.

The *Porcupine* stayed discreetly out at sea, while a tender rowed the incoming party to shore. Paddy was accompanied by a wireless operator, Sergeant Matthew White, and Yanni Tsangarakis, a runner for Ralph Stockbridge, who had volunteered to return as Paddy's guide. Each of them was carrying a heavy load as they disembarked in a rough sea, and Paddy's boots were ripped apart as he scrambled over the wet rocks to the beach.

The officer in charge of the tender made it clear that he could not accommodate all those awaiting passage, and the sea was too rough to attempt more than one journey back to the *Porcupine*. Only Satanas and his family were evacuated that night, leaving the other kapetans and their entourages seething with anger and resentment. This was reflected in Paddy's first signal, which began with the words: 'SITUATION HERE UGLY'.

It would have been uglier still, had the kapetans known that GHQ Cairo had already decided not to attempt to liberate Crete, nor to assist any guerrilla uprising. A Joint Planning Staff meeting in Cairo had recommended that 'The patriot leaders [of Crete] must be clearly informed that no military support other than supplies of stores, ammunition and food agreed upon in advance, and possibly some air action, can be given.'[5] Yet events were unfolding so fast that even this minimal commitment looked optimistic.

The great fortress of Tobruk had fallen after a fierce battle on 21 June 1942, leaving General Erwin Rommel's forces a clear path into Egypt. On the day of his arrival Paddy was told that the German garrison had held a victory parade through the town of Tymbaki, 'under the eyes of a despondent crowd', to celebrate its capture.[6] On 25 June, Rommel's troops were pouring into Egypt. The early days of July were known as The Flap: the warships and other Royal Naval vessels in Alexandria harbour were moved, without warning, from Egypt to Beirut and Haifa. For about a week there was intense anxiety among the SOE operatives in Crete, as signals from Cairo suddenly dried up. By the time the signals came trickling in again, the situation had stabilized: Rommel was held in a bottleneck at El Alamein, with the sea on one side and the treacherous wastes of the Qattara Depression on the other.

Xan Fielding and Paddy met in Yerakari, a large village celebrated for its cherries, which sits at the head of one of the two valleys of the Amari. This area was so green and fertile that British officers coming down from their harsh life in the mountains called it 'Lotus Land'. It was not their first encounter. Both remembered that they had met several years before, probably in the summer of 1933, when Paddy was dining with a friend in the Café Anne in Bloomsbury: Xan was trying to make money by drawing sketches of the diners, just as Paddy was to do in Vienna some months later. At that time they had talked for less than five minutes. In Yerakari, they embarked on a friendship that was to last until Xan's death in 1991. 'Like [Paddy],' wrote Fielding in his war memoir *Hide and Seek*, 'I had tramped across Europe to reach Greece. Like him, I had been almost penniless during that long arduous holiday – but there the similarity between our travels ended, for whereas I was often forced to sleep out of doors, in ditches, haystacks or on public benches, Paddy's charm and resourcefulness had made him a welcome guest wherever he went.'[7]

On 5 August 1942 Xan left Crete to escort Colonel Papadakis, now on the Germans' most-wanted list, to Egypt with his wife and son. It was an unexpected move, which left Paddy to fill the gap and take charge of the western part of the island. He made his way into western Crete with his wireless operator, a young man from the Dodecanese called Apostolos Evangelou, and immediately ran into difficulties. No one in the Chania and Rethymno networks knew that Xan had left, and they had not been warned of Paddy's arrival. It took time to gain their confidence and re-establish links, and he had very little money. He could not afford to hire mules, so wireless sets, chargers, ammunition and anything else that needed moving had to be shifted by him and Evangelou and any other human backs they could borrow.

It was at this time that he met George Psychoundakis: 'George, who was in a muck-sweat from a long run over the mountains, handed over half a dozen letters from agents in western Crete, all twisted into compact billets and carefully hidden in various parts of his clothing; they were produced with a comic kind of conjuror's flourish, after grotesquely furtive glances over the shoulder and fingers laid on lips in a caricature of clandestine security precautions that made us all laugh.'[8]

While trying to establish contact with the intelligence gatherers, Paddy was also preparing a sabotage mission in Suda Bay. A parachute drop of limpet mines was arranged for 8 September, in the White Mountains. They landed safely, along with some much needed cash, though without the wire-cutters Paddy had specifically asked for. Paddy and Yanni Tsangarakis set off, with the limpets on their backs – huge and heavy, 'like studded bowler hats'.[9] They hoped to use them on a large petrol tanker moored in the harbour, but by the time they arrived the tanker had left. They also discovered that it was impossible to break through the perimeter, which was guarded by dog patrols and electric fences. Dunbabin was finding the same in Heraklion. The harbour was too well defended, and no one was prepared to swim out to an enemy ship with a great metal weight strapped to their chest.

Sabotage remained a top priority for SOE, but it was constantly impeded by other demands on the time and energy of those on the ground. Days and nights were spent waiting for messengers, or the next wireless schedule, or parachute drops, usually postponed because of the weather. Moving the wireless sets in their suitcases involved back-breaking marches through the night. There were also marches to the coast to meet incoming craft, marches through the mountains to secret conferences, marches to gather information. The Cretan terrain is among the harshest in Europe, and distances on a map bear no relation to the ground that has to be covered. When asked how far it was from one place to another, a Cretan would reply by saying it was 'ten cigarettes away', or however many he thought would be smoked en route.

Inevitably there were also days of tedium when there was nothing to do but wait, for a message or a runner. But for someone like Paddy who enjoyed singing and poetry, the Cretans provided a rich seam of distraction. He picked up a range of Cretan songs, and was always ready for a round of *mantinades*, improvised rhyming couplets that were taken up by one person after another in the circle. Many of the older shepherds could recite great chunks of the *Erotokritos*, a seventeenth-century romance in the Cretan dialect, the recitation of which could go on all night.

Since the SOE operatives took special care not to enter villages except in very rare circumstances, they relied on their guides and the local people for food. 'When I first arrived the food situation was poor, though I cannot claim ever to have gone seriously hungry.'[10] It was a monotonous diet of yoghurt, sheep's cheese, bread, with beans and tomatoes and lentils in the summer; but there never seemed to be any shortage of wine, *sikoudia* or home-grown tobacco. Years later, he told a friend that the only civilized item he missed on Crete was his toothbrush:[11] these were almost unknown outside the main towns, and had he been captured in possession of a toothbrush his cover would have been blown instantly.

At the end of September Paddy, along with Vangeli Vandoulakis and the wireless operator Evangelou, moved their equipment to a hideout east of the village of Photineou (Fotinos), home of Yanni Tsangarakis. The area was close to a large enemy supply dump and many Germans were billeted nearby, so it was a good place from which to spy on them – though sometimes they came rather too close for comfort.

When a hundred and fifty Germans moved into the area and began a firing exercise, Nikoli Alevizakis (son of Father John Alevizakis of Alones, a great figure in the resistance) thought that they must be looking for the wireless set. As he took to his heels to warn Paddy and the others, the soldiers stopped their exercise and began firing at him. Paddy and Yanni Tsangarakis moved quietly to higher ground; but the wireless in its cave became increasingly vulnerable as the Germans fanned out. Evangelou the operator, Paddy wrote, 'bent over the wireless with the earphones on, failed to see them, but kept tapping Morse while three Germans passed between him and our cave, a hundred yards away . . . Yanni Tsangarakis and I, meanwhile, lay down with our rifles cocked, in case they should spot the set. Yanni, who knew his village was in danger of being burnt down, kept crossing himself and repeating, "O, my poor village . . . "' It was a heart-stopping moment, but they were lucky:

'The Huns walked straight past, up the hill. It was wonderful. We packed up quick and beat it.'[12]

By the end of October, western Crete had two wireless stations. Good news was also coming from North Africa, where Montgomery's massive attack on the Germans at El Alamein was at last pushing them westwards, out of Egypt and back into Cyrenaica. In fact, thought Paddy, 'everything was going swimmingly at last. I was getting to know all the big boys, and . . . I felt I was getting somewhere.'[13]

The following month, however, the Germans holding Fortress Crete launched a big counter-espionage drive. On the night of 18 November the Germans surrounded the villages of Vaphes and Vrysses, and took thirty-seven prisoners. Among them were Andreas Polentas, Perikles Vandoulakis, and Evangelou – who was caught in the house of Nicos Vandoulakis, where the radio was hidden. His pockets were filled with incriminating papers; but Elpida Vandoulakis, Uncle Nico's daughter, managed to take his jacket and help him into another one before the police took him away. She stuffed the papers into her dress, and later that night, carried the heavy wireless and batteries out to a field and buried them. Thanks to her, the wireless was saved; but Polentas and Evangelou were kept in the notorious Ayia prison in Chania, where they were tortured and eventually shot.

Paddy was profoundly shaken when he heard the news, and all his Cretan friends and helpers went to ground. For the first time, he was alone and unescorted. He had papers in his pocket made out in the name of Mihali* Phrangidakis, aged twenty-seven, but he still had to be careful: 'I rattled along all right in Greek, but could fall into terrible give-away blunders.'[14] Yet in some ways being without a guide was a relief, since they always tried to keep him away from the Germans. Now he was free to wander about and listen in on enemy conversations, all the more enjoyable since the enemy's morale was very low.

The Battle of Alamein had turned the German advance into a retreat, and the Afrika Korps was now being hounded out of Cyrenaica. There were tales of bad discipline, failure to salute officers

---

* Paddy was always known as Mihali in Greece, during and after the war. If he used his first name it tended to be shortened to Petro, which he found irritating. 'Mihali Phrangidakis' was just one of several aliases he used.

and drunkenness. Paddy reported spending a long evening in Aghios Konstantinos, an area of Rethymno, in the room next door to two German sergeants. They were feeling wretched, above all at the prospect of spending the fourth Christmas '"*weit von der Heimat*" . . . Then, to my astonishment, they started an English lesson. I felt like correcting their pronunciation through the door. When they went out to dinner I went into their room with a petrol lighter and hunted round. (I pinched the manual of a German W/T set, which may or may not be interesting.) I dropped the lighter and had a feverish hunt on all fours for it and the door, and got back to my room just before they came back, slightly drunk.'[15]

Tom Dunbabin, Xan and Paddy did all they could to prey on German fears and frustrations. They dropped leaflets in German, stamped with swastika-bearing eagles as if they had been made by disaffected German soldiers. Xan and Paddy also began a chalk-scrawling campaign, enlisting young Cretans to help. 'WIR WOLLEN NACH HAUS!' (we want to go home) and 'WO IST UNSERE LUFTWAFFE?' (where is our air force?) and 'SCHEISSE HITLER' (shit Hitler) were the most common scrawls, but Paddy also took advantage of the rumours that Communism was spreading through the sullen German ranks. Some slogans read 'HEIL STALIN!' or 'HEIL MOSKAU!' accompanied by a defiant hammer and sickle. The success of his graffiti could be judged by the arrest of German soldiers, and searches of their billets and incoming parcels. The following year the graffiti campaign was backed up by a secret printing press, which distributed black propaganda in German.

On 27 November, Xan returned to Crete with another SOE officer, Captain Arthur Reade, who had trained as a barrister before the war and was later part of the prosecuting team at the Nuremberg trials. He, Xan, a radio operator called Alec Tarves, and Nikos Souris, Tom Dunbabin's right-hand man who had completed the training course at Haifa, returned to Crete by submarine. It was a difficult landing in rough weather, and they were almost smashed on to the rocks. Arthur Reade had been sent to Crete with one objective, the sabotage of Suda Bay, but in a job where it was essential to blend into the scenery, Reade's appearance was a liability. He was so tall and English-looking that he could never have passed for a Cretan shepherd, and when he grew his beard it came out fan-shaped and bright red.

During the night of 6–7 December, the villages of Kourites, Nithavri, Apodoulou and Platanos in the Amari were raided. The Germans turned up in huge numbers, with machine guns and even mortars. The men were herded into the school, the women into the church, and here they were kept for forty-eight hours while the Germans searched and interrogated. They found nothing, thanks to a well-developed network of lookouts, and no one gave anything away.

Had the enemy mounted a raid on Yerakari that Christmas of 1942, however, they would have bagged most of the British officers on Crete; but the Germans took Christmas seriously and stayed in their garrisons for the feast. Paddy, Xan, Arthur and Tom 'reeled happily from house to house',[16] enjoying the hospitality of their Cretan comrades, and celebrating the German reversals at Alamein and Stalingrad. Paddy was looking particularly dashing in his new Cretan waistcoat, 'of royal blue broadcloth lined with scarlet shot-silk and embroidered with arabesques of black braid'.[17]

Xan was always surprised by the high sartorial style that Paddy managed to maintain in the roughest conditions.

> Though we all wore patched breeches, tattered coats and down-at-heel boots, on him these looked as frivolous as fancy-dress. His fair hair, eyebrows and moustache were dyed black, which only added to his carnivalesque appearance, and his conversation was as gay and witty as though we had just met each other . . . at some splendid ball in Paris or London. His frivolity was a salutary contrast to Tom's natural gravity and my own temper . . . It was also a deceptive quality, for although it enhanced his patent imaginative powers, it concealed a mind as conscientious and thorough as it was fanciful.[18]

Yanni Tsangarakis brought some bad news early in the New Year of 1943. An enemy patrol had surrounded Alones. There had been enough time to hide the wireless and its batteries while, with help from Tsangarakis, the radio operators had slipped through the German line and disappeared. But the patrol had arrested Siphi Alevizakis, one of the three sons of Father John, and on him they found two letters, in English, to Paddy. They had taken him away, and he could expect no more mercy that Apostolos Evangelou and Andreas Polentas. 'Grim tales were coming in of the goings on at [Alones] – arrests, beatings-up etc. A friend saw Siphi the Vicar's son being taken through Argyroupolis, with blood streaming out of his mouth.'[19]

Pleased with their haul, the Germans left and returned the following day; by which time the charging engine and all other incriminating evidence had been spirited away. A few days later they raided the village of Asi Gonia looking for George Psychoundakis, with an informer who was hidden under a raincoat. George managed to escape, but several of his family were arrested and interrogated.

Keen to stamp out this hotbed of clandestine activity, German patrols intensified their search of the Alones–Asi Gonia region. It was now vital to move the wireless set that had been hidden on the day following Siphi's arrest. Paddy and Xan met Siphi's father, Father John Alevizakis, in a cave overlooking Asi Gonia: 'he brushed aside our expressions of sympathy with a phrase that came constantly to his lips: "God is great." Then, as he took out a bottle of raki he had brought with him, he asked us all to drink to the toast: "May the Almighty polish the rust from our rifles!"'[20]

The wireless, batteries and charging engine were moved in the course of one freezing January night, by Paddy and eighteen men, most of whom were cousins of George Psychoundakis. Their destination was the Beehive, a round cheese-hut near Gournes. This had been the hideout of Arthur Reade and Alec Tarves, his wireless operator, since they arrived on the island in November. It was a gruelling march: 'Every now and then we sat down to smoke a cigarette, and only the cold kept us all from falling asleep where we sat.'[21] They were exhausted when they reached Reade and Tarves at the Beehive, but there was no time to rest; they could hear the sound of rifle and machine-gun fire from the villages below. The wireless had already been moved to a remoter spot, and as they scrambled higher, they saw a party of over a hundred Germans moving up the gorge. It was time to hide.

George and Alec Tarves went over the watershed while Paddy, Yanni Tsangarakis and Arthur Reade scrambled into the woods and hid in a thick cypress tree. They spent the rest of that freezing day (it was 25 January) in its branches, scarcely daring to move. The German patrols went to and fro, shouting to each other; some soldiers passed almost directly beneath them. But in the late afternoon the Germans gave up the search when a mist rolled in and snow began to fall. Emerging from the tree stiff as planks and chilled to the bone, Paddy, Yanni and Arthur Reade scrambled uphill, spent the night in a damp hole, and made their way to the village of Kampos. Paddy referred to their narrow escape as 'Oak Apple Day'[22] – the name commemorating the several hours that Charles II spent in an oak tree avoiding the Parliamentarians after the Battle of Worcester.

Tom Dunbabin left Crete in mid-February 1943 with a large party of Cretans, including George Psychoundakis who was sorely in need of a rest. Xan had returned to his position in western Crete, so Dunbabin made Paddy responsible for the Heraklion area. This was not what he wanted to hear. 'I now feel as if I were starting on an op. in Crete all over again, far from all the friends and contacts I had gone to considerable pains to make (which is one of the most important parts of work here, in my opinion) in an area I have no feeling for at all.'[23]

As it turned out, the Heraklion sector was not as bad as he had expected: it was certainly less arduous, as he admitted in his report to SOE in Cairo:

> Working in this area, after my former haunts, is like settling down to a Jane Austen novel, after leaving a thriller by Sax Rohmer half-way through. Merely the struggle for existence [in western Crete] is a full-time job. On looking back, my six months seem to have been one long string of battery troubles, faulty sets, transport difficulties, rain, arrests, hide and seek with the Huns, lack of cash, flights at a moment's notice, false alarms, wicked treks over the mountains, laden like a mule, fright among one's collaborators, treachery, and friends getting shot.[24]

All Paddy's reports from Crete describe the people involved in gathering information, their relative efficiency, the tension between the resistance leaders and the machinations of the Communists; but everything comes into sharper focus once he moves to Heraklion. The Cretan desire to expel the invader was as strong as ever, but sooner or later Crete would be liberated. Politically, those involved in the resistance were looking to the future.

In the first week of March Paddy entered the city dressed as a shepherd, his moustache and eyebrows freshly darkened with burnt cork, on one of the last days of Carnival. He spent the next eight days in a borrowed suit with a collar and tie, involved in 'a succession of conferences all day with work far into the night',[25] designed to iron out rivalries and improve lines of communication. At the same time, he was doing his best to neutralize the influence of the Communists.

On Crete as on the mainland, the Communist goal was to control all strands of the resistance and thus position themselves to dominate the post-war settlement. Yet EAM (the National Liberation Front: a coalition of different left-wing organizations, now controlled by the Communists) failed to make as much headway on Crete as it had on the mainland, and the non-Communist Cretan Resistance (EOK: the National Organization of Crete) viewed EAM with deep suspicion. The Communists still managed to spread a good deal of anti-British propaganda, claiming that the British had no interest in liberating the Cretans from the German yoke and kept a presence on the island only to ensure that Crete became a post-war base for their imperialist activities.

The Communist figurehead on Crete was General Mandakas of the Greek army, but EAM were also very keen to recruit kapetan Manoli Bandouvas. As a patriotic peasant with a large following among the people, his support would be a public relations coup, while Bandouvas himself was sympathetic to their cause, particularly when he saw how it rattled the British. It was to try and keep him out of Communist hands that SOE gave Bandouvas the splendid title of Chief of the Francs-Tireurs.

Paddy wandered around Heraklion after sundown. He saw how every road leading down to the sea ended in a wall eight or ten feet high, guarded by machine guns, 'and between them and the sea lies a jungle of wire into which land-mines are sown'. When the time came to leave, 'I borrowed a raincoat and a wonderful velvet trilby and bicycled out of town . . . I looked the image of a spy – just like the ones in the Careless Talk poster, I thought . . . My bike had a little tin swastika on the front.'[26]

Over those eight days in Heraklion, Paddy said he had never worked so hard in his life. But over those past months, during the long days of enforced idleness in caves and sheepfolds, one might wonder what he had been writing or drawing for his own amusement. Paddy gives some idea when he had to report the loss of his briefcase, in the scramble to hide from a German raiding party on his mountain headquarters in April. The briefcase contained nothing incriminating, he reassured Cairo. However, he was sad to lose 'some comic drawings of British military life', and 'an exercise book containing verses (my own in English) and others in French, Greek and Rumanian from memory'.[27] There was also a wish-list, seven pages long, of all the guns, weapons and ammunition he felt were needed in Crete. If it made the Germans think that such a splendid armoury was on its way, so much the better.

At the time of the raid Paddy had been on his way to Mylapotamos on the north coast, to coordinate the arrival of Ralph Stockbridge of ISLD. Stockbridge, who had been the first covert wireless operator on Crete, was now returning with the rank of Captain. Although SOE and ISLD were deadly rivals in the internecine struggles of GHQ Cairo, Paddy and Ralph got on extremely well. To avoid duplication of effort, they decided that Stockbridge would take charge of all intelligence work in central and eastern Crete: a task made easier by the efficient information service in Heraklion, run by young men barely out of their teens. When their leader's cover was blown he was replaced by a young lawyer called Micky Akoumianakis.

Stockbridge and his operator, John Stanley, landed on 12 May from the Greek submarine *Papanikolis*. It was not the smoothest arrival but, met by Paddy, they were taken to a sheepfold belonging to the Dramoundanis family above Anoyeia. This village, perched like a ship on a great spur of rock, was serving as a muster station for many andartes and intelligence agents for whom life had become too dangerous.

At dusk on 25 May, about ten people – including Paddy, Stockbridge, Stanley and Yanni Tsangarakis – were sitting around the sheepfold when there came a warning. Three hundred Germans, coming from Anoyeia, were heading towards them. This happened so often it aroused no particular alarm; but Paddy told everyone to get packed up and reached for his rifle. It had been cleaned and oiled that morning, and he thought it was empty. He was unaware that some of the company 'had been amusing themselves by doing Greek and British arms drill with my rifle, and practising loading and unloading'.

> I drew the bolt backwards and forwards, easing the springs to see if it was working smoothly after being oiled (without realizing it, I had put a round in the breech). I pressed the trigger and the round hit Yanni, who was sitting by the fire a little distance away doing up his sariki, through the left hip . . . [the round] had passed twice through his leg before entering the body. There were six wounds in all. We bound them up, but it was no use, and he died about an hour later, shedding very little blood. He did not seem to suffer a great deal, and said some very kind words to me before he died that I shall never forget.

They buried him at dawn under two ilex trees, about a quarter of a mile from the camp. Yanni had been one of Paddy's closest Cretan friends, and 'the best and hardest worker we have ever had here'.

Those who had witnessed the scene knew it had been an accident. They tried to ease Paddy's shock and distress by reminding him that similar things happened all too frequently among the Cretans, whose approach to gun safety was casual to say the least. 'Everyone was extremely decent to me about this horrible accident,' he wrote, although his own remorse was not so easily assuaged. 'No amount of writing about it will bring Yanni back to life, nor excuse my not examining the magazine before closing the bolt, and I am not going to attempt it.'[28]

His first instinct was to go straight to Photineou, Yanni's village, to tell the family and beg their forgiveness, but the Cretans, who included one of Yanni's cousins, dismissed the idea at once. It would cause untold trouble in the present climate, and enemies of the Tsangarakis clan might whisper that Paddy had shot him 'for treachery'. Until the moment was right to reveal the truth they insisted that Paddy tell a different story, which they all swore to uphold. Their party had run into a German ambush, and Yanni had been shot while trying to make a break for it. 'I want to say that I did not agree to this hateful fiction out of a wish to shirk my responsibilities, but for the sake of Yanni and his family, and our work on Crete . . . If pensions are granted to the families of people who die in our work in Crete, please lay this on for Yanni.' Paddy also asked that £100 of his own back pay should go to Yanni's nephew, whom Yanni was planning to support while he underwent training in Egypt.[29]

The annual SBS sabotage raid began on 4 July, and to coincide with the attack on the airfield Paddy made another attempt to sabotage shipping in Heraklion harbour. He and Manoli Paterakis smuggled the limpets into the city by donkey, strapped them on, and managed to get into the harbour, but it was too well guarded for them to be able to proceed further. The SBS raid attacked two airfields and blew up a large fuel base; but on returning to the boats they ran into a German patrol, lost two men and took two German prisoners. 'Fifty hostages were executed in reprisal,' wrote Tom Dunbabin, and most of these 'had no standing or connection with our work; they included most of the small Jewish community of Heraklion.'[30]

The SBS raid had also been designed to foster the impression that an Allied landing on Crete or Greece might be imminent. This possibility was never far from Cretan minds, but after the invasion of Sicily in mid-July 1943, followed by the fall of Mussolini's Fascist regime, many felt the day to be drawing closer. The Germans were appalled at the speed with which the situation in Italy had changed, and on Crete their relationship with their co-occupiers had become very uneasy.

The Germans ruled the central and western areas of Crete while the eastern parts of the island, Lasithi and Siteia, were under Italian control. The Cretans viewed the Italians with great hostility at first, remembering the unprovoked Italian invasion of Greece in 1940. Yet as time wore on, they proved more humane as occupiers than the Germans – perhaps in part because of the peaceful nature of the eastern Cretans, who were not such inveterate troublemakers as their compatriots in the mountains. But Lieutenant Franco Tavana, head of Italian Security, was proud of the fact that he had not been responsible for a single Cretan death.

When news of the fall of Mussolini reached Crete in late July, it was greeted with relief and rejoicing: 'the Italians had ripped off their black shirts – or had them ripped off – tore down every photograph of the Duce and declared their hatred of the Germans and the war.'[31] At the same time General Angelo Carta, head of the

Siena Division and the 32,000-strong garrison of Lasithi, was in a very difficult position. The Germans suspected that the new Italian government of Marshal Badoglio would soon approach the Allies to negotiate an armistice, which would throw the occupation of Crete into turmoil. Carta feared that at any moment the Germans might move in, disarming and interning every Italian on the island. Carta was, in Paddy's words, 'a comfortable, plump, monocled and rather worldly figure',[32] yet he was also anxious and indecisive. He depended on the advice of Lieutenant Tavana, who had been a customs official before the war and now served in the *Alpini* Corps. Tavana's views were clear: he loathed the Germans, and believed that the sooner Italy joined the Allies the better.

Paddy was in the Amari valley when he received a message from Micky Akoumianakis of the Heraklion intelligence network. Lieutenant Tavana wanted a meeting, for his superior was not willing to allow the Germans to disarm or intern him. Paddy was picked up in a taxi (the first car he had been in for over a year), and driven to Knossos. The next day, Paddy and Micky bicycled into Heraklion to meet Tavana in the flat of a dentist, Dr Stavrianides. The dentist immediately ordered Paddy to strip and take a bath, while his clothes – stiff with weeks of accumulated dirt and lice – were whisked away to be washed. They were still being laundered when Lieutenant Tavana appeared early for the meeting, so Paddy had to greet him in his host's dressing-gown and a pair of scarlet pyjamas. Tavana and Paddy got on well, but since setting up the meeting Carta had changed his mind; General Bräuer had done much to soothe his fears, and he was now reassured that he was in no immediate danger of a German takeover. Paddy urged Tavana to arrange a talk between him and Carta. He wanted to convince the General that 'some British help would be forthcoming in the event of a clash',[33] and Tavana, who believed the 'clash' would come sooner or later in spite of Bräuer's soothing words, was just as keen to arrange it – but Carta still baulked.

The Cretans had observed the tension between the occupiers with considerable interest. Again and again they asked whether Paddy thought there would be an Allied landing on Crete, which would naturally be followed by a general uprising. On orders from GHQ, 'I did what I could to discourage great expectations.' At the same time, he could not supress his natural optimism: 'in spite of my growing doubts about the immediate future, I hoped and felt that sooner or later, there would be a landing (wrongly, alas!) but I said, as I had been told to do, that we would all be given the right amount of warning for all our efforts to be combined for the best.'[34]

On 12 August Paddy and Manoli Paterakis left Heraklion to see the andarte leader Manoli Bandouvas, for whom he had arranged an arms drop. Given the kapetan's unpredictable nature and what was to follow, one might ask why he did so – though there were good reasons at the time. Bandouvas and Tom Dunbabin had clashed on the subject of distributing previous drops, and there was a distinct coolness between them. Yet at this critical moment, it seemed vital to Paddy that 'everybody fighting the Germans should be friends'.[35] Paddy had plans to make a series of arms drops to the other kapetans as well, but Bandouvas was the most prominent. If there were to be an Allied landing on Crete, it was important to have him well armed, on friendly terms with SOE, and not under Communist influence.

Bandouvas had installed himself in a well-appointed camp on the Viannos plateau, which included an armourer, a tailor and a cobbler. He had around a hundred and sixty followers, more were joining him every day, and he claimed he could summon another two thousand men should the need arise. The arms drop took place on 20 August and went without a hitch. Firing their guns in exaltation, Bandouvas and his men returned to their lair with the spoils. The drop had included not only guns and ammunition but British–issue soft caps, bush shirts and web belts: equipment that would enable the band, should they be called on to fight in support of the Italians, to look more like a regular unit.

The news of the long-expected Italian armistice, announced on 8 September, was celebrated with rapture by the Italian troops who thought they were about to go home. Their joy was short-lived. General Friedrich-Wilhelm Müller, the divisional commander who had a reputation for being hard and intransigent, immediately took over the Italian area. All Italian troops were given the choice of fighting under German officers, joining 'non–combatant units' (in other words, labour gangs), or being interned. An all-night meeting between Paddy, Tavana and General Carta achieved nothing. Cairo had not repeated their offer of a bombing raid to help the Italians, and Paddy could not promise Allied support if Carta resisted the Germans. In the circumstances, Carta was unwilling to hand over his weapons to the Cretans – though they were given some eighty rifles and a number of hand grenades.

Despite the swift German takeover of the Italian sector, many Cretans believed that the Italian armistice would inevitably be followed by Allied landings on Crete. One of those who believed this most fervently was Manoli Bandouvas, whose force had increased to some three hundred men, and whose frequent motto was 'the struggle needs blood'.[36] According to Paddy, Bandouvas had been repeatedly reminded that his orders were to hold himself in readiness to support the Italians, should that become necessary; and that whatever happened, he was not to move without orders from Cairo.

On 9 September, Paddy was in his hideout at Kastamonitza – equidistant from Heraklion and Neapolis, the regional capital of Lasithi – when he was joined by Tom Dunbabin, who had returned from Cairo with the news that there would be no Allied landing on Crete. All efforts had been diverted to the islands of the Dodecanese in an effort to keep them in Italian hands, but the attempt had failed, and the islands were now under German control.

At about the same time, a runner appeared from Bandouvas with a message so badly written that it took some time to decipher the alarming words: 'When are the English landing to help us fight the Germans?'[37] The kapetan had convinced himself that liberation was at hand, and was on the point of initiating an uprising. Dunbabin went to deal with Bandouvas, while Paddy returned to his discussions with General Carta. Since it was now certain that there would be no Allied invasion of Crete and a German takeover of Italian positions looked inevitable, Carta wanted to be evacuated from the island. Paddy made the arrangements, and a motor launch was arranged to meet him and the General on the south coast at Treis Ekklisies.

On 10 September Bandouvas attacked and killed two Germans picking potatoes at Kato Symi; a third escaped to raise the alarm. This was followed up by the annihilation of the enemy garrisons of Ano Viannos and Arvi, and Bandouvas then pronounced a full-scale mobilization of the Heraklion area. This was immediately rescinded on his arrival by Dunbabin, who told Bandouvas to stop his attacks, but it was too late. Two days later a large detachment of Germans overran the area, determined to destroy the nest of andartes. Bandouvas and his men scattered into the hills, but not before killing a further twenty Germans and taking some prisoners.

The reluctance of the Italians to fight beside the Germans, the fear that they might join the Cretans and provoke an uprising, and now the attacks from Bandouvas, all persuaded General Müller that the time had come for exemplary punishment. Between 15 and 16 September, the Germans slashed through seven villages in the Viannos area. Every building was bombed, animals were driven away, fodder burnt, and over eight hundred and fifty people were taken hostage. Every house in every village was reduced to rubble, and over five hundred people were killed, including women and children.

Meanwhile the plan to evacuate General Carta and his staff was under way, though Tavana would not be of the party. He had elected to stay in Crete, to organize a fifth column among the Italians who were now fighting under German command He destroyed every document that could possibly be of use to Müller, and put all papers that might be of use to the Allies into a bulging satchel and gave it to Paddy. On no account, said Tavana, should General Carta be aware of the satchel: it should be given, in secret, to the captain of the motor launch who could pass it on to Allied HQ. To lay a false trail, Tavana took the General's car and abandoned it near an inlet where a submarine might have surfaced.

On 16 September, General Carta and his staff were smuggled out of Neapolis. They made their way south-west to Tzermiado, where they met up with Paddy, Manoli Paterakis and Grigori Khnarakis, a long-serving member of the resistance who knew the Lasithi and Viannos regions very well. The march took three days, spurred on by swigs of Triple Sec from the General's water bottle. As well as entertaining Paddy with anecdotes about high life in Rome and Paris, 'he is informative and entertaining about Bräuer and Müller and German officers in general, and he gets on with all the mountain folk.'[38]

They were woken on the first morning of their march to the

coast by a Fieseler Storch reconnaissance plane, dropping leaflets. Manoli picked one up, and handed it to the General. 'The Italian General Carta, together with some officers of his staff, has fled to the mountains, probably with the intention of escaping the island. FOR HIS CAPTURE, DEAD OR ALIVE, IS OFFERED THE REWARD OF THIRTY MILLION DRACHMAS.' The General waved it about with glee, exclaiming, 'Thirty pieces of silver! It's a contract of Judas!'[39]

Having successfully avoided a number of German search parties they reached the sheepfold above Tsoutsouros on 21 September, and walked down to the beach the following night. Here they found Tom Dunbabin and Manoli Bandouvas, with about forty of his men. Forced westwards by the Germans, Bandouvas was now hoping that the launch that was coming for the General would take him and his entourage off the island too.*

General Carta and Kapetan Bandouvas sat peacefully playing cards while waiting for the motor launch, which appeared in the early morning of 24 September. The wind had risen and there was a choppy swell on the water. A rubber dinghy was lowered to bring the new arrivals to the island: Father John Skoulas of Anoyeia, known as the Parachute Priest, and Captain Alexander (Sandy) Rendel and his wireless operator who were to set up in the Lasithi sector. The sea was so rough that Rendel's briefcase and the recharger for the wireless set were swept overboard. Once they had landed General Carta boarded the dinghy, followed by Paddy and Manoli Paterakis. Ostensibly they wanted to see the General safely on board, but Paddy also had to deliver Lieutenant Tavana's satchel full of documents to the skipper, Bob Young.

The handover did not take long; but by the time Paddy and Manoli were ready to leave, the sea had turned so rough that Bob Young decided it was too risky to take them back. Without warning and without goodbyes, Paddy wrote, 'We were heading full tilt to Africa. Everything had changed.'[40]

---

* As things turned out, Bandouvas did not get off the island until the end of October, by which time he had fought the Germans again at Mt Tsilivdikas: see N. A. Kokonas, *The Cretan Resistance 1941–1945* (Rethymnon, 1992), p.181.

9

Setting the Trap

When the boat reached Mersa Matruh on the Egyptian coast, Paddy and Manoli, together with the General and his entourage, were taken back to Cairo to be debriefed. From there they went their separate ways. Paddy hurried towards the centre of Cairo and the bright lights while Manoli, eager for news of what was happening in Greece, headed for the villa in Heliopolis that had been set aside for the use of Greeks and Cretans working for SOE. In urban areas all over Greece, people depended on the distribution of food coming in from the villages, but since the occupiers were more interested in stripping the country for their own use than feeding the inhabitants, town and city dwellers were living on the edge of starvation and thousands died of malnutrition: and 'the acute shortage of food . . . created the conditions for widespread political mobilization.'[1]

The organization that harnessed these new political forces most effectively was the Communist-dominated EAM and, from December 1941, its military wing, ELAS (the National Popular Liberation Army). It demanded absolute loyalty, any failure of which invited a swift and bloody retribution. But its Robin Hood tactics, particularly evident in the early days of its existence, won growing support in both urban and rural areas. Bands of ELAS andartes would raid government warehouses and distribute the contents, while tax offices were burnt down and tax collectors attacked. At a time when inflation was soaring and barter was almost the only means of survival, EAM/ELAS kept roads safe and protected the peasants from bandits (though they were quite capable of banditry themselves). There were also two much smaller non-Communist resistance formations operating within Greece,

EDES and EKKA;* but they stood little chance against the power of EAM/ELAS which, with its formidable organization, became 'a state within a state of chaos'.[2]

In July 1943, a delegation representing each of the three main resistance parties in mainland Greece had come to Cairo. The delegation's arrival had been arranged by SOE, and was supposed to be secret, but since its members stayed in Cairo for two months, it did not remain so for long. Each of the parties had one representative, except the Communists who had three.

These men had not come, as Monty Woodhouse put it, 'for a friendly chat and a pat on the back'.[3] They had come to demand that the King should not return to Greece without a plebiscite, and that their appointees should hold the key posts in the post-war government. They saw themselves as the political leaders of occupied Greece, claiming an authority that put everyone off-balance. The British, the Greek king and his government-in-exile 'simply could not understand that the overwhelming majority of those who were prepared to engage in active resistance were not prepared to do so on behalf of what they saw as a discredited monarchy and political system'.[4] The result was that the delegation went back empty-handed, and the one opportunity to bridge the gap between the government-in-exile and the bulk of the population in occupied Greece was lost.

The other worry for SOE was that now the Allied high command had decided to strike enemy-occupied Europe through Sicily rather than the Balkans, resistance operations in Greece were going to be scaled down if not put on ice. Cairo expected the resistance groups to go to ground obediently, and hold themselves in readiness to attack the Germans again when the time came for their withdrawal. Yet the urgent political demands of the delegation, and their barely concealed rivalries, revealed all too clearly that before long the Greek resistance groups would start fighting each other.

Paddy lost no time celebrating his unexpected leave, but he had much to think about. The successful evacuation of General Carta

---

* EDES: National Republican Greek League. EKKA: National and Social Liberation.

now prompted him to consider the idea of kidnapping a German general: and not just any general but the hated Müller, responsible for the butchery of the Viannos villages earlier that month. Supposing he were kidnapped and whisked off the island? At a time when Greece was beginning to feel like a backwater as the war pushed up through Italy, an operation of this kind would generate a lot of noise and publicity: it would make the Germans look remarkably foolish, and give a terrific boost to Cretan morale.

He had arrived in Cairo with fifteen months' worth of back pay to his credit. But the cost of living in Cairo had risen sharply now that the desert war was effectively over, and GHQ was swollen by an influx of officers supporting their war-substantive ranks with desk jobs. In the endless round of pleasure, Paddy was always happy to spend the dregs of a night on someone's sofa; but at the same time, he did rather hanker for a room of his own.

Through Amy and Walter Smart at the Embassy Paddy had met Countess Sophie Tarnowska, a beautiful Polish woman who founded the Cairo branch of the Polish Red Cross. She had married her kinsman Andrew Tarnowski, but this marriage was almost over by the time she and her sister Chouquette escaped from Poland. When Paddy saw Sophie again, she introduced him to the man she had fallen in love with: a tall young officer in the Coldstream Guards by the name of William Stanley Moss.

So far, the war had been good to Billy Moss. When just out of Sandhurst, he had had a spell guarding Rudolf Hess. He had met and dined with Churchill at Chequers, and been part of the victorious army that chased the Germans out of Africa after the breakout at El Alamein. Back in Cairo, he had found himself a desk job in SOE. The work was hardly exciting, but he was well placed to listen out for anyone recruiting volunteers for secret missions.

Billy too was looking for lodgings. When he heard that there was a palatial villa on Gezira Island for rent, large enough to include a garden and a ballroom, he seized the opportunity and set about filling it with congenial fellow-lodgers. Sophie Tarnowska was to become the presiding muse of the house, and to protect her reputation they invented a sad lodger called Mrs Khayatt, who was in very poor health and rarely left her room. Then came Arnold Breene, 'a rubicund and youthful Pickwick'[5] who worked in SOE, followed by Paddy. The last to join the group were Billy Maclean of the Scots Greys, and his second-in-command, David Smiley of the Blues. They had been in the wilds of Albania since April, and moved in to the villa at the end of October.

The villa was christened Tara, after the legendary seat of the high kings of Ireland. The place became notorious for its wild parties, sometimes fuelled by a lethal cocktail of prunes marinaded in raw alcohol (bought cheap at the local garage), which was mixed in large quantities in the bath. On one particularly rowdy night, all the glasses in the house were smashed. Then Andrew Tarnowski, Sophie's ex-husband, picked up a vase of flowers and threw it through the biggest window in the ballroom. That autumn, the young warriors of Tara were bathed in a dangerous glamour that no other Cairene coterie could emulate. They were invited everywhere, and to be seen at their parties was to be part of a charmed circle.

Everyone at Tara talked about everything they had ever read, seen or done, and everyone they had ever known – though never about their post-war plans: that seemed to be tempting fate. Paddy talked more than most, yet David Smiley noticed that when others spoke of parents and home, he talked of Rumania, Balasha and Băleni; he seldom mentioned his immediate family. Paddy was also a serious fire hazard. Unless he fell asleep in the arms of his girlfriend Denise Menasce, he had a dangerous habit of dozing off with a lighted cigarette in his hands. One night he burst into Billy's room in a panic, having set the sitting-room sofa ablaze.

Paddy had first outlined his plan to kidnap General Müller to Jack Smith-Hughes, of SOE's Cretan desk. Smith-Hughes reacted positively to the idea, as did his commander, Brigadier K. V. Barker-Benfield. He was given the go-ahead, promoted to the rank of Major and told to put together a team. His instinctive choice for the job of second-in-command was Xan Fielding, but two things made that impossible. The first was that Xan was in Crete, doing other things. And while Xan was small and dark enough to pass for a Cretan, he would never make a convincing German. Whoever was chosen must look obviously Aryan, and it was essential that he should know how to handle a car. At the same time, Paddy knew that he had to have someone he could get on with; friction or rivalry would become unendurable once the mission was under way.

Paddy had already approached two different people for the post of second-in-command. It was only after they had both turned down the opportunity that he offered the job to Billy Moss, who accepted with alacrity. He was tall, blond, an excellent driver, easy company, and he looked up to Paddy as a hero. From his Russian mother he had learned Russian, and he also knew a little French; but he knew not a word of German or Greek.

Everyone in Tara knew about their supposedly secret operation, and they often discussed ways and means. David Smiley recalled one morning in their steaming bathroom, where Paddy and Billy Moss, along with Billy Maclean, were shaving and bathing and padding about in towels. Smiley had considerable experience in staging an ambush involving moving vehicles. 'It's quite a technical business. You have to make sure that there's someone to warn the others when the party is coming, and you also have to have a covering party, in case there's a fight.' The most important thing to be considered was the point of attack. 'I remember drawing a rough map on the steamy bathroom wall, demonstrating how an assault should be sprung on a narrow bend in the road, and indicating where the warning and the covering party should be.'[6] Paddy went off for a parachute training course in Haifa, but he was back in Tara for Christmas – the highlight of which was a turkey stuffed with benzedrine.

Although SOE had given its backing to the plan, not everyone was convinced of its value. Bickham Sweet-Escott, one of SOE's most experienced executives, was in Cairo at the time. Just after Christmas 1943 he was asked whether or not the operation should go ahead.

> I made myself exceedingly unpopular by recommending as strongly as I could that we should not. I thought that if it succeeded, the only contribution to the war effort would be a fillip to Cretan morale, but that the price would certainly be heavy in Cretan lives. The sacrifice might possibly have been worthwhile in the black winter of 1941 when things were going badly. The result of carrying it out in 1944, when everyone knew that victory was merely a matter of months would, I thought, hardly justify the cost . . .[7]

Nevertheless the plan went ahead, and Paddy and Billy Moss were told to be ready to go on 6 January 1944. A car came to pick them up from Tara in the early hours of the morning, and drove them to Heliopolis to pick up Manoli and George Tyrakis. Manoli was tall and aquiline, with a jutting nose and chin and penetrating eyes; Tyrakis was a shorter and more cheerful figure, who proved to be a brilliant lyra player. They sat in the back, in high spirits at the thought of going home, singing Greek and Cretan songs – Paddy joining in at the top of his voice. The party was accompanied by a cargo of stores which included a consignment of Marlin guns and four thousand pounds' worth of gold sovereigns.

They flew to an airstrip east of Benghazi, where they spent two miserable weeks in sodden tents waiting for the weather to clear. Since it refused to oblige they were flown to Bari, hoping for better flying conditions there. On 4 February Paddy, Billy, Manoli and George took off from Brindisi for Crete, aiming for the Omalo plateau, a tiny shallow bowl in the jagged, snow-covered peaks in the mountains south of Neapolis. For the pilot, the zone was so restricted that the team could not be dropped in a 'stick' formation – he would have to circle and come in again four times, dropping each man off individually.

Snow and loose cloud swirled around the open bomb-bay, and far below they could see the dropping zone marked by three pinpricks of light formed by three signal fires. Paddy was the first to jump. Welcoming Cretan hands hauled him to his feet, and then all eyes turned again to the snow-streaked sky. Paddy gave the all-clear with a torch to signal his safe arrival, but the clouds were thickening and the pilot could no longer see the signal fires: he was forced to turn back.

Paddy spent the next seven weeks in a cave with Sandy Rendel, the SOE officer in charge of the Lasithi area, who took great pleasure in his company.

> Best of all was the singing. Paddy could sing folk songs in half a dozen languages, but mostly he would sing with the rest of us the local songs, in particular *Philedem*, the old Turkish tune which became a form of code-name for him with the Cretans. In fact, throughout

the . . . island they would refer to him as 'the *Philedem*' – as a
Highlander might speak of 'The Mackintosh'.[8]

A month later, after several attempts had been made to drop the
rest of the team, Paddy was told they would have to come in by
motor launch. Then, in late March, came news that threw the whole
mission into question. Their intended victim, General Müller, had
been posted to Chania to replace General Bräuer as commander of
Fortress Crete. In the face of this disappointment, 'All the delays
seemed, retrospectively, more bitter.'[9] SOE Cairo was informed, but
decided to go ahead with the operation anyway. After all, the aim
was to boost Cretan morale and damage German confidence; from
this standpoint, one general was as good as another. The new target,
who had succeeded to Müller's post in Heraklion, was General
Heinrich Kreipe. No one knew much about him, except that he
had just arrived from the Russian front.

Billy, Manoli and George finally reached Crete on 4 April, near
Tsoutsouros on the south coast. It was a happy reunion, but Paddy
was busy overseeing the unloading of stores and the stowing of four
German prisoners who were being taken back to Egypt. He seemed
a different person from the recklessly ebullient partygoer of Tara: 'I
saw him go off,' wrote Moss, 'and watched him as he gave orders,
commanded men to do this and that . . . he seemed to have the
whole situation at his finger-tips and was capable of coping with
anything.'[10]

They spent the rest of the night and next day near the beach,
and with the stores mounted on the backs of four mules, they began
the long march towards Heraklion. Trying to slip past the villages
on the road was impossible, since every dog in every yard began
barking. On these occasions Paddy enjoyed laying a false trail by
shouting orders in German, and singing 'Bomber über England', 'Lili
Marlene' or the 'Horst Wessel Lied'. This had the added advantage
of keeping the villagers safely in bed.

At Kastamonitza they were joined by two experienced resistance
men whom Paddy had worked with in the past: Antoni Papaleonidas
came from Asia Minor and had worked as a stevedore in Heraklion,
while Grigori Khnarakis had been involved in General Carta's

evacuation. Paddy had also summoned Micky Akoumianakis, who ran the intelligence network in Heraklion. He lived in Knossos, near the Villa Ariadne – which had been built for the archaeologist Sir Arthur Evans, and was now the residence of General Kreipe. Micky's father Manolaki, who had died fighting the Germans in 1941, had been Evans's overseer and Micky had known the villa all his life.

A long conference between Paddy, Billy and Micky followed, during which Micky was told the aim of the operation. So far, this was known to no one but the four core members of the team, others being told only when it became necessary. The effect, as Paddy described it, was always 'electric' – a gasp of astonishment at the sheer audacity of the plan, followed by excitement and apprehension in equal measures. While Billy, George and Manoli stayed in hiding Paddy and Micky took the bus to Heraklion.

Here Micky contacted Elias Athanasakis, a young student involved in the intelligence network, to help with the planning. Their first idea had been to abduct the General from the Villa Ariadne itself, but it was too well guarded. The only alternative was to set an ambush for his car. The General usually made two trips a day to his divisional headquarters at Ano Archanes, some five miles south of Knossos. After spending the morning at work he returned to the villa for lunch, and then set off to work again from about four till eight. Sometimes he stayed on to play a few rubbers of bridge with his staff, and on those evenings he would not get back to the villa till nine or ten.

The only possible abduction point was on the last stretch of the way from Archanes, where a downward slope would oblige the car to reduce speed before it joined the main road to Heraklion. Woody ground rose to one side, and there were plenty of hiding places among nearby rocks and bushes. Since it would be dark, it was vital not to miss the car. Elias undertook to study it closely, so that he could recognize the sound of its engine and the slits of light from its blacked-out headlamps. As soon as he saw the car leave Archanes he would bicycle hard to a point where an electric buzzer had been installed on a long wire, to signal the lookout on the higher ground. Three flashes from a torch from the lookout would tell the team to get into position.

'The risk of passing traffic still remained, possibly of trucks full of troops. Here we would have to trust to improvisation, luck, speed and darkness, and, if the worst happened, by a party of guerrillas – un-lethal bursts of fire, flares all over the place, shoutings, mule-carts and logs suddenly blocking the road to create confusion . . .'[11] Even if they succeeded in kidnapping the General, there was the prospect of having to drive the stolen car past the Villa Ariadne, and straight through the centre of Heraklion. This was the quickest way to get off the enemy-infested plain and into the hills.

To minimize the risk of reprisals, it was vital to convince the Germans that the abduction was planned by regular forces controlled from Cairo, and not the act of local 'brigands and terrorists'. To underline the point, Paddy would signal Cairo as soon as they were safely away. The BBC would then broadcast the abduction, and the RAF undertook to drop leaflets over the island.

Since the mission would have to take place at night, it was essential that the team, as well as the back-up force – to be provided by Athanasios Bourdzalis, a local kapetan – were well hidden in the vicinity. Micky found a house near the village of Skalani, close to a shallow gorge at the bottom of which was a dried-up river bed; it was owned by Pavlos Zographistos and his sister Anna, who were willing to shelter the main part of the team, while Bourdzalis and his men could hide in a cave the other side of the gorge. The house was about a half-hour walk over rocky fields to the abduction point.

Micky and Paddy then spent several days in Heraklion, studying the street plan and examining entrances and exits. Paddy took the opportunity to hold several meetings with resistance leaders, which were not directly concerned with the operation, and he made contact with the group that disseminated news from the BBC by hand. 'After months in the mountains,' he wrote, 'there was something bracing about these descents into the lion's den: the swastika flags everywhere, German conversation in one's ears and the constant rubbing shoulders with the enemy in the streets. The outside of Gestapo HQ,* particularly, which had meant the death of many friends, held a

---

* The interrogation and torture of suspicious Cretans was undertaken by the Geheime Feldpolizei, not the Gestapo, who were never in occupied Crete.

baleful fascination.'[12] Back in Knossos, they had another brush with the enemy. They were in the house of a friend when three tipsy German sergeants came in. Wine was produced, and Micky offered them a cigarette – from an English packet. Not missing a beat, he told them the cigarettes were black-market loot from the battle of the Dodecanese: 'A deluge of wine covered up this contretemps, followed by attempts, bearishly mimicked by our guests, to teach them to dance a Cretan *pentozali*.'[13]

Paddy, Micky and Elias all left Heraklion together and rejoined Billy and the others in the sheepfold above Kastamonitza on 16 April, Orthodox Easter Sunday. Four days later Bourdzalis arrived with his men. Manoli and George Tyrakis were very disparaging: the oldest had no teeth, the youngest had barely started shaving, and while they were all 'armed like lobsters' as the Cretans say, their guns were poor. Still, one could not fault their willingness. Refusing a meal, the party set off at once for what became a two nights' march to Skalani.

They reached the Zographistos house after dark, on 23 April. The surrounding fields were planted with vines, but well-used footpaths lay across the landscape like a web. The four main members of the group sheltered in the house, while Bourdzalis and his men walked further down the dry river bed to a small cave that contained a wine press. It was a squeeze, but the German presence in and around Heraklion was such that no one could afford to be seen in daylight.

Paddy and Billy composed the letter they planned to leave in the car. It was addressed to the German authorities in Crete, and dated 23 April 1944.

Gentlemen,

Your Divisional Commander, General Kreipe, was captured a short time ago by a BRITISH Raiding Force under our command. By the time you read this both he and we will be on our way to Cairo.

We would like to point out most emphatically that this operation has been carried out without the help of CRETANS or CRETAN partisans and the only guides used were serving soldiers of HIS HELLENIC MAJESTY'S FORCES in the Middle East, who came with us.

Your General is an honourable prisoner of war and will be treated with all the consideration owing to his rank. Any reprisals against the local population will thus be wholly unwarranted and unjust.

Auf baldiges Wiedersehen!

PM Leigh Fermor, Maj., O.C. Commando

CW Stanley Moss, Capt 2/i.c.

P.S. We are very sorry to have to leave this beautiful motor car behind.

Seals from their signet rings gave the final touch to what Paddy hoped would be seen as a very British production.

Micky Akoumianakis arrived from Heraklion with two German uniforms, lance corporal's stripes, and a traffic policeman's paddle with a red and white tin disc. Paddy had just shaved off his moustache and Micky was photographing them in the uniforms, when suddenly four Germans were seen approaching the house. Paddy and Billy waited, their Colt pistols drawn, but the soldiers were only trying to scrounge some food from Pavlos's sister. She was an anxious woman, and this brush with the enemy did nothing to steady her nerves.

More men were brought in to reinforce the ambush team. Niko Komis from Thrapsano and Mitzo Tzatzas of Episkopi were both quiet mountain men, who had acted as guides on the way to Skalani. Strati Saviolakis was a policeman from Annapolis in Sphakia. In his uniform, he could provide a good smokescreen while the party made its getaway. They also took on a young man called Yanni, who would guide them to Anoyeia.

The ambush was to have taken place on 23 April, but on that day the General returned to Knossos earlier than usual. Then Strati the policeman reported that some of Bourdzalis's men, stiff from being cooped up in the wine-press cave, had come out to stretch their legs, and news of their presence was spreading. Reluctantly, Paddy had to tell Bourdzalis to take his men home. Having lost his back-up, he was delighted when an experienced resistance fighter called Antoni Ziodakis appeared out of the dark that night. Ziodakis was an old friend whom Micky had found in Heraklion, and he and Paddy talked and smoked till dawn.

The team moved out of the house on the 24th (Anna had decided their presence was too dangerous) and into the shelter of a clump of plane trees at the bottom of the steep-sided river bed. There were rumours of large German patrols sweeping the area, and no one dared move. Even more alarming was the letter from the local head of EAM, the Communist resistance, addressed to Paddy in person as 'Mihali'. The letter hinted that EAM knew where the team was hiding, and threatened to turn them over to the 'authorities' if they did not remove themselves, for they posed a serious danger to the area. 'I sent back a quieting and ambiguous answer,' wrote Paddy, 'hoping the guerrillas' departure [i.e. Bourdzalis and his men] would lend colour to the words.'[14] Paddy hoped above all that the abduction would take place that night, but the General spent the whole day in his villa. The plotters grew anxious, since with every passing day more people knew of their whereabouts.

The following day, the 26th, the General was driven to his head-quarters at Archanes at the usual time. Billy and Paddy changed into their German uniforms at dusk. Manoli, George and the others took their Marlin guns, and together they set off across the fields, arriving at the abduction point at about eight in the evening. It was the first time that Billy had been there, and he noticed at once that the pitch of the road as it approached the junction was much steeper than he had expected. If the driver used the footbrake rather than handbrake to stop the car, it might be in danger of rolling away as its occupants were hauled out – but it was too late to do anything about it now.

10

The Hussar Stunt

Hidden among the rocks and bushes were Manoli and George, Paddy and Billy in their German uniforms, and Micky Akoumianakis. Meanwhile Mitzo and Strati climbed on to the bank, ready to receive the signal the moment the General's car had left Archanes and was on its way back to the villa. 'During the hour and a half of our vigil a few German trucks and cars drove past at intervals . . . very close to us, all coming from the south and heading for Heraklion, nothing from the minor Archanes side road. Nice and quiet; but time seemed to pass with exasperating slowness . . . On the tick of 9.30, Mitzo's torch flashed clearly three times.'[1]

The General later admitted to Billy that he had always felt rather uneasy about that junction; that if anything were to happen to him in Crete, he felt it would happen there. So perhaps it was reassuring to see two corporals in field grey step out of the darkness. He did not have time to notice the odd details of their uniforms that would have given them away instantly in daylight: the commando daggers, and Billy's puttees, which had not been worn in the well-booted German army since the First World War.

Billy waved his disc and I moved my red torch to and fro and shouted '*Halt!*' The car came to a standstill and we stepped right and left out of the beams of the headlights, which, in spite of being partly blacked out, were still very bright, and walked slowly, each to his appointed door . . . I saluted and said '*Papier, bitte schön.*' The General, with an officer-to-man smile, reached for his breast-pocket, and I opened the door with a jerk – (this was the cue for the rest of the party to break cover) – and the inside of the car was immediately flooded with light. Then I shouted '*Hande hoch!*' and with one hand thrust my automatic against the General's chest – there was a gasp of surprise – flinging the other round his body, and pulling him out of the car.[2]

More men poured out of the darkness. Armed with coshes and guns, Manoli, Grigori and Antoni Papaleonidas helped Paddy to restrain the General, who was shouting, swearing and lashing out for all he was worth. Handcuffs were forced on to his wrists and he was shoved into the back of the car. Meanwhile, Billy had yanked open the door on the driver's side. The driver, Alfred Fenske, reached for the Luger at his belt. Billy struck him on the head with a cosh which knocked him out, and he was pulled from the car and dragged to the side of the road. Billy moved swiftly into the driver's seat. The engine was still running, the handbrake was on, the fuel gauge indicated that the tank was almost full – and Paddy was sitting beside him, wearing the General's hat. In the back of the car, General Kreipe was firmly wedged between Manoli, Strati and George Tyrakis, who held a knife to his throat.

It was a moment of pure elation, with the kidnappers laughing and shouting and slapping each other on the back, while Micky leant through the window, cursing Germany and the General in a frenzy of pent-up hatred. Seeing the inside of the car still lit up like a beacon, Paddy smashed out the bulb with his pistol butt, and they set off towards Heraklion. Elias and Micky were left to remove all traces of the operation. Grigori, the two Antonis and Niko, who were in charge of the driver, set off across country more slowly than they had hoped: Alfred Fenske had regained consciousness, but still needed support when walking. They would meet up with the rest of the team on the slopes of Mount Ida in two days' time.

In the car, Paddy addressed the General in German. 'Herr General, I am a British major. Beside me is a British captain. These men are Greek patriots. I am in command of this unit, and you are an honourable prisoner of war. We are taking you to Egypt.'[3] This came as a relief to the General, as did the assurance that he would eventually get his hat back, but he was astonished to hear that they proposed to drive him straight through the centre of Heraklion. For this part of the journey, the General was ordered to crouch down in the well between the front and back seats: he still had George's knife at his throat, and as the checkpoints came up, hands were clamped over his mouth.

Billy drove through no less than twenty-two German checkpoints. Two factors tipped the odds in their favour. General Kreipe did not like checkpoints and used to growl at sentries who kept him waiting, so when they saw his car with its two unmistakable metal pennants they tended to wave him through. The blackout also came in handy. Although the streets were crowded with Germans, everyone looked like shadows; only odd chinks of light escaped from doors and windows. Billy 'calmly and methodically hooted his way through the mob . . . collecting many salutes as the soldiers cleared out of the way'.[4] To anyone peering in, the back of the car would have been impenetrably dark. In the front, Paddy made sure that the General's hat with its gold braid was visible, and not his face. The last checkpoint at the Chania Gate was heavily defended, and it looked as if the sentry with the red torch meant business. Billy slowed down smoothly, giving the guards enough time to recognize the Opel. The barrier was still down; but as Paddy barked, '*Generals Wagen!*' Billy began to accelerate, and the barrier came up just in time. It worked like a charm.

As soon as they were out of Heraklion and on to the coast road, a mood of riotous jubilation broke out in the car. Paddy also took the opportunity to introduce Billy, George, Manoli and Strati to the General, 'and for a moment the four figures behind all seemed to be formally bowing to each other'.[5] A little further on, the General said, 'Tell me, Major, what is the object of this hussar-stunt?'[6] Even Paddy had to admit that there was no easy answer to that question.

At Yeni Gave (now Drosia), Billy stopped the car. The handcuffs were taken off the General's wrists, and he was asked to give his word not to try and escape – which, rather to Paddy's surprise, he did. But when the General saw him getting back in the car, he had a moment of panic. 'You are going to leave me alone with these . . . people?'[7] Knowing how most Cretans felt about the Germans he did not trust andartes to follow the Geneva conventions, even though his countrymen had hardly set a good example. Paddy reassured him that he would be well looked after, and got into the car with George.

Paddy had learnt the rudiments of driving, but he was happier with horses than he was with cars. The Opel jerked forward in low gear, and he managed to drive it to the top of the track that ran past the hamlet of Heliana to the submarine bay that looked on to the tiny island of Peristeri. The car was left prominently on the road, with its accompanying letter. Paddy and George kicked up the track, scattered a chocolate wrapper, a cigarette tin and a few more butts, and before leaving, broke off the car's two metal pennants that had served them so well. Then, under a new moon, they set off to walk to Anoyeia.

Anoyeia, well known as a centre of defiant resistance, had been united under the leadership of Stefanoyanni Dramoundanis. Shortly after Paddy had stood godfather to his daughter, the Germans had encircled the village and caught him. With his hands tied, Dramoundanis jumped over a wall and tried to escape, only to be shot in the back by the enemy. Normally, Paddy would have been welcomed; but since he was still in the uniform of a German corporal, he was given a taste of the Anoyeians' hatred for the occupiers. Doors and shutters slammed, while the warnings rang out from house to house: 'The black sheep are in the wheat!' – 'Our inlaws have arrived!' At the café the old men fell silent, pointedly turning their backs. He did not reveal himself till he found the wife of the priest, Father Charetis, who was terrified. 'It's me, Pappadia!' he whispered. 'It's me, Mihali!' – 'Mihali? I don't know any Mihali!' she cried, backing away. She finally recognized him by the gap between his front teeth, and hustled him and George into the house.

Paddy's godbrother George Dramoundanis soon arrived, along with Father Charetis, and couriers were found to take messages to Sandy Rendel to the east, and to Tom Dunbabin, who was the other side of Mount Ida. It was a matter of vital urgency to get news of the abduction to Cairo, so that the BBC could broadcast the announcement and the RAF drop leaflets.

Meanwhile Billy and Manoli, guided by Strati, had brought the General within sight of Anoyeia though they could not risk entering the village. It had been a long night. They had found no water till 3 a.m., and the General moved slowly – his leg had been badly hurt, he said, as he was dragged from the car. He was also very hungry, having had no lunch: yet what upset him most was the loss of his Knight's Cross, won in the push against Leningrad on the Russian front. Strati went up to the village and made contact with Paddy, and returned with a basket of food and wine. The kidnappers had to scramble up to a small cave with the General when they heard that Germans were in the village, a warning no doubt set off by Paddy in his corporal's uniform.

A Fieseler Storch plane dropped a stream of leaflets at about 5.30 p.m. They were hastily printed in Greek, and told the Cretans that if General Kreipe were not returned within three days, 'all rebel villages in the Heraklion District will be razed to the ground and the severest measures of reprisal will be brought to bear on the civilian population'.[8]

In Anoyeia, Paddy was still at the priest's house when the leaflets fluttered down. 'The room was convulsed with incredulity, then excitement and finally by an excess of triumphant hilarity. We could hear feet running in the street, and shouts and laughter.' Paddy does not say so, but the news must have been received with anxiety too: the enemy's threats were very real. 'I seemed to be the only one in the room undisturbed by the German threat,' wrote Paddy, such was his faith in the RAF leaflets and the BBC news, which would soon be reporting the General's evacuation from the island. '"And you'll see!" he told the villagers. "Those three days will go by and there won't be any villages burnt or even shooting!"'[9] An old man in the room reassured him that they were willing to make the sacrifice. As a Cretan proverb put it, 'You can't have a wedding feast without meat.'

Paddy joined Billy and the General at sunset, and they set off on the long climb up Mount Ida. All were on foot but for the General, who rode a mule and wore Strati's greatcoat against the cold. In the small hours, they took shelter in a conical shepherd's hut: Paddy and Billy had not slept since the operation began. It was still dark when they got going again, and before long they were hailed by a lookout from a rocky ledge above. They had reached the hideout of Mihali Xylouris, one of the best and most reliable resistance leaders in Crete who had taken over as kapetan from the brave Dramoundanis. He was surrounded by armed Cretans, and three SOE operatives: John

Houseman, John Lewis, and Tom Dunbabin's wireless operator, who had the set nearby.

It was a day of disappointments. After an hour of trying to send the coded message, the operator discovered that the wireless set was irreparably broken. There were two other stations on the island, but only Tom Dunbabin knew where they were and he seemed to have vanished. They now sent a fresh flurry of appeals: to Sandy Rendel again, to Dick Barnes on the north coast, in charge of the Rethymno area, and to Ralph Stockbridge. They must contact Cairo immediately and ask for a motor launch to meet the abduction party on 2 May, which would give them six days to cross the island. If contact were not made on the 2nd, the launch should be prepared to stand by for the following four nights. The Germans were out in force, looking for the General: there were reports of troop movements in several places, while columns of dust were heading towards Mount Ida.

More bad news was brought by the two Antonis and Grigori, who had been responsible for escorting the General's driver. From the outset, Alfred Fenske was so badly concussed that he could scarcely walk; and when truckloads of Germans started moving in open order across the landscape, his abductors realized they had no choice but to kill him. The enemy were too close to risk a shot, so – Antoni Ziodakis made a slicing gesture across his throat. Deeply shaken, Paddy feared that Fenske's death had cursed the whole enterprise. As for the General, he was never informed. When he asked what had happened to his driver, he was told that Fenske was ill but was being looked after in hiding.[*]

Paddy, Billy and the General shared a blanket that night, with Manoli and George on either side, nursing their guns and taking it in turn to sleep. They had hoped to have additional clothes and blankets delivered by Pavlos Zographistos, who had undertaken to

---

[*] Years later, Alfred Fenske's son Manfred came to Crete to learn more about his father's end. He was accompanied by Annette Windgasse, who wrote to Paddy about the visit. 'I have heard', she wrote, 'that you have been worried about the driver's death. And, though there have been sad moments for his son to face the place where his father died, he accepted this as a consequence of the war and feels in peace with you.' (Annette Windgasse to PLF, Wuppertal, 15 July 2008.)

bring up the rest of their kit; but they never saw him or the kit again. No one slept well that night, and as dawn broke and the sun illuminated the great snow-streaked hump of Mount Ida, the General murmured a line in Latin: '*Vides ut alta stet nive candidum Soracte . . .*'

It was one of the few Odes of Horace that Paddy knew by heart, and which he had translated at school. Taking up where the General had left off, he went on to the end of the poem.

> The General's blue eyes swivelled away from the mountain-top to mine – and when I'd finished, after a long silence, he said: '*Ach so, Herr Major!*' It was very strange. '*Ja, Herr General.*' As though, for a long moment, the war had ceased to exist. We had both drunk at the same fountains long before; and things were different between us for the rest of our time together.[10]

This was one of the defining moments of Paddy's war, the one he was most fond of recalling in interviews. In *A Time of Gifts* and 'Abducting a General',* Paddy sets the scene in the cave of Mihali Xylouris. From this area, honeycombed with caves, the rising sun in spring strikes Mount Ida at a breathtaking angle. On a later occasion, however, Paddy said he had only used Xylouris's cave for convenience: the event had actually taken place in a cave near Aghios Ioannis in the Amari.

Climbing ever higher, they left the protection of Mihali Xylouris and, in a few hours, a friendly shout told them they were now in the territory of Kapetan Petrakogeorgis. Here they were given food and guides, as well as news of considerable enemy activity. The Germans had not fallen for the story that the General had been evacuated by submarine. They thought it far more likely that the abductors were holding him in the mountains, and that their goal was the south coast. German patrols were pouring into the southern foothills to cut them off. Yet for all their strength the enemy clung

---

* 'Abducting a General' was commissioned by the historian Barrie Pitt for a part-work called *The Purnell History of the Second World War* (1967–8), see Vol. 5, No. 7. But what should have been an article of 5,000 words turned into an account of 36,000 words, most of which remains unpublished. The full story is told in Chapter 19.

to well-known trails, and never ventured far into the mountains where they knew andarte snipers lay in wait.

Antoni Ziodakis left the team and went on ahead; he planned to cross the watershed and find a place on the southern slope where they could all meet up, somewhere near the village of Nithavri. With the Germans busy making a cordon round Mount Ida, it would not be easy. Antoni was accompanied by two runners to take messages back to the main party, and it was agreed that bonfires would be used to guide the team to the rendezvous.

When the rest of the team set off again, it was dark and the way became considerably steeper. The General's mule had to be sent back, and the party had to continue on foot 'up a slippery and collapsing staircase of loose boulders and shale and scree'.[11] The General made the ascent with agonizing slowness, having to stop every ten minutes. Billy and Paddy thought he was doing well, for he did not complain and had he refused to go on, things might have been considerably harder. The Cretans, however, thought he was dragging his feet. Perhaps they expected too much, accustomed as they were to the wiry agility of their own fathers; but they did little to hide their ill-feeling. Except for Manoli, the General stayed out of their way. He sensed that if anything happened to Paddy or Billy, there were others in the party who would happily slit his throat or push him down a crevasse.

For Kreipe, being on the other side of the occupation was an eye-opener. He had had no idea that the Cretans and the British were working so closely together, and he was appalled by how many of his captors had German papers, giving them permission to travel about. When George Tyrakis wanted to go and see his parents in Phourphoura and asked if anyone could lend him an identity pass, two or three were immediately produced. The incident was recorded by Giorgios Phrangoulitakis (known as Skoutello, or Scuttlegeorge), who joined the team in early May and later wrote his war memoirs: 'The General turned to Lifermos and said, "Have they all got our identity papers? See what people we have to deal with!" Lifermos translated it to us and we all laughed.'[12]

The trees thinned out and vanished altogether. As they crossed the saddle of Mount Ida, 'mist surrounded us and rain began to fall.

We stumbled on, bent almost double against the blast . . .' The descent, as steep as a ladder in places, was even worse. 'It was appalling going for everyone; for the General, in spite of our help, it must have been an excruciation. There was not a glimmer of Antoni's guiding fires in the dark void below.'[13]

They took shelter in a cave, which proved to be 'a measureless natural cavern that warrened and forked deep into the rocks, and then dropped, storey after storey to lightless and nearly airless stallactitic dungeons littered with the horned skeletons of beasts which had fallen there and starved to death in past centuries . . .'[14] Billy was sure it must be the legendary cave supposed to be the childhood home of Zeus, and it says much for his energy and Paddy's that they ventured to explore it at all. Since they had left Petrakogeorgis they had eaten nothing but a little bread and cheese given them by a friendly shepherd, and since then nothing but wild herbs. It was the last day of April. On that night, and the one after, the BBC announced that General Kreipe had been captured and 'is being taken off the island'. Considering their circumstances, a past tense would have been more helpful. The RAF leaflets, which Paddy was waiting for so eagerly, never materialized.

The kidnappers were hiding in the cave when they received a message from Antoni: 'In God's Name come tonight.' They set off after dark, hoping the thick mist and pouring rain would keep them hidden since there was no hope of seeing any fire. On reaching the rendezvous, they found no sign of Antoni. After several anxious hours, they pulled out the message again. A second reading revealed, 'In God's Name *don't* come tonight.'[15] They spent the day in a ditch about half an hour from the village of Aghia Paraskevi, with the rain still pouring down. George went to the village and fetched Antoni, who could not believe what they had done: against all the odds, they had somehow stumbled through the German lines in the dark. George and Antoni returned to the group, carrying a huge basket of much-needed food and wine.

They were now in the Amari: a valley high above sea level, contained by the slopes of Mount Kedros to the west and Mount Ida to the east. Along the valley lay a string of villages, known for their loyalty to the resistance. All of them had provided clothes, food and hiding places to Allied soldiers after the Battle of Crete, and now did the same for the kidnappers. There was some good news: no villages had been burnt, even though more than three days had passed since the abduction. On the afternoon of 2 May a German plane came over, dropping leaflets. 'It had now been ascertained, we read, that the kidnapping was the work of "hired tools of the treacherous British and the Bolsheviks. Those who were responsible would be mercilessly hunted down and destroyed." '[16] This was a terrific relief to Paddy, for it seemed to exonerate the Cretans from having taken part in the abduction.

The enemy were everywhere, although reports of their positions and strength were shifting and contradictory. Messengers brought news that German troops were swarming around the lower folds of Mount Ida, calling 'Kreipe! Kreipe!' as they went. The team did not tell the General how close his compatriots were, in case he tried to make a break for it: he was feeling very downcast at the thought that they were making almost no effort to find him. Paddy and Billy still had no idea what had happened to the messages they had sent from Xylouris's cave, asking for a motor launch for their evacuation. If only they could find Tom Dunbabin, he could put them in touch with the other wireless stations.

Tom later claimed that, having sent his set and operator to Paddy at Xylouris's cave, he went down with an attack of malaria and was obliged to lie low till he had recovered. Paddy had his doubts. Though kept informed, Dunbabin had not been party to the plan when it was hatched in Cairo; it was not necessarily an escapade he would have approved of, and as head of station he might have stopped it. Yet he did not, and later wrote a report that expressed no reservations about its success. But while that success still hung in the balance, Paddy had the feeling that Tom did not want to be too closely identified with the abduction.

Yet if the messages had got through and the launch were preparing to meet them on 2 May, then it could already be lying to off the coast. It might still be possible to evacuate the General. The night of 2 May was hard to bear. Everyone lay awake in an agony of suppressed excitement, hoping against hope that a messenger would arrive to say that the launch was waiting.

No runner came, and by the next day it was too late. A force of two hundred Germans had moved into Saktouria. The beach was now unusable, and their way to the south coast was blocked. Billy Moss and Paterakis were once more left to guard the General, while Paddy and Tyrakis set off to try and locate another wireless and gather information about other possible beaches. They spent the first night in George's village of Phourphoura. No sooner had Paddy and George left than Billy received two messages: one from Dick Barnes, the other from Sandy Rendel. The launch would indeed be there for the next four nights, though it seemed increasingly unlikely that the party would be able to reach the south coast in safety.

Paddy and George headed northwards through the Amari valley. Being able to move freely in bright sunshine made everything look better, but their cheerful mood did not last. On 4 May, at about noon, the Amari valley shook with a noise like distant thunder as four villages were razed to the ground. The following day, an announcement appeared in the German-controlled news-paper *Paratiritis*, listing a series of 'crimes' that had unleashed this punishment:

> The brazen and criminal deeds of the outdoor bandits who abducted and spirited away General Kreipe brought about the inevitable meas-ures against these elements; elements guilty of illegal activities against the security of the occupation forces and the general peace of the area . . . Especial severity has been brought to bear on three moun-tain regions in the Heraklion area . . . The villages of Lochria, Kamares and Margarikari were surrounded by German troops on 3 May 1944 and emptied in the course of a large-scale operation waged against the bandits of Mount Ida. After the evacuation of the villagers the villages themselves were razed to the ground.

Reasons for the destruction were given in detail. These villages had 'adopted a treacherous posture' to the occupying forces, and had given food, shelter and every possible help to the 'bandits' Petrakogeorgis, Bandouvas and other andartes. Not only that, but the villagers had turned out in force for the funeral of Petrakogeorgis's mother. This showed that the Germans had plenty of other grudges against these villages, apart from the abduction. Yet the Kreipe

Operation was so theatrical, so celebrated both in Crete and abroad, that many saw it as the chief cause for the reprisals.

While Paddy was trying to make contact with Dick Barnes and his wireless station, the presence of more and more Germans in the area forced the General's captors to move on. In Patsos they found shelter in a stone-walled hut, surrounded by trees and built against the side of a cliff. The place belonged to the Haracopos family, who gave them food and wine in abundance though they were far from rich. They had a son, George, who spoke a little English and was involved in the resistance: he wanted to go to Cairo, so as to train and join the Greek brigades in Egypt.

On 8 May a message arrived from Paddy. A contingent of Raiding Forces, under George Jellicoe, was due to land on the Saktouria beach to contact the abductors and, if necessary, help them to fight their way off the island. Paddy had signalled Cairo to say that this force had to be stopped at all costs, for Saktouria was now held by a strong enemy force.

Paddy joined Billy the following night, and next morning came a message to say that the raiding party had been postponed. Their communications with Cairo were now re-established, and the runners – particularly George Psychoundakis – were covering huge distances to bring the messages while their news was still fresh. Yet they still had to find an isolated beach, at a time when the Germans were reinforcing the south coast with more and more men. Psychoundakis contacted a friend, who undertook to find a cove free of Germans. For the moment, all they could do was to stay out of sight and move westwards.

Before leaving Patsos, Paddy approached their host, Efthymios Haracopos, and tried to give him some money. The family had been more than generous, and Paddy was taking his only son to Egypt. The General, who had been watching this scene, was impressed by the way the old man flatly refused payment. Over the days of his captivity he had seen how the Cretans treated the British as friends, while they loathed the Germans. The contrast had come as a revelation.

They set off in good spirits, with a mule for the General. They were marching to the village of Photineou when the beast lost its footing and the General was sent tumbling down a steep precipice. He was in considerable pain, and his captors thought he had damaged a shoulder blade. A sling was arranged, which he kept on for the rest of the journey. The cumulative strain of the past week was beginning to tell on some of the others too. Antoni Ziodakis was doubled up with sciatica, while Paddy was beginning to experience a numbness and tingling in his right arm.

As they approached the south coast they were under the protection of Yanni Katsias, who had returned to Crete on the same boat as Billy, Manoli and George in April. He had a fearsome reputation as a bandit, murderer, and veteran of innumerable vendettas, and was accompanied by two of the shiftiest-looking sheep rustlers the party had ever seen. According to Billy, 'they moved with such swift silence, such uncanny goat-footed agility, that they appear to do a job which would normally occupy a dozen scouts.'[17]

By 11 May the team were outside the village of Vilandredo, a few hours north of Rodakino beach, which – so far – remained undefended. Their hideout was a cave 'that clung to the mountainside like a martin's nest', as Paddy put it.[18] The last hour of the climb was particularly hard going: they had to scramble to a point above the cave, and then let themselves down, clinging on to trees and creepers, till their feet found the narrow ledge. Here they were given a wild welcome by Paddy's godbrother, Stathi Loukakis (during his first months on Crete he and Xan had baptized Anglia, his little daughter) and his brother Stavro. Dennis Ciclitira, who had replaced Xan, was asleep nearby, and his wireless set was a few miles away at Asi Gonia. They got to work at once, writing signals and planning the next stage. With a deserted beach and a functioning wireless nearby, the operation might succeed after all.

Dennis left the next morning for Asi Gonia, to send the signals. Stathi then moved the party thirty feet higher, to a far more spacious and commodious cave with cushions and coloured blankets, where a spectacular feast was laid on. According to Billy Moss, it was the first bedding they had seen since the abduction; he estimated that none of them had slept more than three to four hours a night in the last two weeks.

In the late afternoon, the Loukakis brothers came running up to the cave: seven truckloads of Germans – over two hundred men – had just detrucked in Argyroupolis, the old road terminus less than an hour away. Over the next few hours the group moved three times, trying to find better shelter; and it was well after dark when the General stumbled on the path, and fell about twenty feet. Billy described how he raved and swore, then 'relapsed once more into that whimpering state of self-pity'[19] – or, as Paddy put it: 'Utter depression succeeded the fury unleashed by this last mishap.'[20] The night was bitterly cold: they gave the General all the coverings they had, and everyone else sat and shivered through the dark hours. At 5 a.m., Stavros and Stathi appeared with bread, cheese and raki. They asked a runner to take a message to Dennis, but the runner refused: it was too dangerous.

They did not hear from Dennis till mid-morning on the 13th. Whilst there were a great many Germans in the vicinity, he reported, none were too close for comfort. He had also had a message from Cairo: they would try and send a boat the following night but the plan was provisional, subject to confirmation that afternoon. Paddy had another severe attack of what felt like rheumatism: he could now hardly move his right arm, a condition not helped by the bitter cold of the night before.

The Loukakis brothers brought them food and blankets, so the night of the 13th was more comfortable than the one before. They settled down to sleep, only to be woken at ten o'clock by Dick Barnes, who had arrived in person to give them a message from Cairo. The boat was coming the following night, and would wait for them off Rodakino beach. He gave them a map reference, and the code: the launch would approach only when they flashed the letters 'S.B.'

They rose hurriedly, for several hours of darkness had already been lost and the General, battered and bruised from two falls, could not be expected to complete the long march to the beach in a hurry. Once again the team was split, partly to disguise their numbers as they moved over relatively open country. Paddy, Manoli and the General would take the longer, safer route, though it would still be hard going. Billy and the others, led by the sheep-thieves, took the more strenuous and dangerous path, and reached the rendezvous at dawn. It was perched high among the rocks and still several miles from the beach, and afforded a sweeping view of the coast. Just below them was a German coastal garrison behind a barbed wire fence. Through his binoculars, Billy watched them hanging out their washing and playing leapfrog.

Paddy and the General arrived a few hours later, and considering the General's exhaustion, Billy was amazed they had been able to make it so swiftly. But he had had the support of both Manoli and Paddy when he stumbled, and 'he moved across the landscape in a sort of trance.'[21] Billy was more worried about Paddy. '[He] is walking very stiffly,' wrote Billy, 'and his cramp seems to be getting much worse.'[22]

The team began its descent towards the beach in mid-afternoon, moving off in ones and twos at twenty-minute intervals. They lay up in a little vegetable garden among the rocks with a natural spring, about a quarter of a mile from the beach. An old man came to water it, but he asked no questions. They left him at dusk, tending his beans.

At nine they reached the shore, and an hour later Billy got out the torch, to start flashing the code letters 'S.B.' They both knew the Morse code for 'S' – as in S.O.S. – from their schooldays, but then came the terrible realization that neither of them knew how to flash the letter 'B'. The only hope was to flash a confident S, followed by a few 'non-descript electrical blobs'. 'It occurs to me now', wrote Paddy, 'that we ought to have asked the General. He must have been as eager to go now as we were. Did we not think of it, or was it shame at our amateur status?'[23]

They heard the sounds of muffled engines approaching, and flashed their S's and blobs in mute appeal, only to hear the engines gradually receding. At that moment Dennis Ciclitira appeared, with three German prisoners whom he wanted to send to Cairo. He seized the torch and began signalling 'S.B.' repeatedly. The engines approached again, and soon a dinghy was making its way to the beach. In it were a group of heavily armed members of the Raiding Forces led by Bob Bury, all eager for a fight and bitterly disappointed to discover that they were on one of the few beaches that were entirely free of Germans.

Bob Bury had brought enough weapons and rations for a small campaign; and while he refused to give their weapons to the Cretan andartes on shore, he was willing to leave them his rations. All the Cretans who had taken part in the abduction accompanied the General to Egypt, except for Antoni Ziodakis, who decided to stay behind and continue the fight. Before embarking in the launch, those departing from Crete followed the practice of leaving behind their boots, jackets and weapons for those remaining. Soon they were on board in a state of wild euphoria, revelling in unlimited supplies of whisky, English cigarettes and lobster sandwiches, too exhilarated to sleep. The General was very quiet, and kept himself apart from the revelry. As the boat approached Egypt he went up on deck, and spent a long time gazing out to sea.*

The launch drew into Mersa Matruh around midnight, and General Kreipe was greeted with a smart salute by Brigadier Barker-Benfield who spoke excellent German. The General was pleased by this reception, and over a dinner of pilchards and a prune, he and Barker-Benfield discussed this war and the last. Kreipe also gave a lively account of his kidnapping, but bewailed the loss of his Knight's Cross. (The Brigadier looked suitably grave, and said he would issue a £5 reward for its return.) The General went on to say that Paddy and Billy had treated him 'with chivalry and courtesy'.[24]

Now that the whole operation was finally over, Paddy thought his symptoms might improve; but neither the joyous reunions at Tara nor the news of an immediate DSO could mask the fact that they were getting worse. The following night, at a dinner with the King of Greece, Prince Peter had to help Paddy cut up his food since his right arm was completely paralysed. By now he had a fever, and the joints in his arm were throbbing.

On 19 May, he was admitted to the 15th (Scottish) General Hospital. His temperature was very high, and the symptoms in his arm were spreading to his legs. At first, the doctors thought he was developing polio; but as his wrists, shoulders and ankles became

---

* The General was sent to London for interrogation, and to a POW camp near Calgary, in Canada. He was returned to England where he was treated for diabetes, and was then sent to Island Farm Special Camp 11, near Bridgend in Wales. He was not repatriated to Germany until October 1947. (See www.specialcamp11.fsnet.co.uk.)

swollen and painful, they revised their diagnosis to polyarthritis. 'With vigorous treatment', wrote a doctor on his service record, 'the condition of the joints gradually improved and muscle power in the limbs was restored.'[25] Yet it took a long time: Paddy was in hospital for almost three months. During this time he was visited by General Paget, who pinned the Distinguished Service Order on to his battle-dress jacket, worn over pyjamas.

Billy Moss, who had been awarded the Military Cross for his part in the operation, came to see Paddy in hospital full of plans for what to do next. Billy wanted to make use of the large number of Russian POWs on Crete; he would train them as guerrillas, and then unleash them in a series of coordinated raids on German fuel dumps. He also harboured another, secret plan to capture General Kreipe's successor.

Moss returned to Crete on 6 July. Basing himself with Mihali Xylouris in the mountains near Anoyeia, he put together a unit that included some members of Xylouris's band and a few Russian POWs. Their most dramatic action was to ambush a German detachment at Damasta. The events leading up to this raid began on 7 August, when a German unit marched into Anoyeia demanding labourers. The unit was attacked by a band of ELAS fighters, who captured about ten Germans. They hoped to exchange their hostages for Cretan prisoners, but when that came to nothing, they shot their captives. Realizing that the Germans would soon return to destroy Anoyeia, the villagers fled.

The following day, 8 August, Billy Moss and his unit of eight Greeks and six Russians took up ambush positions under a bridge at Damasta, on the Heraklion–Rethymno road north of Anoyeia. As the Germans drove over the bridge, Moss and his team disabled three 3-tonners and a small truck. These were followed by another truck carrying a detachment of German soldiers, escorted by an armoured car. Most of the soldiers were shot, while Moss himself destroyed the armoured car by approaching it single-handed, and lobbing a grenade into the turret.

For this action, a bar was added to Moss's MC, while at Damasta a monument beside the bridge commemorates the event. Initially, Paddy seems to have applauded the action. In a letter to Iain Moncreiffe he describes Billy as 'green with fresh laurels and a bar to his MC in the air, having ambushed a Hun column, knocked out ten trucks, taken fifteen prisoners, killed fifty, and put an armoured car out of action by jumping on it and throwing Mills bombs down the turret until the cannon stopped firing. We had planned the op. together, but I was still too ill to take part.'[26]*

In later years, however, Paddy took a more ambivalent view of the episode. 'I wish the Damasta ambush hadn't taken place!' he wrote decades later to Ralph Stockbridge.[27] In the margins of the letter, Ralph wrote, 'So do I: this refers to Moss's totally undesirable attack on the Germans at Damasta, which ambush must have contributed to the destruction of Anoyeia.'

The village had already been abandoned by its inhabitants; but on 13 August the Germans returned and razed Anoyeia to the ground, along with a number of outlying villages. Damasta was also sacked, and thirty men were killed. This was the start of weeks of sustained violence that spread throughout Crete. From having been relatively passive, suddenly the occupiers were bent on doing the maximum possible damage to those villages they suspected of aiding the Allies.

Between 22 and 30 August, the Germans poured into the Kedros side of the Amari valley and began the work of systematic destruction. On 25 August, as the shooting, burning, blowing-up, looting and beating was at its height, the German-controlled Greek newspaper *Paratiritis* made the following announcement.

> In the month of April 1944, the German General Kreipe was abducted by a British Commando force with the help of Greek bandits.
>
> The Commander of Fortress Crete had asked the whole population . . . to assist in questioning to discover the perpetrators. This invitation has however had no effect . . . It has been proven that the British Commando force was supported not only by Greek bandits but also by the population of the villages of Anoyeia, Yerakari, Gourgouthi, Vryses, Ano Meros, Kyra Vrisi and Saktouria near which he was concealed, making them equally guilty, being as they were fully aware of his concealment. These villages and their inhabitants have been visited with the threatened punishment.

* Presumably Paddy is referring to the formation of the unit and its use on fuel dumps, for neither of them could have predicted the attack on Anoyeia, nor the Damasta raid.

While this might seem conclusive, the fact that the Germans used the Kreipe Operation as an excuse for their savagery was merely window-dressing. Their real motives were not of the kind that could be announced in *Paratiritis*, and the Amari villages were not the only ones under attack at this time. In the words of Tom Dunbabin, 'the destruction was spread over the whole of western and eastern Crete. This was the last act of German barbarity for most of Crete. The object was to cover their imminent withdrawal by neutralizing the areas of guerrilla activity, and to commit the German soldiers to terrorist acts so that they should know that there would be no mercy for them if they surrendered or deserted.'[28]

The Germans had indeed been worried about rising levels of desertion and surrender in their ranks, and turning every man into a looter and a killer guaranteed that no German deserter would be helped by the Cretans. At the same time, an organized withdrawal from occupied territory was bound to go more smoothly if the civilian population had been cowed and beaten into submission. At the end of August the violence stopped. In the first week of September, the Cretans watched as the Germans began pulling out of eastern and central Crete, blowing up roads and bridges behind them as they went.

For all the violence of these reprisals, Paddy drew comfort from the words of Alexander Kokonas, the schoolmaster of Yerakari, who saw his village destroyed and suffered the loss of nine members of his family. As Paddy recalled in a letter to Ralph Stockbridge: 'I have always been touched by the fact that he [Alexander Kokonas] wrote that, though he wasn't in favour of General Kreipe being captured, not a single house less, nor a single inhabitant of the Amari would have been spared if the abduction had never happened.'[29]

That summer, representatives of all the political parties in Greece gathered in Beirut. The idea was to bring together both sides, Communist and monarchist, left and right, which had polarized so dramatically during the German occupation. As EAM accused the non-Communists of collaboration and right-wing parties accused EAM of murder and theft, the tensions were all too clear. But for nine months they managed to have a government of national unity, headed by George Papandreou, in which six ministers were Communists. Paddy was also in Lebanon, convalescing. He spent that summer in the mountains as the guest of the writer Mary Borden, who was married to Major-General Sir Edward Spears, and was sent back to Crete in October.

Given the political turmoil in mainland Greece Paddy was relieved to conclude, from the evidence he could gather, that the Communists were not in a very strong position in Crete. As for the Germans, they had retreated to the far west of the island where they held Maleme airport, Suda Bay and Chania. They were well supplied, and in no hurry to leave: their only imperative was that they would not surrender to the Cretans.

Paddy's arrival was the signal for jubilant reunions and endless feasts among his Cretan friends, but he was appalled by the destruction of the Amari villages. The only excitement came on 8 December, when the Germans launched an attack on his headquarters at Vaphes. They arrived with seven tanks and about four hundred infantry, but people emerged from all the neighbouring villages to attack them, 'with such spirit that at about 1700 hours they were forced to retreat after having killed only four Cretans and destroyed only two houses. The German losses amounted to about thirty . . .'[30] Paddy was also pleased that this feat had been accomplished by exclusively non-Communist bands.

He had one other, difficult task to carry out before he left. He felt honour bound to travel to Photineou to visit Kanaki Tsangarakis, brother of Yanni, and explain the facts of Yanni's death. The story that he had died in a German ambush had not lasted beyond the end of the war, and now Paddy felt he must see Kanaki face to face and tell him exactly what happened.

Kanaki came down from his house to see Paddy, who was waiting for him by the old fountain. Without any preamble he said: 'Mihali, is it true that you killed my brother?' Paddy replied, 'Yes, Kanaki, it was a terrible accident, it was me.' – 'That's all I wanted to know,' said Kanaki, who turned on his heel without shaking hands.[31]

Paddy moved from Vaphes to Heraklion in mid-December, and left the island on the 23rd. He reached Alexandria on Christmas Eve, in time to take part in the last Christmas at Tara. There was a twilight feeling about Cairo, for all the action had moved to the Far East and many of his friends were headed in that direction. Billy Moss and David Smiley were parachuted into Siam, Billy Maclean spent over a year in Sinkiang.

Xan Fielding had been parachuted into the south of France in the summer of 1944, and it was a miracle he was alive at all. He and Francis Cammaerts, one of the most experienced SOE officers in France, had been caught at a roadblock at Digne and thrown into prison. They were rescued by the legendary Christine Granville, who persuaded their gaolers that, since the Allies were on the Riviera, it would be foolish to kill these two suspected *résistants*. When Xan and Cammaerts were led out of their cells, they thought they were about to be shot, but at the prison gates they were welcomed by Christine, who drove them away to safety. Back in Cairo, Xan too applied for a posting in the Far East. He spent some months in Cambodia, and then on the border of Tibet.

Paddy was eager to join this exodus to the Orient, and did his best to persuade SOE to send him east. To his great disappointment, they refused; perhaps they did not think he had fully regained his health. Having nothing better to do, Paddy enjoyed the last days of wartime Cairo; and, shortly after Christmas, he met a woman called Joan Rayner.

11

The British Institute, Athens

Whether she was at a crowded party or relaxed among her closest friends, Joan Rayner seemed somehow detached, and in touch with a private inner self. Alan Pryce-Jones, to whom she was briefly engaged, described her as 'very fair, with huge myopic blue eyes. Her voice had a delicious quaver – no not quite quaver, an undulation rather . . . her talk was unexpected, funny, clear-minded. She had no time for inessentials.'[1] Her clothes were plain and well made, and when not having to look smart, she liked wearing men's shirts and riding breeches. Three years older than Paddy, she was widely travelled, a tireless reader, and a very good photographer.

Her mother, Sybil Eyres, had inherited a fortune in woollen manufacturing. On marriage, her husband Bolton Monsell added her name to his, becoming Bolton Eyres Monsell. He pursued a successful career in politics, holding the posts of Chief Whip for the Conservatives and First Lord of the Admiralty; he was created the 1st Viscount Monsell in 1935.

Joan and her sisters, Diana and Patricia, had a conventional upbringing, but Joan was a natural intellectual like her elder brother Graham and gravitated towards his friends, among whom were writers and musicians such as John Betjeman, William Walton and Constant Lambert. In 1937, Joan married a journalist and typographer, John Rayner,* who had been instrumental in creating the energy and style of the *Daily Express* in the 1930s. The marriage

---

* There was a curious link between him and Paddy. Elizabeth Pelly, to whom Paddy had lost his virginity, had been the bride in a celebrated mock wedding that had taken place at the Trocadero in 1929, and scandalized the press. Her 'bridegroom' was John Rayner. See D. J. Taylor, *Bright Young People* (Chatto & Windus, 2007).

did not last. Joan suffered a bad miscarriage, which put a strain on a relationship that was already at breaking point, and the war gave it the *coup de grâce*. She took a cypher training course at the Foreign Office, and worked in England until 1943. After postings to Algiers and Madrid she came to Cairo in early 1944, when Paddy was in Crete. Most of the cypherenes and secretaries whom the war had brought to Egypt tended to live in the capital's westernized areas, but Joan preferred its medieval Arab heart. She lived with the writer Patrick Kinross and Eddie Gathorne-Hardy, David Balfour and the painter Adrian Daintrey, in an old house attached to the Ibn Tulun mosque.

Paddy was on Crete in early December when his attention was first drawn to her by a letter from Billy Moss. 'A good thing turned up in the shape of Joan Rainer [*sic*],' Billy wrote, 'and we have seen quite a bit of her recently. She's got a good brain and talks about bull-fights and Spanish poets. I think you would like her.'[2] Joan was aware of Paddy's existence too. 'I kept hearing rather too much about him,' she recalled. 'Everyone was telling me how marvellous he was, how he'd captured a German General and all that . . . and I was rather determined not to be dazzled.'[3] They met at a party given by Marie Riaz, at which Paddy was smitten almost immediately. Joan did her best to remain undazzled, but it was a losing battle.

Joan had been offered a job at the Embassy in Athens, and Paddy was keen to return and explore the country further; but although the Greeks now had a government of national unity, the political divide was so acrimonious that there was talk of civil war. A massive demonstration called by the Communists on 1 December led to clashes with Greek police and army units, supported by British troops. This resulted in several casualties, and provoked the *Dekemvriana* – over a month of heavy fighting between the Communist forces and the Greek government, backed by British troops. In early 1945 a ceasefire was agreed, and a month later ELAS, the military wing of the Communist resistance, was demobilized. The threat of civil war had subsided, but not gone away.

Paddy made the long journey back to England at the end of January 1945. During his two months' home leave, spent between London and Weston with the Sitwells, he applied for permission to visit Rumania, but this was refused. At the end of March he was ordered to join the recently formed Special Allied Airborne Reconnaissance Force, or SAARF, based at Sunningdale golf course. Now that the capitulation of Germany was inevitable, SAARF's task was to rescue thousands of POWs who might be either marched off and slaughtered, or used as hostages and bargaining counters in the final days of the Reich.

The plan was for a three-man team with a wireless set to be dropped near the target camp, dressed in tattered uniforms. Then, having quietly joined one of the work gangs, they would infiltrate the prison camp, contact the senior British POW, establish communications with the advancing Allied troops, arrange for air cover and an arms drop, and then overpower the garrison or strike a deal with the camp's commandant.

With another team headed by Henry Coombe-Tennant, who was later to become a monk at Downside, Paddy's team pored over aerial photographs of their target: Oflag IV-C, otherwise known as Colditz. The fortress had a fearsome reputation for impregnability, and housed some of those VIP 'bargaining counters' known to the Germans as *Prominente*.* Then Paddy heard that Colonel Miles Reid MC, who had been held in Colditz before being released as part of an exchange of prisoners, was back in Britain. Paddy had met Reid during the Greek campaign, when he had commanded the Phantom Reconnaissance Unit. With the permission of SAARF's commandant, Brigadier J. S. 'Crasher' Nichols, Paddy borrowed a staff car and drove down to Haslemere where Reid and his wife were living.

Reid thought the plan insane, and was appalled that anyone should even consider it. 'Had we learnt nothing of the impregnability of the fortress, had we no idea of the thoroughness and rigour of checks and counter-checks of working parties, not heard of the scrutinies and the roll-calls? There was absolutely no hope of the plan succeeding . . . and instead of good, untold harm would ensue.'[4] Paddy drove back to Wentworth feeling very downcast, and the following day Reid himself turned up demanding to see Brigadier

* Among them were Viscount Lascelles, later Earl of Harewood, a nephew of George VI; George Haig, the son of Field Marshal Earl Haig; and Giles Romilly, a nephew of Winston Churchill.

Nichols. They remained in his office for some time, and both emerged looking furious. 'Crasher' Nichols was adamant that the mission was viable and would go ahead, but Reid had his way – largely because the plan was overtaken by events. The POWs in Colditz were freed by Patton's advancing armour on 16 April, though no *Prominente* had been left behind; they had all been moved before the Americans arrived.

Paddy had one other task, which was to see Billy Moss's account of the Kreipe Operation safely through the censors. Moss was in London at the time, so it seems odd that he left this to his friend: but perhaps he felt that Paddy's name and contacts might give the project a better chance. The censor (unnamed) was not impressed, describing it as a 'manuscript of questionable taste and no literary or documentary value'.[5] Paddy was aware of its shortcomings, particularly an 'attitude of patronage to the Cretans that hints that they are only fairly gentle savages . . . However the publishers are going to make some pretty drastic editorial revisions, so it may eventually emerge as what it should be: a young man's unpretentious account of an exciting adventure.'[6]

One might also ask why it was Billy, not Paddy, who wrote the story of the Kreipe Operation. Yet it had always been agreed that Moss should write up the mission, and as it turned out, only he had had the time to keep notes. Moss had spent days of enforced idleness, guarding the General with a handful of Cretans in mountain caves, unable to have more than a halting conversation with any of them; whereas Paddy was working flat out trying to liaise with Cairo, keep out of German hands, and bring the party to an isolated beach. There were other considerations too. Paddy had been with the Cretan resistance for most of the war, and for better or worse, he had become an important figure in its history. A book by him would have had a huge impact on the island, and despite all his efforts to be fair to everybody, it would inevitably have offended some people. And there would have been unpleasant repercussions if some mischief-maker dragged up the Tsangarakis tragedy. As far as Paddy was concerned, it was not worth the risk.

With the Colditz operation cancelled, Paddy and Henry Coombe-Tennant – still wearing SAARF badges on their uniforms – were flown to Luneburg Heath in Germany, and stationed in the bombed-out ruins of Hamburg. They were now part of a team whose mission was to seek out and pursue war criminals, and to inspect the local tribunals set up to regulate claims and administer justice. They were ordered not to fraternize with the Germans, and instructed to look out for the so-called *Werwolfen* – doomed young Nazi fanatics, whose tactics were thought to include stretching wire across the road to decapitate people.

Paddy was in a car with two others, driving near Itzehoe in Holstein, when he noticed a signpost pointing to Schloss Rantzau. Hoping to get some news of his old friend Josias who had been so kind to him in Bucharest, they drove up to the castle. Like every other manor house and schloss in the area it was filled with refugees from Hamburg, but Paddy managed to find a relative of Josias, and the news was not good. He had been taken by the Russians when they marched into Bucharest in August 1944, and no one knew what had become of him. Paddy later discovered that he had been deported to the USSR, where he died in captivity some five years after the end of the war. His lover, Marcelle Catargi, committed suicide.

Paddy spent three weeks in Denmark after leaving Germany, and came home with four sporting guns which 'someone had looted and then gave to me' (probably Paddy's way of saying he had looted them himself). He was back in London in time to celebrate Victory in Europe Day, on 8 May 1945.

At a time when every man of military age was defined by what sort of war he had had, Paddy's celebrated adventures meant that he was much in demand. One of those who took him up was Emerald Lady Cunard, who lived in a lavishly appointed suite in the Dorchester where she entertained politicians, generals, bemedalled soldiers, musicians and writers. It was here that Paddy met Ann Rothermere, later Fleming, with whom he made an instant bond; and the writer and critic Peter Quennell, who was to publish some of Paddy's earliest work in the *Cornhill* magazine. More often he was to be found at the Gargoyle Club, which had survived the war with its Matisse-mirrored walls and tiny dance floor intact. Here he saw a lot of Xan Fielding, back from Cambodia, Nepal and Tibet.

Billy Moss and Sophie Tarnowska had married in Cairo that

spring, and though Paddy was sad to miss the occasion, he was glad that Joan had been able to attend. Soon after, she set off on a long journey into Lebanon, Syria and Iraq with her friend, the artist Dick Wyndham. Paddy was perhaps not quite so happy about this, but Joan came and went as she pleased.

She returned to England that summer, and invited Paddy to come and stay at her family home in Dumbleton, Worcestershire. Dumbleton Hall is a large neo-Jacobean house bristling with gables, chimneys and cupolas, designed by Humphry Repton in 1837 and set on the edge of the Malvern Hills. Joan's mother Sybil was welcoming but painfully shy, the opposite of her husband who radiated confidence and authority. Among the guests were two of Joan's oldest friends. Lady Dorothy ('Coote') Lygon was a friend of Evelyn Waugh, and the model for Lady Cordelia Flyte in *Brideshead Revisited*. Round and owlish in appearance, she was to spend many years teaching in Athens. She had been a debutante in the same year as Joan, as had Wilhelmine (Billa) Harrod (née Creswell). Happily married to the economist Roy Harrod, Billa would devote much of her life to saving the churches of East Anglia; but at that time, she was better known for being the inspiration for Fanny, the narrator in Nancy Mitford's *The Pursuit of Love*.

Both Billa and Coote approved of Paddy. Joan's brother Graham Eyres Monsell was harder to impress, but there too he succeeded. Graham was tall, elegant and a gifted pianist. Like Paddy he had served in the Intelligence Corps, seen action in Africa and Italy, and had left the army with the rank of Lieutenant Colonel. He was devoted to Joan, with whom he shared a strong resentment of their father, who had denied Joan a proper education and had forbidden Graham to study the piano to professional level. In Lord Monsell's mind 'only pansies played the piano',[7] and he felt that Graham's homosexuality was somehow linked to his love of music. Graham often suffered from bouts of severe depression, and in these moments he relied on Joan. Billa Harrod once said that she had never seen a brother and sister so close.

In early September Joan set off for Athens and her job at the Embassy, where she was secretary to Osbert Lancaster, then press attaché at the Embassy. They knew each other through John Rayner, who first commissioned Lancaster to draw regular pocket cartoons for the *Daily Express* which appeared, with few interruptions, from 1939 to 1981. Paddy was eager to join Joan in Athens, and began looking for a job that would base him in Greece.

London was crowded with recently demobbed men like himself all looking for jobs. Paddy's enviable war record had certainly improved his prospects, but he was now thirty years old, had never been to university and never been in regular employment. He heard that Sir Louis Greig was looking for a tutor to the young King Faisal of Iraq and applied for the job, but he decided not to pursue it. Then he heard of a vacancy in Athens, for the post of deputy director for the British Institute of Higher English Studies, which had been set up the previous year by Maurice Cardiff under the auspices of the British Council.

Paddy was interviewed for the job by Colonel Kenneth Johnstone of the Council, whose methods were rather baffling. Paddy realized he had been accepted only when the Colonel rose to his feet, shook hands, and said, 'Don't worry my boy, everything will work out splendidly.'[8]

Although the Germans had blown up the docks and harbours of Piraeus before their retreat, Athens had not been too badly damaged during the war. Far more severely affected were the Athenians, who had lived in a state of semi-starvation since 1941. One of the results was that almost everyone kept chickens, even those living in apartment blocks in the city centre. The crowing of cocks, added to the cries of street vendors, blaring radios and the metallic cacophony of antique trams, was enough to convince Osbert Lancaster that Athens was one of the noisiest capitals in Europe. In 1946 the Acropolis still dominated every prospect, for most people lived in modest two-storey houses. In the poorer parts of town, below Mount Hymettus, the walls were covered with Communist slogans in red.

Paddy's immediate superior was the unfailingly affable Rex Warner, a Greek scholar who was considered one of the most promising novelists of his generation. Maurice Cardiff remembered them both. 'At a midnight contest in a taverna, given quite difficult rhymes, he and Paddy produced passable sonnets in minutes, but Rex's was the more perfect and metrically correct.'[9] As Director of the Institute Warner was answerable to Steven Runciman, whom Paddy had met in Sofia in 1934 and who was now the British Council's Representative. Tall, fastidious and a brilliant linguist, Runciman was then working on the *History of the Crusades* which made his name; but his chief recreation was collecting scandals and stories. 'Royal gossip is very good,' he once said, 'and political gossip is even better; but my dear, *nothing* beats Vatican gossip.'[10]

They all worked in the same building in Ermou Street, and Runciman had vivid memories of Paddy. 'He looked very good in an office,' said Runciman, 'but none of us could think of anything to do with him.' Cardiff recalled that Paddy was not at work very often and when he was he seemed to be throwing a party, sitting with his feet on the desk and entertaining a stream of Cretan visitors. The Cretan economy had been almost destroyed by the occupation, and there was very little work. Paddy found menial jobs for both Manoli Paterakis and George Psychoundakis in the Institute; they and others often spent the night on the floor of his room at the Grande Bretagne, and later, in the flat he was lent in Kolonaki. His office was always blue with cigarette smoke, and the sound of loud talk, Cretan songs and rollicking laughter echoed down the passage.

This did not make him popular. 'There was a very insensitive side to Paddy,' said Cardiff. 'He was very bumptious, a bit of a know-all, and his enthusiasm and noisiness could be rather wearing.'[11] Steven Runciman, too, had his reservations about Paddy. Cardiff said that this was because he resented the fact that Paddy knew more Greek royals than he did; but Runciman also saw how Paddy disturbed the peace of the office. 'All the girls were in love with him,' he said. 'He used to borrow money from them – and I have to tell you, they weren't always paid back. There were occasions when I had to sort out Paddy's little irregularities myself . . .'[12]

One of Paddy's closest friends at this time was George Katsimbalis, whom he had met on his first wartime posting to Athens. Among his many literary projects, Katsimbalis was editing the *Anglo-Hellenic Review* – a literary magazine which had been given a home in the British Institute. They met almost every day: at Psara's at the top of the Anaphiotika steps, or in the Platanos taverna in the still tourist-free Plaka. Katsimbalis 'was expert in three languages and hardly a Greek, a French or an English-speaking poet seemed to have existed . . . of which he couldn't recite, without a hesitation or a mistake, dozens of pages by heart'. He was also a brilliant raconteur, of living stories rather than rehearsed party pieces. 'New facets would be revealed each time because each time it was a live experience being drawn from a deep and fresh reservoir of memory.'[13]

Katsimbalis was at the heart of a group of friends that included Joan's boss Osbert Lancaster; Monty Woodhouse, who was advising on Greek affairs; the painter Nico Ghika, who with Yanni Tsaroukis and Yanni Moralis was evolving a new vision of Greece; and George Seferis, a quiet, thoughtful diplomat who was also the greatest poet of his generation. The ache of exile was a frequent theme in his poetry, using ancient myths to illuminate both the past of Greece and its very uncertain future. Lawrence Durrell had published poems by Seferis in *Personal Landscape* and, with Rex Warner, translated his work into English.

The parliamentary elections that took place in Greece in March 1946 were the first in ten years, but they were boycotted by the Communists and the political parties of the left. The result was a victory for the monarchists, and over sixty per cent of Greeks voted in the plebiscite for the return of the King on 1 September. The Greek Communist Party (KKE) had not been outlawed; but in a right-wing backlash, gangs of armed men with grievances born of the occupation had taken their revenge on known Communists, particularly in the Peloponnese. Meanwhile the Communists began to regroup in Epirus and Thessaly, though at this stage with no plan beyond that of defending themselves and consolidating their support. 'Most contemporary accounts', wrote Monty Woodhouse, 'agree in depicting the descent into civil war as a gradual deterioration, which took its gravest turn much later in the year.'[14]

A few days before the elections took place the British Ambassador, Sir Rex Leeper, was succeeded by Sir Clifford Norton. Having been Ambassador in Poland, Norton understood the potential threat from Soviet Russia, and in the years that followed, he was instrumental in maintaining British support for Greece while the civil war raged.

His wife, Noel Evelyn, was always known as Peter. A passionate collector of contemporary art, she brought in her wake two young and promising painters: Lucian Freud and (in May 1946) John Craxton, who in years to come was to design the jackets of almost all Paddy's books.

Craxton became a great friend of Paddy's, and was able to put Lady Norton straight about his sexual orientation. Because he had never refused floor-space to a Cretan looking for work, Lady Norton had heard that Paddy's rooms were filled with young men, and like many others she had leapt to the wrong conclusion. Craxton decided to settle in Greece for a while, and it was Paddy who suggested the island of Poros, opposite Lemonodassos.

One visitor to Greece that year was Maurice Bowra, classical scholar, poet, and Warden of Wadham College for over thirty years. Cyril Connolly described him as 'a person sculpted out of a harder, grander material than anybody else'.[15] Bowra had come to Greece in his capacity as Chair of the British Council Humanities Advisory Committee as well as to lecture, so he was introduced to the staff of the Institute. Although he became one of Joan's most devoted admirers, Bowra was not so sure about Paddy; in a report written on the Council's work in Greece, Bowra wrote: 'A misfit is Mr P. Lee-Fermore [sic] who has many excellent gifts but is unfit for office work. With his experience in Crete he has many unusual Greek acquaintants, which is a great asset, and he might be better employed on a roving commission of making contacts, for which he is admirably fitted.'[16]

With this in mind, Steven Runciman suggested that Maurice Cardiff and Paddy (who was joined by Joan) should visit the British Council's recently established outpost in Salonika, and see some of the larger towns. They had no political brief beyond talking to people, testing the temperature of pro-British feeling, and finding out what they could about the Communist resurgence.

As they drove north, Paddy told stories of his participation in the Greek campaign in 1940, and the Venizelist revolution in 1935. Maurice was not entirely sure he believed it all; but in a village near the Albanian border, a man came up and embraced Paddy saying, 'Do you remember when the Germans were coming and the Papas put up the white flag, and we grabbed the old bastard and made him pull it down?'

'He had a passion for words,' Cardiff continued. 'Crossing a high pass over the Pindos range we came across some Vlach shepherds with their flocks . . . Paddy had picked up Romanian on his travels. Now he tried it out on the Vlachs with some success in general conversation and triumphantly in an extended haggle over a magnificent black sheepskin cloak . . .'[17] They celebrated their return to Athens with a drink in the bar of the Grande Bretagne, with a group of friends including Nico Ghika and his first wife Tiggy (short for Antigone). Cardiff recalled how Joan mentioned the sheepskin cloak, and begged Paddy to get it. He returned with the cloak over his arm, adopted a Byronic pose and flung it round his shoulders, in a magnificent gesture which swept all the drinks into Tiggy's lap.

As there was still nothing for him to do at the office, Paddy volunteered to do a lecture tour round Greece, to introduce the glories of British culture – Lord Byron, for example, or the Pre-Raphaelite Brotherhood – to a Greek audience. Since it seemed as good an excuse as any to get him out of the way, Runciman agreed.

As Osbert Lancaster was about to leave the Embassy, Joan was once more free to accompany Paddy. At first the lectures were held in sparsely attended halls, where a handful of students and one or two elderly ladies listened respectfully. All this changed in Corfu, where the British Council's work was in the hands of a remarkable woman called Maria Aspiotti. She had Paddy and Joan to stay in her house for a day or two, and put the word about that Major Leigh Fermor, the hero who had captured the German general, was going to give a lecture. Paddy gulped when he heard that she had hired an enormous cinema for the event, but on the night it was filled to bursting, with shouts of 'Kreipe! Kreipe!' from the eager audience. As Maria Aspiotti had guessed, there was only one story the audience wanted to hear from Paddy, and it had nothing to do with the Pre-Raphaelites.

At the lectern Paddy had a carafe and a glass, from which he took repeated sips as he told the story. When it was nearly empty, he refilled it from the carafe. A roar of approval went up from the crowd as what remained in the glass turned milky-white – Paddy had been drinking neat ouzo. The lecture was a huge success, and from then on, Paddy talked no more about British culture. At a time when the Communist press was doing everything possible to stir up anti-British feeling, lecturing on the Kreipe Operation was the most useful thing he could do. As one American officer put it to Maurice Cardiff, 'he's the best bit of propaganda you've got.'[18]

Everything became more comfortable and more fun once Paddy and Joan had met up with Xan Fielding in the Peloponnese. He had come to Greece as part of an international observation team, set up to oversee the revision of electoral registers and supervise the elections. With his work done, Xan was now on a spell of prolonged leave and had managed to borrow an army jeep.

The three of them drove to Kalamata, where the summer heat was fierce, and found a table by the waterfront. 'The stone flags of the water's edge . . . flung back the heat like a casserole with the lid off. On a sudden, silent, decision we stepped down fully dressed into the sea carrying the iron table a few yards out and then our three chairs, on which, up to our waists in cool water, we sat round the neatly laid table-top, which now seemed by magic to be levitated three inches above the water.'[19] Their waiter had no hesitation in wading into the sea to serve them their grilled fish, while the neighbouring diners, delighted by this spectacle, sent can after can of retsina to their table.

When they reached Crete, they were treated like heroes. Paddy and Xan lectured first in Heraklion, then Chania. In both cities the cinemas they appeared in were packed, and everyone wanted to shake their hands. The most physically stressful part of the journey, however, was their triumphal cavalcade through the villages of the White Mountains and the Amari, as they made their way slowly back to Heraklion. Joan was a traveller who took heat, cold, discomfort, bad food and fleas in her stride, but she almost collapsed under the abundance of Cretan hospitality.

> We had had days and days of feasting and drinking, everyone in each village trying to give us a meal, so the moment we had finished coffee in one house we started with sikoudia again at the next, and

as they had all killed their best lamb or chicken it was impossible to refuse. The families that we couldn't go to stood on the road with trays of raki and meze (usually a bit of old goat's head) and we had to have a drink from each one. No sleep, of course, lyras, dancing, singing and drinking all night, feux de joie and indeed whenever our cavalcade arrived in a new village, it sounded as though a battle was going on. It was the most glorious journey and so moving to see how much Paddy and Xan were loved . . .'[20]

The Communist papers did their worst. This lecture tour was just another propaganda exercise, to cover up the fact that Paddy and Xan were little better than spies. The death of Yanni Tzangarakis was dragged up again, only now the truth was out: he had not been killed by Germans but by Paddy, probably because Yanni knew 'all the secrets of the English'. Paddy felt he had to see Kanaki again, to try and explain events once more. He arranged to meet Xan and Joan at the Villa Ariadne at Knossos, now safely back in the hands of the British School of Archaeology. Asking the taxi to wait on the Rethymno road, Paddy walked up to Photineou and Kanaki's house, which was high on the mountainside. Paddy knocked and went in. 'He stood up saying, "What do you seek here Mihali? We are not friends," laying his two first fingers on the butt of the pistol in his sash. It was no good, so I left, very sad.'[21]

After a few days on Santorini they went to Rhodes, where Lawrence Durrell was living with his second wife, Eve Cohen, in the Villa Cleobolus – a little house almost submerged in a tangled garden, within which was a Turkish graveyard. 'It was an amazing sojourn, spent in talk and music and feasting,' wrote Paddy. 'Strange things always happened in his company and one afternoon, in the ruins of ancient Camirus, wine-sprung curiosity set the four of us crawling on hands and knees through the bat-infested warren of underground conduits. We climbed out covered in droppings and dust and cobwebs . . .'[22]

With their clothes so torn and filthy, it seemed like a good idea to take them off. They walked on naked, and came across a stone that looked just like a sacrificial altar. A tableau was made, photographed by Joan: Paddy lay across the stone and Larry held the sacrificial victim's penis, while beetle-browed Xan wielded an enormous knife. Then, still naked, they walked along the top of a high wall, which enclosed a series of twelve-foot Doric columns that once supported a ceiling. Someone dared Xan to jump on to the top of the nearest column, which stood two yards clear of the wall. Xan didn't think twice. A tremendous leap and he was there, 'while the [column] rocked frighteningly on its stylobate for several seconds'.[23]* He struck an Eros pose, immortalized in another photograph by Joan whom Durrell called 'The Corn Goddess'. As for Paddy, he was described as 'a wonderful mad Irishman . . . quite the most enchanting maniac I've ever met'.[24]

They were back in Athens when, in early November, General Müller and General Bräuer were sent to stand trial. As they had commanded the forces of occupation in Crete Paddy was curious to see them, and he and Joan attended the initial proceedings in the public gallery. Here they were recognized by a journalist, who insisted that Paddy meet the two defendants. He was taken through to a lobby full of lawyers and officers of the court, where the two well-guarded generals sat on a bench.

The journalist introduced Paddy as the English major who had kidnapped General Kreipe. General Müller, who had killed so many Cretans and who had been the original target of the operation, looked up. '*Mich hätten sie nicht so leicht geschnappt,*' he said with a smile.[25] 'You would not have snatched me so easily.' Considering that the generals were staring death in the face, they looked far more self-possessed than Paddy, who was overcome with nerves and embarrassment. He pulled out a packet of cigarettes and offered them round, but had no matches. General Bräuer had, and as he lit Paddy's cigarette, Paddy noticed that his hands were perfectly steady. The two generals were interested to meet him. They said they had known there were some British officers up in the mountains, and asked questions about SOE's organization. When Paddy left, they said, 'Come and visit us in prison.' They were found guilty in December, were sentenced to death, and executed by firing squad in May the following year. Paddy was unhappy that Bräuer had suffered the same fate as Müller, for he was nowhere near as brutal or sadistic a commander.

---

* The photograph appears on page 3 of the second plate section.

Paddy's time at the British Council was almost over. He was summoned to Steven Runciman's office. While acknowledging that the lecture tour had been successful propaganda, Runciman added that it had been a considerable expense to the Council. His services were no longer required. 'I'm leaving in about a fortnight,' Paddy wrote to Lawrence Durrell on 18 December, 'feeling angry, fed up, and older than the rocks on which I sit. Fucking shits.'[26]

By the end of 1946, no one was in any doubt that the Greek civil war was intensifying. The Communists, now rebranded as the Democratic Army of Greece (DSE), had about 16,000 partisans, supported by Yugoslavia and Albania, though not the USSR: Stalin gave them no support at all, beyond some encouraging noises for the DSE in the press. He was happy to leave Greece to the British and Americans, and in return expected no interference in his take-overs of Poland, Czechoslovakia, Rumania, the Baltic States and Bulgaria.

In one sense, Paddy lost his job with the British Council at just the right moment. While in Greece in 1946, he had seen the graffiti on the walls, the newspaper reports of atrocities committed by either side, the impassioned leaflets. Now the Greek army, supported by the British, were fighting the Communists in Epirus, Thessaly and the Peloponnese. Paddy's departure, however painful to him, meant that he did not have to watch Greece tearing itself apart.

12

The Caribbean

Back in London in early 1947, Paddy, Joan and Xan installed themselves in a topsy-turvy flat immediately above Heywood Hill's bookshop, not far from Paddy's old stamping ground of Shepherd Market. In his mind this period came to resemble a 'never-ending party' at the Gargoyle Club, which acted as a second home for some of the most interesting people in London. Among those milling about in the cigarette smoke were Dylan Thomas, who was supposed to be working at his cottage in Wales; artists including Lucian Freud, John Minton and Ben Nicholson; Cyril Connolly, Peter Quennell, the philosopher Freddy Ayer and the poet Stephen Spender, whom Paddy had met through Costa; and Robert Kee, who was at that point working as a journalist for *Picture Post*.

Another engaging friend from this period was Philip Toynbee, once a Communist but still a wild idealist, whose intellect was as prodigious as his intake of alcohol, and who like Paddy had been in the Intelligence Corps during the war. After one epic evening at the Gargoyle, he dossed down in the flat. 'He woke up, utterly at sea as to where he was. It had been a late evening . . . He stayed two or three days, which we spent talking and pub-crawling . . .' On another occasion, they had both Philip and Dylan Thomas tucked up on their sofa. 'It was a marvellously exhilarating time: hangovers were drowned like kittens the following morning in a drink called either a Dog's Nose or a Monkey's Tail: a pint of beer with a large gin or vodka slipped into it, which worked wonders.'[1]

That Easter Paddy and Joan took a bicycling holiday in the south of France, aiming for the great gathering of gypsies and the horse fair at Saintes-Maries-de-la-Mer in the Camargue. The town was so crowded with horses, gypsies and tourists that at one point they thought they might have to sleep out in the open; in the end they slept head-to-toe with another couple in the only bed they managed to find. Paddy wandered among the gypsies, trying out his Rumanian with varying degrees of success and attempting, if not to learn, then at least to get to grips with the basic elements of Roma. For all that, the fair was a disappointment: the gypsies he saw in the Camargue were not as wild as those he had seen in Rumania before the war.

Over the coming months, he began to get an idea of just how much Rumania had been weakened. Heavily backed by Moscow, the Rumanian Communists had taken power in 1945 and set about turning the country into a Soviet satellite. Its resources were stripped for the benefit of the Soviet Union while its people were infiltrated at every level by the secret police. *Ci-devant* aristocrats like the Cantacuzenes were described as 'elements of putrid background',[2] to be ostracized and closely watched.

Since Rumania was an enemy country during the war, Paddy and Balasha had been unable to exchange letters. The one he wrote to her in June 1947 was sent through Bill Bentinck, whose post as Ambassador to Poland was about to end in scandal.* Paddy's letter had reached Rumania in the diplomatic bag, addressed to Iris Springfield, a friend of Balasha's who worked in the British Legation. For Balasha, this was the first direct news of Paddy since 1940. However, she had heard of his military achievements, and his medals, from Tony Kendall – with whom Paddy had spent Christmas 1934 in Burgas, recovering from malaria. She had no illusions that their pre-war affair would revive in the post-war world, and was happy that he had found Joan. She wrote him a long letter in July, telling him what had happened since they had parted in 1939.

Balasha had survived the long, arid years since their parting living mostly in Bucharest, with her friend and cousin, Alexander Mourouzi, whose estate at Golásei was close to Băleni. A violent earthquake in 1940 had destroyed most of the lovely house that Paddy had known; but although it had been partially repaired, the estate was ruined. The Communists had confiscated all the Cantacuzene lands,

---

* Bill's wife Clothilde, who had run away with Balasha's husband Paco, was divorcing Bill – ironically enough – on the grounds of infidelity with Balasha.

supposedly for redistribution among the peasants, but the peasants were no better off; in fact they were starving. 'This is the third bad crop,' wrote Balasha. 'The whole village is dying of hunger. They have been eating boiled acacia leaves at Băleni . . . There is absolutely no hope to live on [sic] the land now. Every day there is a new requisition, or arbitrary measure – we are forced to till the land, yet our horses, tractors, sowing and mowing machines have all been taken, the oxen also. Those who have sheep are forced to give up all the wool. There is no hope wherever you turn . . .'

She and Mourouzi were doing everything they could to escape Rumania. 'It will be extremely difficult,' she continued, 'not only when we get somewhere else, but to leave here at all. Sometimes, Paddy, I wake with such a burning, jumping in my stomach at the idea of getting out. We have tried so often. Now, building a small craft, we hope to leave in a month's time. The expense is terrific, yet we're ready to spend our last penny on it.'³ They hoped the boat would take them to the Turkish coast, after which they would make their way into Greece – although by then they would have nothing left to live on. Balasha begged Paddy to alert all her friends, so they could send whatever money they could spare to Athens.

In the second week of August, Balasha and Alexander sailed out into the Black Sea from a place near Costineşti, south of Constanţa. Accompanied by a sailor who had agreed to take them to Turkey, they had gone little more more than a few hundred metres when they saw a light, heard a motor boat approaching, and their hopes of escaping Rumania were dashed. They were arrested and imprisoned. Mourouzi was lucky not to have been sent to work on the Danube–Black Sea Canal, a useless trench in which over 100,000 'undesirables' died. Balasha was held in a cell with ten other women, with little water and almost no food. She was released two weeks later without explanation, as was Mourouzi. 'I'm still afraid of being taken again,' she wrote to Paddy on 6 September. 'Those two weeks were hell. We fathomed the horror of human nature at its worst.' There was very little food outside prison too; and this, combined with the failure of their escape and her dread of incarceration, had left her in a state of profound anxiety and depression.

No letters exist from Paddy to Balasha at this time – the earliest dates from 1948, and is addressed to Alexander Mourouzi, who evidently still hoped to escape with Balasha to Greece. Paddy told him that all Balasha's friends were being mobilized and 'together, we shall be able to scrape up something – but so horribly little compared to what is needed . . . I beg you not to think that, just because I am nicely established on this side, I lack the imagination to understand . . . the difficulties you face, and the humiliations and miseries that surround you.'[4]

In London in the summer of 1947, Paddy was looking for a publisher who might give him an advance on the book he still planned to write on Greece. Peter Quennell introduced him to the *Cornhill's* owner and publisher John Grey Murray, known to his friends as Jock. The firm of John Murray had been founded in 1768, Jock being the sixth to bear the name in direct descent. The second John Murray had published Jane Austen, Walter Scott and Byron; while the third had published Charles Darwin's *On the Origin of Species*. When Jock joined the firm it was famous for its scholarly Handbooks, indispensable for the serious traveller; but he soon developed a keen eye for up-and-coming authors. Freya Stark, Kenneth Clark and John Betjeman were all in the Murray stable, as was Osbert Lancaster. Jock was a man of great charm and humour; but the main reason he attracted and kept such talent was that he was the perfect publisher. In the age before the literary agent he did everything he could for his authors, being willing to act as banker, promoter, psychiatrist, pen-pal or editor as occasion demanded.

On 27 August 1947, Jock Murray wrote himself the following memo:

> PLF called. I said that we would be very interested in the possibility of the book of his Greek travels, and that it seemed wise to intersperse his war experiences through a travel book rather than to write a book on War Exploits. He is going to work out a table of contents with a rough synopsis of what the chapters would contain, and an Introduction . . . There is no doubt that he can write though sometimes rather incoherently. The main problem will be to get such a book into some shape and to give it a sense of purpose.

Soon after that, another opportunity emerged. The publisher
Lindsay Drummond had commissioned Paddy's friend Costa
Achillopoulos to produce a book of photographs of the islands of
the Caribbean. Costa was looking for a congenial travelling
companion who would write the photo captions and text for the
book, as well as spin-off articles to help finance the trip. He urged
Paddy to join him and when he protested that he did not have the
funds, Costa replied that he could have the whole of Lindsay
Drummond's advance – which came to £250. It was too good an
opportunity to miss, especially since Joan decided to come too.

On 30 September, Jock Murray saw Paddy again, now preparing
for his journey to the Caribbean. 'He has not had time to do the
synopsis or any more writing on the [Greek] book before he leaves
for South America. So it will have to hold over for the present.'[5]

One other thing happened between the time he came back from
Greece and left for the Caribbean: a catastrophe hardly comparable
to what had happened to Balasha, but which could have been
avoided altogether. It concerned the two trunks which he had left
with Catherine d'Erlanger before the war. They had contained
rolled-up paintings by Balasha, all the letters he had written to his
mother between the Hook of Holland and Istanbul, sheaves of
sketches that he had sent back to her for safekeeping, and possibly
one or two of the diaries he had written at the time. But while
Paddy was fighting with the resistance in occupied Crete, the
Baroness had sold her house in London and moved to New York.
She wrote to Paddy, telling him that the trunks had been sent for
safekeeping to Harrods Depository in Hammersmith. He had never
received the letter.

Paddy had not thought about the trunks for years when he heard
that Harrods was trying to get in touch with him, requesting him
to claim his property and pay the £90 owed in storage charges or
it would be sold at auction. Paddy went to the warehouse, and even
saw the trunks; but 'As I had not got the sum needed to pay for
the storage at once, the very helpful manager said the sale could
be held over until I could settle the matter.'[6] Paddy came back, he
wrote, 'in a month', though it may well have been longer. Whenever

it was, he was too late. The trunks had been sold, the contents dispersed, and Harrods could give him no clue as to who had bought them. When he told Joan the story, she said she could have given him the money on the spot.

Left luggage was something of a recurring theme in Paddy's nomadic existence. A few years later the Secretary of the Travellers Club, of which he had been a member since the end of the war, reported to the House Committee that Mr Leigh Fermor owed 'over £100 for storage, if bye-law 6 were to be strictly enforced'.[7] What happened next is not recorded in the archives of the club; but the sale of the trunks from Harrods Depository, said Paddy, 'still aches sometimes, like an old wound in wet weather'.[8]

Costa, Paddy and Joan set off for the Caribbean on 1 October 1947. The *Colombie* had been a troopship during the war, and then a hospital ship, which meant that almost all its fittings had been ripped out. Apart from a sprinkling of French civil servants, most of the passengers were black. At first Paddy, Joan and Costa planned to travel third class, though this intention did not hold. Joan reported that there were seventy passengers in the women's dormitory, the noise was incessant, one could not walk upright because of the cat's-cradle of washing lines draped with wet clothes, and the lights were never switched off. Compared to this, the men's dormitory was quiet as a tomb; but they decided to travel second class after all, and hang the expense. The voyage lasted well over two weeks, but the food was good and there was plenty of wine.

They did not like Guadeloupe. Raoul, a cheerful Martiniquais who owned the guest house and took them on picnics, was the best thing about this island, which seemed 'baking, shadowless, empty, hostile, dejected'.[9] They grew to loathe Pointe-à-Pitre. 'It was hard to choose between the day − the dust, mud and the vacuity of the streets − and the night, those interminable hours of damp torpor under a mosquito net.' At Paddy's request, Raoul guided them through the steaming tropical jungle to the summit of the Soufrière, a traditional name for volcanoes in the Antilles. Paddy saw the brilliance of the flowers, the architectural beauty of the tree-ferns, the lianas and the acomas, the strange absence of birdsong; but he could not shake off the sense of seething decay that sustains the forest floor in its sodden and noxious splendour.

Martinique's Fort-de-France was a lot more lively, though Paddy had not expected to feel so close to America. Cars, fridges and wirelesses were much in evidence, and the aggressive advertising for Coca-Cola left him stunned. 'It is on a scale that nobody who has not crossed the Atlantic can hope to grasp. They are printed on almost everything you touch. Everywhere the beaming heroines of these giant advertisements smirk and simper and leer.'[10] Yet while the inhabitants drank so much Coke that the metal bottle-tops littered the streets, they were more likely to vote Communist than anything else.

The book that the travellers relied on most for everyday information was Sir Algernon Aspinall's *Wayfarer in the West Indies*, published in 1930. Paddy had also brought with him a new edition of Father Labat's *Voyages aux Isles de l'Amérique* (1722), which was his constant companion. Greedy, sadistic and ruthless, Father Labat was a remarkably gifted Dominican monk who could turn his hand to military engineering, irrigation, business, torture or cookery with equal ease. In twelve years he had not only strengthened the defences of the islands held by the French but also built a string of schools, convents, refineries and hospitals. He reorganized the watercourses of his order's failing sugar plantations and turned them into profitable concerns in a matter of months. In his free time, he noted everything he could about the food, music, dancing, superstitions, magic and healing arts of the African slaves, whom he would question at length. Curiosity satisfied, he would either reward them, or treat them with appalling severity.

In Martinique Paddy found the first in a series of excellent local libraries, the Bibliothèque Schoelcher. Here he read memoirs and journals that described the celebrated carnivals and balls of Saint-Pierre, the former capital of the island. It was destroyed by the eruption of Mont Pelée in 1902, wiping out the entire population bar one: a catastrophe that was to become the heart of Paddy's only novel, *The Violins of Saint-Jacques*. Some of the names he gave to his characters come from the poignant catalogue of slaves of the estate of La Pagerie – ranging from Théodule, aged seventy (estimated at 3,000 livres), to Sabine, aged two (400 livres) – who were sold following the death of Madame Rose Tascher, mother of the Empress Josephine.

Holding this list in his hands was another reminder of how raw the wounds of slavery still were, how understandable the slogan 'À BAS LES BLANCS!' scrawled on the walls. On reading the poems of Aimé Césaire, the mayor of Fort-de-France, Paddy had been aware of the poet's 'constant and burning sense of the sorrows and injustices of the African race in the Antilles'.[11] Yet the slave list was shown to him by Dr Robert Rose-Rosette, a man who felt that dwelling on the sorrows and injustices of the blacks was holding people back. Dr Rose-Rosette was mulatto: a man who, like many of the islanders, was descended from both slaves and slave owners. He and his circle promoted a tolerance based on a desire to lay to rest the 'age-old lamentation' of slavery, while taking pride in their African roots and abandoning the 'age-old grievance' against the whites.[12]

Being a natural optimist with a generous view of humanity, Paddy felt that the doctor's views were admirable, and indeed the only way forward. Yet as he travelled further into the Antilles, he found that the 'deadening effects of slavery in the same place, of generation after generation of it, with no hope of change' had gone deeper and done more damage than he could have imagined.[13] Slavery had been abolished for over a hundred years; yet, with the islands' economic decline, the descendants of slaves felt they were being robbed of the opportunities to which, in a just world, they were entitled.

Paddy spared no effort to search out groups of people he had heard of, often living in remote, sometimes dangerous places: the poor whites or 'Red Legs' of Barbados, the Rastafarians and Maroons of Jamaica, and the Caribs of Dominica. He noted the fact that both the Ashkenazi and Sephardic communities cooperated to build the synagogue in Kingston, and listened hard to the languages he heard: Creole French, where every 'r' becomes 'w'; Carib, Arawak (spoken by Carib women: the language of the tribe the Caribs conquered), and Papiamento.

What a strange trio they must have made: Costa, incessantly active, his cameras and lens cases dangling from his neck, 'the whole figure, one of charm with a dash of comedy';[14] Paddy, ruddy and sweating, his natural ebullience sometimes turning to irritation as he grappled with an alien culture and uneasy thoughts; and Joan, her eyes usually invisible behind thick dark glasses. In the few of Costa's photos where she appears, she is wearing simple cotton dresses; and, in one where she is crossing a rope bridge, she is carrying a rather incongruous handbag. She must have felt rather left out at times, for in Paddy's notebooks she is not always with him and Costa as they set off for a night in the sleazy bars, rum shacks, hash dens or red-light districts of whichever island they were visiting.

For a purely European sensibility like Paddy's, almost untouched by the cultural currents of the Americas, much of this new world was baffling and unpredictable. At a *Bal Doudou* where people came to drink and dance to a biguine band, Paddy watched the girls, as brightly clothed and made-up as exotic birds. He regretted the ubiquity of Western clothes, and celebrated the details of the traditional *'gwan wobe'* (gran' robe) with its brilliant colours, generously flounced skirt and gold jewellery.

In St Kitts, where Horatio Nelson had married Mrs Nesbit, he found a French–Carib dictionary in the local library. In Trinidad he noted the flowery elaboration of calypso songs, and the exaggerated elegance of the Saga Boys with their tight jackets, voluminous trousers and snap-brimmed hats. In Grenada, in the town of Gouyave, they read an announcement for a sweepstake, in which the first prize was a free funeral for the lucky winner. The town apparently boasted a lilac-coloured hearse, emblazoned with the words *Bon Voyage*. The incongruity of Georgian architecture in a West Indian landscape always hit him afresh: the capital of Dominica looks like 'an Antillean Cranford'[15] while St George in Grenada (where it was raining) looked like 'a beautiful eighteenth-century Devonshire town in mid-winter'.[16]

In Haiti Paddy witnessed a riot in a theatre, where the black audience were outraged by the lifeless acting of the *'sale mulatres'* (mulattoes, of mixed race) who made up the company. Yet for the French missionary Father Cosme, racial tension was not the most frightening thing about Haiti; it was the rise of Voodoo. Until recently Voodoo had been violently suppressed by the missionaries, but the current government positively encouraged its practice.

Night after night, Paddy, Joan and Costa, drawn by the beat of the drums, pressed their way through the crowds around the *tonnelle*, an open circle of beaten earth with a central pillar where the rituals took place. Here the faithful danced themselves into a hypnotic trance, hoping to be possessed by one of the Lwas, the powerful deities of Voodoo: Legba, Damballah Wédo, Zaka, Agoué Arroyo, Erzulie Fréda Dahomin, Ogoun Feraille. The possession might go on all night before the god left, leaving its human shell drained and exhausted. All had their symbols and, not surprisingly, images of the Catholic saints were easily brought into the Voodoo pantheon, as were chunks of church liturgy. At the edge of the tonnelle was a little hut, *le caye Zombi*. They flashed a torch inside where, amongst many other objects, they saw a cross on which hung an old frock coat and a battered bowler hat. A totem seen in every Voodoo temple, it represents Baron Samedi, God of the Cemeteries and Lord of the Dead.

Paddy became utterly absorbed by Voodoo: its fusion of gods that had been traced back to Guiana, Congo and Dahomey, its patchwork language of French, Creole, Latin and tribal African, its inexplicable rituals – 'It seemed impossible to talk or think or read about anything else.'[17] No one seemed to object to their presence in the tonnelles, and no one asked for money, though it was appreciated when they brought a half-bottle of rum to contribute to the audience's common supply.

The books on Voodoo that Paddy found were by French, American and German academics, whose main aims were to codify this religion and trace the origins of its gods and rituals. But in trying to put Voodoo on an academic grid, they seemed to miss its very essence.

> It was developed instinctively to lead the slaves to a private liberty that the state of things in their world forbade. The open air and the sunlight meant the cane-fields, the sweat, the chains, the whip, the endless toil and misery of a slave's existence. So, like children who build up a dark and secret world of freedom and womb-like intimacy out of chairs and carpets, and sit there in felicity for hours, the slaves went warrening back into the darkness, farther and farther away from the heartless glare. There they crouched in the warm secrecy of their own sounds and spirits and joys and terrors, and, above all, with memories of Africa which grew, with every passing generation, dimmer and more wonderful.[18]

Wherever the travellers went, all human interaction was contaminated to a greater or lesser extent by what, at that time, was known as 'the colour question'. They were both amused and appalled by the French civil engineer who loathed the bread-fruit tree because it 'keeps the black alive without working. It lets them grow fat without doing a hand's turn . . . And who's to blame for *that? You,* sir . . . Not you directly, but your Bligg!'[19] ('Bligg' turned out to be Captain Bligh, the captain of the *Bounty*.)

More sinister than this lunatic was the mealy-mouthed apartheid practised on the island of Barbados. Rather than adopt an overt segregation, Barbadian whites had ensured that all the establishments they patronized were designated as 'clubs', from which blacks were automatically excluded. As whites, Paddy, Joan and Costa were automatically members, even though 'we had never been elected and it was impossible to resign'.[20] No wonder they were made to feel so unwelcome when, all unwitting, they walked off the street into a local bar.

Paddy tried to wriggle out of the straitjacket of colour prejudice but it was not always possible, and he was often frustrated by the way it put him in a completely false position. In the streets,

> men shout out 'Hey I want to talk to you.' You give no sign of life, you are talking to somebody else, then 'You white guy don' want to talk to a nigger, eh?' in an offensive defensive voice. What is one to do? Gallop back, shake his hand . . . in an élan of ersatz camaraderie, and say 'My dear friend, I am entirely lacking in colour prejudice and you are a great guy, but you put me in an impossible position, because I'm in a terrible hurry. I'd love to stay and talk, but I can't.' What happens? Either a lachrymose shaking of the head ('I'm onto a sucker') or 'You're a gentleman, Sah! I got de very girl for you!'[21]

As for the Rastafari of Jamaica, Paddy was told that they hated white people with a passion. They lived in a huddle of huts made of newspapers and the rusting skeletons of cars, on a patch of ground in the slums of Kingston called the Dunghill, pronounced Dungle. Paddy was greeted with open hostility but, by handing round his cigarettes and pretending to be a complete innocent, they thawed. He was taken into a hut, where he was told about their culture and beliefs while a boy rolled him a reefer. The only authority they were willing to acknowledge was their king, Haile Selassie, the Lion of

Judah. He was going to come and conquer the West Indies, drive out the white man and take the Rastafari back to Ethiopia. When Paddy ventured to suggest that all the slaves brought to the Caribbean came from west rather than east Africa, he was told it was all lies, written in white history books. 'We're from Abyssinia. We got wise men, and they tell us the truth.'[22]

While in Jamaica Paddy, Joan and Costa spent a day at Goldeneye, as guests of Commander Ian Fleming and his not-yet wife, Ann Rothermere, whom Paddy had met through Emerald Cunard. Although Ann and Fleming had been lovers for years and she was about to leave her husband Esmond Rothermere for him, the proprieties had to be observed. Ann was making her first visit to Goldeneye chaperoned by Loelia, Duchess of Westminster.

The house was modest, Spartan, surrounded by trees on all sides except where two great glassless windows looked out over the sea. Loelia was swimming languidly in the bay when they arrived, while according to Ann, Ian had not yet emerged from the study where he spent his mornings on the typewriter, 'bashing away at a thriller'. This was his very first Bond book, *Casino Royale*. When he emerged from his study Paddy described Fleming as having 'a strong sneering face, but not a sneering character'.[23] Much later Ian Fleming was to borrow heavily from Paddy's description of Voodoo in *The Traveller's Tree* for another Bond novel, *Live and Let Die*.

For all the hybrid eclecticism of the Antilles and their calypso colours, Paddy was glad when they left the Caribbean for British Honduras. 'All the Caribbean islands have something wrong with them,' he wrote in a notebook. 'All are founded on bloodshed and slavery, and are now miserable, subsidized, impoverished places, stiff with political friction and repression, or rich places exploited up to the hilt, pleasure haunts for the rich.'[24] In British Honduras, on the other hand, 'the colour question' vanished. The Indians they met as they made their way down the river Belize were 'calm, gentle, friendly and laughing easily, with a dignity and normality and equality that is a tremendous relief . . . There was none of the suspicion on both sides, the touchiness, the banter, the begging, the jeering, the awkwardness.'[25] They made their way south by sea, threading their way through the maze of little reefs and islands which fringe the coast, while Paddy read Sir John Thompson's *Civilization of the Mayas*.

Costa left them at Punta Gorda, travelling by sea to Puerto Barrios in Guatemala. From there he made his way to Guatemala City, to meet Anne-Marie Callimachi who had come out to see him. As a Greek Costa could travel freely, but British citizens coming in from British Honduras were forbidden to enter Guatemala. For years the Guatemalans had laid claim to British Honduras, a territory which would have given them half the eastern seaboard of the Yucatan peninsula. The argument had been allowed to drop during the war, but now the sabre-rattling resumed. Britain was on the point of despatching troops to defend its territory, while Guatemala had closed its frontier with British Honduras to the British.

'Joan and I have formed the insane plan of attempting to get into Guatemala overland,' wrote Paddy in his notebook in mid-February, from a remote Indian settlement called San Antonio in the far south of British Honduras.[26] The proposal appalled the local *alcalde*, Don Diego, who kept saying that it was '*imposible por la pobra Señora*'. He also told them that the roads were impassable: a hurricane two years before had destroyed some, while the rest were probably still blocked by landslides and fallen logs. On the map, the Guatemalan border was only a few miles away to the west; but the dense Petén jungle was scored with ravines, and no one knew the state of the few roads. However, there were a number of Indians in San Antonio who had come from the Guatemalan side. They found one who had just made the journey. 'Dark, enthusiastic, cheerful man, a *chiclero** in a red bandana and long cutlass, leggings and boots . . . We asked his name, and it was his answer which decided us more than any proper reason. It was Exaltación Puc.'[27]

With a couple of mules and Exaltación, they embarked on a twelve-hour trek through the jungle. Bent almost double for hour after hour as they followed Exaltación and his machete, they squelched through thick mud, slithered down steep gullies and scrambled pain-fully up the other side. The hostile, spiny undergrowth caught at

---

* *Chicleros*: poor men who worked deep in the jungle tending the *chicle* trees, which produce gum: hence 'Chicklets', an American brand of chewing gum.

hair and clothes and blotted out almost all light. The mules were abandoned, sold to a band of *chicleros*. One of their number was deputed to carry the luggage, but he soon abandoned them too, after which Exaltacíon carried almost everything. He also cooked their tortillas and bean mash flavoured with chili peppers, and that night – Paddy and Joan were too sore to move – he built them a shelter of leaves to sleep under. Eventually the jungle began to give way to little stands of maize, and they came across a *chiclero* encampment, big enough to form a ragged village round a little airstrip. A day or two later Paddy and Joan were on the plane, which was filled with people taking their chickens and pigs to market.

In Guatemala City they met up with Costa, and set off westwards a few days later to Panajachel, which became their base for the first half of March. Here they hired horses, and rode through the villages that are strung around Lake Atitlan, and Paddy finished reading William Prescott's *The Conquest of Mexico* – 'as stupendous as Gibbon'.[28] They made an expedition to the north of the country to clamber up the vertiginous Mayan ruins of Tikal, smothered in roots and lianas and guarded by screaming monkeys swinging from branch to branch, 'like furious black footballs of fur'.[29]

Leaving Panajachel they went south once again, and crossed the border at Santa Anna into El Salvador. It was 21 March, Palm Sunday, and the streets were filled with palm-waving crowds. After three days they moved into Honduras and spent the rest of Holy Week in the capital, Tegucigalpa. 'For the whole week the town was one enormous wound,' Paddy wrote to Jock Murray, 'and every itch in the palm seemed to herald the stigmata.'[30]

From El Salvador they made their way through Nicaragua, sailing down the San Juan river; but the journey had become slow, hot and claustrophobic. At Barra del Colorado in Costa Rica, the air was almost solid with insects. Costa left while Paddy and Joan were out riding, having found a boat going to Puerto Limón. He hoped they would follow the next day, but they missed the boat – and Costa had all the traveller's cheques. In Panama, waiting for money, they were saved from starvation by a Greek hot-dog vendor called Stavro. When the money finally arrived, he refused all payment – he had fed them purely for the pleasure of talking about Greece.

Their passage home took about three weeks, on an Australian boat, the *Rara Tiki*, which docked at Tilbury on 20 May. On leaving the boat they bought a newspaper, where Joan was shocked to read that her friend Dick Wyndham was dead. He had been covering the Arab-Israeli War for the *Sunday Times*, and was caught in a burst of machine-gun fire just outside Jerusalem. It was a bitter homecoming.

13

Writing *The Traveller's Tree*

In the spring of 1948, Paddy found himself with almost too much work. From Panama he had informed Jock that 'I have not written another word of the Greek book since leaving England, and have had a terrible time keeping up to date with notes and diaries about the Caribbean and Central American Balkans, and a series of articles. But as soon as I have sloughed off the literary commitments of the journey, I long to resume writing about Greece . . .'[1] The articles were part of the agreement he had with Costa who wanted to place his photographs in as many magazines as possible. Since most magazines required a story to accompany the illustrations, Paddy found himself having to write articles for *National Geographic, Contact* magazine and *Picture Post,* among others; and once back in England, he could not put off the task any longer.

So Paddy made no demur when, that August, Joan set off on a tour of south-western France with Cyril Connolly. They had always agreed that their relationship would never be fettered by possessiveness; freedom and friendship came first. Joan was above sexual jealousy, and so was he – unless it took the form of a joke, or a way of expressing how much he had missed her.

Connolly was in a strange mood. He was beginning to tire of Lys (Mrs Ian) Lubbock, a member of the *Horizon* staff whom he lived with, relied on and had once loved. As for *Horizon*, he was disenchanted with the magazine and editing its pages was becoming a chore. When Harper & Row commissioned him to write a book about south-western France, he had asked Dick Wyndham to keep him company and take the photographs – but now Dick was dead. So he had asked Joan, 'a person with whom I have almost everything in common – friends, tastes, intellectual interests – and very beautiful . . .'[2]

As they walked and drove over the Massif Central and into the Dordogne, the ever-susceptible Cyril fell rapturously in love. 'She was indeed very remarkable,' he wrote of her in his unfinished novel 'Happy Deathbeds', in which she appears as Jane Sotheran. 'She did what she liked, she kept moving, she had few possessions, no husband, a lover in several capitals, old friends, a good palate, a talent for photography, a love of art and exploration, a safe private income. Paying her share formed an intrinsic part of her character and contributed to the defeat of all her lovers . . .'[3]

Joan did not enjoy the sexual tension, and felt that her bohemian values somehow obliged her to release it. 'Why do these complications have to spoil things so often?' she wrote to Paddy. 'I feel like a boringly monogamous bourgeois bitch but I can't do anything about it. It seems so easy to make everyone happy, but I can't.'[4] And when, in the wild gorge of Bramabiau, Connolly suggested that they perform a mock-wedding, she was willing to play along with him. Connolly felt that the stones loosened by a party of Boy Scouts high above them were the work of a Cyclops whom he called 'Paddy-Phemus'.[5]

After some time in England struggling with his articles, Paddy moved to Paris where he took a room in the Hotel Louisiane. He does not mention his fellow guests, but at this stage they included Simone de Beauvoir and Juliette Gréco. Around the corner were the Café Flore and the Deux Magots, where Jean-Paul Sartre and de Beauvoir worked and held court. Not far away was Le Bar Vert which stayed open all night, and Le Tabou, the hottest new nightclub in Saint-Germain-des-Prés. In fact he had installed himself in the heart of existentialist Paris, and it is perhaps a miracle that he did any work there at all. Yet somehow he despatched all his articles from his room at the Louisiane, where the window looked out on to the backs of three gold horse's heads belonging to the horse butcher below, which gave him the impression that he was riding a troika.

Once the articles were out of the way, he took up an invitation to Gadencourt, near Pacy-sur-Eure in Normandy, and a farmhouse that would become a regular refuge in the future. His old friend Amy Smart, who had been so much a part of his life in wartime

Cairo, had bought the property before the war with Allanah Harper, writer, muse, and founder of the Paris literary quarterly *Echanges*. It was set in an orchard, every room was stuffed with books; and while Amy and Walter Smart still passed their winters in Egypt, they spent much of the summer in Normandy. Paddy's fellow guest that summer was Patrick Kinross, another old friend from Cairo.

Here Paddy began writing the book that Costa had already entitled *The Traveller's Tree*. He felt it was a good choice. This particular fan-like palm tree is found throughout the Caribbean, though its original home was the islands of Mauritius and Reunion; displacement featured in the history of every ethnic group to be found in the Antilles, all of whom (including the Caribs) had originated elsewhere. Paddy set to work on the book with application and enthusiasm. 'I love this life', he wrote to Joan, 'and hate the idea of leaving it. I've discovered that I can write absolutely the whole day long with the utmost enjoyment, settled quietly in the country . . . How different writing a book is to writing articles! If ever the Muse flags, I nip into the dining room and swallow a *coup de rouge* . . .'[6]

He stayed at Gadencourt as long as he could, and then returned to Paris and the Louisiane. When not writing, he was rereading Gide – *Paludes* and *Les Caves du Vatican*; and it was around this time that he discovered the work of J.-K. Huysmans, who was to have a profound effect.

Joris-Karl Huysmans (1848–1907) had been a follower of Zola and the Naturalists, until his novel *A Rebours* shocked Paris with its misanthropic decadence. He went on to plumb the darkest pits of depravity in *Là-Bas*, a fictional study of Satanism, and eventually returned to the Catholicism he had abandoned in his youth. Yet he held modern priests in contempt, with their veal-broth sermons and their bourgeois God, venerating instead the saints of the medieval church, who practised years of self-mortification in order to curb the cravings of the flesh.

Huysmans' works led Paddy into a study of French monasticism and religious ecstasy, which – in different form – he had witnessed in Haiti. Above all, he was exhilarated by the author's style. Here was someone who could take eight pages to describe the effects of dawn breaking inside Chartres Cathedral, with an almost hallucinatory intensity; someone who, like Proust, used lists of things to build up layers of images; someone who could describe plainchant as architecture, just as (decades later) Paddy was to describe the Baroque architecture of Melk in musical terms.

They had another bond; for Huysmans, like Paddy, struggled with bouts of depression. The confident start he had made on *The Traveller's Tree* at Gadencourt had turned into a jumble of fragments: in fact he had so much material that he felt he could make a further two books of it, one on Central America and one on Mayan civilization. Part of his absorption with Huysmans and religion was, he knew, an escape. The pleasures of Paris at night were also becoming dangerously addictive. He had always resented going to bed, and revelled in the smoky world of tarts and nightclubs, all-night cafés, seedy bars and chance encounters. Nor had he lost his taste for *pastrouma*, the pungent dried meat he had first eaten in Bulgaria. 'A lump of camel', as he called it, was often on the menu of the small Cretan restaurant where he was a regular.

Someone had told him that the abbey of Saint-Wandrille in Normandy took in non-paying guests, even if their reasons for staying did not include religious retreat or instruction. In late September, he took a train from Paris to Rouen. The abbey had been founded in the seventh century, and its periods of prosperity alternated with periods of pillage, destruction and fire. During the battle for Normandy in 1944, its seventeenth-century buildings had been partly destroyed; but it was still home to some sixty or seventy monks.

When Paddy turned up on the doorstep unannounced one Sunday afternoon, he had no idea whether the monks would be willing to take him in or not. But he was allowed in and shown to a cell, a high seventeenth-century room overlooking a courtyard. It contained a bed, a prie-dieu, a crucifix and a table. Meals were taken in silence, in the enormous refectory hall. Working at the coalface of salvation, the monks spent several hours a day in church, and several more in study, private prayer and meditation. All that was required of the guests was to obey the rules set out for them.

How different the Benedictines were to the raki-swigging, pistol-packing, ballad-singing monks he had known in the monasteries of wartime Crete. These pale cowled figures, who were never seen to smile or frown, seemed to him barely alive. It was impossible to work in this suffocating, tomb-like place. By nine o'clock – just when his friends in Paris were beginning to think about how to spend the evening – the whole monastery was asleep. Paddy slept badly the first few nights, falling into deep wells of hopeless misery. By day he was restless and tired. This was followed by a period of intense lethargy, when he found himself – for almost the first time in his life – spending more hours asleep than awake.

He emerged from this period of narcolepsy feeling not only refreshed, but revitalized in a way that was quite new to him. He began to understand how the monastic rule conserved energies that, in real life, were dissipated in 'conversations at meals, small talk, catching trains, or the hundred anxious trivialities that poison everyday life. Even the major causes of guilt and anxiety had slid away into some distant limbo . . . This new dispensation left nineteen hours a day of absolute and god-like freedom.'[7] Paddy spent it walking in the autumnal forests around the abbey, while at night he worked in front of the pile of manuscripts, maps of the Caribbean islands, and photographs of the Central American jungle.

Almost a month was spent at Saint-Wandrille, which went from being a sepulchre to a sanctuary. He felt he could not impose on the monks much longer, but work was progressing and he did not want to break the monastic spell. It could also be that he was rather nervous of the direction Joan wanted their relationship to take. 'I got the curse so late this month', she wrote in one letter, 'that I began to hope I was having a baby, and that you would have to make it into a legitimate little Fermor. All hopes ruined this morning.'[8]

He returned to Paris filled with resolution, but soon felt the need for another monastic immersion. This time he went to the great monastery of Saint-Jean-de-Solesmes on the river Sarthe, where the tradition of plainchant had been revived under its founder, Dom Prosper Guéranger. Again the monks welcomed him, but 'I'm not enjoying Solesmes quite as much as I did Saint-Wandrille . . . There are many more monks here, everything is much more organized and impersonal.' The long cold passages, and the swing doors with frosted glass panes, gave him that sinking feeling of going back to school. However, 'I am working like anything at the moment, and in spite of Benzers [benzedrine tablets, sent to him by Joan] I feel absolutely exhausted.' In between bouts of writing he read in the vast and well-catalogued library. The books included 'a Flemish medieval mystic called Ruysbroek, and St Angela of Foligno, who even surpasses Marie de l'Incarnation . . .'[9]

During his stay a nervous young English monk arrived at the monastery. His name was Henry Joseph Campbell, and Paddy described him in *A Time to Keep Silence*. 'Shot down in the war in the bomber he was piloting, he had studied, after his release from a German prisoner-of-war camp, for the Anglican ministry. He had then gone over to Rome and plunged into the depths of a Trappist monastery.'[10] His letter to Joan filled in the details of the young monk's experience at Timadeuc, the most austere of the Trappist foundations in France. 'It wasn't the dead silence . . . that got him down, so much as the gruelling work in the fields . . . living the life of a navvy without a single moment's solitude . . . He looks a nervous wreck, wild eyes, chapped hands and broken nails, talks the whole time . . . He has the most dreadful doubts every now and then, and careers into my cell to ask for advice.'[11]

While Paddy was listening to this troubled young man, Joan was missing her lover. 'I was beset with doubts and gloom at the thought that you must be concocting some appalling letter saying you never wanted to see me again . . . Darling Angel I am longing to see you again so much and I do think it would be lovely to get married awfully soon. I don't think we will ever get anywhere the way we live at the moment and I'm sure we shan't feel any more tied than we are already.'[12] Paddy, struggling with his own demons and uncertain if he would ever succeed as a writer, was in no mood to respond.

In the second half of December, he spent ten days in the monastery of La Grande Trappe in Normandy, home to the Cistercian Order of the Strict Observance. The Trappist life is one of continual prayer and total silence. Even Huysmans, when he came to La Grande Trappe, warned his spiritual adviser that it would be a short visit: he had heard that the vegetables were cooked in nothing but water.

Paddy was shown into a bare, freezing cell; he had no contact with the monks; his cheerless meals were eaten alone, listening to the reading from the refectory on a loudspeaker. The Trappists spent seven hours a day standing or kneeling in their Victorian Gothic church, which Paddy described as 'a great, dark, north-Oxford night-mare'.[13] Yet two days of low spirits gave way to a calmer mood, and 'a kind of masochistic enjoyment of the sad charm of the Trappe'.[14]

He understood that every monk's life was one of perpetual penance and sacrifice, accompanied by titanic struggles with doubt and temptation – torments that no monk was ever free from. Thinking of Henry Campbell, Paddy wondered what damage such stress might inflict on the psyche. 'Can so many human instincts be seized like a handful of snakes, tied up in a sack, and locked away, alive and squirming, for a lifetime?'[15] Yet the guest master and the Abbot, who were the only monks permitted to talk to him, seemed remarkably healthy and normal.

It was almost Christmas when he left La Grande Trappe, and travelled back to Paris by bus with the Abbot. As the rain scuttled across the steamy windows, the Abbot spoke of his brief wartime service as an infantry officer and a POW, till he returned to his abbey at the armistice. 'Everything in his face', wrote Paddy, 'and the slight Breton accent of his voice revealed a thoughtful and sober alacrity, leavened occasionally by a deep quiet laugh.'[16]

In the articles he wrote about these three monasteries, Paddy's own religious feelings are scarcely mentioned. He was grateful to the abbots, guest masters and librarians with whom he conversed for never raising so embarrassing a subject, and silently hopes his reader will show the same tact. Almost none of his subsequent writings show anything like the same level of introspection, and certain passages seem to yearn for a deeper spiritual experience, like a thirsty man in the desert gazing at what might be an oasis or a mirage. For the monks the oasis was very real but for Paddy, in spite of his yearnings, it remained a mirage.

Yet the weeks he spent in these French monasteries had made a profound impression. From time to time throughout his life he would re-immerse himself in their austere tranquillity, and something in his nature needed these retreats. He found the company of monks both restful and intellectually exhilarating, and he admired and respected the choice they had made. Above all, they made him aware of how much better he worked when away from the bright lights. From now on he would try and do all his serious writing in a quiet place, removed from bustle and temptation.

In *Enemies of Promise* (1938), Cyril Connolly advised the ambitious writer to resist the temptation to find a day job, that sapper of creative energy, no matter how broke he was. It was never much of a temptation to Paddy. All his life he had lived on a shoestring, and he was not afraid of penury or discomfort. But over the next year or so, he was under great strain to complete his first book. At the same time he had no money coming in, and was relying on Joan to tide him over: it was not an easy time for either of them.

Joan wanted to marry him; but Paddy, while delighted to make it a marriage of true minds, saw several impediments to the real thing. While they remained single her help was a gift, freely given and gratefully received, and if she became disillusioned or lost patience, she could walk away. At the same time he did not want to lose her, nor did he want her to think that he was dragging his feet. In early 1949 he wrote: 'Darling, I like the glib way I talk about getting married; I do hope you'll still have me! I have been such an empty bore these last weeks, that perhaps you are thinking better of it. Darling, please don't! I'll be alright again as soon as [the book]'s finished, I promise!'[17]

Yet if they did marry, some might say he had only done it to secure a safety-net: and there were people who, usually because they worshipped Joan, took a dim view of Paddy. Maurice Bowra was one of those who bore him a grudge, and put it into verse. 'The Wounded Gigolo', written in April 1950, is addressed to Balasha Cantacuzene and suggests (wrongly) that she dismissed Paddy. Joan is the subject of 'On the Shores of Terra Fermor', written a month later. Bowra sees her sighing and stranded, having made the mistake of giving her heart to someone who is rarely there.[18] It was essential that they wed as equals, and for that to happen he had to prove himself as a writer. Joan knew it too, and after 1949 her mentions of marriage and babies tail off.

In February 1949 they drove through France and Italy with Hamish St Clair-Erskine, Nancy Mitford's first love who was once described as living 'entirely on personal charm'.[19] The party split up in Tuscany.

Hamish and Joan drove on to Sicily, where she was to take photographs for an article Peter Quennell was writing on the sculptor Giacomo Serpotta, while Paddy settled down to what he hoped would be a productive spell of writing in Pienza. 'Darling, we are absolutely broke,' wrote Joan from Taormina, 'so do try and live for ages on what you have . . . I don't know how we are going to get home, but I am hoping for a miracle . . .'[20]

Paddy moved into an inn on the tiny main square, looking over the Duomo and the palace built by Aeneas Silvius Piccolomini, later Pope Pius II. 'The little albergo-trattoria looked snug enough. But it was March, when a wind from Siberia blows into the Tuscan hills, and in a day or two, fingers were turning to icicles; no question of holding a pen; so I went to the bar and found it full of woodsmoke and dramatically cloaked herdsmen from the Abruzzi drinking grappa at high speed; it was the only thing to do.' When he returned, the landlady said she had put 'a priest' in his bed – which proved to be a charcoal brazier, kept above the bedclothes by a wooden cage. 'When I had clumsily lifted the whole thing out, I felt lucky, after all that grappa, not to have set that beautiful little town on fire.'[21]

Having spent perhaps more than he should on grappa he moved down to Rome where, true to form, he soon found some friends attached to the Embassy. On hearing of his search to find somewhere to write, Cécile and Mondi Howard suggested the old Franciscan monastery of San Antonio near Tivoli. Paddy was allowed to move into its deserted splendour, and here – with the help of the kindly baroque angel painted in flight over his bed, which 'brought me luck' – his work seemed to go better.

'One evening, I started writing at sunset, worked, as I thought, for an hour or two, and suddenly there were odd sounds and something queer about the light. It was dawn breaking and the birds waking up.'[22] Years later, writing to Ann Fleming, the ghost of that intense period of productivity was still alive: 'I moved in [to the monastery] and wrote *The Traveller's Tree* before you could say knife.'[23]

That was a bit of an exaggeration; but Paddy always felt that the act of writing should begin with a creative torrent of words and ideas, coming so thick and fast that he could scarcely keep up with them. He set great store by the initial surge of writing, for the words put down at this point glowed with life and energy. If this part had gone well, it could be subjected to hours of unpicking and refashioning without (he hoped) losing the freshness of the original. Yet these moments of creative possession, when the self is lost and time becomes meaningless, were rare. When asked which particular passages in *The Traveller's Tree* had sprung up in this way he was reluctant to offer an answer. It was the moment that was precious, not the work produced.

Ever since he had struck out on his own, just being abroad brought a spiritual and imaginative release. The act of writing always flowed better abroad, and now Paddy embarked on a ten-year odyssey in which he was rarely in one place for more than a month or two, shifting mainly between Italy, Greece, England and France. Amy and Walter Smart allowed him to live at Gadencourt whenever it was empty, and here he was looked after by their Breton housekeeper, Marie, who cooked for him. He spent some time there that spring, and in the summer moved to the Easton Court Hotel in the village of Chagford, Devon. Patrick Kinross had told him about this fourteenth-century inn, which was run by an American lady called Mrs Postlethwaite-Cobb and her partner Norman Webb. They dispensed a generous but reasonably priced hospitality to an appreciative literary clientele, including Evelyn Waugh when he needed to get away from his family. Paddy was by now frantic to finish the book, and the strain was showing.

'Darling old Mole,' Joan wrote to him:

> Don't get gloomy and depressed and don't write me any awful letters saying we can't even talk or get on, as I do love you so much. I was furious and miserable last night at leaving you as we don't seem to have seen each other properly alone for ages – but then I think I shall feel like that until the book is finished as I keep feeling you should be writing instead of just talking to me. You sounded so sweet this morning and I am desperately addicted to you at the moment.[24]

Another friend came to the rescue. Barbara Warner, who had left her first husband Victor Rothschild for Paddy's old boss Rex Warner, told Joan that summer that she could have the use of a flat at 76 Charlotte Street which belonged to her mother, Mary Hutchinson.

'The only blot is Mrs H[utchinson] whom I am terrified of,' wrote Joan,[25] but the flat became their London base for a number of years.

Paddy's article on Saint-Wandrille appeared that summer in the *Cornhill* magazine, which had been under the editorship of Peter Quennell since 1944. The *Cornhill*, as Quennell himself admitted, was never in direct competition with Cyril Connolly's more influential *Horizon*. '*Horizon* was dedicated to the spirit of the age, to new ideas and discoveries . . . while in the *Cornhill* I merely assembled whatever I considered worth printing . . . Mine was an individual, perhaps a dilettante choice.'[26] Paddy's second article, 'From Solesmes to La Grande Trappe', appeared the following spring.

On 9 September, Jock Murray took Paddy out to lunch. In a memo to himself he wrote: 'He has finished his Caribbean book for Lindsay Drummond, it is roughly 200,000 words and they want him to cut it down. When he has finished the two travel books on Central America, he will get down to the Greek book and promises to let us see a synopsis and additional material. He is also completing a second contribution for the *Cornhill* on a Trappist monastery.'[27]

He was also hoping to write a life of the great conquistador Pedro de Alvarado. The idea was suggested by Edward (later 1st Lord) Shackleton, the younger son of the explorer, who was putting together a series of books on great travellers and explorers. 'I ought to be able to do it fairly quickly,' wrote Paddy, 'by March at the outside, probably sooner.'[28] Paddy was willing to do it for £100 advance and £50 on delivery since he was so short of money, but the project came to nothing.

Disaster struck at the end of January 1950. Paddy had already corrected galley proofs of *The Traveller's Tree* and was awaiting page proofs when he was told that the firm of Lindsay Drummond was filing for bankruptcy, leaving Paddy with no publisher. His only hope was Jock Murray, to whom he wrote on 10 February 1950: 'I have written to them saying that you might like to have a look at it . . .'[29] He added that, as promised, he would shortly be sending Jock what he had written of his book on Greece, which had been heavily revised and retyped.

To his profound relief (and that of Lindsay Drummond's creditors) Jock Murray decided to take on *The Traveller's Tree* and undertook to pay the receivers 'advances to the Author and costs incurred'[30] which came to £350. Part of the 'costs incurred' were Paddy's heavy corrections at the galley stage, and they were just as heavy when Paddy returned the page proofs. Few other publishers would have allowed Paddy such freedom of action at such a late stage in production: Jock Murray was very indulgent. But since there was a big advance to pay back, it meant that Paddy could expect no money on publication.

Billy Moss's *Ill Met by Moonlight* was published in March. Billy had sent Paddy the proofs, to which the latter had made endless corrections and little changes of style – but still he was not happy. As well as Billy's rather tactless treatment of the Cretans, Paddy felt he had been unsympathetic to the General. Billy disagreed. It was a diary, written under difficult conditions, and should be accepted as such.

The reviews were kind, paying tribute to two very brave young men who had pulled off an extraordinary feat; but Harold Nicolson agreed with Paddy. Writing in the *Observer* he remarked that '[Moss] did not fully understand the self-sacrifice of the Cretans who, in assisting with the operation, were exposing their homes and families to savage reprisals. Nor was he sufficiently sensitive to the agonies of humiliation that General Kreipe must have suffered.'[31]

On 14 March, accompanied by Joan, his sister Vanessa and his mother, Paddy went to Buckingham Palace to receive the military OBE from the hands of King George VI. After the ceremony the King passed down the line of honorands, stopped in front of Paddy, and fingered the medal. 'So where did you get that then?' asked the monarch – to which Paddy was tempted to reply, 'Your Majesty, you've just put it there.'[32] After the investiture, they all repaired for a celebratory lunch at the Café Royal. Joan had been dreading it, knowing how Æileen had hated the very idea of Balasha; but she was funny and charming, and the event passed off more happily than Joan had dared to hope.

That spring Paddy took a boat to Oporto and travelled round Portugal before going to stay with the anthropologist Julian Pitt-Rivers, in the Andalusian village of Grazalema. Between 1949 and 1952, Pitt-Rivers lived among the villagers whose customs and traditions he described in *People of the Sierra* (1953). At Grazalema he was joined by Joan, and together they went on to Madrid – where things had not gone well. From Dumbleton she wrote: 'I just wanted to say what an angel you have been the whole time – so sweet and patient while I was so beastly as usual . . .' It seems as if her bad temper was due in part to anxiety about his financial dependence.

> Darling, it must be so wretched arriving in England and having no money. I propose to pay into your bank £30 from June for the rest of the year and an extra £50 to start you off, and then you need not have all the bother and hell of asking me. It sounds terribly little darling but I do think you ought to try and make some money for yourself – I cannot think why really, but it would be much better for you from every point of view. Also it's about half of what I really must try to live on. Please don't think I'm doing this so that we can see less of each other, but only so that we needn't be so much bothered by it all.[33]

In other words, Joan was going to support Paddy with up to half her allowance for the rest of the year, and probably beyond. She hoped that he might earn a little money to augment this, because while an allowance of £720 a year was generous for one person, it would be hard to make it stretch for two. It was an act of great generosity.

14

Travels in Greece

With *The Traveller's Tree* now finished and ready for publication in December, Paddy could finally turn back to the book on Greece, for which he felt a lot more research was needed. This would come out of the advance paid in three tranches of £100, and over the next two years Jock often had occasion to write to the Bank of England for permission to transfer more than the permitted £50 into Greek drachmas and Italian lire.

The Ambassador Clifford Norton and his wife, Peter, had Paddy and Joan to stay at the Embassy when they arrived that summer, and took them for 'a heavenly day bathing and drinking and talking' at their cottage near Piraeus.[1] Freya Stark remembered it too: 'Yesterday we had a cheerful party down here,' she wrote to her husband, Stewart Perowne, 'with Paddy Leigh Fermor and Joan . . . Paddy looking in this wine-dark sea *so* like a Hellenistic lesser sea-god of a rather low period, and I do like him. He is the genuine buccaneer . . .'[2]

From Athens Paddy and Joan went to Istanbul, which he had last seen in 1935, and from there they made the long dusty journey into central Anatolia and the town of Ürgüp in Cappadocia – a place they had been urged to visit by George Seferis. Just to the east of the town lies a geological phenomenon: an arid lunar landscape in which families of conical rocks erupt out of the desert. Between the fourth and the eleventh centuries, monks and hermits were drawn here. Into the rock they carved hundreds of cells and churches, complete with vaults and pillars, apses and domes, all painted with saints and scenes from the life of Christ. From the evidence of painted prayers and scrolls, the monks who lived here were not great scholars, though Paddy notes that their 'phonetic spelling provides additional proof that tenth-century Greek was pronounced exactly as it is in Athens today'.[3] 'The Rock Monasteries of Cappadocia' was the third of his articles on monasteries for the *Cornhill*.

The plan was to explore Thrace and Macedonia, which he had not visited since before the war. From Istanbul they went by rail to Adrianople (now Edirne), and another train took them to the coastal town of Alexandroupolis, from where they hoped to board the ferry to the island of Samothrace.

The town was welcoming, but in the uneasy years following the civil war, local officialdom was wary of independent foreigners wandering about on no specific business – particularly when they spoke the language well. The harbourmaster did not like the look of Paddy and Joan, and refused to let them board. Paddy, who saw himself as an honorary Greek, was indignant at being treated like a spy and a furious row ensued; but everyone who had gathered to watch the argument took his side, and eventually they were allowed to cross to the island. It was late September 1950 when they returned to the mainland, and not long afterwards they attended a Sarakatsan wedding. Many years later the wedding at Sikaraya, some two hours north-west of Alexandroupolis, was to be the subject of the opening chapter of *Roumeli*.

They went to Sikaraya in an antiquated train. Attached to the back was a cattle truck which carried the bridegroom and his friends, all shouting and singing and waving guns and banners. The ritual 'abduction' of the bride took place at a railway halt, where she was waiting with her bridesmaids. To the sound of triumphant whoops and gunfire she was passed like an effigy into the truck. Paddy was fascinated by the women's elaborate woollen costumes, stiff as armour with pleated skirts and embroidered sleeves: descriptions that relied on the photographs Joan took at the time.

After the church service, the Sarakatsan clans gathered in a house among the conical tents, recently built by the groom's father. Dressed in black with their crooks over their shoulders, the men all sat on a long low divan. Low tables were brought in, laden with wine and roast lamb, and as the celebrations got under way the men began singing Klephtic songs. But although the bridegroom was busy looking after his guests, there was no sign of the bride. She, it turned

HODOPE MOUNTAINS

Edirne

Xanthi

vala Komotini Sikaraya

THRACE

Alexandroupolis

THASSOS

SAMOTHRACE

ount
thos

Constantinople Bosphorus

SEA OF
MARMARA

Hellespont (Dardanelles)

Çanakkale

Troy

DES

AEGEAN
SEA

TURKEY

Smyrna (Izmir)

Kuşadasi

CYCLADES

PAROS

DODECANESE

Greece, Albania and Turkey

out, was standing in silent vigil in an upstairs room with her companions, her dowry ranged behind them. Paddy and Joan were taken to
see her, and she accepted their greeting with a silent bow of her
head.

From Komotini, a town with a large Turkish population, Paddy
now wanted to visit the Pomaks of the Rhodope mountains. It took
some time, for they had to apply to the Greek army authorities before going into such uncertain territory; but on 30 September,
they made the journey by truck to a Pomak village called Kedro.

The Pomaks are a Slavic group of Sunni Muslims, supposedly
converted to Islam by the Ottoman Turks; and there are Pomak
communities in Bulgaria, Macedonia and western Thrace. The
Pomak language has elements of Greek, Bulgarian and Turkish, but
only the women spoke it. Their host, Daoud Ali-Oghlu Mehmet,
spoke Turkish and Greek, and lived in a traditional Pomak house,
with great flat slabs of stone on the roof: conventional roof tiles
simply blew away. Paddy and Joan sat on woven homespun rugs on
the floor with their host, hand-rolling excellent tobacco into cigarettes and drinking endless cups of coffee. Daoud and his friend
Suleiman were happy to talk about the Pomaks, who call themselves
Achriani – as in *Agrianes*, an old Thracian race. Daoud told him the
story of the Prophet Nüh Ali es Salaam (Noah), and – in a lowered
voice – about the civil war. The Reds had looted his house, taking
wheat and corn, destroying jars and looms. He also hated the bandits
who roamed the mountains, who he said were all Bulgarians. Paddy
and Joan slept that night on the floor of Daoud's house, wrapped
in blankets.

Xanthi felt like Babylon after the Pomak village: a thriving town,
filled with promenading crowds and illuminated shops. It was the
first time for several days that they heard Greek in the streets rather
than Turkish, and they were glad of it. In Kavala they visited
Mohammed Ali's house, and then took a boat to the island of Thassos.
After a happy week spent climbing over ruined temples, talking to
French archaeologists, eating honey and cheese with a bee-keeper
who had become a Jehovah's Witness in Istanbul and swimming
every day, they returned to Kavala on 8 October.

Wherever they went, Paddy asked people if they had heard of

the Anastenaria, or Nistinari: a strange Orthodox sect whose particular pantheon is dominated by St Helena, discoverer of the True Cross, and her son St Constantine – known to them as the Grandparents. 'Their rites', Paddy wrote to a friend a year later, 'are a hash of garbled Christianity with the Orphic Mysteries, which still survive in odd forms along the Hebrus River, down which Orpheus floated as a corpse . . .'[4] The feast of SS. Constantine and Helena, 21 May, is the day the *Anastenarides* – the devotees – perform their feats of fire-walking. To the music of the lyra, drum and shepherd bagpipes, they prepare for the ordeal by dancing for hours, holding icons of the Grandparents above their heads, until they enter an ecstatic trance. A great fire is lit, and when it has burnt down the coals are raked into a circle; the devotees then dance barefoot across the coals, protected by the saints.

No one on Samothrace had heard of the sect and Daoud's friend Suleiman did not believe they existed. But in the town of Drama they found a beer-seller, who knew someone in the village of Mavrolefki who was a Nistinari. The beer-seller had also heard whispers that they held wild orgies, at which blindfolded men and women coupled with whoever they bumped into.

On 10 October, Paddy and Joan set off to the village of Mavrolefki. Here they had been told to wait at the café, and Uncle Mihali Zoumis would come and meet them. But someone wanted to register their hostility to the Nistinari, and to the unhealthy interest they had aroused in the foreigners. When Uncle Mihali turned up, he was distraught: the icon of St Constantine had been stolen, and he had a pretty good idea it was the work of the mayor or the priest. In the early 1950s, the Greek Orthodox Church and local government were agreed that certain ancient customs should be stamped out: Greece was transforming itself into a modern country, and these primitive, backward, heretical traditions created a bad impression.

They spent that night with Uncle Mihali and his daughter, and the following day he took them to meet Grikou, an elderly devotee of the Grandparents who was very upset about the theft of the icon. 'Everybody hates us, and despises Grandpa,' she said, wiping her eyes on her scarf and crossing herself frequently. She went on to describe the joyful old days when several villages would get together to dance and sing. 'We used to dance in the fire for hours, holding the saints in our hands. The saint gets hold of us, and leads us like a rider leads a horse – we can't help ourselves.'[5] As far as he could tell, the old woman's feet looked neat and undamaged. Paddy did not dare broach the subject of orgies.

That afternoon the Mayor took them to visit a Sarakatsan encampment nearby, and by the time they returned the icon had been found: but its frame was broken, the faces of the Grandparents defaced. 'The Mayor fingers [the icon] disparagingly,' wrote Paddy, '[he] obviously hates it, and I hate him.' Back in Drama, they paid a visit to the Archimandrite and asked what he thought of the Nistinari. 'He leant back and stroked his beard. "Idolaters, my child. Good people, but idolaters."'[6*]

Paddy's second notebook devoted to this journey begins in Ziakas, in Macedonia, which they reached on 20 October. This was the time of year when hundreds of Vlachs left their summer pastures in the Pindus mountains, and began their annual migration to the winter pastures in Thessaly, which lay between Elassona and Tirnavos. 'Vlach' is one of those difficult words that Paddy enjoyed turning over and over. Greeks will sometimes use it indiscriminately, when referring to herdsmen who are either settled or semi–nomadic. When they speak of true tent- and hut-dwelling nomads, they will use the word 'koutsovlach' – though this should apply only to a group of Latin-dialect-speaking Arromans. Vlachs are far more numerous than the Sarakatsani, who think of themselves as the elite of the nomadic world.

On the way to the Vlach village of Samarina they passed empty villages, gutted by the civil war. 'The whole population has gone, the broken houses might have been empty 100 years ago, only the white gigantic slogans, the hammers and sickles, snarl with life. EVERY BOY AND GIRL TO THE COMMUNIST YOUTH MOVEMENT; OUT WITH THE ENGLISH and LONG LIFE TO GENERAL MARKOS. Men, women, children all gone.'[7] These were the scars of a civil war that had left over a hundred thousand people dead, and a quarter of a million homeless.

---

* Although they did not see the firewalkers at Mavrolefki, Joan did photograph the Nistinari rituals at Langada on another occasion.

Grevena was full of Vlachs on the move. It was a five days' journey for the families, but a trek of twenty or thirty days for the men driving the flocks. 'Black-hooded old men, talkative children, hens, sacks of blankets, many cats either under children's arms or with heads projecting from bags . . . More than ever convinced, listening to Vlach conversation ("Dumnetzeu", "Dracu", "Ceapa" etc) that resemblance between Vlach and Rumanian more than a coincidence, terminal augmentations etc . . .'[8] Kalabaka too was crowded with Vlachs, and here Paddy saw the Abbot of St Baarlam, whom he had last seen eleven years before. They followed him back to the monastery where he lived alone with Father Bassarion, and spent the next few days exploring the monasteries of the Meteora. Scarcely a dozen monks and even fewer nuns still perched on the steep crags; many of the monasteries were abandoned altogether, some no longer accessible. 'They disintegrate in mid-air, empty stone caskets of rotting timber and slowly falling frescoes that only spiders and owls and kestrels inhabit . . .'[9]

Then they crossed the plain of Thessaly to Larisa, and wandered down the vale of Tempe, where the river ran a pale green between plane trees turning gold. Back in Athens, a finished copy of *The Traveller's Tree* was waiting with the Nortons at the British Embassy. On 1 December, Paddy wrote to Jock from Delphi: 'I think the *Tree* looks magnificent, and everybody I have shown it to is most impressed . . . I can hardly believe I am connected to such an impressive tome!'[10] He was sad not to come back for the book's publication on 6 December, but the next leg of the journey would take him south into the Peloponnese, all the way to its southernmost point at Cape Matapan, at the very tip of the Mani. Then he planned to go north again, into Epirus.

> I've already filled several notebooks, and it's pretty unusual material, most of it, which I don't think has been covered before. Joan's photographs are splendid. I think that it ought to turn out a pretty interesting book. Joan returns to England for a month, during which time I may retire somewhere to write a chapter or two. Murray's Guide [to Greece], for which many thanks, will be most useful. Do you think you could discover one for Turkey, to cover those parts of Macedonia, Epirus etc that belonged to the Ottoman Empire till the Balkan Wars?[11]

The reviews of *The Traveller's Tree* were everything Paddy could have hoped for. The *Times Literary Supplement* wrote that 'Mr Leigh Fermor never loses sight of the fact, not always grasped by superficial visitors, that most of the problems . . . of the West Indies . . . are the direct legacy of the slave trade.'[12] It also praised his tireless zeal in tracking down any minority whose ancestry, dialect or religion bore witness to the tumultuous history of the islands. Both the *Evening Standard* and the *Scottish Daily Mail* called it the best travel book of the year, though the latter did remark that the exuberance of his style was sometimes too much of a good thing: 'Only now and then . . . does a wild tangle of images and epithets seem to call aloud for the editorial brush and comb.'[13]

Joan quizzed Cyril Connolly on what he had made of *The Traveller's Tree*. To Paddy Joan reported that he was, in general, very enthusiastic though he felt the book lacked shape and, 'unprompted by me, that you had some of Norman Douglas's less good tricks – that you seemed to be influenced by him and it was a pity as when you were really yourself it was the best and very good indeed . . . Don't mind me telling you any criticisms – you will see so much praise – and it may all help.'[14] Douglas's 'less good tricks' presumably refer to his long and elaborate sentences as much as his love of digressions.

Paddy spent that Christmas in Athens, and in early 1951 met Louis MacNeice, who had just been appointed British Council Representative there. They had many Gargoyle friends in common, most notably Dylan Thomas. Over the coming months Louis and his wife Hedli, a professional singer, spent many evenings with Paddy, reading aloud and talking about poetry with friends such as George Seferis, the classical scholar Professor E. R. Dodds, and Kevin Andrews.

Andrews, who was half American and half English, was a classical scholar who was equally familiar with modern demotic Greek. On a fellowship from the American School of Archaeology in Athens, he made a study of Crusader ruins of the Peloponnese at a time when Greece was going through the final stages of the civil war. Andrews took no sides; but in remote mountain villages he knew people who had undergone appalling brutalities at the hands of their fellow villagers, and witnessed the revenge and recrimination that followed the war. None of this altered his love of Greece,

which he looked on as his adopted country – even to the extent
of dressing as a Greek shepherd, and living as they did. As Paddy
put it, 'Andrews always brought a tang of curds and woodsmoke
back with him to Athens.'[15]

Paddy and Kevin Andrews introduced the MacNeices to the
tavernas of Athens, 'where', as Paddy recalled, 'the minstrels with
violin, accordion and lute wandered from table to table singing
mountain songs which one could join in' (he never failed to do this)
'or old ironical and romantic numbers from long-forgotten musical
comedies'.[16] This was the mainstream end of taverna life. But Paddy
also wrote of visits to less respectable haunts, where the songs, known
as *manghes*, were very different:

> urban, low-life and dockside with a special rather apache-like delivery,
> originating among Asia Minor refugees, accompanied by long-necked
> mandolins . . . and short, tortoise-shell-bowled baglamas, accompanied
> by very intricate dances scanned against the beat . . . with hands
> linked on shoulders while the words recounted some hard-luck story
> or feud or ill-starred love . . . I had a passion for such haunts, felt I
> was plumbing the mysteries of the east, merging the Ottoman world
> and Byzantium and intrepidly advancing into a maze of louche and
> delinquent life.[17]

Towards the end of January, while still in Athens, he spent an
evening with Michael Powell, one half of the Michael Powell and
Emeric Pressburger film partnership. Powell was keen to make a film
of Billy Moss's *Ill Met by Moonlight*; Paddy was not so convinced by
the idea, but he did not want to spoil any opportunity that might
bring money to Billy and glory to the Cretans. 'I sent him to all
my old friends [in Crete],' he told Jock, 'who dragged him all over
the mountains, filling him with wine and playing the lyra and firing
off rifles. He came back, after three weeks of footslogging, wild with
excitement, and determined to start shooting in May.'[18]

Powell's description of Paddy, on the night he took the film-maker
on one of his marathon taverna-crawls, approaches hero worship.
'We ate very little and drank a great deal . . . Everywhere Paddy
had friends. Everywhere, he was greeted as *Mihali!* . . . Except for
Lord Byron, I don't think that any foreigner has captured the love

and imagination of the Greeks so much . . .' This was especially true in a Cretan tavern, where 'Paddy got a boisterous welcome. Someone was playing a bouzouki . . . They started to sing an interminable song' (a round of *mantinades*), 'each man capping the other with a verse, arms flung out, fingers pointing, eyes flashing, as the point of the joke was made. Paddy was very good at this . . .' Walking under the walls of the Acropolis at about two in the morning under a full moon, Powell suggested they scale the cliff on the north side and creep in. After a hundred feet of scrabbling they were on top of the hill, and headed for the main temple. 'We heard voices, and the quick steps of soldiers. "Sit down in the shadow," said Paddy. "In the bright moonlight they can't see us." Years of hunting and being hunted, years of narrow shaves were in these simple words. Two armed soldiers passed us without seeing us, about fifty feet away . . .'

Their luck did not last. As they left the temple, the two interlopers were apprehended and marched off to the guardhouse. But when it emerged that the officer on duty that night was a Cretan from Rethymno, another round of jubilant celebration began. 'We drank to the eternal friendship between Britain and Greece. We drank to Lord Byron. We drank to John Murray, Paddy's publisher, as well as Byron's ("Murray, my Murray"). We drank to Major Patrick Leigh Fermor, DSO. We even drank to General Kreipe.'[19]

Paddy did not like this time of year in Athens. 'For the last three weeks I've been in the throes of a real attack of chronic solitary gloom . . . sloth and lassitude hang in the air, hot blasts from Africa . . . alternate with icy winds, filling one with depression and sloth . . .'[20]

He took the advice of an Athenian friend and headed to the island of Salamis, where he hoped to find shelter and a place to work in the monastery of Panaghia Phaneromeni. Much to his astonishment, the monastery was now inhabited by nuns. The Abbess allowed him to stay for two days but dared not have a man in the convent any longer, for fear of getting into trouble with the bishop. But surely, she asked, he knew the poet Sikelianos? He had a house just outside the convent walls.

Angelos Sikelianos was one of Greece's most celebrated play-wrights and poets, and is associated with Delphi where he inaugurated a short-lived Delphic Festival. His house on Salamis consisted of a single thick-walled room with a high ceiling, containing little more than a bed, a washstand, and a huge table covered in books. Paddy, who had met him in Athens, telephoned Sikelianos who was delighted to lend him the house, and asked the nuns to look after him. 'A nun trots along three times a day with bread, rice, cheese etc. They're sweet.'[21]

From here Paddy despatched an SOS letter to Jock, asking for a further £100. 'I knew it would take some time before I actually got any royalties,' he wrote, but he was expecting some dollars, sooner or later.[22] This last was no boast. Cass Canfield of Harper & Row in New York had seen an early copy of *The Traveller's Tree* and enjoyed it: 'While the book is somewhat overlong for American readers, Fermor writes with great distinction and charm,' he reported to Jock Murray.[23] He was very keen to see the Greek book.

On 6 March Joan wrote to say that Jock had stumped up £100, and 'I'm asking for another £200 from the Bank of England. I can't ask for more but I think we'll manage.'[24] By now Paddy was once again in Thessaly; and on 12 March, he took a bus from Larisa to Tirnavos.

It was the Monday before Lent, known as 'Clean Monday', and he had come to see the traditional *bourani* celebrations, for which the town was famous. Bourani is the name of a soup made of spinach, herbs and beans to which no oil is added. Though sounding rather austere and penitential, side by side with the Lenten ritual went a fertility rite dating back to the worship of Dionysus. Bourani is made in huge cauldrons, and stirred with phallus-shaped ladles of wood and clay. Before the war, the women of the town were forbidden to leave their homes on the night of Bourani; if they did so, they risked being subjected to dreadful indignities.

At first Paddy was told that all such primitive customs had been stopped, condemned by Church and state. But after lunch he followed a general movement to a hill outside the town. Here were gathered most of the town's population, including women and children, and a group of about fifty young men who were drinking and dancing. 'Then a giant clay phallus was produced, filled with wine and everybody drank out of it, after which it was placed on the grass and blessed with signs of the cross, kisses and prostrations'[25] – though Paddy noticed that it was quickly hidden when the police turned up.

Paddy joined the young men on a drunken drive on two tractors, to the village of Ambelona. As night fell, the men began brandishing small clay phalluses and shouting obscenities. They stopped men on the road and obliged them to 'kiss the cock'. Then everyone returned to Tirnavos, to a drunken evening with much singing and dancing in the taverna.

Paddy stayed the following night in Tirnavos, where people told him more stories of the campaign against Bourani. Only the week before, a preacher had attacked the custom in the public square, saying that anyone caught participating in the abominations would be exiled. 'Is all this progress?' wrote Paddy. '. . . *mangika* songs* being stamped out or castrated, persecution of the Anastenari, no masks at carnival . . . Do they want to turn Greece into a milk bar?'[26] This was what Paddy feared most: Greece losing its ancient identities in an all-pervasive, industrialized Americanization, her music drowned by the constant homogenized pap of the radio. He need not have worried: movies on You-Tube show that neither the Anastenari's fire-walking nor Clean Monday with the Tirnaviots is in any danger of being stamped out.

From Tirnavos he made his way westwards to Metsovo and so to Yanina, the capital of Epirus, which 'looks wonderful at the moment – brilliant spring weather, with Aly Pasha's domes and minarets reflected in a bright blue lake'.[27] This was part of the landscape of *Childe Harold's Pilgrimage*, and from the Zitza monastery, where Byron and Hobhouse had stayed twice in October 1809, he wrote to Jock: 'It's a very beautiful derelict thing, on top of a hill north of Yanina near the Albanian border, surrounded by the snow-capped peaks of the Pindus. The region teems with memories of Byron, some rather disconcerting . . .'[28]

Paddy travelled south to Missolonghi, then along the north coast

---

* The songs of the *manghes*: the gambling, drug-taking wideboys of the Greek underworld – see p.251.

of the Gulf of Corinth. At Naupaktos (Lepanto) he headed into the Aeolian mountains, 'to an extraordinary remote valley where all the villagers have been professional beggars from time immemorial . . . I filled a notebook about them, also with their curious secret language.'[29] Although in *Roumeli* Paddy refers to them as the Kravarites, this term refers only to the Kravara, their barren and mountainous homeland. They called themselves *boliárides*, and their secret language, *ta boliárika*; *boliarévo* meant, more or less, 'outwitting the mugs'. They were skilled at conjuring and trickery, and as children were taught to twist their limbs so as to look severely maimed. 'Can you blame them?' said the villagers. 'Nothing grows here, you couldn't graze a mouse!'[30]

Paddy describes his experiences among the descendants of the *boliárides* in *Roumeli*, but never tells the reader exactly where he is: partly because he is condensing more than one encounter, and partly out of tact. Among the villages known for these ancient skills were Aghios Dimitri, Platanos and Symi, but in 1950s Greece begging was seen as something shameful. Yet once the subject is broached (the face-saving formula being that it all happened a long time ago) the villagers produced old 'Uncle Elias', who was delighted to tell him how his forebears made a living, wheedling money out of gullible foreigners who should have known better. For this craft was not practised in Greece: the *boliárides*, with their traditional woven bag and hollow staff for carrying coins, travelled north to find their prey in Albania, Bulgaria, Russia and Rumania.

Paddy took down as many words as he could. He had only to say something in Greek or point to an object and a chorus of villagers would sing out the word in Boliaric. Most were variations on the Greek, but Paddy thought he could detect traces of Slav and Turkish, while some were pure invention. He came down from the Kravara in the highest of spirits, with a notebook full of treasure.

He was back in Athens on 1 April and met up with Joan, who had been in London. She brought good news. Ian Fleming, a director of Lord Kemsley's Dropmore (later Queen Anne) Press, said they would like to print a de-luxe limited edition of the first two articles on monasteries. Paddy had hoped to write many more articles on the subject, eventually to be gathered into a book, but Fleming was willing to pay £150, which would be very welcome for further travelling in Greece. An even more agreeable surprise came from the Royal Society of Literature, with the news that *The Traveller's Tree* had won the Heinemann Foundation Prize. It meant not only another £100 tax free: it put Paddy on the literary map, and marked him out as a writer whose career would be worth following.

From Athens, Paddy and Joan set off to Nauplia, via Mycenae with a detour to Epidaurus, and then sailed down the eastern coast of the Peloponnese. From Astros, where they waited for mules to take them into the interior, Paddy wrote to Jock:

> It's a fascinating wild and remote mountain region, the only place in Greece where a sort of ancient Greek is spoken, owing to the isolation of the district – it's a kind of Doric-Laconian, quite incomprehensible to the rest of Greece . . . I'm finishing a long Meteora article for *Cornhill*, which will follow this hot-foot . . . Joan sends love – she is knitting something out of rust-coloured wool the other side of this tin table.[31]

Joan is often mentioned in Paddy's letters and notebooks, usually as a quiet presence. Sometimes he sees her reading, and notices the book and what she is wearing; sometimes he glances at her sitting opposite him, brows furrowed, deep in concentration over her pocket chess set. (Joan played chess to a high standard, but never with Paddy who was too impatient to be any good at the game.) Sometimes, in a notebook, he will comment that they had had a row that made them both miserable, though he never mentions the cause. It was probably money. Joan had to bear the strain of his extravagance as she tried to make her allowance stretch for two, and sometimes even her patience snapped. It is interesting to note how often Paddy was attracted to older women, and he was younger than the two great loves of his life. Yet he was not looking so much for a mother, as for someone to be Wendy to his Peter Pan; someone who would keep his feet on the ground, and at the same time do the tiresome, grown-up things so that he would not have to.

Joan took on these responsibilities, while at the same time being an almost perfect travelling companion. In any café or house where they stopped, she noticed things that Paddy – singing, drinking and smoking with the locals – might well have missed. He relied on her social antennae, too: she knew how to tell him to be quiet without putting him down or hurting his feelings. Yet if Paddy and his hosts were in the mood to laugh and talk all night, Joan would never have tried to drag him away. She would either leave on her own, or fold herself into her thoughts till he was ready to go. When they were alone together, she was the best listener he ever had: funny and responsive, always ready to tease or pull him up if he got carried away, never allowing him to get away with sentiment or sloppy thinking. He also needed her in his fits of depression, when her encouragement and sympathy were the surest way to regain his habitual bounce.

Joan might have made more appearances in Paddy's two books on Greece, but as a fiercely private person and his initial editor, she did not encourage mentions of her presence. That is left to her photographs. Landscapes predominate, and there are several in which people are photographed at a distance or from the back – sign of a certain reserve in a photographer; but some of her portraits, of Father John Alevizakis for instance, or Father Christopher of St Barlaam's monastery, show that she could also approach within inches of someone's face.[32] Although she had a good camera and was technically adept, Joan never set much store by her photographs, often referring to them dismissively as 'my snaps'. Many remain in the envelopes in which she picked them up from the developer. The ones she took on her travels with Paddy were placed in chronological order and numbered, the subjects noted, the negatives kept; yet instead of pasting the positives into albums, they were glued into two cheap, lined exercise books as if their prime purpose was to be a visual reference for Paddy. Seeing how well thumbed they are, they seem to have been put to good use.

Having crossed the Peloponnese to Cape Malea, Paddy and Joan sailed to Crete. Paddy was too excited to sleep – 'Couldn't believe I was back in Crete, sat up watching dawn break, drinking in the Cretan accent, lovely . . .' They went on by bus to celebrate a rowdy Orthodox Easter with Manoli Paterakis and his family at Koustoyerako, where Paddy was impressed by how unsentimental they were about the destruction of their village and the losses they had sustained.

'Each has a father killed, limps from a machine-gun burst, arm bust, house burnt. Let them burn them again!'[33]

From there they went to visit George Psychoundakis in Asi Gonia – 'bald with a huge moustache'. Here the celebrations continued, and Paddy was rather embarrassed by the way he was expected to live up to a war-hero image that was, to him at least, no longer real. 'In Crete I have to conform to an outgrown tradition of myself – how one changes! What a traitor one is to one's own past!'[34]

Psychoundakis, on the other hand, had not been able to shake off his past. In spite of having fought so hard for the Cretan resistance, and in spite of the commendations he had received in official British reports and the British Empire Medal he had been awarded in 1945, the authorities found that his service record was not in order. He was arrested and imprisoned as a deserter, and spent months of bitterness and misery in the jails of Piraeus and Macedonia. 'I was locked up in cells . . . with brigands and Communists and all the dregs of the mainland,' he told Paddy, and all his hair fell out during the ordeal.[35] He had to do two more years of service in the Pindus before being released, and on reaching home he found his family poorer than ever. He took a job first as a charcoal-burner, and then as a road-mender.

It was while in prison that George had begun to write down everything he could remember about the war and the occupation, a task that was eventually finished while he worked on the roads, writing by candlelight in the nearby cave where he slept at night. Paddy asked if he might see the result, 'and without a word he dived into his knapsack, fished out five thick exercise books tied in a bundle, and handed them over'.

Together the notebooks were called 'Pictures of our Life during the Occupation', and Paddy read them over the next four days. They were written with passion, clarity and truthfulness, and represented a unique document of the time. 'Dozens of accounts by officers who were dropped or infiltrated into enemy-occupied country have appeared . . . but there has not been a single one, as far as I know, by any of the millions of men who formed the raw material of the Resistance in occupied Europe.'[36] Paddy decided that he would translate George's book, and try and find it a publisher. It would never make its author a fortune, but George needed every penny he could earn – he had gone back to being a charcoal-burner, and was still miserably poor.

As Paddy and Joan proceeded on their triumphal progress through the villages, they saw that Cretan hospitality had lost none of its over-abundance, and only the long walks and mule rides from one place to the next gave them an opportunity to rest their digestions. Groups of armed mountain men greeted them outside each village, and welcomed them with volleys of shots fired into the air.

There was also another man with a gun, though he was not mentioned in Paddy's introduction to *The Cretan Runner,* nor indeed in his notebooks. At Alones they had spent a few days with Father John Alevizakis and his sons, prior to attending a feast in Rethymno. They were warned not to go on: Yorgo, the son of Kanaki Tsangarakis, had heard Paddy was there. 'He was waiting,' wrote Paddy, 'with rifle and binoculars, to pick me off when I left the village.' The blood feud was still alive, and the only way out of the village was through a deep ravine.

> Yorgo was on one side, our way out on the other . . . I asked whether he was a good shot and Levtheri, Father John's son, laughed and said 'Yes, the blighter can shoot a hole through a 10 drachma piece at 500 metres,' which made us all laugh rather ruefully, including Joan . . . The only thing to do in such a case is to be accompanied by a neutral figure, head of a rival clan or family in whose company nobody can be shot without involving the whole tribe.[37]

A suitably friendly figure agreed to accompany them to safety, and 'under his protection Joan and I crossed the blank hillside, looking across the valley at Yorgo sitting on the rock, binoculars round his neck and gun across his knees; but unable, by Cretan ethics, to blaze away . . .'[38] In Vilandredo they were received like kings by Paddy's god-brother Kapetan Stathi Loukakis. When Stathi heard that the Tsangarakis men were lying in wait for his guest, he too took steps to protect them. Joan noticed that when they left the village they were guarded by lookouts posted at key points, who could challenge anyone who came within firing distance.

Back in Athens towards the end of May, they came across the

painter John Craxton. He, the ballet dancer Margot Fonteyn and the choreographer Frederick Ashton were guests of a rich American attorney, Thomas Hart Fisher, and his wife Ruth Page, also a dancer and choreographer. They had chartered a boat called the *Elikki*, which was more of a large caique than a yacht. It was not luxurious: the one loo on board could only be reached by walking through the hosts' cabin.

Paddy and Joan were immediately invited to join the party; and although this would prevent Paddy from receiving the Heinemann prize in person, it was an excellent opportunity for him to refresh his memory of the Cyclades for the Greek book. It was not only the joy of Paddy's company and his knowledge of Greece that made him an ideal dragoman for the cruise, he was also the only one with sufficient Greek to communicate effectively with the crew. 'Paddy told the captain where to go,' wrote Ruth Page, 'and we went to all kinds of islands where no tourist had ever set foot.'[39]

It was July by the time they returned to a sweltering Athens but they were soon on the road again, taking a lift to Corinth in a truck full of ouzo. Travelling south through Mycenae, Argos, Nemea and Tripoli, they were heading for the Taygetus mountains and the deep Mani, the most barren and rocky region of the whole of Greece.

In Sparta ('that Potsdam of the Peloponnese', as he called it[40]) a local man led them to some mosaics which he brought to life by sloshing a bucket of water over them. One of the mosaics showed a buxom Europa and the bull. 'How pleased Zeus is to have her on his back,' said the policeman. 'See, he's smiling to himself.'[41] From there they were given a lift in a jeep by the son of a bank manager, who planned to take them all the way to Kalamata, till he discovered it was a seven-hour drive. Instead he took them as far as the village of Anavryti, inhabited – so the rumour went – exclusively by Jews. When he heard this rumour in Sparta it had immediately sparked Paddy's interest, since the only Jewish communities he knew of in Greece were in the north.

The villagers, it turned out, were not Jewish at all; their reputation, they told him, was due to the fact that they were so much cleverer than the dim-witted plain-dwellers: 'we can nail horseshoes on a louse . . . We could sell you the air.'[42] A bed was made up for the travellers on the floor of a house belonging to a family called Adamakos, and the following day they were woken early by their guide, Panayoti, who was to take them over the mountains. The Taygetus mountains rise eight thousand feet, dividing the Laconian from the Messenian plain. Perhaps midwinter might have been a worse time to set out, but midsummer was not ideal either:

> A vast slag-heap soon shut out the kindly lower world; the sun trampled overhead through sizzling and windless air. Feet became cannon-balls, loads turned to lead, hearts pounded, hands slipped on the handles of sticks and rivers of sweat streamed over burning faces and trickled into our mouths like brine . . .[43]

The ordeal went on for hour after hour before they reached the watershed; but once they had crossed the inferno, they found themselves in greener country, a place quite unlike the rest of Greece.

The Maniots are believed to be the closest descendants of the classical Greeks, and they remained pagan for centuries after the rest of Greece became Christian. Paddy learnt all he could about their customs and superstitions, their culture of the vendetta, and the beautiful metrical dirges sung by the women at funerals. They had maintained a precarious independence while the rest of the country was under Ottoman rule. 'Terrible tales of massacres, battles, bullets, slit throats – "The Turks never got hold of us, nor did the Communists!"'[44] The prevailing political feeling was defiantly royalist. In Kardamyli, where Paddy and Joan were eventually to settle, he noted how conscious the people were of the antiquity of their village.* The blinding light and barren rocks of their land had made the Maniots tough and resilient, but there was plenty to grumble about. 'If only we could find a merchant who bought stones,' said one of them, 'we'd all be millionaires.'[45]

'Well,' Paddy wrote to Jock from the island of Skopelos:

> the notes for the Greek book are assembled at last! I will be heading for home at the end of this month, after getting back to Athens and spending a few days winding things up and a day or two in the National and Gennadion libraries. I've got a formidable amount of

---

* In his *Geography*, Strabo names it as one of the 'seven fair cities' promised by Agamemnon to Achilles.

material, all of it fascinating. I hope to be able to borrow Amy and Walter Smart's cottage in Normandy to do the writing in – it's only a few hours away from Victoria – but in case that falls through, you couldn't ask all your pals about a pleasant and *cheap* cottage for the winter, suitable for a hermit embarked on a major literary enterprise, could you?[46]

Jock at one point suggested that, if he were really serious about looking for a place free from diversion or temptation, he might consider a small boarding house in Aberdeen.

15

Byron's Slippers

Paddy's article on the Meteora, 'The Monasteries of the Air', was published in the summer of 1951 in the *Cornhill*. He spent much of the following winter working at Gadencourt, while preparing to translate George Psychoundakis's Cretan war memoir. The original notebooks were being typed up in Athens, and he hoped to start work on the typescript in the new year.

In February 1952 Paddy was in Paris, elated by the fact that Amiot-Dumont were going to publish *The Traveller's Tree* in a French edition, called *Au-delà de la Désiderade: les Caraïbes d'île en île*. In a long letter to Joan he also described a day with Freya Stark. They spent a happy afternoon going round the Musée de Cluny, which houses the celebrated Unicorn tapestries. After browsing round the bookshops and getting caught in a snowstorm they had tea in her room in the Bristol Hotel, where Freya (then just short of sixty) told him that she was learning to draw. 'She spends all day at the Académie Julian charcoaling away from the life – quite astonishingly well.' Her husband Stewart Perowne turned up, and after dinner Paddy vaguely suggested they go on to a cabaret. Freya seized on the idea, and they ended up at 'an elaborately camp joint in Montmartre called Madame Arthur, with an endless transvestitist [*sic*] cabaret . . . Freya got pleasantly watery-eyed and tipsy, and very excited like a small girl seeing LIFE for the first time; Stewart rather excited too . . . We got to bed at about 5am.'[1]

Back at Gadencourt, Paddy told Jock that the Greek book was 'going like a fire hydrant',[2] but this was interrupted in mid-March when he received the proofs of his translation of two novellas by Colette. The work had been commissioned by Secker & Warburg, through the good offices of Raymond Mortimer of the *Sunday Times* who knew Paddy was short of money. Colette wrote *Chambre d'Hôtel* (translated as *Chance Acquaintances*) and *Julie de Carneilhan* between 1940 and 1941, and neither is considered among her best work. Paddy regretted that he never met her (she died in 1954) and could remember very little about the stories, which he had 'struggled through' while in Greece the year before. Although he usually enjoyed her writing, having to correct the proofs in a rush soured him for Colette. 'It's like some awful imposition at school . . . I'm beginning to think she's fearful rot,' he wrote.[3]

The letter was written to a relatively new friend, with whom he was to correspond for the rest of his life: Lady Diana Cooper. They had first met in London in the late forties, and again in Paris, at a lunch given by Bertha Lady Mitchelham, perhaps in the latter part of 1951. Paddy sent her a copy of *The Traveller's Tree*, and soon after that she invited him for a weekend at her house near Chantilly. When Sir Alfred Duff Cooper had retired as British Ambassador to Paris in early 1947, he and his wife had decided to remain in France, taking a lease on the Château de Saint-Firmin, an eighteenth-century house set amid the woods and lakes of the grounds of the Château de Chantilly. Duff was happy to sit quietly, reading and writing books, but Diana dreaded inactivity. She filled the house with friends, planned picnics and expeditions, and tried to maintain her pre-retirement levels of excitement.

Paddy and Diana each discovered that the other was the sort of person they liked best. He was good-looking, entertaining, ready for anything, had had 'a splendid war', and was someone all her friends would enjoy meeting. He could illuminate any subject under the sun, and had a memory that had retained most of the thousands of books he had read over the years. He knew all her favourite passages from Browning, Shakespeare, Donne, Tennyson, Meredith and Keats off by heart, and much more besides – whole evenings were spent singing and reciting poetry. He rejuvenated Diana, quickened her excitement and curiosity; but while Duff would certainly have appreciated his passion for verse, he was probably not quite so taken with his noisy ebullience.

As for Paddy, he worshipped Diana – not just for her indestructible beauty (though its disintegration was painfully obvious to her) but for the original cast of her mind, the flourish of her phrases, and the blind eye she turned to convention. Like him, curiosity was driven by energy: she was ready to jump into a car and go exploring at a moment's notice.

Joan was never threatened by Diana or any of Paddy's women friends, since they occupied such different spheres of Paddy's existence. She was always the magnet, the one he came home to. With her he could while away an afternoon, stroke a cat, read a book, listen to music and never be bored. Joan asked for nothing, and gave him the space in which he could work. But while she was passionately devoted to her friends, she never shared his desire for revelry.

Diana wanted to see as much of Paddy as she could, with or without Joan, and he spent many weekends at Chantilly. 'I hated moving off to gloomy old Paris,' he wrote to Diana on 14 March, 'where I wished like anything we were still sitting in front of the fire talking about slaughterhouses and public executions and other comfortable topics . . .' He collected stories to amuse her. In Paris again after another weekend at Chantilly in early May, he told her about a long night's ramble where he had ended up

in a fairly louche place called the Café de l'Echaudé, just off the Place de Furstenberg where Delacroix's studio is. At the next table sat five immense negroes – jet black, with beautifully shaped heads, talking quietly together in some African dialect . . . I scraped acquaintance, of course, and learnt that they were four Woloffs from Dakar, the other a member of the warlike Fong tribe of Dahomey, where most of Voodoo comes from. After a few *fines à l'eau* they were all singing, very quietly, a southern Saharan war song, and tapping the tom-tom measure with those long fingers. The Fong told me that he came from a grand family that ruled once from Abomey . . . to the Haute Volta river, and that on the ruler's birthday 100 years ago, sometimes as many as a thousand tribesmen were beheaded – one after another with huge scimitars. Towards the end of the ceremony the Prince would sometimes get bored, and move off to dinner while the holocaust went on . . . [4]

The typescript of George Psychoundakis's book arrived from Athens that spring, but he still had to convince Jock Murray that it would be worth publishing. To strengthen his case, he sent the

PATRICK LEIGH FERMOR

typescript to Professor Richard Dawkins of Exeter College, Oxford,
who – though a classicist – was intrigued: 'This man Psychountakis
[*sic*] writes a rather interesting and very colloquial demotic which,
to be easily understood, almost needs to be read aloud . . . It is a
style a long way off the cultured demotic of Athens.'[5] His enthusiasm
grew as he read on. In an undated letter which Paddy passed on to
Jock, Dawkins wrote: 'What a book! What a man! I do congratulate
you on finding him and encouraging him in the right way . . .
George's book although without being too harrowing makes one
feel all through the utter brutality of the Germans and their attack
on Crete.' Tom Dunbabin, too, was enthusiastic; and, thus encouraged, Jock Murray decided to go ahead and commission Paddy to
translate 'Pictures of our Life during the Occupation' – called in its
English edition *The Cretan Runner*.

Paddy and Joan were back in England in June, where the highlight
of the season was the Black and White Ball at Longleat. They stayed
with Henry and Daphne Bath at their house in Sturford Mead, in
a wild party which included David and Virginia Tennant, Henrietta
Moraes, Xan and Paddy, Lucian Freud and Kitty Epstein.

Paddy had first met Henry and Daphne Weymouth at the
Gargoyle Club before the war, when they seemed to live in a
perpetual party. After the war Henry became Marquess of Bath and
inherited a debt-ridden estate – but the party went on. Evelyn
Waugh described the chaotic atmosphere of Longleat as one of jazz
all day, drinking all night and children running wild.[6] Now the
Bath marriage was crumbling. Henry Bath was seeing a great deal
of Virginia Parsons, who would not be Mrs David Tennant for
much longer; while Daphne had begun an affair with Xan, who
was her junior by over a decade. She and Xan had spent that spring
travelling around Crete, where she took photographs for his forthcoming book *The Stronghold* – an account of four seasons in the
White Mountains of Crete.

The ball was 'great fun and unbelievably rowdy', wrote Paddy.
'Xan and Daphne had just arrived severally from Crete, looking like
a couple of Mohicans, and seemed more gone on each other than
ever – all very harmonious and congruent at the moment, as Henry
is happily involved with Virginia. I do hope they've all got the sense

266

to keep it so . . .'[7] But Henry had married Virginia just after the ball, while Daphne married Xan the following year.

Given his delight in magnificent parties, it was no surprise that Paddy agreed to contribute a chapter to a book with the eye-catching title *Memorable Balls*. The editor, James Laver (who at one point had rented the flat above his mother's in Piccadilly), asked him to write about the Creole assemblies of the French Antilles, of which the most celebrated were those of Martinique. This was the holiday task he had in hand when he and Joan, who had just acquired a long black 1932 Bentley, set off for Italy that summer.

In Rome, they joined forces with an American scriptwriter, Peter Tomkins, and his wife Jeree and drove north to travel round Tuscany. They were staying in San Gimignano when Paddy settled down to write his chapter for *Memorable Balls*; but on rereading it, he found the piece dull and lifeless. So he began inventing characters, giving them names and describing their lives; and before he was even aware of it, a slim novel had emerged – he later admitted that no book had come to him so quickly and easily. Joan announced the event to Peter Tomkins by saying, 'Paddy's laid an egg.'[8]

They left Italy and Paddy took his egg to Paris, and put the final touches to it while staying with Duff and Diana at Chantilly. 'I've forgotten to tell you', he wrote to Joan, 'that except for two paragraphs I have at last finished the story of the Antillean ball, and I feel terribly excited about it . . . and I would like it to be printed as a small book. I don't know what it's like, really, but I think it is exciting and alive and rather odd. Did I tell you that it is called *The Violins of Saint-Jacques* – do you like that as a title?'[9]

The story of Paddy's only novel, *The Violins of Saint-Jacques*, was inspired by the great eruption of Mont Pelée which destroyed Saint-Pierre, the capital of Martinique, in 1902. 'The inhabitants of Martinique', he wrote, 'still ascribe to this event nearly all the handicaps under which the island now labours, for all that was precious morally, materially, intellectually and politically had been centralized in the old capital; and all obliterated in the space of a few minutes.'[10]

The tale begins in present-day Greece, where the narrator meets an elderly woman called Berthe who tells him the story of the island

of Saint-Jacques. The thunder and smoke of the impending catastrophe are, at first, merely dramatic noises in the background, while
a duel and an elopement are taking place amid the splendours of a
magnificent masked ball. But the force of the eruption splits the
island apart, and within a few hours, nothing is left. Berthe, who
was in a boat on her way to intercept the eloping lovers, could only
watch as Saint-Jacques and everyone she loved sank beneath the
waves. Her parting gift to the narrator is an elaborate silver spoon,
the only thing that was left of an entire way of life: a detail inspired
by the half-melted bits of cutlery he saw in the Musée Volcanologique
that he had visited on the outskirts of Saint-Pierre.

The experience of being the only survivor is what shaped Berthe's
life, and to a certain extent it shaped Paddy's too. He had been
cut off from his friends in Germany, Austria, Czechoslovakia,
Hungary and Rumania, and most painfully, Balasha and her family
at Băleni. 'When war broke out, all these friends vanished into
sudden darkness. Afterwards the uprooting and destruction were
on so tremendous a scale that it was sometimes years after the end
of it all that the cloud became less dense and I could pick up a
clue here and there and piece together what had happened . . .
Nearly all of them had been dragged into the conflict in the teeth
of their true feelings and disaster overtook them all.'[11]

When Paddy returned from Italy with a fully-fledged novel rather than
the chapter commissioned, he thought he might be honour-bound to
offer *The Violins of Saint-Jacques* to Derek Verschoyle, the publisher of
Memorable Balls. Before doing anything he turned to Jock Murray for
advice. Jock's reply was a masterpiece of tact and reassurance.

> I am sorry you are in a dilemma. It will surprise them when they
> were expecting an article of 3,000 words to receive a fiction of 35,000
> words. But at the same time if they liked it very much it would be
> very embarrassing, because we like to think of ourselves as your
> publisher and indeed probably have an option on your next book
> . . . However there will obviously be a way out, but do send me a
> copy of the typescript as quickly as you can. And then forget all
> about it until you have finished George's book.[12]

Paddy was also keen for Diana Cooper to read *The Violins*. 'It's about 160 pages long and needs a great deal of polishing and pruning . . . if you liked it at all, I'd love to dedicate it to you as a sort of present.'[13]

Most of January 1953 was spent at the Travellers Club, though visits were paid to Julian Pitt-Rivers and Professor Dawkins in Oxford, for more talks on Greece. He also attended a charade party given by the zoologist Julian Huxley in Hampstead:

> . . . a whole room full of marvellous dressing up things, Aztec, Inca, Central Africa, the Solomon Islands etc: tremendous brainy charades, involving the coelacanth, Philemon and Baucis, the siege of Troy . . . It was fun seeing an eminent zoologist getting over-excited about the sit of a grass skirt, and struggling with his wife for the ownership of a Papuan mask with red parrot feathers.[14]

The Queen Anne Press edition of *A Time to Keep Silence* was reviewed in the *Times Literary Supplement* by James Pope-Hennessy. 'Seldom,' he wrote, 'if ever, can Benedictine rule have been analysed and discussed with such respect, good humour and good sense by a writer not a member of the Roman Catholic Church.'[15] (It was also, he was pleased to report, considerably shorter than *The Traveller's Tree*.) Paddy himself saw the book as a token of his gratitude and admiration for the monks who had been so kind to him. But in an introduction to the Penguin edition of 1982, he says that there were some reproving voices, who felt that it would have been more tactful to preserve the monks' privacy.

His friend Henry Coombe-Tennant, who had become a monk at Downside Abbey after the war, felt that Paddy should not be too upset. 'There is only one requirement of guests – that they should not disturb the life of the monastery by their numbers or their demands. It did not occur to me when I read your book that you might have been a disturbing influence . . . but I can understand monks of the older school who might feel that it isn't right to visit monasteries and then write a book about it.'[16]

That spring Paddy went to France again, to work in seclusion at Gadencourt; but before doing so, he treated himself to a brief stay at Chantilly. 'Being alone with you is what I like best, a delight of which I can never tire,' he wrote to Diana Cooper, after spending a few 'ice-bound, isolated days of lolling interminable chat and crosswords, reading aloud and trumpoil-* or fireside-meals.' But after the companionable warmth of Chantilly, the move to frozen Gadencourt induced a period of deep gloom. It was bitterly cold, and Paddy was assailed with 'terrible onslaughts of misery and loneliness that only Bach, Mozart, Beethoven and Ravel managed to thaw a bit . . . It was the year's nadir.'[17] The gloom had been intensified by a book called *Personal Religion Among the Greeks*, by André Jean Festugière. One particular passage, suggesting that those whose restlessness barred them from inner peace were doomed to take refuge in crowds, rang horribly true.

Cheering news came in late February, when the Rank Organization expressed interest in the film rights to *The Violins of Saint-Jacques*. If they took the rights they would pay Paddy £1,500 – 'nothing compared to what people got before the war, but Golconda to me'. But Rank could not make up their minds. Warner Brothers were also interested: 'If I remember rightly,' wrote Mrs Mary Dilke to Jock Murray from their Wardour Street office in March 1953, 'you described it as being the story of an island which blows up, and I feel sure this has potentialities for us.'[18] Her bosses would probably require a more cheerful ending than the one supplied, but in the event, Warner Brothers lost interest. Paddy was also approached by Alan Jefferson, representing George Posford – a composer of musicals whose hits had included *Goodnight Vienna*, *Balalaika* and *Zip Goes a Million*. Paddy liked the idea of *The Violins* becoming a musical, but this too came to nothing.

Compared to the progress of most books, that of *The Violins of Saint-Jacques* seemed to have taken place back to front. The film rights were being fought over even before its publication in the *Cornhill* magazine, where it took up almost three-quarters of the issue for Spring 1953. The book itself, published jointly by John Murray and Derek Verschoyle, only appeared later in the year. Lawrence Durrell, who read it two years later, wrote to Paddy saying, 'It is madly, intoxicatingly overwritten but the sheer barbaric wealth of material in it would furnish a dozen ordinary novels.'[19]

---

* The dining room at Chantilly was adorned with *trompe-l'oeil* panels by Martin Battersby.

Paddy had decided to spend that spring in Italy, and rented rooms in the Casa Sabina in Tivoli which belonged to a Miss Edwardes. 'Tremendous weeks of work ahead, which makes me feel very excited.'[20] It appears that Paddy really did apply himself, for on 10 April he told Joan that 'I finished [*The Cretan Runner*] this morning, after having translated 20 to 30 pages of the typescript a day, which is a tremendous amount . . . It is a great weight off my mind, and now all is clear for Greece at last, and I'm about to plunge into it.'[21]

Before doing so, he decided to take up Peter Quennell's suggestion of a walking tour of Umbria. This had been discussed after a boozy dinner at the Etoile with Ann Fleming, when they had repaired to Charlotte Street and drank (as Paddy confessed to Joan) 'over half a bottle of your Armagnac . . . I really will try and return a bottle.'[22] The appearance of a much-delayed *Sunday Times* cheque made up his mind.

Paddy and Peter Quennell met in Siena on 22 April. From there they went by train to Perugia, where they bought knapsacks and began a walk (broken by the occasional train ride) that took them to Assisi, Spello, Spoleto, Todi, Gubbio and back to Perugia. As they made their way south into the foothills of the Apennines, Quennell's borrowed boots became more and more uncomfortable; while Paddy 'was usually a hundred yards in front, leaping from rock to rock, and chanting a wild Greek song, like Byron on the field of Waterloo'.[23] On arrival in a town at dusk, Paddy would stop passers-by to ask whether they knew of a modest restaurant serving surprisingly good food and wine, preferably set into the ancient fabric of the walls and commanding a magnificent view.

Paddy had been afraid that Quennell's expensive tastes would demand grander hostelries, but Quennell proved an easy and congenial companion. Settled in some approximation of Paddy's ideal trattoria after a day of torture in his boots, Quennell wrote:

> I immediately received my reward . . . His capacity for enthusiasm, one of his greatest gifts, is supported by a huge supply of miscellaneous knowledge; and, when we talked of buildings we had just seen, his conversation would revolve at dragon-fly speed around a vast variety of favourite subjects – now the difference between Guelf and

Ghibelline battlements; now the use of the acanthus leaf, particularly
the 'wind-blown acanthus', in the sculptured capitals of Byzantine
churches. Umbria, he reminded me, was the dark-green motherland
of the mysterious Etruscan people . . . [24]

On parting from Quennell in Perugia in early May, Paddy took
a bus to Sulmona in the Abruzzi where he came across an old friend
of his, Archie Lyall. Like Paddy, Lyall had travelled in the Balkans
and served in the Intelligence Corps during the war. He had also
written books on the Balkans, Rome and southern France. When
Paddy found him, 'he was drinking his tenth solitary grappa in the
Piazza del Duomo.'[25]

Lyall had been looking for Paddy, with whom he wanted to go to
the feast of St Dominic of Sora in the village of Cocullo, just inland
from Ortona on the Adriatic coast. St Dominic protects his devotees
from snake-bites, and for weeks before the event still-hibernating
snakes had been collected from the surrounding countryside. Their
venom drawn, the snakes – dropped from windows, draped round
people's arms, and coiled in great loops round the statue of St Dominic
– become the focus of a great procession, which attracted hundreds
of pilgrims as well as sightseers like Paddy and Archie Lyall.

Once the saint was back in his niche, the snakes were sold off.
Paddy wrote that one quack from Bologna bought a whole sackful,
which he was going to boil down and make into an ointment for
rheumatism. Paddy bought one too, for 400 lire – 'a beauty, speckled
grey and green, one and a half yards long, with clever little black
eyes'.[26] Archie Lyall drove him back to Rome with the snake writhing
all over the car and Lyall complaining, 'Your bloody puff-adder's
getting up my arse.'[27]

In Rome, Paddy's wallet was stolen with fifty pounds worth of
traveller's cheques – a disaster he could ill afford. With cash borrowed
from various friends he headed north-west to Porto Ercole, where
he found a perch in the bowels of the massive Aragonese fortress
that dominates the peninsula. 'I live in two rooms – rather dark
hell-holes – for 1,000 lire a day, which isn't bad. About thirty peasants live a troglodytic life in various dungeons and holes dotted
about the castle, and the whole thing is owned by a hunchback

spinster – a schoolmistress from the Abruzzi – who acquired it twelve years ago in settlement of a debt.'[28]

He found it hard to work in these uncongenial surroundings, and was depressed by how difficult it was to pick up the threads of the Greek book, which he had abandoned for months while working on *The Cretan Runner*. Another worry was his mother, who relied on his sending her five pounds a month, a sum that had (he hoped only temporarily) dried up. He wrote an apologetic letter to Vanessa, who was now the only breadwinner in her family, since her husband had become an alcoholic and lost his job. She had worked in the administrative side of Heal's department store till head-hunted by the firm of Josiah Wedgwood, and her salary was as good as a woman could expect at that time. But she had two children to raise; she could not be expected to support her mother as well.

> The only bother about this erratic and disorganised life is that it is beset with financial doldrums which I can nearly always overcome by stop-gaps or going to earth somewhere, but while I'm working on a book, precious little comes in, and sometimes nothing, with the result that poor Mummy suffers by the bank not paying her the wretched weekly sum I'm supposed want to give her . . . Do explain this when you see her, and tell her I'll do everything I can to set matters straight as soon as poss . . . I think I'd better take a regular job on some newspaper soon, so as to be of more help. But it'll probably mean goodbye to other writing for the time being.[29]

Another film company was interested in buying the rights to *The Violins*, and as Paddy wrote to Jock,

> it would solve so many problems. a) Constantly straining your very generous help about advances etc. b) Freedom from worrying and possibility of finding a permanent cottage or something in which to do nothing but write, and stop living in suitcases and constantly losing things. c) Entirely for your private ear . . . Other members of my family are not behaving quite as well as they should about my mama; I do what I can, but it's not much at the moment, and she's rather hard up. It's a frightful worry and the extra pennies would settle it for ages.[30]

'Other members of my family' is a reference to Sir Lewis Leigh Fermor, who had retired to Surrey with his second wife Frances.

His granddaughter Francesca recalled that he never spoke of Æileen without a certain tight-lipped bitterness. His little house (named 'Gondwana') near Horsell was scarcely luxurious, but it was still better than the squalid flat near Leicester Square where Æileen lived. Paddy and Vanessa both felt he could have done more for their mother but Æileen, throwing her purple cloak over one shoulder, remained resolutely buoyant.

Paddy might have felt worried and guilty about Æileen, but had no intention of changing his own life to ease hers. The loss of a notebook covering his travels in northern Greece in 1950 now provided him with the perfect excuse to revisit Epirus – 'one of the wildest, steepest, rockiest parts of Greece . . . The place, like Crete, is stiff with vendettas and every mountain is the scene of some skirmish in the Greek War of Independence.'[31]

He and Joan travelled to Greece towards the end of June with their American friend Peter Tomkins and his wife, who had a jeep. In Yanina, the Turkish capital of Epirus, Paddy 'did a certain amount of Ali Pasha research, and took a good look at the remains of Byron's house', and visited the monastery of Zitza, where Byron and Hobhouse had stayed. At Souli, Paddy left the party for a two-day walk to the cliff of Zalongo. When Souli fell in 1808 to Ali Pasha's Arnauts, its women and children fled across the mountains to this cliff; and then, dancing to the rock's edge, the women threw themselves and their children into the void.

Paddy had hoped to drive through the Acarnanian mountains to Missolonghi; but Joan came down with a fever and, to spare her the jolting of the jeep, he took her there by boat. When she had recovered they set off on a quest to find a pair of slippers, which were said to have belonged to Lord Byron.

That a pair of Byron's slippers still existed in Missolonghi had come to Paddy's attention the previous year, in a crumbling country house in Sussex: Crabbet Park, the home of Judith, 16th Baroness Wentworth, who was Byron's great-granddaughter.

Paddy's acquaintance with Lady Wentworth had come about at a time when Jock Murray was trying to collect all Byron's letters, to make a complete edition of his correspondence. Jock knew that there was a great hoard of hitherto unseen Byron papers at Crabbet, but owing to a row between his grandfather and the Lovelace family, Byron's direct descendants, all contact had been severed. Ever keen to help Jock, Paddy mentioned that his friend Michael Holland was on good terms with Lady Wentworth. A plan was therefore made for Paddy and Michael Holland to visit her for lunch, and perhaps find out more about the Crabbet Papers. It is also possible, given the mention of 'Ali Pasha research' and visiting Byron's house in the letter above, that Paddy was thinking of writing something about Byron.

Lady Wentworth was almost eighty when Paddy met her, but she was not the sort of woman who made concessions to time. She came to greet them wearing a long skirt and tennis shoes, having just had a game of squash with her farm manager, and her mass of improbably auburn hair was piled up under a mob cap. She still ran the magnificent stud of Arabian horses set up by her parents, and had published several books: on Arabian horses, thoroughbred racing, toy dogs, as well as several volumes of verse – 'They're no great shakes, I fear – it doesn't always run in families,' she admitted to Paddy.[32] Her house was filled with Byron memorabilia, which included paintings, costumes, and trunks full of letters and documents.

Paddy found her fascinating – not least because she used turns of phrase that had last been fashionable in the Regency. Deploying all his charm, he hinted that he would very much like to see what were known as the Wentworth and Lovelace Papers. Lady Wentworth was not encouraging, but he hoped she would eventually come round to the idea.*

Yet his knowledge of Greece had reminded Lady Wentworth of some letters she had received from an Australian sergeant during the war, who had met a man in Missolonghi who had a pair of slippers belonging to Lord Byron. The slippers' current owner felt they should be returned to the poet's family, and he too had written her a letter; but since the letter was in Greek, she was unable to read it and had never heard from him again. Through Michael Holland she forwarded all the letters to Paddy, and asked if he could find out anything more.

---

* It was not until some years later that Lady Wentworth allowed Doris Langley Moore full access to the Papers: see Doris Langley Moore, *The Great Byron Adventure* (New York: J. B. Lippincott Company, 1959).

Now he and Joan were in Missolonghi, Paddy realized that he did not have the letters with him, and that he had forgotten the name of the man they were looking for. They spent a hot and frustrating day trudging round the town, asking whether anyone had heard of a man who might have Lord Byron's slippers. No one had, but word spread. On returning to the hotel they found a young woman waiting for them, who said that the slippers were in the possession of her uncle, Charalambos Baiyorgas.

Mr Baiyorgas was then in his seventies, and the story of how he had acquired the slippers is told in full in *Roumeli*. Made of thin red tooled leather with yellow silk uppers and turned-up toes, 'something about them carried instant conviction . . . the worn parts of the soles were different on each. Those of the left were normal; the right showed a different imprint, particularly in the instep.' The owner, who did not know about Byron's clubbed right foot, was not very interested in this discovery; but for Paddy, 'I believe I saw my hands trembling as I held them.'[33] Had they been shown to Paddy as part of Lady Wentworth's collection it would not have been such a moment of wonder; but to find them here, at Missolonghi, made '*Lordos Vyron*' seem very close. He sketched the relics, while Joan took photographs of them – for Mr Baiyorgas admitted, with some embarrassment, that he could not bear to let the slippers go after all.

The resemblances between Byron and Paddy began with a certain physical likeness, and once the connection was made, they multiplied. Both had an idealized vision of Greece before they ever set foot there. Both felt that in England their spirits were fettered while in Greece they were freed, and both were known for being scholars as well as men of action. In writing, both believed in immediacy, although they corrected their work obsessively and demanded as many sets of proofs as their respective John Murrays would allow. While careless of comfort when abroad they both loved dressing up, and had the reckless courage and panache that the Greeks call *leventeia*. When Hobhouse wrote that Byron 'seemed always made for that company in which he happened to find himself', he could have been writing about Paddy.[34]

On a deeper level, their differences are more apparent. Byron's moods took him to far greater extremes of despair than Paddy ever experienced, resulting in greater poetry and considerably more emotional damage to those around him. Paddy's looks were a part of his physical confidence, while Byron thought his beauty botched by his hated limp. He went through much of his life feeling bitter and cursed, whilst Paddy never lost a certain joyful innocence and believed himself profoundly blessed.

He was always rather exasperated when people compared him to Byron, whom he admired very much. Byron had given everything for Greece: his fortune, his health, and eventually his life. The Greeks had taken him to their hearts, and every subsequent Englishman, including himself, benefited from the association and basked in his glory.

From Missolonghi, Paddy left Joan with the Tomkinses and took a bus eastwards to Naupaktos on the Gulf of Corinth 'where Lepanto was fought and Cervantes lost an arm', as he wrote to Diana.[35] He revisited the Kravarites, and made further notes on their secret language. 'I collected some amazing stories,' he wrote to Jock, 'also a vast glossary of their very peculiar thieves' cant.' He did not regret losing the notes: 'I got very much more and newer stuff this time, and it was well worth it.'[36]

In August 1953, the Ionian Islands were struck by the worst series of earthquakes in their history. Over the course of several days, more than a hundred tremors tore the fabric of the islands apart, leaving hundreds of people homeless and the economy of the islands in ruins. Since Paddy was in Greece he was asked to write about what had happened for the *Sunday Times*, and he was pleased to hear that Philip Toynbee was coming out to cover the story for the *Observer*. Thanks to Paddy's friend Panayiotis Canellopoulos, whom he had met during the Greek campaign and who was now Minister for National Defence, Toynbee and Paddy travelled to the islands on a Greek air force plane. In Zante they found 'two British frigates laden with aid to the quake-struck, commanded by a dashing young captain called Geoffrey Crick . . . We all clicked at once, and helped as much as we could . . .'[37]

Back in Athens, Paddy and Toynbee repaired to neighbouring tables in a café to write their copy. 'As we had been inseparable throughout, our pieces were nearly identical, so we had to go through them, docking similar adjectives and adjusting our phrases, so that the rival newspapers' reports came out respectably different.'[38] That done, they could relax. One evening was devoted to an orgy of talk with Katsimbalis and George Seferis, while on another occasion (he and Paddy were both very drunk) Toynbee found himself in the mood for a more traditional sort of orgy. They were in a flat belonging to two pretty but prim girls who worked at the British Embassy. 'As usual, Philip behaved like a centaur at a wedding breakfast, grasped one of them, and said "Now, let's all have a great deal of SEX! And, just in case anybody's feeling shy, I'll get the ball rolling and kick off by buggering Paddy."'[39]

Cyprus was hit by an earthquake a month later, and once again Paddy was sent by the *Sunday Times* to cover the event. Maurice Cardiff, who had been a colleague at the British Council in Athens in 1946, was then working for the British Council in Nicosia. He and his wife Leonora, and Paddy who was accompanied by Joan, went out to dinner on two or three occasions, during which Cardiff noticed Joan's unusual relationship with Paddy. One evening, Leonora and Joan left the restaurant earlier than the men. As Joan stood up to go, she took a handful of notes out of her wallet and gave them to Paddy saying, 'Here you are, that should be enough if you want to find a girl.'[40] When this story was told to one of Joan's closest friends, she was not surprised. 'A moment came when Joan told Paddy she no longer wanted to sleep with him,' she said, 'but she never expected him to remain celibate.'[41]

Nor did he; but his weakness for the sleazier pleasures of the night sometimes led to a nasty surprise for his more respectable girlfriends. When one complained that she had found an embarrassing parasite on her eyebrow (let us not ask how it got there) Paddy told her she was making a fuss about nothing. 'They're perfectly easy to get rid of . . . I expect I picked them up from a tart in Athens.' On another occasion, however, his mortification at having passed on the same sexually transmitted vermin gave rise to a letter so funny that it must be quoted in full.

> I say, what gloomy tidings about the CRABS! *Could* it be me? I'll
> tell you why this odd doubt exists, instead of robust certainty one
> way or the other: just after arriving back in London from Athens, I
> was suddenly alerted by what *felt* like the beginnings of troop

movements in the fork, but on scrutiny, there was nothing to be seen, not even a scout, a spy or a despatch rider. Puzzled, I watched and waited and soon even the preliminary tramplings died away, so I assumed, as the happy summer days of peace followed each other, that the incident, or the delusive shudder through the chancelleries, was over. While this faint scare was on, knowing that, thanks to lunar tyranny, it wouldn't be from you, I assumed (and please spare my blushes here!) that the handover bid must have occurred by dint of a meeting with an old pal in Paris, which, I'm sorry to announce, ended in brief carnal knowledge, more for auld lang syne than any more pressing reason.

On getting your letter, I made a dash for privacy and thrashed through the undergrowth, but found everything almost eerily calm: fragrant and silent glades that might never have known the invader's tread. The whole thing makes me scratch my head, if I may so put it. But I bet your trouble *does* come from me, because the crabs of the world seem to fly to me, like the children of Israel to Abraham's bosom, a sort of ambulant Canaan, I've been a real martyr to them . . .

There's some wonderful Italian powder you can get called MOM which is worth its weight in gold dust . . . Don't tell anyone about this private fauna. Mom's the word . . .

As well as noticing Joan's generosity in funding Paddy's post-midnight prowls, Maurice Cardiff also observed (not for the first time) how oblivious he could be to the reactions of people around him. On another evening in a taverna Paddy, already pretty drunk, began singing his repertoire of Greek songs. 'The tension in the room was hardening by the minute: the Cyprus question had not blown up, but there was a lot of anti-British feeling and they did not think it was right for an Englishman to sit there pretending to be more Greek than the Greeks – but Paddy had no idea, he just kept on singing.'[42]

Yet his songs had the very opposite effect in the village of Bellapaix, near Kyrenia, where Lawrence Durrell had a house. He and Joan were once again in Cyprus in November 1953, after one of their gastronomically punishing tours of Crete and the strongholds of the Cretan resistance. 'It was as joyous a reunion as we ever had in Rhodes,' wrote Durrell.

After a splendid dinner by the fire he starts singing, songs of Crete, Athens, Macedonia. When I go out to refill the ouzo bottle at the little tavern across the way I find the street completely filled with people listening in utter silence and darkness . . . 'What is it?' I say, catching sight of [a neighbour]. 'Never have I heard of Englishmen singing songs like this!' Their reverent amazement is touching; it is as if they want to embrace Paddy wherever he goes.[43]

With Joan at Dumbleton Paddy spent Christmas 1953 in Ireland, at Luggala (pronounced Luggalore), the house of Oonagh Oranmore and Browne. Luggala was a Gothic Revival toy of a castle, though its innocent exterior belied the reckless goings-on inside. Paddy described the atmosphere as 'a mixture of a night-club, the Hons' cupboard and the Charge of the Light Brigade, so tremendous was the pace, even for me, all day and all night . . .'[44] Oonagh, who was one of three Guinness sisters, had married the 4th Baron Oranmore and Browne in 1936, but at that stage she was passionately involved with the journalist and historian Robert Kee.

They were still at Luggala when Paddy read that Duff Cooper had died on New Year's Day. He put off writing to Diana for days, waiting in vain for the moment when the words would flow of their own accord – which of course never came. When he finally wrote to her on the 11th, he recalled Duff 'having to stop reading *Vile Bodies* out loud by the fire, to mop away the helpless tears of laughter that were streaming down his face. None of the obituaries I've seen quite got the point . . .'

He spent a few days recovering from the excesses of Luggala at Birr Castle with Michael and Annie Rosse and Michael's sister, Bridget Parsons, followed by a visit to Dublin where 'I did some agreeable pub-crawling with Robert Kee, and made friends with the poet Patrick Kavanagh and Sean O'Faolain, drinking Guinness in Joycean pubs.'[45] He and Robert then returned to Luggala, which was quieter now than it had been over Christmas and New Year. The only party on the horizon was the Kildare Hunt Ball to which nobody wanted to go, least of all the hostess; but Paddy was convinced it might be fun, and cajoled everyone else into accepting the invitation. Before leaving for the ball, Oonagh summoned the butler and asked him to bring her one of her pills which, she remarked, would make a tiresome evening a bit more bearable. A pill the size of a hornet arrived on a silver salver and Paddy, intrigued, asked if he could have one too.

In the early hours of the morning, Paddy – now revved up on a mixture of alcohol and the contents of the hornet – began deliberately to antagonize Tim Vigors, one of the tallest and broadest of the pink-coated Kildare huntsmen. When Paddy asked Vigors if it was true that the 'Killing Kildares' were in the habit of buggering their foxes Vigors punched him to the ground, while a few of his friends decided that this insufferable Englishman needed a lesson he would not forget.

'There we were, all slamming away at each other like navvies,' wrote Paddy to Diana. 'I was being dealt with by half a dozen great incarnadined Nimrods; Robert Kee came to my rescue, only to be brought down by Roderick More O'Ferrall, and the scarlet mael-strom surged over them and me. The Macgillicuddy of the Reeks's sister-in-law plunged into the middle and fetched me one on the top of the head with her ringed fist . . .'[46] This resulted in a cut on his head, which began to bleed profusely.

The person who pulled him out of the melée was Ricki Huston, a beautiful Italian-American dancer who was the fourth wife of the film director John Huston. Seizing him by the arm, she ordered Paddy, supported by Robert Kee, into her chauffeur-driven car: 'I'm taking you to a doctor,' she said, 'you need sewing up.' Her driver was bitterly disappointed to have missed the fight: 'If only we'd known, Sir, me and the boys would have come and sorted 'em out for you . . .'[47] They drove to Dublin, where a surgeon was woken to give Paddy three stitches on the top of his head.

Duff's death plunged Diana into a morass of grief and gloom from which the only escape was travel. Her first stop was Rome, where Paddy joined her for a fortnight towards the end of February. From Rome they went by train through Latium and Tuscany, where they stopped off to visit Bernard Berenson at the Villa I Tatti in Settignano, where Diana had spent part of her honeymoon. Berenson loved Diana, and wept as she told him simply how Duff had died. Paddy remembered him waving his stick majestically across the valley, telling them that this was the very landscape that appeared in Benozzo Gozzoli's *Journey of the Magi*.

From Italy Diana moved on to Greece, where Paddy had given her introductions to everyone he could think of. He made his way back to England, realizing on his return that he had lost all the letters (mostly replies to condolences on Duff's death) that Diana had given him to post. He sent her an apologetic letter from Wantage in Berkshire, where he was spending the weekend with John and Penelope Betjeman. 'We had great fun last night looking up obscure poets – South Africans, Australians, Canadians etc – and reading them in the appropriate accents . . . Penelope's Catholicism has evidently split the household. There is a certain amount of doctrinal bickering and smart rejoinders, surreptitious reading of the *Catholic Herald* (stuffed under a cushion if John comes into the room).' At one point Paddy caught a glimpse of Penelope's room: 'a grotto of images, rosaries and crucifixes . . . [Their household is] a sort of microcosm of Reformation England inside out.'[48]

, On 22 March Paddy was once more at Crabbet, to tell Lady Wentworth about the discovery of Byron's slippers in Missolonghi. This time he went with Michael Holland's son Anthony, and after lunch Lady Wentworth suggested a game of billiards. They played in silence as the weather outside grew wild, with the wind roaring down the chimney as Lady Wentworth 'scored breaks of 50, 70, 95, and once, 108 . . . On and on it went, like something in a terrifying Norse legend, gambling for one's life with a man-eating witch in a dim, shadowy cave at the bottom of a fjord as the hours passed. I could see Anthony was thoroughly rattled too. We were losing by larger and larger margins with each successive game, and still the grim work went on . . .'[49]

The news that Mary Hutchinson would be leaving the flat in Charlotte Street, which had been Paddy and Joan's London base for the past five years, filled them with dismay. He and Joan packed up their belongings and, once again, he found himself having to beg storage space in the houses of various friends. What struck him most was the feeling that the one solid base in their lives was gone: 'It was as if somebody had climbed a tree and beat a rookery to bits so that all of us flapped away into the dark. I've moved into the Travellers, where I have been for the last ten days, feeling pretty gloomy on the whole.'[50]

It was not just the loss of Charlotte Street: Paddy's father Lewis was dying. 'We had only met twice during the last six years,' he wrote to Diana, 'and corresponded as little . . . I felt wretched at not feeling more strongly.' Paddy had been down to see him several times, and was very upset by his appearance – 'hollow-cheeked, grey-green, with enormous unmoving and luminous eyes, talking very slowly and almost inaudibly . . . The only consoling thing is that he has no idea he is dying ("Such a bore being cooped up when all the flowers are out . . . ")'[51]

These sad meetings with his father left Paddy in a turmoil of guilt and regret that produced terrifying nightmares. 'I had a brute last night, full of allegorical monsters . . . like one of those really murky *zuppa di pesce*'s, when your plate is a writhing mass of scales and spikes and backbones and overflowing, sucker-studded tentacles and balefully accusing eyes.'[52] Paddy escaped as he always did: by plunging either into the murkier dens of late-night London or into books – at this time he was reading *The Wilder Shores of Love* by Lesley Blanch, and Enid Starkie's *Petrus Borel*, about a strange group of Romantic poets in Paris in the 1830s. Lewis Leigh Fermor died on 24 May. 'What a strange business Daddy's funeral was, a sort of nightmare,' he wrote to his sister Vanessa. 'I'm so glad you were there too – I don't think I could have taken it if there hadn't been your eye to catch now and then!'[53]

The need for a semi-permanent base was met by their friend, the painter Nico Hadjikyriacou-Ghika. The most celebrated Greek painter of his day, he had studied in Paris and was happy in a handful of languages; but his work was grounded in the landscape and traditions of Greece. His seafaring family's house in Hydra had been built in the middle of the eighteenth century, and the craggy rocks on which it was constructed had given it a series of nine terraces. Nico and his wife Tiggy spent most of their time in Athens, and only used the house for a few weeks a year. Paddy and Joan had stayed the previous summer, and now they were urged to make themselves at home for as long as they liked. The offer was gratefully accepted.

The pair moved in in June 1954. 'It's a great white empty thing,' wrote Paddy, 'on a rocky, cactussy hillside among olives and almonds and fig trees. Thick wall and wooden ceilings, full of charm. The only drawback is that it's ten minutes down to the sea, fifteen or twenty up, and jolly steep . . .'[54] Sometimes Paddy felt as though he were living in a colossal, three-dimensional Ghika painting: 'The eccentric terrain really does tilt towns and panoramas to the angle of those Byzantine backgrounds stretching upwards in height instead of receding in depth . . . Likewise the sea, which should fade as it recedes and induce a feeling of the earth's roundness, does the reverse. Equally intense at horizon and shore, it stands bolt upright . . .'[55]

The galley proofs of *The Cretan Runner* appeared in July, and he worked on them in between bouts of energetic entertaining. 'Patrick K[inross] came for three days,' Paddy wrote to Jock Murray, 'then Cyril Connolly and his bride [Barbara Skelton], which was not as difficult going as it might have been. The great Eroica Rawbum' (an anagram of Maurice Bowra, who was accompanied by Ann Fleming) 'comes out next month.'[56] He was not sure he was going to get on with 'Rawbum', and the feeling was mutual. 'Dear Paddy will be there,' Bowra told Billa Harrod, 'and I have decided to be angelic to him and treat him like a great writer.'[57] Next came Diana Cooper, Freya Stark and his pre-war friend Tanti Rodocanachi, among others. 'Don't be disturbed about this,' Paddy continued in his letter to Jock, 'as I seclude myself for *seven hours a day* in my hermitage in the bowels, and am working like anything, and allowing nothing to interfere. My diligence fills everyone with awe. I'm allowing myself a week's hol at the beginning of Sept, but till then the grindstone and my nose cohere.'[58]

Joan went back to England towards the end of August, having limped through southern Italy with Maurice Bowra in a car that kept breaking down. He was not the easiest of travelling companions, and by the end of the journey her nerves were in shreds. 'God how I loved Hydra,' she wrote to Paddy. 'Do let's always live in Greece with a mule and caique . . . I really hate anything else now and love being with you most, in spite of everything, always.'[59] Joan's idyllic vision assumed that they would always be welcome in Greece, and as individuals, they were. But as the struggle for Cyprus intensified, Anglo-Greek relations were strained to breaking point – a situation that the two of them found very hard to bear.

16

Cyprus

In the years after the war, Britain took a long time to adjust to the fact that it was no longer a world power. Although it had little empire left and had lost its grip on Palestine and Egypt, it was still bent on keeping a huge garrison in the eastern Mediterranean, and the focus of this effort was the island of Cyprus.

The British had taken control of Cyprus from the Ottomans in 1878 and in 1925, by the Treaty of Locarno, it became a British Crown Colony. Turks numbered about eighteen per cent of the population, but the Greeks who made up the rest were in no doubt about the island's identity: Cyprus was culturally, ethnically and incontrovertibly Greek. It had been so since prehistoric times, while the Orthodox Church on Cyprus – founded within fifty years of the death of Christ – was one of the oldest outposts of Christendom. This conviction was shared by every Greek on the mainland. Sooner or later, they thought, Britain would be forced to accept the Cypriot claim for *enosis*, union with Greece.

Yet the British were in no mood to relinquish their sovereignty over Cyprus, which they wanted to hold at all costs as a 'Commonwealth Fortress'.[1] Any local protest at Britain's rule and its reinforcement of the island was ruthlessly suppressed. When the Greeks took the case for *enosis* to the United Nations in September 1954, Britain's protests gained little sympathy. But since the Turks were against *enosis* they voted with Britain, and the Greeks failed to get the support they needed. On 19 December, Greek students rioted in Athens, Nicosia and Limassol.

Paddy arrived in Athens just before Christmas 1954, in a bid to persuade the King of the Hellenes to come to Crete to unveil a monument dedicated to those who had lost their lives during the occupation. He stayed with the new Ambassador, Sir Charles and Lady Peake. Whilst the Ambassador could not support *enosis*, he felt that his government's refusal to discuss a measure of self-determination for Cyprus was, to say the least, unwise. Paddy, on the other hand, was in no doubt. Scribbling his thoughts in a notebook for a possible article, he wrote: 'Greeks right and we are wrong. Up to us to make step.'

For Paddy, a direct descendant of the Philhellenes – those passionate young men from all over Europe who 'went off to serve the cause of Greek freedom with copies of Byron in their pockets'[2] – Greece and Britain were bastions of freedom who had always been on the same side, and in occupied Crete this conviction had underpinned his everyday survival. He had been willing to die for both Greece and England, and now he was forced to watch these two countries throwing away two centuries of goodwill. But while he had no doubt that Britain was in the wrong, he was enough of an Englishman to deplore the threats and bombastic demands made by the Greek government, and the way the Greek newspapers compared the British administration of Cyrus to the Nazi occupation of Greece. 'I do wish the whole [Cyprus] thing was settled,' he wrote to Lawrence Durrell. 'It makes both the English and the Greeks conduct themselves like complete lunatics, and grotesque caricatures of themselves.'[3]

Progress on the book ground to a halt as he embarked on fresh avenues of research and fretted about Cyprus. George Seferis was worried that he had been at it far too long already. He confided his fears to Joan, 'my last friend in England' as he called her. 'I was rather uncomfortable when I saw a letter from Paddy in the *Kathimerini* . . . asking the readers of this paper to send him information about the [*manghes*],' he wrote. 'I'm afraid he is too much PENELOPE-IZING* with that book.'[4] He wrote to the compulsive rewriter as well. 'Stop writing letters to *Kathimerini* or you are going to be submerged by letters like this . . . Paddy, Paddy, I am certain you

---

* In the ten years that Penelope had to wait for her husband Odysseus to come home from the Trojan wars, a number of suitors had gathered round her. She kept them at bay by telling them she would make her choice when she had finished her tapestry; and every night, she would unpick the work she had done that day.

don't need any more material for your book. Shut them off and even shut the windows.'⁵

Paddy had no intention of doing either and never regretted his letter to the newspaper, which put him in touch with a scholar called Kosta Papadopoulos.

Since then we have been in constant correspondence, and the last letter is *50 pages long*, answering questions about Lazi, Pomaks, Kitzilbashi in Thrace, the Paulicians, the Cumans and Pechenegs [*patzinaki*] and the possible Jewish origin of the Lacedaemonians (see Chapter 12 Second Book of the Maccabees in the Apocrypha – but don't worry, I'm keeping it dark!), the Trapezuntine crypto-Christians, the crypto-Muslims of Asia Minor, the Pelasgo-Phrygian descent of the Tsebekides etc. etc. He seems to know Ancient Greek as well as Turkish, Persian and Arabic. George K. is absolutely enthralled, as he's a complete mystery man. He's asked everywhere, and discovered that he is a well-known scholar (according to someone in the National Library) married to a 'well-known actress' that no one has ever heard of.⁶

In January Stephen Spender – poet and current editor of *Encounter* magazine – came to stay in the house in Hydra with his wife Natasha. They were there at the same time as the art historian Roger Hinks. Hinks had been involved with the disastrous cleaning of the Elgin Marbles in 1939, after which he had resigned as Assistant Keeper of Greek and Roman Antiquities at the British Museum. His attitude to the Greeks made Paddy squirm with anguish and embarrassment. 'The Greeks bore him stiff, and he says so without any inhibitions at all . . . He and George [Katsimbalis] no go of course. When George mentioned the Marbles, I begged him to keep it dark, but, of course, he'd had lots of fun with it already . . .'

Paddy had been afraid that Roger would not get on with the Spenders either, but all went well – 'in fact nothing but jokes, laughter and fun the whole time, Stephen twinkling away like an overgrown Peter Pan'.⁷ Before setting out by car for Hydra that January, Joan had written that 'I find myself doing the fatal thing of saying vaguely to lots of people do come and stay. I expect we shall be fuller than ever. Warners, Harrods, Campbells all seem iminant [*sic*]. And Maurice wants to spend the whole of next summer there. I will keep them all at bay if you don't want them . . .'[8] But neither she nor Paddy were very good at keeping friends at bay.

Later that spring, they spent several days travelling by bus round the Peloponnese with 'the Gas-Bag of Attica', as Paddy called George Katsimbalis. The journey began in Tripoli, 'a lightless, drizzling, pot-holed Balkan town, block-house built of ferro-concrete'. Their spirits rose only when they found a restaurant where George unearthed a wine so rare that the bottles they drank were probably the last in existence: 'it was like shooting the last dodo.' They followed the road south as far as Sparta, then west to Mistra, made a loop round the Messenian peninsula, before they moved northwards to Pylos, site of the Battle of Navarino and guarded by a great Venetian fortress. They made their way back along the west coast for two final days at Olympia, 'escorted all the way by George's unstaunchable and, I must say, wonderful story-telling'.[9]

The following month (May 1955) Paddy went to Cyprus, where Lawrence Durrell had persuaded him to give a lecture for the British Council. By now the anti-British guerrilla organization EOKA,* under the leadership of Colonel Grivas, was increasing its activities, bombing and attacking British targets and service personnel. Paddy joined Durrell in Paphos, to witness the trial of a group of EOKA rebels who had been captured while waiting for a caique loaded with guns and ammunition. The crowd outside was smashing windows and shouting for the release of the accused. Paddy doubted the British would ever win, though Durrell did not think that the Cypriots 'by themselves would have the stamina for a long conflict'.[10] Either way, it was very depressing. 'Cyprus was detestable,' Paddy wrote to Diana, 'the Cypriots sullen and, in a wet way, disaffected, the English the sweepings of the Colonial Office, well-intentioned, unimaginative, blundering, stubborn and fifth-rate.'[11]

He and Joan travelled on to Beirut, where George Seferis was then serving as Greek Ambassador to Lebanon. Spurred into action by his accusations of 'Penelope-izing' at Christmas, Paddy had come to 'read great lumps of my book out to George . . . whose opinion

* National Organization of Cypriot Fighters.

I value more than anyone else's about literature dealing with Greece'.[12] To his relief, the great poet's reaction was encouraging.

He did not go to London for the publication of *The Cretan Runner* in May, but followed its progress closely. Thanks to early and enthusiastic reviews by Dilys Powell in the *Sunday Times* and Peter Quennell in the *Daily Mail*, it sold over two thousand copies in the first two weeks. But an interesting review by Rodis Roufos, which appeared when the book was published in Greek, showed a very different response. Whilst Roufos admitted that Psychoundakis was a courageous patriot, 'unfortunately, he cannot write'; his style, as one might have expected from a poor islander of limited education, is influenced 'by bad journalism and popular serials'. Paddy the Philhellene, wrote Roufos, saw only a primitive storyteller unfolding his tale with dazzling immediacy. Roufos recognized that his motives were good, but he felt Paddy had done no service to the Greeks, who appear as 'quite nice native servants to the Allied officers they were called on to serve during the war'.[13]

June was a busy month. The run of visitors on Hydra included Patrick Kinross, Eddie Gathorne-Hardy, Coote Lygon and Nancy Mitford. 'The house became a carilloning belfry, [Nancy's] private peal fortunately harmonizing with the goat bells outside. She was in tremendous spirits, and very good at ragging Nico [Ghika] (which he loves) . . .'[14] One of their last guests that summer was Cyril Connolly, alone this time, for his wife Barbara Skelton had eloped with the publisher George Weidenfeld; 'the poor chap looks pretty glum and more like a wounded football than ever.'[15]

Jock Murray and his wife Diana also came to stay on Hydra, though Jock's real purpose in coming was to prise a manuscript out of Paddy's hands. Originally, Paddy's outline for the book went as far as Constantinople, and included almost every island in the Greek archipelago. It was probably in Hydra that Jock began to argue that the Greek book would only become manageable if it were divided into two volumes, and from the work so far, the first would be the one about the southern Peloponnese. He left with a great sheaf of manuscript, to begin the long task of turning what was already a labyrinth of amendments, additions and corrections into a book. Its working title was *The Dark Towers*, but a book with a similar title appeared just before Paddy's went to press. Instead, Paddy decided to call it by a single, resonant name: *Mani*.

One spur to completing the work was the prospect of joining Diana Cooper, who had been lent the *Eros II*: Stavros Niarchos's second-best yacht, that is, with a crew of eight to take Diana and her friends anywhere she wanted to go. For this Diana had to thank her friend Pamela Churchill, who was having an affair with Niarchos (after her break-up with Elie de Rothschild, and before her marriage to Leland Hayward). Diana had asked Paddy to help her construct the itinerary and join the party, and he was very keen on the idea. 'I have hopes of being finished by then, and ceasing to be a bore to you, Joan and all one's friends. It has been really intolerable . . . I've got to shed my burden (like Christian after the Slough of Despond) before being free again. I wish I wrote faster.'[16]

Paddy had been based in Hydra now for over a year. The Ghikas begged him to stay on but he was beginning to feel stale there, and the Cyprus situation was poisoning everyday life. When an official in the Greek Aliens Office attempted to have him and several other British nationals expelled, he took the matter straight to his old friend Panayiotis Canellopoulos, then vice-premier. Canellopoulos 'was furious. So all is well now. But it was awfully worrying and humiliating and angering and illogical while it lasted.'[17]

On 12 September, the voyage of the *Eros II* began. On board were Diana; her son John Julius, a young diplomat recently posted to Belgrade, and his wife Anne; Paddy and Joan; and Frank and Kitty Giles, who had known Diana in her embassy days when Frank had been Paris correspondent for *The Times*. Paddy's itinerary took them through the Cyclades and the Dodecanese, to Chios and Psara off the west coast of Turkey, and, Syros, Skopelos and Skiathos in the northern Sporades. For John Julius, Paddy's company was a revelation. His knowledge of Greece was encyclopaedic, but 'nobody has ever carried his knowledge so lightly, nobody has ever seemed less like a scholar.'[18]

The English visitors were not always welcome as they toured the islands, for the problem of Cyprus was entering a new and darker phase. In late August Harold Macmillan, the new Foreign Secretary, had called a conference on Cyprus with Britain, Greece and – for the first time – Turkey at the table. By including Turkey, Macmillan hoped to internationalize the discussion and weaken the Greek position. In the end, it weakened the British position too, and created a new set of tensions. The cordial relations that had existed between Greece and Turkey between 1930 and 1955 turned to ashes in the wake of savage anti-Greek riots in Istanbul in September, where Greek churches were singled out for destruction. Meanwhile, anti-British resentment in Greece rose to new levels of bitterness.

Sometimes, as they entered a taverna, people would stop talking and a chill would fall around the strangers. On one or two occasions, a lone voice would start singing the 'Hymn to Freedom', and every Greek would stand up and join in. The Greek national anthem consists of the first two verses of this long poem by Dionysios Solomos; but when Paddy joined in, he sang a great many more verses – belting them out with his hand on his heart as everyone lapsed into uncomfortable silence. Did this emphatic display of support for Greece make the English interlopers more popular? John Julius, a devoted fan of Paddy's, thought it did; Frank Giles thought the opposite.

Cyprus had also come between Paddy and Katsimbalis, who were now embroiled in what Seferis called 'Homeric quarrels'.[19] In one particularly heated exchange, Paddy supported, if not the British government's position, then at least its good faith. But Katsimbalis was outraged by his 'infinite admiration for Mr Macmillan and Mr Eden, and your blind loyalty to English diplomacy. It was impossible for you to accept that . . . the Foreign Office planned and provoked the Turks to act against us so they can hide behind them and never solve the Cyprus problem.'[20] Another bone of contention was the EOKA rebels. Paddy considered them terrorists, whilst Katsimbalis thought they had as much right to use violence as Paddy and the Cretans had during the German occupation. Seferis agreed: he believed that EOKA was 'a resistance movement of the pure type which has been experienced by Paddy and so many others when we were fighting together'.[21] Even Crete seemed anti-British now. Paddy had given a friend of his, the diplomat Fred Warner, a letter to open doors as he walked around the island: 'Apart from the villages where I sent him, where they were polite and hospitable, there was coldness, suspicion and hostility all the way.'[22]

Joan poured out her misery to Seferis: 'I am in such despair about it all, I find it almost impossible to write to you and anyway you may tear the letter up unread. George Katsimbalis refused to dine with Paddy and me on my last night in Athens, which upset me dreadfully . . . What are we to do? I can't think about it any more without bursting into tears . . .'[23]

Seferis did not tear up her letter. 'All of us in Greece have been through very difficult moments since September,' he wrote back, 'and the despairing thing is that the situation does not improve. I have never felt more than now the need of friends, and you are Joan, one of my best.'[24] Paddy too could think of little else. As he wrote to Jock, 'the mess we have both (but mostly we) made of it begins to develop into a kind of obsessive and paralyzing compound of anger and gloom. I find myself struggling with a long article (I don't know who for) about Cyprus – roughly, a plea that we should change our entire policy there – I don't think I'll be able to do anything until it's off my chest.'[25]

The article appeared in two parts, on 9 and 16 December 1955, in the *Spectator*. It was the most passionately political article that Paddy ever wrote. He argued that the British position in the eastern Mediterranean would be far stronger with Greece on our side, and Britain's refusal to discuss the matter 'seemed evasive, graceless and insulting'. He deplored the 'incendiary broadcasts' made from Athens to Cyprus, which had raised the level of anti-British hatred.

> But it was depressing, at the trial in Paphos last year, to see that the caique-skipper, the sailors and the shore party in the dock for running explosives into the island for use against the British were exactly the same hardy type of Greek . . . that used not only to help us run guns and agents against the Germans . . . but befriend and shelter the straggling remnant of our defeated army at appalling risk.[26]

Evidently Seferis and Katsimbalis had gone some way to revising his opinion, if not of EOKA's methods, then of the purity of its intentions. The only just and sensible way out was to cede Cyprus to Greece without further ado. Yet his condemnation of the bloodshed and destruction caused by current British policy in Cyprus suggests to the reader that it was perhaps too late for such a civilized solution.

He stayed on a week in Athens after the *Eros* party broke up, and made up his quarrel with Katsimbalis. They lunched together three times: 'he a bit hangdog and ashamed of his outburst', Paddy reported to Diana in October 1955. Paddy also had to supervise the return of his books to England. He had several crates made, including one to contain his most recent purchase: the twenty-seven quarto volumes of the *Great Greek Encyclopaedia*. With this unwieldy luggage he now planned to cross Europe by train, and soon he was feeling like 'a man carrying a grand piano across the Gobi desert'. The packing cases caused nothing but trouble and went astray in Belgrade, where John Julius was left to sort out the tangle of paperwork and send them on.

The article on Cyprus was written from Gadencourt, where he had settled down to what he hoped would be a long and productive bout of writing. He was cheered by the fact that the Rank Organization had finally bought the film rights to *The Violins of Saint-Jacques* — up to now they had only purchased options. This brought a windfall of about £1,000, which meant he could contribute more towards his mother's maintenance — although as he explained to Vanessa, 'a lot goes in taxes, and arrears of income tax of which I've never paid a penny, and debts which have been haunting me for years.'[27]

Despite the attention it received when it first came out, *The Violins of Saint-Jacques* was never made into a film. But a decade later its dramatic possibilities inspired the composer Malcolm Williamson, who turned it into an opera with a libretto by William Chappell. Paddy was very excited, and implored Diana to come and keep him company on its first night, at Sadler's Wells, on 29 November 1966. 'After all, it's dedicated to you . . . which sort of makes you a sort of part-owner. I do wonder what it'll be like.'[28] The music critic Paul Conway described the score as 'one of the composer's most enjoyably eclectic, ranging from Brittenesque seascapes and Bergian Expressionist to Sullivan-like melodies', which gives one an idea. It has never been revived.[29]

In the spring of 1956, Paddy made his first visit to Lismore Castle in Ireland, a romantic fortress that dominates a stretch of the river

Blackwater in County Waterford. Built by King John and lived in by Sir Walter Raleigh, Lismore was the Irish country seat of the Dukes of Devonshire.

He had been invited to stay by his new friend, the young Duchess (Andrew Cavendish became the 11th Duke on the death of his father in 1950, his elder brother, William, having been killed in action in 1944). Born Deborah Mitford and known as Debo, it was said by her sister Nancy that she was stuck at the mental age of nine. Debo did not mind. The youngest of seven children, her siblings had given her no reason to believe that growing up made one any wiser. Paddy was to become a great friend of both Devonshires, but he did not appreciate the full range of Debo's originality till he came to stay at Lismore.

He described her as 'funny, touching, ravishing and enslaving . . . With all this, there was another quality that I like better than anything, a wonderful and disarming unguardedness in conversation, and an intuitive knack . . . for people's moods and feelings.'[30] Since she was five years younger than Paddy and as pleased with him as he was with her, many people have wondered whether they were lovers at some point, but the balance of informed opinion seems to doubt it.

From Lismore he returned to Gadencourt, where he set to work revising the text of *A Time to Keep Silence.* Jock Murray wanted to republish this the following year, since Paddy was still so embroiled in *Mani* that there was no hope of that book coming out in the spring. He had also been working on two other pieces. One was a long essay on Nico Ghika, in what Cyril Connolly would call the Mandarin style, which was published in *Encounter* the following year as 'The Background of Ghika: Thoughts on a Greek Landscape'.[31]

The other was called 'Sounds of the Greek World', a long prose poem which he had begun in Hydra. Every city, island, mountain and valley that Paddy can think of holds a 'sound': not just something heard, but an image or an allusion to something read or experienced:

> Salonika is an argument over a bill of lading, a Ladino greeting outside a synagogue; Volo, the smack of backgammon counters, Patras, the grate of cranes unloading, Samos, the bubbling of a narghilé. Kalamata is the heel slapped in the Romaïc dance . . .

Bassae and Sunium are the noise of the wind like panpipes through fluted pilars, Nemea the rumble of a column's collapse. Naoussa is the thud of a falling apple, Edessa a waterfall, Kavalla the drop of an amber bead. Metsovo is a burning pine cone, Samarina a voice in Vlach, Tzoumerka a wolf's howl.

The climax of the poem is a list of linguistic, semantic and metrical terms that reflect the richness of the Greek language:

for the flexibility of accidence,
the congruence of syntax
and the confluence of its crasis;
for the fluctuating of enlitic and prolitic,
for the halt of cæsuræ and the flight of the digamma,
for the ruffle of hard and soft breathings,
for its liquid syllables and the collusion of dipthongs,
for the receding tide of proparoxytones
and the hollowness of perispomena stalactitic with subscripts,
for the inconsequence of anacolouthon,
the economy of synecdoche,
the compression of hendiadys
and the extravagance of its epithets,
for the embrace of zeugma,
for the abruptness of asyndeton, for the swell of hyperbole
and the challenge of apostrophe, for the splash and the boom and
       the clamour and the echo and the murmur of
       onomatopæa . . . [32]

All find their echo in the million different sounds of the sea as it washes over the stones and pebbles, rocks and chasms of the Greek coastline. And yet, although the poem is filled with human songs and sounds and activities, it is devoid of people: as though he was describing Greece with his eyes closed, looking at an inner landscape filled with fragments of experience, poetry, books, myths – a landscape of memory, in other words. A Greek landscape that existed before the Cyprus débâcle left its bitter taste on everything, and might exist again.

17

In Africa and Italy

Michael Powell and Emeric Pressburger had bought the rights to *Ill Met by Moonlight* and wrote the script in tandem, but it was always Powell's project. He was passionate about the story, and very disappointed that they had been forbidden to make the film in Greece, because Cyprus was still poisoning Anglo-Greek relations. Instead they decided to shoot it in the Alpes Maritimes, in the rocky country above Menton.

Paddy was flattered that Dirk Bogarde was chosen to play the part of Major Leigh Fermor, and gratified that the job of technical adviser had, on his recommendation, gone to Xan Fielding. Xan, his wife Daphne (who was 'a bit gone on Dirk', as Paddy reported to Debo[1]), with Dirk Bogarde and his life-long partner Tony Forwood, made an inseparable quartet that summer.

In mid-August Paddy joined the film set, and was rather alarmed when Powell told him what was being planned.

> Some bits – not yet filmed, unfortunately – turn Bogarde-Fermor into a mixture of Garth [strip-cartoon hero in the *Daily Mirror*] and Superman, shooting Germans clean through the breast from a dentist's chair, strangling sentries in an off-hand manner – *all totally fictitious!* I'm having a terrific tussle getting them to change these bits in the film, not because I really mind, but because anyone who also knows anything about the operation knows that it's all rot.[2]

After a week he moved south-west to Auribeau-sur-Siagne, to a little inn where he had worked on *The Traveller's Tree*. When it grew too hot, he would plunge into the dark pools of the river Siagne that curled below, but most of his waking hours were involved in what he called 'the death-grapple with my book'.[3] This burst of industry was brought to an abrupt end by a telephone call from Ann Fleming.

Ann had been invited to stay at the Villa Mauresque on Cap Ferrat by Somerset Maugham, then in his eighties and living in retirement with his partner, Alan Searle. On her arrival she found a letter from Paddy, urging her to arrange an invitation. Paddy was duly invited to lunch, and arrived (according to Ann) with 'five cabin trunks' (according to Paddy, all he had was one zippered holdall), 'parcels of books and the manuscript of his unfinished work on Greece strapped in a bursting attaché case'.[4] Paddy made himself very agreeable at lunch. He and Maugham exchanged memories of the King's School, Canterbury, and Maugham asked him to stay on for a few days. All went well until dinner that night.

Maugham had lived with a pronounced stammer since childhood. In his novel *Of Human Bondage*, which deals with the misery of his schooldays, the stammer is turned into a limp. Paddy knew the book and had been hearing the stammer all day, but neither sufficed to stop him from putting his foot in it. The first jokey reference to stuttering passed without comment, but the second was more serious. Maugham had just staggered through a sentence to the effect that all the gardeners had taken the day off because it was the Feast of the Assumption. At this point, Paddy recalled being in the Louvre in front of a painting of the event, with his friend Robin Fedden (who also had trouble getting his words out): 'and Robin turned to me and said "Th-th-that's what I c-c-call an un-w-w-warrantable assumption." There was a moment's silence – the time needed for biting one's tongue out.'[5]

The evening was wrecked. When the other guests left, Maugham turned to Paddy and said, 'G-goodbye, you will have left by the time I am up in the morning.' After their host had retired, Ann described Paddy breaking the silence with a cry of anguish, as he slammed his whisky glass on the table 'where it broke to pieces and showered a valuable carpet with blood and splinters'.[6] Ann helped Paddy pack the following morning, and as he picked up his bag and walked to the door, Paddy heard 'a sound like an ogre's sneeze'. The monogrammed linen sheet had caught in the zip, leaving a great tear a yard long.

Ann Fleming and Diana Cooper, who was staying nearby, persuaded Maugham to have Paddy back to lunch to make up. 'It was really a gasbag's penance and I, having learnt the hard way, vouchsafed no more than a few syllables.'[7] Maugham was perfectly polite, but he had had enough of Paddy. He was later heard to describe him as 'that middle-class gigolo for upper-class women'.

Stavros Niarchos had once again lent Diana his yacht, the *Eros II*. This time the party consisted of Diana, Paddy and Joan, Frank and Kitty Giles, and Alan Pryce-Jones, editor of the *Times Literary Supplement* who had briefly been engaged to Joan. The *Eros* took them into a part of the Mediterranean that Paddy had never explored: to Corsica, Sardinia, Elba and the little islands in between. In Corsica he visited the village of Cargese which had been colonized by emigrants from the Mani in the seventeenth century, and he was very excited to find two old women who still spoke fluent Greek. 'A number of Corsican words had crept in but it was unmistakably Maniot, with many rustic turns of phrase that have been lost in the Mani.'[8]

The filming of *Ill Met by Moonlight* was finished that autumn at Pinewood Studios, which he visited from Devon where he had gone to write. He made light of it to Diana and Debo: 'I've just spent two days trying to teach Cypriots . . . to talk Cretan dialect (which involved changing the syntax of the whole dialogue) with a Cretan accent, which is like teaching someone from Lincolnshire to speak in the accent of Co. Galway.'[9] He also had to do 'all the Greek-speaking bits done by Dirk, i.e. he makes the shapes with his mouth, laughs superciliously, lifts his eyebrows or shouts at the top of his voice – all in dead silence – while I, concealed in a bush, make all the noises . . .'[10]

In a letter to Billy Moss, he sounds more anxious. 'You and I are absolutely OK, we emerge as charming, intrepid chaps . . . It's really the Cretans I'm worried about. They are all Cypriots, and far too shrill and agitated.' He also regretted 'a patronizing touch about you and me and our relationship to [the Cretans], a slight suggestion of their relegation to the role of picturesque and slightly absurd foreigners constantly in a state of agitation, coolly managed by these two unruffled and underacting sahibs.'[11]

The film achieved the distinction of being spoofed on *The Goon Show* as *Ill Met by Goonlight*, but even Powell had to admit that it was not a good film. This he blamed on the tensions between himself and Dirk Bogarde. Powell had wanted 'a flamboyant young murderer, lover, bandit – a tough, Greek-speaking leader of men'. But Bogarde, like Paddy, had served as an intelligence officer in the war. He knew how British officers behaved, and insisted on playing his role with a light-hearted nonchalance to which Powell attributed much of the film's weakness. 'All the other actors took their tone from him,' wrote Powell. 'It's a wonder that Paddy didn't sue both Dirk and me.'[12]

Paddy and Billy Moss barely saw each other again, after their encounters at Pinewood Studios. Moss had by then written several more books, and in the year *Ill Met by Moonlight* was filmed he published *Gold Is Where You Hide It* – an investigation into what the Nazis had done with the treasure of the Reichsbank. But something in Billy seemed unable to adjust to the post-war world. Leaving Sophie and his two young daughters in London, he travelled to Antarctica, and after that sailed round the islands of the Pacific. By the time he settled in Kingston, Jamaica, he was drinking heavily. Despite the urgings of his friends he refused to seek help, and died there in August 1965, aged only forty-four.

Keen to get on with *Mani*, Paddy had moved into the Easton Court Hotel in Chagford in mid-September. He often admitted that he could never have written the book without Joan – sometimes even referring to it as 'Joan's book'. It was to her that he read out passages and thought aloud, she had been with him on most of the journeys and taken photographs of what he described, and he relied on her encouragement to push him on.

They both longed for a permanent base, and now they no longer had the Charlotte Street flat, Joan persuaded her trustees to let her buy a small house at 13 Chester Row in Pimlico. 'It will be wonderful to have somewhere for both of us to assemble scattered books, clothes, papers etc,' wrote Paddy to Diana, 'and a proper base to be nomadic from. It's rather demoralizing, always returning to improvisation.'[13] Given the fact that he found himself incapable of any sustained work in London it might seem an odd choice. But Chester Row was never seen as a permanent home – it was, as he described it, 'a base to be nomadic from'. They always planned to spend most of the year abroad. It also did not bring the prospect of marriage any closer. Paddy had once told his sister Vanessa that the disaster of their parents' union had made him very wary of matrimony, and that 'Joan and I have got into this pleasant habit of intermittent concubinage, with vague intentions of getting married sometime. We often talk of it, but then always seem to forget.'[14]

From the room on the ground floor of the Easton Court Hotel where he was supposed to be working, he wrote vivid letters about the Devon woods and the wilds of Dartmoor to Diana and Debo. On a black horse called Flash he rode through the wet woods, beside banks trailing the last of the summer flowers. He described the steep hills, dark streams crossed by old stone bridges, and the wild ponies of Dartmoor. One moonlit night he watched them pour off the hill and gallop through the village, their hooves thundering on the cobbles. He joined a group of men who were rounding up ponies for the annual pony fair, their Devon accents all but incomprehensible. With the Mid-Devon hunt he rode to hounds for the first time since the war, and Flash flew over the fences. As they pelted across the country the hounds were occasionally joined by a herd of heifers and, at one point, a troop of ponies, their manes streaked and dripping with rain. The Devon he described is hardly the contemporary Britain of the late 1950s, but a rural vision of ancient walls sunk in damp greenness, with a pervasive smell of earth, rain and wet horse. Yet there are few moments in Paddy's writing when he felt so connected to England, or described it with such delight.

By the new year he had finished *Mani*, and he could not decide whether it had at last come together or still required a great deal of work. In January 1957 his frustrations spilled over in a letter to Diana Cooper, who had asked for his advice as she was about to embark on writing her memoirs. It was vital, he told her, to have a clear idea of who she was writing the book for.

> The military maxim about having only one objective for an operation is absolutely sound. My ghost objective in *The Traveller's Tree* was a composite figure: Joan, a dash of Cyril . . . Professor Dawkins at Oxford and the shade of Norman Douglas. *A Time to Keep Silence* was a straight post-facto juggle of about twenty letters I wrote to Joan . . . *The Violins* had you in mind throughout. I'm making such a *fucking mess*, and a long drawn out and a painful one, of the book I'm finishing at the moment, because my objectives are mixed – i.e.

Greece and England, the Cyprus balls-up, let's not go into it; but it's an excellent warning.[15]

In February 1957, while busy correcting the latest typescript of *Mani* in the monastery of Saint-Wandrille, Paddy was summoned to the telephone. Calls to the monastery were rare, and Paddy was even more astonished to find that the caller was the film director John Huston. They had met in Ireland, probably at Luggala, and now Huston was ringing to ask whether Paddy would consider working on the script of his next film. It was based on a novel by the French writer Romain Gary called *The Roots of Heaven*, which had won the Prix Goncourt the year before. Darryl F. Zanuck, one of the founders of Twentieth Century-Fox, had bought the rights soon after and persuaded Gary to write the script, but Huston was not satisfied: he proposed that Paddy should take over and rewrite it.

When consulted, Joan was strongly opposed to the idea. A project like this was a mere distraction, when he should be getting on with the companion volume to *Mani*. Paddy agreed, but he could not resist the combination of a fat fee plus the opportunity to spend several weeks in equatorial Africa. The first John Murray edition of *A Time to Keep Silence* appeared in May, and the following month he handed in the final corrections of *Mani*. Then, with excitement and trepidation, he went to Paris in August to take up his new job.

The Roots of Heaven is a complex novel, in which long passages of monologue explore the economic and political tensions of post-colonial Africa. The book revolves around a maverick loner, Morel, who is determined to stop the slaughter of elephants by big game hunters and ivory poachers. He is joined by a black freedom fighter, an American journalist, a disgraced army officer, and Minna: barmaid, prostitute, and the only one who shares Morel's real love of the elephants.

It was not the easiest novel to turn into a film, but Zanuck put Paddy through a crash course in scriptwriting. They worked in a top-floor suite in the Hotel Georges V where the air must have been eye-watering, for Zanuck was never without a cigar in his mouth and Paddy was then smoking between sixty and seventy cigarettes a day. Here they would march up and down for hours, establishing the plot lines from which Paddy would build the script. In a long and funny letter to Debo, Paddy described Zanuck's approach to the novel. 'It's a swell book, Mr Feemor . . . The best bit is when they bump off all those elephants. But we'll run into difficulties here because of all that goddam humanitarian hooey in England and America. I'd like to do the thing properly and shoot a whole lot of them . . .'[16]

The film crew made its way to Africa in the early part of 1958, with Paddy joining them in late January or February. The first part of the filming was done at Fort Archambault (now Sarh, in Chad), where they spent three weeks in suffocating heat. When it became unbearable they moved several hundred miles north-west to the town of Maroua, in Cameroon, and then to Bangui, now on the southern border of the Central African Republic.

The film's leading actor, Trevor Howard, was 'a charming man, not at all intelligent but a wonderful actor'.[17] He drank nothing but whisky from morning till night, and Paddy felt he was profoundly depressed. Errol Flynn joined them in Maroua, preceded by an enormous hamper from Fortnum & Mason filled with tinned grouse and quail. 'Errol Flynn and I have become great buddies,' Paddy wrote to Xan Fielding. 'He is a tremendous shit but a very funny one, and we sally forth into the dark lanes of the town together on guilty excursions that remind me rather of old Greek days with you.'[18] (The third big star of the film, Orson Welles, only joined the filming in Paris after Paddy had left.)

Despite the fact that *The Roots of Heaven* was a plea to save the elephants, John Huston was very keen to shoot one, since he had not managed to do so while filming *The African Queen* a few years earlier. The back of his Land Rover was an arsenal of shotguns, rifles and ammunition, and it was obvious that he lived not for the film, but to slope off into the bush with a gun. His lack of commitment to the project had its effect on morale too: Paddy noted that Huston's 'lackadaisical . . . nonchalance is oddly un-galvanizing'.[19]

The script never rose above serviceable, and Huston was notorious for demanding endless rewrites. 'The changes in the script', wrote Paddy to Joan, 'can be either an exciting challenge to one's talents and skills in marquetry; or a deadening, heart-breaking mortician's work, rougeing and curling a corpse, when one goes over a scene for the fifth or sixth time. Apart from the pennies, I think it's an utter waste of time . . .'[20] His consolation was a miniature walk-on part. As Morel and his companions march down the road to what might be their death, Paddy dashes into an open-air café, shouting: 'Listen everybody! He's been spotted, on the road to Biondi!'

In a company that included many different cliques and nationalities, Paddy had found a home in the French clique which revolved around Juliette Gréco, one of the most celebrated singers of post-war Paris. She was playing the part of the barmaid Minna, who in the novel is a German blonde – the exact opposite of Gréco's dark Levantine beauty. She had been given the role because of Darryl Zanuck's infatuation with her; his feelings were not returned and she had only agreed to take the part on condition that she could bring a large entourage of friends.

Of the company, Paddy wrote, Juliette was 'the most interesting by far – oddly beautiful, utterly bohemian, erratic, very well-read and brilliant, and with a tremendous sense of humour. We became great pals at once . . .'[21] 'Jujube', as she was known, was equally attracted, admitting that she had '*un sérieux penchant*' for Paddy: she describes him speaking French with an irresistible accent, while words 'jostled to escape from his mouth, so eager was he to offer them, to throw them like flowers at the feet of a beloved. He loves talking and has lots to say in a dozen languages . . .'[22] Juliette's romantic trysts – with Stephen Grimes the artistic director, and possibly with Paddy – had to be undertaken with the greatest caution. Zanuck was still in the grip 'of a wild, insane and pathological jealousy . . . which spreads through the whole camp from the heart like a blight'. One evening 'he knocked her out cold, revived her by throwing a bucket of water over her, and sobbed for an hour.'[23]

With the director and producer of the film so preoccupied with other concerns, it is hardly surprising that the film was a disappointment. 'The depths of the novel were untouched,' Huston admitted to his biographer Lawrence Grobel. 'It became, in our hands, a kind of adventure story, a shoot-up. It could have been a very fine picture . . . but the fact remains, it wasn't.'[24]

Paddy spent that Whitsuntide in Spain, where Xan and Daphne Fielding, an American couple called Billy and Anne Davis, and Debo

Devonshire were planning to attend the great feast of Nuestra Señora del Rocío, near Seville. From all over Spain, pilgrims and brother-hoods devoted to the Virgin of el Rocío assembled in the fields around the little village, and it had not occurred to the English travellers that every available room would be taken. The whole party was obliged to doss down in a shed with an earth floor already occupied by several other pilgrims. Debo spent a sleepless night since, despite her shoving and pinching, Paddy snored the whole time. 'He sounded like some rusty machine, making an almost mechanical noise with maddening regularity.'[25] The following day, he was astonished by the violence of the struggles that broke out among the different brotherhoods, as they fought for the privilege of bearing the miraculous statue around the village.

From Spain he and Joan returned to Greece where, on the island of Paros, Paddy finished correcting the page proofs of *Mani*. Free at last of the book he had been dragging around like an iron ball for so long, and his bank balance in the black thanks to the money made on *The Roots of Heaven*, Paddy was in a mood of godlike freedom. It seemed a good moment to climb Mount Olympus, which neither he nor Joan had ever done. Their expedition was joined by Alan Hare, a fellow member of SOE who had spent much of the war in Albania and had been a frequent guest at Tara, and Roxanne Sedgwick, the Greek wife of Alexander Sedgwick, Middle East correspondent of the *New York Times*. 'It took four days and nearly did us all in,' Paddy reported to Debo. 'The last day was real hand-over-hand stuff, till at last we were on the highest point of S.E. Europe, with the whole of Greece below like a map.'[26] An exhausted Joan announced that if she slipped down a crevasse and died, her body was to be left where it fell. Paddy composed her epitaph:

> Bury me here on Olympus
> In the home of the lonely wall-creeper
> Don't take me back to Athens, please
> Stretched out on a second-class sleeper.

Joan spent most of that September on Hydra, while Paddy flitted backwards and forwards to Athens. The novelist Compton Mackenzie, who had served in Greece in the First World War and was a passionate supporter of Cyprus's claim for *enosis*, had been commissioned by the BBC to do a series of three programmes called *The Glory that was Greece*, and invited Paddy to join him for a day's filming at Thermopylae. Mackenzie found him to be 'a man after my own heart . . . He did not resemble Norman Douglas either in looks or conversation but his company brought back the mood of days spent with Norman Douglas more nearly than anybody has done.'[27]

Paddy and Joan might have spent longer in Greece that autumn, using Hydra as their base; but then something happened that pulled his thoughts abruptly westwards. Pope Pius XII, aged eighty-two, died at his summer palace of Castelgandolfo on 9 October 1958. The old Pope had reigned for almost twenty years, the last few blighted by illness and nervous exhaustion, and for the Vatican his death felt like the end of a very long chapter. The election and coronation of the next pope would be a new beginning and a spectacular event, and Paddy was determined not to miss it.

He arrived in Rome towards the end of the month, and made his way to the flat on Tiber Island where Judy Montagu lived. The only child of politician Sir Edwin Montagu and Venetia Stanley, confidante of the prime minister Herbert Asquith, Judy had politics in her blood; but she also lived life with a gambler's recklessness. Her friends ranged from the very grand – she was a close friend of Princess Margaret – to the artistic and bohemian. She had had a brief affair with Paddy a year or two before, which had left her broken-hearted. But her heart was now mended, and fixed on the photographer and art historian Milton Gendel whom she married in 1962.

Gendel was irritated by Paddy's sudden reappearance, and (as Judy reported to Diana Cooper) 'retreated in a sombre state of green-eyed sulks . . . Milton is in on everything but slopes off early, while the hero and I gallivant like mad whizzing around nightclubs and jabbering – in complete purity but vast cosiness – till broad daylight (Old 7 o'clock again) . . .'[28]

Judy formed part of a close group of three English women who acted as a magnet to friends passing through Rome. Like Judy, the other two were the daughters of illustrious parents. Jenny Nicholson's father was the poet Robert Graves; a journalist on *Picture Post* and the *Spectator*, she was married to Patrick Crosse, bureau chief of Reuters in Rome. Whilst Jenny was the most practical and professional of the three, Iris Tree was easily the most eccentric. Iris had grown up in the theatre – her father was the actor-manager Herbert Beerbohm Tree. She was a true romantic, a poet and actress who had never allowed either comfort or common sense to interfere with her life. Her son Ivan Moffat, a film producer, had been a friend of Paddy's since Cairo days.

In the company of these friends Paddy met a young and beautiful woman, Lyndall Birch, who was working as a proofreader for the UN's Food and Agriculture Organization. She had been emotionally terrorized by her mother, the writer Antonia White; and while she loved her father Tom Hopkinson, the celebrated editor of *Picture Post*, there had been little room for her in his life. Men flocked around Lyndall; but having little experience or self-confidence, she found their attentions as alarming as they were flattering. She had made an impetuous marriage at the age of twenty-three to Lionel (Bobby) Birch – then editor of the *Picture Post* – which had lasted only a matter of months.

She and Paddy were drawn to each other, and began meeting in her tiny flat in the Via del Gesù. He had to climb up several flights of stairs on tiptoe so as not to attract the suspicions of the landlady – 'I did love that. It gave everything a wonderful feeling of conspiracy and romance.'[29] Lyndall had never met a man who was less predatory, and whose company she enjoyed so much – although it did make her rather quiet: she was in awe of his learning and did not want to give herself away as being uncultivated. She need not have worried. Paddy was happy to do all the talking and never minded anyone's lack of culture, as long as they responded to him with warmth and enthusiasm.

Lyndall had never been so in love, for which her older friends gave conflicting remedies. Diana Cooper's was brutally practical: forget Paddy, marry for money (Lyndall had a rich admirer at the time) and divorce with a large settlement. Judy also advised her to get over 'the hero', since from personal experience she knew that he would never leave Joan. Besides, neither of the lovers had any money, so nothing but disappointment could come of their affair.

Iris Tree, on the other hand, dismissed such practical considerations. What could it matter if they had no money? Run away with him, urged Iris, find a Greek island and live for love on bread and water.

On 28 October the conclave of cardinals declared that their choice had fallen on Cardinal Angelo Giuseppe Roncalli, and on 3 November he was crowned Pope John XXIII. In the last half of the twentieth century, incoming pontiffs reduced the ecclesiastical pomp and pageantry of their coronations; but in 1958 the Vatican could still put on a magnificent display, and Paddy was not disappointed. 'Ah, Diana,' he wrote, sending her a postcard of the new Pope, '. . . the silver trumpets, the ruffs, the cloaks with Maltese crosses, the morions and slashed doublets . . . I'm swooning . . .'[30]

Paddy returned to England for the long-awaited publication of *Mani*, whose difficult gestation was rewarded by enthusiastic reviews. The *Times Literary Supplement* recognized the author as a 'literary trailblazer' in a region of Greece that few people knew anything about.[31] And as *Mani* was promoted as the first of a series of books on Greece, the *Times* reviewer wrote that 'Mr Leigh Fermor will be hard-put to keep up his own level in the sequels.'[32] In a letter of congratulation, Lawrence Durrell wrote of 'its tremendous truffled style and dense plumage. You've written us all (Greek Dept) into a cocked hat, by God. Bravo!'[33]

The book opens with Paddy and Joan making their way from Sparta into the deep Mani, and the tone of the book is free and unconstricted. Paddy follows his inclinations, writing about the vagaries of Greek surnames, the Maniot diaspora, piracy and the slave trade, and helmets that double as cauldrons – but always he is brought back to the person who sparked off the last train of thought, and to a specific place. He is intensely aware of how few resources the Maniots have, how harsh their life is. Yet the endurance of these people, their stories and traditions, their ghosts and legends, all fill him with joy; while their violent past and rigid codes of honour are contrasted with a hospitality as simple and natural as it had been in the days of Homer.

At the same time as celebrating the Maniots, he is yearning for another, more complete, more spiritual Greece; one that was not entirely obliterated with the end of the Byzantine empire, but had entered another dimension. This is the idea behind the extraordinary flight of imagination, sparked by a poor fisherman in Kardamyli who might have been the last of the Palaeologi: over seven astonishing pages, Paddy describes the return of the last Emperor of Byzantium to the throne of his ancestors, in a resurrected Constantinople that a magnanimous Turkey has given back to Greece. It is likewise the refrain when he describes the paintings of Mistra that seemed for a brief moment to fuse all that was best in the sacred art of Eastern and Western Christendom. If only it had had a chance to flourish, it might have given rise to another Golden Age.

'This sudden shining mist of impossible surmise', he writes, 'is one that floats again and again before the eyes both of Greeks and of strangers who look for more in these seas and islands than the dispersed and beautiful skeleton of the ancient world.'[34] He asserts his faith in this eternal Greek spirit, and if only others could share his conviction, perhaps even the Cyprus problem might be resolved. This thorny subject is finally broached as he sits in a café in Layia, among a group of old villagers. '"Don't go," one of them said, "there's no hurry. Sit here and take it easy, like Gladstone."'[35] O Gladstonos is remembered, with more affection than accuracy, as the statesman who persuaded the British government to cede the Ionian Islands to Greece.* It was the perfect, oblique way to indicate Paddy's answer to the Cyprus question: if the British government could relinquish a whole archipelago in 1863, to Greece's lasting gratitude, surely it could make a similar gesture now by returning Cyprus to its rightful owners?

He agreed with the old men in the café that the reason both Greece and England were in this mess was that neither country had politicians of sufficient authority and vision to deal with it, while the newspapers and radio only whipped up anger and made things worse. But in front of their quiet reproaches (no Athenian demagogues here), Paddy the Philhellene is left feeling miserably embarrassed to be English. And this, as he told his readers, was before the British government brought the Turks into the negotiations, after which Greek resentment had grown fiercer.

---

* Gladstone sympathized with the Ionian islanders' claims for union with Greece, but his mission was not a success. The islands were ceded to Greece in 1863 by a government led by Lord Palmerston.

The warmth with which Paddy championed the Greek cause did the book no harm: probably the reverse. *Mani* became the Book Society Choice for December, which meant they took 9,000 copies; by the following February further sales had earned Paddy £1,200. Flushed with cash and confidence, Paddy bought himself his first car: a dark blue Standard Companion, in which he planned to drive to Rome. Joan had had to drive it to Dover, since he had failed his first driving test; but he was allowed to drive in Europe on a provisional licence granted by the AA.

He drove with the handbrake on all the way from Le Touquet to Chantilly, which Joan would have prevented had she been with him. But she was driving out to Greece with one of her oldest friends, Janetta Jackson. As a protégée of Ralph and Frances Partridge, Janetta had absorbed many of the values and tastes of the Bloomsbury circle, but not its high-minded austerity. Once her second marriage to Paddy's friend Robert Kee was over, she had married Derek Jackson, one of the great scientists of his day who had ridden in the Grand National three times. That marriage too ended in disaster; but despite her turbulent emotional life, there was a clear-eyed tranquillity about Janetta, and a diffidence that resembled Joan's.

Joan and Janetta were driving through Kent to the coast when, in heavy traffic on the outskirts of London, Joan ran into a pram. The baby was unhurt; but because Joan was full of concern for the baby and had offered to pay for a new pram, the mother saw her as a soft touch and took her to court, which upset Joan terribly.

Paddy had made no secret to Joan of the fact that he was yearning to see Lyndall again, and wrote '. . . this entire journey was strange and marvellous . . . there was not a hitch, not a scratch, not an unkind word from the moment I set off from Le Touquet, as if everything were in league to shelter a love affair that couldn't last, all the world loves a driver . . .'[36] He had often thought of Lyndall in the three months they had been apart; but while she had written several letters to him, he had written only one to her — and having been sent with a heavy packet of papers (draft chapters of *Mani*), it did not reach her for several more weeks. Still, he was sure he would be forgiven in the joy of their reunion.

Lyndall had taken time off from her work at the UN to play the part of a young novice in the film of *The Nun's Story*, starring Audrey Hepburn. Filming was taking place in Rome, but Lyndall suggested they go to Assisi for the Easter weekend. She seemed more reserved than he had expected; and it was on that gloomy Good Friday that she told Paddy their affair was over. She had been deeply hurt by the fact that he had never written; and in the face of what looked like a humiliating rejection, she had found other company and had no wish to resume their relationship. Stunned, he could scarcely believe it: the disappointed Paddy now felt that he was as much in love with her as she had been with him the previous October.

A few weeks later, Paddy wrote Lyndall a long and revealing letter.

> You know – you must know – how much I loved our October life. But, in illogical contrast to my vanity and conceit in other ways, a sort of deep-rooted ill-opinion of myself (linked, as far as I can make out, with the . . . knowledge of how little, as far as a life-time goes, I can offer anyone) makes me the most laggard of mortals in thinking anyone could be in love with me.

He goes on to admit to a 'rhinoceros-hide obtuseness', and a 'lack of sensitiveness and lack of twigging about what happens to others . . . I had no idea what harm and unhappiness I was unconsciously inflicting.' He also tried to explain why her letters had been answered by nothing but silence:

> silence caused by the thought that I would be in Rome again almost at once; and by the vanity of waiting for inspiration to write a letter . . . of immense length and loving tenderness and brilliant wit and imperishable splendour . . . You know how ashamed and sorry I am about all this; how bitterly furious with myself, you can't know.[37]

The letter was written from the castle of Passerano, near Palestrina, some nineteen kilometres east of Rome. He had first set eyes on the castle on a picnic with Judy Montagu, when it struck him as 'one of the most beautiful and romantic places I had ever seen, a triangular, Guelph-battlemented castle on top of a green hill plumed with oak trees . . .'[38] Paddy borrowed it from the owner, Count Paolo Quintero, who dismissed any question of rent: the castle had no water, electricity, plumbing, or even glass in the windows.

Undaunted, Paddy borrowed some furniture, ordered some headed writing paper and hired glaziers to put frames and glass in the vast embrasures. Nuns from a convent in Tivoli were commissioned to make a huge fabric hanging with armorial bearings to cover one end of the banqueting hall, and a flag for him to fly from the topmost tower. He imagined it as the flag of 'Don Patrizio, the Black Bastard of Passerano . . . I like to think that when the Black Bastard unfurls his dread gonfalon from the machicolations, all the peasants . . . cross themselves and dowse their rush-lights, hide their cattle and bolt up their dear ones,' he wrote to Diana – and, a little later, in an almost identical letter to Debo.[39] But since he spent quite a lot of time driving the locals to market and little girls to their First Communion, perhaps 'The Black Sucker of Passerano' was more accurate.

Yet even the romantic beauty of the castle and its surroundings could not make up for its discomforts. The weather that summer was unusually wet. Despite stuffing the cracks with pages torn from the *Daily Mail*, the *Times Literary Supplement* and *Il Messaggero*, cold and damp seeped in through the walls. Few people came to visit him from Rome, although Paddy tended to drive there once or twice a week for a dinner or a party. He did not like the aristocratic Romans, particularly since one of them was the new man in Lyndall's life. He complained of their 'breath-taking, staggering vapidity of chat. They are like cooking with the salt left out.'[40] To Joan, Paddy confessed that taking the castle was 'one of the most foolish things I've ever done. It's lovely during the day, but I feel terribly depressed in the evenings . . . I'm getting less good at solitude than I used to be, and my struggle with Volume Two [the first stirrings of *Roumeli*] has been little more than a series of skirmishes and frontier incidents.'[41]

Paddy was now in his mid-forties, and in the gloomy evenings the castle must have looked like an allegory of his life at that point: a beautiful and romantic structure viewed from outside, but damp and chilly on the inside. He was still brooding about Lyndall, and cursing himself for handling the affair so clumsily. He might even have thought about children, or his lack of them. In a letter to Vanessa a few weeks later he writes, 'I envy you having children and grandchildren, and feel a bit of an outcast in my mossless state.'[42] These momentary regrets should not be taken too seriously; he did not often wish for a pram in the hall. What his weeks in the castle had revealed was that he had reached a point in life where he longed for some form of permanent home: not 'a base to be nomadic from', but a place where he could live and work. Ever since Hydra he and Joan had imagined a house in Greece, and now he pined for Greece like an exile.

Iris Tree came to visit the castle in May; and while he was giving her a lift back to Rome a few days later, the car ran out of petrol. It was getting dark, and Paddy stumbled across a cornfield to a lamp-lit farmhouse. A young man called Silvio agreed to help. As he was siphoning off some petrol from his Vespa, he mentioned that he had turned up two odd fragments of marble, while ploughing a field. Would the Signore like to see them? One was a headless statue about fourteen inches tall, roughly carved, of a seated Roman goddess flanked by a lion, later identified as Cybele-Astarte. 'It was very exciting', he wrote to Joan, 'to see her all clogged up with the earth of two millennia, in the lamplight at the kitchen table.' The other piece was the base of a statue, of which nothing remained but the stump of a tree and two delicately carved marble feet – 'a hauntingly romantic object', which then inspired a poem: 'On Two Marble Feet and a Marble Tree dug up by a Ploughman in the Roman Campagna'.

Paddy bought the two pieces for sixty-five thousand lire. He gave them to Joan ('I know I'm always doing this, "giving" you things that I derive an equal delight in').[43] But the poem, which gives voice to a beautiful statue of which only a fragment remains, was dedicated to Lyndall.

He had been longing for Joan's comfort and company, and needed her to coax him out of his depression. She came in July, the weather improved, and soon it was uncomfortably hot. The castle's vermin grew bolder. Paddy watched a rat breaking through the defences Joan had erected round a pat of butter, and hurled a book at it (Arthur Bryant's *The Age of Elegance*, as he noted to Debo). The rat was not much discouraged, and launched another assault on the butter a few minutes later. Within a month the proliferation of rats, ants and scorpions had driven them away. On Iris's recommendation, they decided to spend the rest of the summer on the island of Ischia.

They settled in the town of Forio on the western side of the island, in a flat with a balcony. It looked out over orange trees to the dome and belfry of the cathedral, 'which looks so mosque-like that it's a surprise to see the crosses on top'. Ischia did not succeed in filling him with energy and high spirits 'as most Greek islands do',[44] but at the same time work was going well and he was deep in a chapter about Turkish Thrace. Among their neighbours were Janetta, who was then in Ischia with her lover, Jonathan Gathorne-Hardy. Paddy and Joan also invited a succession of friends to stay, including Ann Fleming, Iris Tree, Debo and Diana Cooper.

Lyndall came at last in late September. Paddy had hoped she could come earlier, but the spare room in their rented house had been occupied by Diana, whose stay was extended by a paralysing bout of depression. Lyndall was astonished at how warmly she was welcomed by Joan, and with what ease and equanimity. Paddy had told her that there was no sexual jealousy between them, and she could see it was true: he and Joan were more like siblings or old friends than lovers, and their private words and phrases were merely the visible surface of a long and deep-rooted companionship.

Just before Paddy left Ischia, he heard that *Mani* had won the Duff Cooper Memorial Prize. This had been set up by Duff Cooper's friends after his death and the panel of five judges did not include Diana, but Paddy felt he could detect her influence. 'I bet you lobbied like Billy-oh for your old pal,' he wrote, 'and a quadrillion thanks.'[45]

When Paddy had set out for Rome that February, he had been in a mood of youthful joy at the thought of seeing Lyndall again. With that dream shattered he had retired to Passerano, and in the weeks of loneliness there had realized how much he needed Joan and how much he missed Greece. From Ischia he headed back to London, knowing that he and Lyndall were free of their ill-synchronized passion for each other – though he continued to write her long affectionate letters and never wanted to lose her as a friend. About her latest admirer, he observed that 'I can watch all this now with an affectionate detachment that will be much more use . . . than the obsessive and gloomy commitment that has dogged my footsteps most of this year.'[46]

18

A Visit to Rumania

Paddy spent the Christmas of 1959 with Debo and Andrew Devonshire, who had now moved into the ducal seat at Chatsworth in Derbyshire. The house had been under dustsheets since 1944: Andrew's parents, heartbroken by the loss of their eldest son, had avoided it after his death. When Andrew inherited, millions were owed in death duties and it was doubtful whether the estate could survive at all. But survive it did: Chatsworth was made into a trust, the family moved back in, house and gardens were opened to the public, and there was much to celebrate.

Joan's Christmas that year was as sad as Paddy's was cheerful. Joan, her brother Graham and their sister Diana Casey were all in London, where their mother Sybil died at her house in Weymouth Street on Christmas Day. Since Sybil had been divorced from her husband, the 1st Viscount Monsell, for the best part of a decade, her fortune passed directly to her three surviving children and their heirs.* The house at Dumbleton had already been sold to the Post Office for the use of its elderly and retired workers, but the land and farms on the estate were left to Graham. The rest of her fortune, which in today's terms would come to some six million pounds, was equally divided between the siblings.

Joan would not come into her inheritance all at once, but her and Paddy's dream of buying some land in Greece at last looked possible, and in the new year she was in a position to give Paddy a large cheque. He wrote to her from the Easton Court Hotel in Chagford, where he had settled down to work after Christmas. 'I've been thinking so much about that tremendous sum of money. It

---

* Joan's sister Patricia Kenward had died in 1957.

314

really is an act of superhuman kindness and generosity . . . I can't
tell you what a difference it makes, and will make, blowing away
dozens of guilty, nagging and haunting worries, all utterly my fault
through neglect, idleness and *oblomovstochina*. (That's the word. I asked
Isaiah Berlin.)'[1]

Mani was going from strength to strength. Although Cass Canfield
of Harper & Row had been doubtful of its prospects, he had had
to print another fifteen hundred copies. Paddy and Joan spent the
next few months in England: she based in her house in Chester
Row, with Paddy dropping in between visits to friends and efforts
to get on with work at Chagford. His writing was interrupted by
the occasional outing with the hunt, and incidental literary capric-
cios such as translating 'Widdecombe Fair' into Italian: 'All shortcomings of rhyme and scansion are richly compensated for by sheer
exoticism, if sung with spirit,' he wrote to Jock Murray.[2] He also
wrote occasional reviews for the *Sunday Times*, and finally passed his
driving test in Newton Abbot.

He and Joan planned to go back to Greece that summer, and just
before they left Paddy agreed to spend the weekend at Bruern Abbey
in Oxfordshire, the home of Michael Astor. Like his parents Waldorf
and Nancy Astor, Michael had been a Conservative MP and moved
easily in the political world of the day; but he was also a keen reader
and collector of contemporary art. Since Paddy said he would be
driving, Astor asked him to pick up his American girlfriend, Agnes
Phillips, better known as Magouche. After her marriage to the
Armenian painter Arshile Gorky who had committed suicide in
1948, she had married a Bostonian painter called Jack Phillips. They
had now separated, and Magouche had decided to settle in England.

Magouche already knew Joan whom she had met through Barbara
Warner, but this was her first meeting with Paddy. He arrived at her
house dressed as he had been for his great walk: in a leather jerkin
with breeches and gaiters, which he told her he had had made in
order to attend a fancy dress ball as Robin Hood. After several drinks
they set off. Paddy drove very slowly, talking all the time while
Magouche lit endless cigarettes for him. 'He was the most English
person I had ever met,' she recalled. 'Everything was *ripping*, and
there was more talk of PG Wodehouse than of Horace or Gibbon.'[3]

Since there were several architectural delights that Paddy wanted to visit on the way, they did not reach Bruern until late in the afternoon. Astor, who had expected them for lunch, was furious – and jealous of their complicity. Yet Paddy was longing to leave the English summer and get back to Greece. 'In spite of all this green pacific beauty,' he wrote to Lyndall, 'it's not my world. It's like living in the heart of a lettuce and I pine for hot stones and thorns and olive trees and prickly pears.'[4]

At the end of the month he and Joan set out for Greece in Joan's Sunbeam Rapier, planning a leisurely drive across Europe. An itinerary set out by John Julius took them through Slovenia and Ljubljana, Zagreb and Croatia. When they ran out of fuel, they were rescued by 'a party of Persian swells, travelling back to Teheran from Claridge's in a caravan of Cadillacs'. The next stretch took them into Bosnia and Sarajevo ('people talk of the archduke's murder as though it happened last week'[5]), Herzegovina and Dubrovnik, Montenegro and its capital Cetinje, and so into southern Serbia, where the people were Albanian. To Debo he wrote of 'baggy-trousered women heavily veiled, and tall, raffish, guarded mountain men in red and white fezzes, all selling watermelons to each other'.[6] They spent a few days exploring the frescoed Byzantine monasteries of south Serbia, before crossing the border.

As a first step to finding a place to live in Greece Joan had recently bought a tiny house, 12 Kallirhoë Street, in the Makriyannis area of Athens, from her friend Gladys Stewart-Richardson. Miss Stewart-Richardson had lived most of her life in the Greek capital, where she had started a business in the 1920s, making fabrics of raw silk. To Diana, Paddy described the house as 'just adequate for a Scotch spinster of austere and secluded habits, but claustrophobic for two untidy people like Joan and me'.[7] They also had to live with the constant noise of pumps, diggers and pneumatic drills since a road was being built yards from their door, 'along the semi-dried up drain which is all that remains of the ancient Ilissos river'.

The search for somewhere to live was launched in Hydra, after a few days in Nico Ghika's house which had been transformed since they had lived there five years before. Nico Ghika had separated from his wife Tiggy, and returned to his ancestral home with Barbara

Warner, who was in the process of divorcing her husband Rex. He was in his mid-fifties, Barbara in her late forties; but they behaved like young lovers, so wrapped up in each other that they could scarcely bear being apart. 'It made one feel protective and a bit sad,' wrote Paddy to Debo: 'such ages since one was in such a plight, at least overtly.'[8] New terraces had been built to reveal new aspects of the bay, scented plants grew in old amphorae, and the once bare walls were covered with paintings – most by Ghika, others by his friends. Later that year, the house that the Ghikas had so lovingly restored was deliberately burnt to the ground by the caretaker, who had been with the family for years: an action prompted by his loyalty to the first Mrs Ghika and his resentment of the second.

From Hydra Paddy and Joan embarked on 'a long slow golden and autumnal journey round the Argolid'. As winter drew in, Joan went back to England and to Graham, as she usually did for Christmas, while Paddy moved into 'a charming old hotel in Nauplia which I've long had my eye on . . . Here I plan to settle for a bit in frugal, abstemious and diligent solitude.'[9]

In the spring of 1961, Paddy was invited to stay in the family house of Evangelos Averoff-Tossizza, the Greek Foreign Minister. A man of literary tastes, Averoff had written Paddy a letter to say how much he had enjoyed *Mani*, and he hoped Paddy would use his house in Metsovo as a place to write. 'It's what they call an ancestral Epirot house,' he told Debo, with 'huge rooms surrounded by divans, with carved wooden ceilings giving one the feeling of being inside a cigar box, jutting out in storey after storey, overlooking the snow-covered roofs of the highest village in Greece . . .'[10]

Coote Lygon and John Craxton both came to stay with them in the 'cigar box', but the guest he was happiest to see was Ricki Huston, with her Madonna beauty and her New York accent, her fantasy and originality. It had been six years since she pulled him out of the fight he had started at the Kildare Hunt Ball; and while they had seen each other now and again, their mutual attraction had intensified over recent months.

The whole party set off on an expedition to the Thesprotian mountains of western Epirus, where they were the guests of a Sarakatsan family called Charisis. Life for the Sarakatsans had changed considerably since that traditional wedding in 1950. Now their stiff black and white costumes were brought out only for big celebrations, and though no longer purely nomadic, they were just as hospitable and keen to produce a feast. Joan and Paddy, who were soft-hearted about animals, persuaded them not to kill a kid: after all, it was Lent. This was a disappointment to their hosts for whom meat was a rare treat, but they were impressed by the piety of the foreigners.

In the description of this visit in *Roumeli*, Joan and John Craxton are mentioned but not Ricki: although her marriage to John Huston was over in all but name, discretion was called for. As for Joan, she accepted Ricki's presence as easily as she had accepted Lyndall's. Paddy had explained to Ricki in advance that Joan would pose 'no hindrance to anything, as I'm sure you'd like her and she you'.[11]

Joan returned to England, leaving Paddy and Ricki to drive south and catch the ferry to Bari. Heading for Rome, they stopped for the night in Naples. As they were eating dinner a fierce wind blew up, sending the street rubbish spiralling into the air. Coming out of the restaurant, Paddy and Ricki pretended they were in a surrealist gallery. As a page of *Il Messaggero* flattened itself against a wall Paddy exclaimed, 'I'll have that, even if it ruins me!' Ricki clutched him and hissed, '*Don't touch it! It's a FAKE.*'[12] They did not part company till they reached Rome. Paddy then drove with Diana, Judy, and the painter Balthus to Paris, skimming over the new Autostrada del Sol and 'blessing those gentle lessons of the Pindus passes'.[13] Ricki's efforts to improve Paddy's driving had given him a new *élan* at the wheel.

At this point, Ricki's main base was St Clerans: a graceful eighteenth-century house in Galway, which she and John Huston had bought in 1953. Paddy contrived to get himself invited to Lismore in May, and once there, he and Ricki set up a clandestine meeting in a Dublin hotel. Ricki was very fond of Paddy, and impressed by him as a lover. To a friend in Rome she said, 'Most men are just take, take, take – but with Paddy it's give, give, give.'[14]

Paddy spent June and July in a little cottage on the Pembrokeshire coast belonging to Barbara Ghika, 'on the edge of a cliff overlooking a deep coombe full of gulls and guillemots and puffins'. Paddy remained hard at work while Joan came and went, but on Barbara's insistence they had to pretend to be married. Paddy liked the Welsh: 'I'm fascinated by their Eurasian accent in English,' he told Ricki, 'and wish I knew some of their language, which they all talk among themselves here.'[15] He thought of her often, remembering the 'fierce moon-flaunting grapples in what seem like half-lit palaces, tents and caves; and gentle and loving recoveries with my hands full of dark silk and warm alabaster'.[16] Ricki was not going to let him get away with that, and sent him a gently mocking reply: 'I tell myself there's been many and many a handful of multicoloured silk, and a good few chunks of alabaster, for after all aren't you a poet, and a loving, grateful man?' she wrote. 'But it can't quite spoil the music of it.'[17]

He left Wales in July, and a month later he was commissioned to write a full-page article on one of the Seven Deadly Sins for the *Sunday Times*. The other six were shared out among W. H. Auden, Cyril Connolly, Edith Sitwell, Evelyn Waugh, Angus Wilson and T. S. Eliot, which put Paddy in an impressive pantheon.

> I was given the choice between Gluttony and Lust, and chose the former because Lust is too serious a matter . . . Apart from this I have been, thank heavens, in the throes of creative frenzy, and the pages are mounting up . . . This is a great relief, as I was beginning to suffer from faint unavowed despair about this book; I'd left it too long and it was beginning to go cold on me; but I seem to have breathed it back again to life at last.[18]

Sadly this burst of progress fizzled out, and the book that was to become *Roumeli* gave Paddy just as much trouble as its predecessor. Paddy thought Brittany might provide the ideal environment, and after a few days of Lust and Gluttony with Ricki in late October, he settled down in a hotel in the little town of Locronan. It was profoundly depressing, particularly on All Hallows Eve and All Saints' Day. The hotel was empty. All the inhabitants of the town, dressed in black, processed through the rain to the graveyard with soggy chrysanthemums, while the church bell tolled for hours.

From his little room, which looked on to a rain-soaked backyard and a few slate roofs, Paddy wrote to Lawrence Durrell in Nîmes, longing for Provence. Did Durrell know of 'a huge and sympathetic room, with plenty of striding space, a large work table, a shaded lamp, a bed, and a view plunging away into the distance, costing practically nothing?'[19] (The sum he had in mind was between £30 and £40 a month.) He had to finish his chapters on Thrace, Macedonia, Epirus and Thessaly within the next three months, before going to Mexico with Joan in February. The Mexican trip would be a fresh departure, and a new place to write about.

Paddy set off for Nîmes without waiting for a reply, and Durrell was away when he arrived – but it had been an interesting journey. At La Rochelle he made friends with the curator of the local museum, and they sat talking over whisky in the curator's library till four in the morning. In Bordeaux, he quoted two lines of Verlaine to the slim, pale maid who was helping him with his luggage, and to his surprise she recited the rest of the poem. The following day, her day off, the maid – whose name was Annie – took Paddy round the sights of the city. They visited Montaigne's castle, and he took her to lunch in Saint-Emilion. She told him the lonely story of her life. Her fondest memory was of a holiday she had spent alone by the Garonne estuary with her dog, swimming out to gather oysters from the oyster beds that lay offshore. When Paddy left the following day, he found a Mozart record in his car, and a note from Annie saying that he had given her 'the happiest hours of my existence'.[20] He was haunted by the image of this young woman, eating oysters alone in the pearly light of the estuary with her dog, and wrote about her in letters to Diana, Debo and Ricki. Like him she was a changeling, living in a world she did not feel part of. But whereas he had managed to escape, she was still trapped.

Paddy's article on Gluttony was a light-hearted tour of food in various cultures, with a glance at church teaching, cannibalism, the punishments of overindulgence and the Baroque's debt to pasta. It appeared on 31 December 1961, neatly sandwiched between Christmas at Chatsworth and a riotous New Year ball, at which Magouche's ex-husband John Phillips threatened to beat him up.

Jock Murray was worried about Paddy. To him it was

quite obvious that PLF had gone stale on the original idea of a sequel to *Mani*. I don't think he will ever finish it in the form originally

Right: Joan Rayner (*née* Eyres Monsell) and the painter and writer Dick Wyndham, with whom she had travelled in the Middle East before the war. The first English paper she and Paddy bought on their return from the Caribbean, in May 1948, announced his death in Palestine

Left: Joan at Epidaurus, 1946. 'Her talk was unexpected, funny, clear-minded. She had no time for inessentials'

Below: Paddy in Ithaca, 1946, taken by Joan, who took all the photographs for Paddy's books *Mani* and *Roumeli*

Paddy with Spiro and Maria Lazaros, owners of the watermill at Lemonodassos

Above: Xan Fielding and Paddy: brothers-in-arms in wartime Crete, and friends ever after

Right: Lawrence Durrell, Paddy and Xan Fielding, acting up in the ruins of Camirus, Rhodes, September 1946

Above left: Xan at Camirus a little later, with much wine drunk and inhibitions shed. 'A tremendous leap and he was there, while the column rocked frighteningly for several seconds'

Above right: Paddy in Cretan dress. On the back he wrote, 'Immediate post-war bullshit photo'

A proud mother: Æileen and Paddy outside Buckingham Palace in March 1950, where Paddy was to receive the military OBE

The photographer Costa Achillopoulos in Egypt, 1943. Commissioned to compile a book of photographs of the Caribbean islands in 1948, he asked Paddy to join him, to write the captions and articles that would accompany his work. The result was Paddy's first book, *The Traveller's Tree*

Sketch by Paddy of a Voodoo *tonnelle*, Haiti

Filming *Ill Met by Moonlight*, left to right: David Oxney, playing Billy Moss; Xan Fielding, technical adviser; Dirk Bogarde, playing Paddy; and Micky Akoumianakis, who had been SOE's key intelligence agent in the Heraklion area

Above: Lyndall Hopkinson. 'I'm determined not to lose you as a friend as well as in every other way,' Paddy wrote at the end of their affair, 'and one of the things about loving people is, after all, to wish them well . . .'

Right: Ricki Huston, on the west coast of Ireland. 'You seemed marvellous to me, blindingly beautiful and funny and adorned with every grace . . .'

Above: Lunch at Kardamyli, in what John Betjeman called 'one of *the* rooms in the world', for the men who built it. On Paddy's left is the master-mason, Nico Kolokotrones, whose wife sits on Paddy's right

Left: John Grey Murray, known as 'Jock', whose patience and skill coaxed Paddy's books into being. Here he is poring over one of Paddy's manuscripts at his desk in Albemarle Street

Right: Paddy with George Jellicoe, in dark glasses. Friends since the war, they had a strong Cretan connection: Jellicoe often led the Allied raids on German air fields and petrol dumps in occupied Crete. Note the *gorgona* tattooed on Paddy's arm

Above: Paddy and Ann Fleming, dressed for the Operatic Ball at Sevenhampton. Ann is the Ghost of the Opera, while Paddy is dressed as André Chénier
Right: Paddy with Diana Cooper, a lifelong correspondent to whom he dedicated *The Violins of Saint-Jacques*

Left: Paddy and Joan on the terrace at Kardamyli. Also visible are the designs he made, picked out in black and white pebbles
Above: Paddy and Deborah Devonshire. 'I've been reading our book,' Paddy wrote on the publication of *In Tearing Haste*, their collected correspondence, 'and it's jolly, jolly good'

Left: Paddy and Pamela Egremont in the Vikos gorge, Epirus, Greece, 2005

Right: Paddy with Elpida Beloyannis

Left: 'I constantly find myself saying "I must tell that to Joan"; then suddenly remember that one can't . . .'

planned. He is genuinely depressed about his inability to do so and feels a sense of guilt and despair. On the other hand, he is longing to get onto a novel and to try fresh fields in Mexico, for which journey he could probably get financial support from the *Sunday Times** . . . As a way out of the impasse, I suggested that we should publish a small book using the material to hand, including parts that could easily be finished . . . At the end he seemed enthusiastic about this plan and promised faithfully to get on to completing it immediately.[21]

Paddy repaired to Chagford after the winter feasts, inspired by Jock's less ambitious plan for the book. At first things went well. On 4 February he told Jock that 'I've been striking oil, from a literary point of view, such a gusher that it's hard to keep pace with it . . . spells like this have something of the insane buoyancy of a love affair.'[22]

A month later he was still buoyant, despite having sustained a multiple fracture of his left wrist in a hunting accident. Jock had warned Paddy about getting bogged down with the story of Byron's slippers, but 'the whole thing got out of control and covers many pages . . . it's full of things I've been longing to write for years, especially about Ld Byron, and I've been enjoying it like mad . . . Remains the beggar chapter, let's wash out the phallic one at the moment, and use the beggars to complete our revised interim volume . . .' What had been holding him up, he said, was 'that great khaki obstacle of Macedonia'.[23]

Mexico was postponed. Paddy and Joan spent that spring in Rome and Sicily, where Paddy floundered in bouts of depression. 'The main cause of all this gloom is my slowness at writing. I wish I could get a move on,' he wrote to Joan from Montepulciano. 'I don't know what's the matter with me. I've got almost half that wretched chapter done, with the utmost fuss and bother, sometimes pacing up and down, putting on the gramophone and mouldering in my chair. I hope I haven't done my brain in with smoking . . .'[24]

That summer, with Joan still in England, Paddy resumed the search for a place in Greece. With him he took Ian Wigham, a friend with houses in Italy and England whom Paddy described as 'one of the funniest people I've ever met'.[25] They set off in a car from Athens,

---

* Mark Boxer, founder of the Sunday Times Colour Supplement, had agreed to give £1,000 towards financing Paddy's trip to Mexico: JGM memo, February 1962.

to look at the possibility of converting one of the old Maniot tower houses in the village of Kardamyli. But the tower had no privacy, and one of the two women who owned the land 'spoke, without a single comma, for one hour and twenty minutes, in a shrill mad terrifying scream, embracing in her discourse the atom bomb, the wickedness of the Turks, the end of the world, the vice of foreigners, the Beast of Babylon with the Harlot on its back, with a cupful of abominations, fire and brimstone. I felt dead at the end of it, grateful to slink away . . .'

They had driven about two miles south of Kardamyli, on their way to the next village of Stoupa, when they spotted a little headland between two valleys ending in crescent-shaped beaches. Later that day they went back to the spot to go bathing. Paddy told Joan how they had left the car on the road and followed a mule track to the sea, 'walking down into a gently sloping world of the utmost magical beauty . . . The view is an enormous sweep of sea, bounded by the headlands . . . The sun is visible until its last gasp.'[26] It was called Kalamitsi, the place of the reeds.

Paddy first saw the land at Kalamitsi on a Tuesday at the end of June. By Friday, he had asked a lawyer friend, Tony Massourides, to begin the long, delicate work of trying to buy it.

Purchase of the land was complicated by the fact that four people had to be in agreement before it was sold, although only one of them lived on the spot. Angela Philkoura occupied a tiny hut on the property with her goats and poultry. She told Paddy and Massourides that she would be willing to give them a long lease and they could build whatever they liked, but she would never part with the land. 'Money's just bits of paper,' she said. 'It flies away like the birds. But if you have land and olives and vegetables and chickens, you'll never starve.'[27]

These negotiations had been watched with interest by a young couple called Petro and Lela Yannakea, who lived in a tiny white-washed house nearby. Lela urged the old lady to accept: bright and energetic, she immediately understood that the arrival of (relatively) well-to-do foreigners in this remote spot would present opportunities that might ease their lives considerably. Paddy too felt that the proximity of Petro and Lela was one of the major attractions of the place.

Joan suggested that they should lease the land for fifty years, which would see them both out; but Paddy was set on buying it, 'rather absurdly, because of the possibility of descendants, unless my absolute idiocy has done for this! . . . not being married seems steadily more ludicrous – and the very possibility of this paradise brings this out in sharper and sharper relief.'[28] – 'Don't make me cry about my descendants,' replied Joan, 'but yours might well be there . . .' Yet she felt that leasing the land might solve everything, 'as I feel really most of the trouble is the Greeks' hatred of selling land . . .'[29]

There was little time for Paddy to dream about leaving land they had not yet bought to children they had not yet conceived. In January 1963, at the age of fifty, Joan went into hospital in London for a hysterectomy. She had long given up hope of having children but the operation left her miserably depressed, and the long-anticipated trip to Mexico was put off yet again. Paddy toiled on, dragging his manuscripts from Gadencourt to Ann Fleming's house at Sevenhampton, and the village of Branscombe in Devon. 'Please don't despair about [Roumeli], in spite of the damning evidence,' he wrote to Jock. 'Miss John sent me back another 70 pages of TS just before Xmas which needed a lot of correcting and a new lick of paint . . .'[30] But then Paddy's attention turned to a new project, which was to push Roumeli into the background for a while longer.

Sometime before, the American Holiday magazine had asked Paddy to write a 2,000-word article on 'The Pleasures of Walking', and it seemed the ideal opportunity to tackle his great journey across Europe. In a notebook, under the heading 'Rome: August 1962', he had sketched out a few ideas; but trusting as he did in the first unfettered rush of writing, he did not plot it out. With great difficulty he managed to compress the first part of the journey into under seventy pages, by which time he had only reached Orşova. Then something snapped. As he describes it, 'an explosion took place . . . and with an enormous sigh of relief, as if I had wriggled out of a straight jacket, I continued the journey at a normal pace'.[31]

'Do let me know your reactions to all this,' he wrote to Jock. 'I really do think it is exciting and odd . . . I'm writing all the time, like mad, it's a very different thing from the grind that my dilatoriness has turned my proper book into! Should be through in a few days . . .'[32] Jock knew him well enough not to bank on it.

After a journey to Morocco with Joan in March Paddy spent the next few months in England, and with summer came the annual migration to Greece. They still had their sights fixed on the little promontory at Kalamitsi, but any future negotiations − or a new search, if it fell through − were hampered by the fact that they were only in the country for a few weeks a year. The situation was resolved by a new friend, who offered to lend them a house on the island of Euboea.

Sir Aymer Maxwell Bt was a few years older than Paddy and had served in the Scots Guards. From his grandfather he had inherited his baronetcy and the estates of Monreith, in south-western Scotland. The wilds of Scotland had never appealed to Aymer, a gentle, bookish character, in the way they had to his brother Gavin, author of *A Ring of Bright Water*. Aymer preferred the Mediterranean. On a yacht called the *Dirk Hatterick* he took himself and his friends round the islands of the Aegean, and he had a property in Euboea just south of Limni, on the site of an abandoned manganese mine. There were two houses: Aymer lived in one, and the other he lent to Paddy and Joan.

They accepted gratefully, but Paddy was dismayed when he first set eyes on it. On one side the house looked out on a pleasant garden overlooking the sea; but on the other side there was nothing but ruined warehouses, rusting machinery and white spoil heaps. He set to work to create the perfect writing place: a pavilion of rush mats and criss-cross lattice work that cunningly hid the industrial debris, leaving views of mountains and sea. He also made a low relief, in plaster, of a merman and the *gorgona* − the dangerous, double-tailed mermaid known to Greek fishermen, who holds a boat in one hand and an anchor in the other.* Some months later, inspired by John Julius who gave him the address of a tattooist in the Waterloo Road, Paddy had the *gorgona* tattooed on his left arm.

* The *gorgona* is known to rise out of the sea and seize a boat by its bowsprit, crying '*Where is Alexander the Great?*' If the sailor answers '*Alexander the Great lives and reigns!*' all will be well. But if she is given any other reply, she will pull the boat beneath the waves and all aboard will perish. See *Mani*, p.187.

Aymer Maxwell's guests came and went as Paddy built his pavilion. Nancy Mitford came with Mark Ogilvie-Grant, and they made several expeditions to the islands of the Sporades in the *Dirk Hatterick*. They were followed by Maurice Bowra and Eddie Gathorne-Hardy, Lyndall and then Janetta and her family, with Julian Jebb and Jaime Parladé, whom Janetta would eventually marry. At the end of the summer, Paddy and Joan were left alone. But when Joan went back to London, Paddy still had one congenial neighbour. The translator and scholar Philip Sherrard, who made a study of the religious and poetic traditions of Greece, had a house nearby. He and Paddy would meet up at the end of the working day, and eat their supper in the almost deserted taverna.

To thank Aymer for his kindness, Paddy now turned his attention to a little raised circular terrace in Aymer's garden which overlooked the sea. With enormous difficulty and the help of several men, he bought a massive granite mill-wheel, which he made into a table and installed on the terrace. He had a great circle of wood made by the local carpenter to increase the size of the mill-wheel table, which he then painted with the points of the compass and a rose of the winds.

On New Year's Day 1964, Paddy wrote a letter to Jock from Katounia about his account of the walk, which now numbered about 84,000 words. 'The book has changed, and I think ripened out of all recognition. Much more personal, and far livelier in pace, and lots of it, I hope, very odd. I wonder what *Holiday* will say . . .' Whatever its editors said, it was probably unprintable. Having waited almost two years for a piece by Paddy on 'The Pleasures of Walking', which had now turned into a book, all they could do was choose a passage of the right length. This appeared as 'A Cave on the Black Sea', in the *Holiday* issue of May 1965.

In its final stages this proto-book was called 'A Youthful Journey', but in early 1966 Paddy nursed the idea of calling it 'Parallax'. Most often used in astronomy, the word alludes to the difference in the appearance of an object seen from two different angles. It seemed a good way to draw attention to the gap between the nineteen-year-old walker and the forty-nine-year-old writer, and it included the letter 'x' which always produced a positive response, or so he felt.

'If *sex* were spelt *segs*,' he explained to Jock Murray, 'I question whether it would have caught on to the same extent.'[33]

Paddy and Joan finally signed the contract for the plot of land at Kalamitsi on 3 March 1964. The price agreed was £2,000 (about 200,000 drachmas), part of which was raised by selling the little house in Athens.

From Kalamitsi, the village of Kardamyli was a twenty-minute walk away. On their property, nothing could be heard but the sea and the almost deafening throb of the cicadas. Standing on the tip of the headland they could look out to an uninhabited island, on which stood the remains of a castle that was gradually being swallowed up by trees. The island stood about half a mile offshore, while on the horizon rested the pale arm of the Messenian peninsula. To their right, the rock face tumbled down to a tiny cove. Turning to the left, they could see the ground sloping off in terraces to a long pebbled beach. Behind them, the coastal olive groves gave way to hillsides covered in pine and myrtle, thorn and ilex, guarded by the slim lances of cypress trees; and hanging above them all were the great grey flanks of the Taygetus mountains that glowed pink and orange at sunset.

They pitched their tents on the high ground in July and created a couple of makeshift shelters. In one they stored water and food, brought from the village; the other was occupied by a table on which they drew and planned and read. They pored over volumes of Vitruvius and Palladio, studied proportion and design, paced out imaginary rooms and argued about dimensions. Each had a fairly clear idea of what they wanted – as Paddy put it, 'a loose-limbed monastery cum farmhouse' with massive walls and cool rooms.[34] He made paper models of how he wanted the house to look, but this was not enough. At some point, a real architect would have to translate their ideas into proper technical drawings.

Their choice fell on Nico Hadjimichalis, who had made a study of Greek vernacular architecture, particularly on Crete and Rhodes where he had been involved in projects to preserve traditional villages. With these skills went a natural ebullience and generosity that endeared him enormously to his new clients. His mother Angeliki

Hadjimichalis was a renowned expert on the Sarakatsans, while his wife Vana was an archaeologist who was for many years attached to the French School in Athens.

The key figure in the day-to-day building work was the local stonemason, Nico Kolokotrones, 'the last of seven generations of master-masons from Arcadia who had all played the violin'. Nico, 'a charming, eager, hulking, bear-like Zorba figure',[35] put together a team of local builders and stonecutters from the surrounding villages, and soon became such a friend that Paddy and Joan stood godparents to his son. Paddy often worked alongside the builders or scoured the countryside, going as far as Kalamata to assemble jackdaw heaps of marble slabs and traditional semi-cylindrical tiles. Kalamata was then in the early stages of modernization, and such things were lying around like scrap for the taking.

Early September was still warm, though the evening showers had them hunkered down in their tent, drinking Grant's Standfast whisky and soda and reading aloud from Mrs Gaskell. By November, work was well under way and the main terrace was taking shape. Paddy had plans for a rose of the winds, 'with the four cardinal points indicated by their Greek initials picked out in black pebbles tightly cemented among white in cunning squares among the grey slabs . . .'[36] Laying patterns of different coloured pebbles is more often seen in houses of the Cyclades and Sporades than in the Mani, but for Paddy the pebbling became an obsession. He copied his designs from excavations at Olynthus and in the Chalkidiki peninsula: patterns of waves, cables, and interlocking vine shoots.

They returned to London at the end of the year, with Paddy now able to enjoy the privileges of White's Club: he had been proposed by Andrew Devonshire (who also put him up for Pratt's) and Michael Astor. He was also a member of the Beefsteak Club, and of course the Travellers. It is strange to think of him one day in shorts at Kardamyli, inserting pebbles into a path, and the next in a suit and tie in London with highly polished shoes; but when in London he looked every inch a clubman as he swung his cane down St James's Street, with a military bearing that many a round-shouldered writer might envy.

He was still trying to finish *Roumeli*. It seems extraordinary that the book gave so much trouble, particularly since in its latest incarnation three of its six chapters had already been published, but in all the excitement of buying the land and starting to build the house, he had worked on it only in fits and starts. That spring, he finished it at last. He wrote to Joan from Chester Row (she was back in Greece, supervising work at Kalamitsi) to say that

> Jock is terribly pleased with me and has told everyone else that he is absolutely delighted with the final result. I do think it has improved out of all recognition, and there is no longer any need to feel ashamed of it, as I would have a couple of months ago. I've hated this period more than any other I can remember, and felt I was going mad, falling to bits, becoming idiotic, tongue-tied, dull, hopeless . . . I'm sure it was all because of guilty conscience.[37]

Now he could embark on his next big commission with his desk and his conscience clear.

Despite their bruising experience the previous year with 'The Pleasures of Walking', *Holiday* magazine recognized that Paddy was an exceptional writer and they were willing to take another chance. They proposed that he take a journey down the river Danube, and write about the river from its source in Germany to its broad delta on the Black Sea. He was hugely excited by the prospect, not least because he hoped it would be possible to see Balasha while he was in Rumania.

Rumania in 1965 was just beginning to open up to the non-Communist world, although a meeting with the Cantacuzene sisters would involve considerable risks. As Paddy put it, 'Mixing with foreigners incurred severe punishment, but harbouring them indoors was much worse . . .'[38] But it was too good an opportunity to miss, and Balasha and her family felt it was a risk worth taking.

By early June he was in Bucharest, now stripped of its pre-war gaiety, and made contact with Pomme's daughter Ina who was then working as a draughtswoman in an architect's office. She met him after work on a borrowed motorbike, and with Paddy riding pillion, they began the eighty-mile journey to the town of Pucioasa in the foothills of the Carpathians. It was a long ride over rutted roads, and by the time Ina let him into the house it was well after dark. They

climbed upstairs as quietly as possible so as not to disturb the neighbours, but it was hard to stifle the cries of welcome that greeted
his arrival at the top of the house.

Pomme, Constantin and Balasha had been sharing an attic studio
since their eviction from Băleni on the night of 2–3 March 1949.
On that evening, a small posse of Communist apparatchiks and police
had arrived in a truck. Pomme and Constantin were forced to sign
a document surrendering ownership of the house, and the family
was told to pack a small suitcase each. They were advised to take
warm clothes, and told they would be leaving in fifteen minutes.
They were taken to Bucharest, where they lived until orders came
through that they were to be transferred to Pucioasa.[39]

'In spite of the interval,' wrote Paddy, 'the good looks of my
friends, the thoughtful clear glance and the humour were all intact;
it was as though we had parted a few months ago, not twenty-six
years.'[40] Hidden behind that carefully worded sentence was the shock
of finding Balasha 'a broken ruin' of her former self. Though only
in her early sixties, she was shrunken by hardship and anxiety;
her black hair was grey, her face lined, and she was very deaf. She
and Pomme managed to survive by teaching English and French.
Constantin, already ill with the heart disease that would kill him
two years later, was too frail to work.

'Their horrible vicissitudes were narrated with detachment and
speed,' he continued. 'Time was short and there were only brief
pauses for sleep on a couple of chairs. The rest of our forty-eight
hours – we dared risk no more – were filled with pre-war memories, the lives of all our friends, and a great deal of laughter.'[41] He
had brought new watches for Pomme and Balasha, and later he set
up an account for her at the Heywood Hill bookshop so she would
never be short of books. He also knew that Balasha had a present
for him. On her last night at Băleni, in the fifteen minutes she had
been given to pack, she had seized a battered green notebook. It
was Paddy's last journal, the one he had begun in Bratislava in 1934;
she now put it into his hands.

The long article Paddy wrote about the Danube reflects the progress
of the river: clear and brilliantly coloured as far as Vienna, its tone

becomes more sombre in Bratislava. Paddy remembered it as a thriving town ringing to a babble of different dialects, with a large Jewish community; now it was grey, peeling, neglected, and the Jews had been wiped out by the Nazis. Budapest is happier: people tell jokes there and they are real people, not just figures in the landscape. In Rumania the river again takes centre stage, as it thunders through narrow chasms and plunges over submerged cataracts that only the bravest and most skilful pilots can handle. But the building of the great dam that was to tame the Danube had begun the year before, and he knew he was gazing on this scene for the last time. Not only was the Turkish island of Ada Kaleh going to be submerged, but the whole valley for a hundred kilometres upstream. The piece ends in the whispering marshes of the delta, among glades of reed and water teeming with birds.

The piece was published by *Holiday* magazine in August 1966, and given another outing in the *Cornhill* the following summer. Elements in 'Journey Down the Danube' point the way towards his future books on the great walk. The Polymath, who comes into the story of *A Time of Gifts* at Persenbeug, appears a few miles upstream at Linz to tell Paddy about the fishes of the Danube; while the created memory of crossing the Alföld on horseback, and the skills of the Danube pilots, will appear again in *Between the Woods and the Water*.

The article also marked a fresh attempt to master typing, though progress was still painfully slow. As he told Joan, 'it still takes ¾ of an hour a page, but I'm getting better every moment . . . I must be mad not to have taught myself earlier. If only I had typed out each day's work from the MS at the end of each day, over the years, I would be a different person today, calm, rich, prolific, famous, rested . . .'[42]

By July 1965 the ground at Kalamitsi had been levelled, and foundations were in place. 'We had a glorious foundation stone party,' Paddy told Jock, which by Maniot tradition required a blood sacrifice: in this case a fine black cock, with iridescent green tail feathers. The cock was 'beheaded by the mason with his trowel on the stone while the priest chanted away and asperged everything with [holy water and] myrtle branches. About eighty people came and we had musicians, lambs on the spit, gallons of wine, dancing and singing . . .'[43]

The walls were made from rough-hewn blocks of stone, blasted out of the flanks of the Taygetus at the top of the valley,

> a secret quarry among the thyme and myrtle. It varies from pale whitey grey, through gold and ochre into pink and deep russet and unites, when laid, into a beautiful serene honey colour. They start by laying dynamite charges, then dash for cover and bang! The sound of a mini-Borodino booms up through the valley, and up showers a fountain of boulders. Up flies, too, a lot of rock nuthatches that nest all round, chirruping sadly: they realize they'll never hatch nuts on those rocks more . . . Then hard-handed men trim them roughly and a little caravan of mules goes to and fro between the quarry and the site . . .[44]

This letter to Diana was written on printed writing paper, even though the house was barely begun, let alone finished. The design of the address barely changed over the coming decades. KARDAMYLI, MESSENIA it read, in Greek letters to the left and Roman to the right. They rarely called the place 'Kalamitsi', not liking the sugary effect of 'mitsi' in English. It was always Kardamyli.

Every aspect of life in the Mani seemed clean and beautiful, and filled him with joy. He described their first olive harvest (old Angela Philkoura had retired to the village after all), 'largely plucked and gathered by Joan and some of the local squaws whose task it is: 17,000 kilos [sic] from 80 odd trees, now mashed into wonderful green oil (about 300 kilos) by the village mill-stones, ready to be poured into a ribbed Ali-Baba jar two robbers could twist in . . .'[45]

At this stage, the only part of the house to be built was the cistern, the cellar and 'a sort of neolithic loggia, enclosed on three sides by fine arches, the end one four yards in span and a yard thick . . .'[46] At first, they had been unsure whether Kolokotrones was capable of making arches. When asked he admitted he had not done very many, but what was required was a good supply of oleanders. Their springy green stems, he said, were just what was needed to make the template for an arch. Oleanders were plentiful, and soon Nico was so adept at arches 'that he now produces them – using several tons of rock with the nonchalance, ease and almost the speed of an expert blowing smoke rings'. Electricity had not yet come to the Mani, so the whole house was built with tools that were biblical in their simplicity. No line was dead straight, no two openings exactly the same – all of which created a lot of bad blood between Kolokotrones and the joiner, Yanni Mastoro. Paddy, however, was delighted by the effect. 'It gives a live and home-made look to the thing,' he wrote, 'like a cottage loaf as opposed to a pre-sliced Hovis.'[47]

He found a marble quarry in the deep Mani from which he hoped to buy a few slabs. The quarrymen told him that since their orders were only for large pieces, he could help himself to whatever chunks he could find lying about; a few days later Paddy returned with six men and a truck, and took away five tons. In a letter to Aymer he described it as 'beautiful, snow-white glittering stuff, hideous when polished but glorious rough-hewn . . .'[48] It was used for steps and windowsills, columns and seats in the outdoor loggias, while the floors were made of grey-green slate from Mount Pelion.

Paddy and Joan were surprised at what a magnet they were for people, even in a half-built, isolated house to which there was no easy access. To Joan in London, he described a particularly trying day. It began with a visit from the carpenter, followed by someone who wanted something translated into English, and then the MP for Hereford who had connections in Dumbleton: he wanted advice about buying property in Crete. That afternoon a Greek friend from Athens turned up, with four companions and a bottle of whisky: he had promised his friends that they would hear the story of the abduction of General Kreipe from the mouth of the abductor himself. The Athenian party had only just left when a boatload of visitors from Kalamata appeared, a young schoolmaster and his family brought by one of the young blacksmiths.

> I made a dash for the typewriter and began a mad *obbligato*, but there they were. I kept up the crashing till they were on me and received them standing. After half an hour [the schoolmaster] said he saw I was busy and would come back when I was a bit freer and talk about all sorts of things . . . We *must* have a high and forbidding wall at the vulnerable points . . . anything else is folly.[49]

Roumeli, the long awaited sequel to *Mani*, appeared in April 1966. Geographically, the word refers to the region between the Gulf of Corinth and the borders of Macedonia. *Romaíoi*, or *Romioi*, is what the Greeks who live here call themselves (*Romiòs* in the singular). The word springs from the time when old Rome was being engulfed by barbarian invasions, and what was left of the empire looked to Constantinople, the new Rome. Over time, the churches of the East and West split. Constantinople became the heart of the Greek Orthodox world, and remained so for a thousand years, during which time 'the Greeks were *Romaíoi* – Romans – as well as Hellenes'.[50]

Greek intellectuals had been exploring the two strands of their cultural heritage, the classical and the Byzantine, ever since the country's independence. The architecture of nineteenth-century Athens paid homage to both. But Paddy took what he called the 'Helleno-Romaic dilemma' a step further, and suggested that it defined the experience of being Greek. All Greeks contain both sides of the argument, but will usually favour one side or the other. The Hellene is urban, intellectual, progressive. He is rooted in the ideals of classical civilization. He believes in technology and innovation, and sees modernization as essential if Greece is to be part of western Europe. The *Romiòs*, on the other hand, is a countryman, whose roots are in farming and flocks. He is conservative, traditional, and keeps the candles burning in front of the icons. He looks with pride on the recent klephtic past, upholds a way of life that the Hellene finds rather backward, and sees Greece as part of the Orthodox world rather than of the West. '"Hellene" is the glory of ancient Greece,' he wrote; '"Romaic" the splendours and the sorrows of Byzantium, above all, the sorrows.'[51] Although the book's subtitle is *Travels in Northern Greece*, one of its most heartfelt passages is about Crete: a place which, for Paddy, was the essence of *Romiosyne*, the traditional Greek way of life.

These two strands are equally valid, equally Greek; sometimes they complement each other, sometimes they are in opposition; but on one point Paddy was sure. He was acutely aware that *Romiosyne* was in decline, and for him it was a cause of great sadness. He imagines the Hellene, wearily asking why the poor should be kept in ignorance, poverty and disease to oblige a few romantic travellers. 'I realize how severely they damage my case,' he wrote.[52] But his was not a solitary voice. There were many Greeks, including George Seferis and Nico Ghika, who saw how much of Greek tradition and identity was being lost as the country developed.

The Times called it 'a worthy stable-companion for *Mani*'.[53] Dilys Powell described Paddy as 'a wandering scholar but with a difference; unlike the celebrated travellers of the past, he has become part of the country he describes.'[54]

Jock Murray gave a party for Paddy at 50 Albemarle Street, which also coincided with the 142nd anniversary of Byron's death. The 'Londoner's Diary' column of the *Evening Standard* described Paddy as 'a chunky, tough-looking man of 51 . . . wearing his erudition under an unimpeachably Hellenistic tan'.[55] Five days later, they asked what he was going to do next. 'I've got ideas for one or two novels I want to do,' he replied. 'I'm written dry about Greece for the moment.'[56]

He still wanted to write about Mexico, but Jock was against it. He felt that Mexico had been done to death and was trying to persuade Paddy to go to Ethiopia, then almost virgin territory from a literary point of view. But while Paddy contemplated the next big project, another assignment lay on his desk.

That March, just before publication of *Roumeli*, he had been approached by the historian Barrie Pitt who was editing a part-work on the history of the Second World War. Pitt asked him to write a 5,000-word article on the Kreipe Operation, and although Paddy was reluctant, Joan urged him to accept. He no longer had the excuse that writing about the operation 'would spoil it for Billy', as he used to say, because Billy had been dead for almost six years. This was a good opportunity to highlight the Cretan contribution to the mission.

They moved out of the house in Chester Row that August, and from then on their commitment to living in Greece was sealed. Back at Kardamyli the following month, Paddy was bombarding Jock about the horrors of the American edition of *Roumeli*. He had assumed that Harper & Row would allow him proofs. But on discovering that it was simply a reprint of the English edition, he had 'pitched the book from the top of the cliff as far as I could throw it'. He was particularly resentful that the dedication to Amy and Walter Smart still had no page of its own, but was relegated to 'a left-hand page mainly occupied with small-type information about copyright and other trade matters. For me, a dedication is like throwing a cloak over someone's balcony before a bullfight; it's distressing to find it hanging, as it were, in the staff lavatory.'[57]

19

A Monastery Built for Two

In years to come, the architect Nico Hadjimichalis always laughed at the way Paddy used to claim he had created the house himself. Yet it took several hours to drive the hundred and eighty miles from Athens to Kardamyli, and Hadjimichalis was not on site very often. Most of the problems that arose day to day were resolved by Paddy and Joan, in consultation with Kolokotrones. Looking at the plans, however, the house seems to have gone up exactly as Hadjimichalis's drawings indicate; and the most important elements – the breath-taking entrance, the gallery, the library, and the loggias on the terrace at the southern end of the house – are so beautifully proportioned that just being there lifts the spirit. The plans show separate bedrooms from the start: Joan's, on the southern end of the house, had a huge internal arch that spanned the room and framed the view over the bay. Paddy's was small and looked north over the garden; but he had plans to build a separate study thirty yards away from the house, which would have its own bedroom and bathroom.

The main room of the house was entered by a big beech double door, for which Paddy had optimistically designed a massive stone door-frame. Though the posts could be assembled in blocks, the lintel was one solid piece of stone about six feet across, and it took the combined strength of several men to get it to the house. A shepherd watched them making their slow and painful way down the hill. 'What are you going to do with that?' he asked. 'We're going to chuck it into the sea,' replied Kolokotrones through gritted teeth, 'just to see if it floats!'[1]

A divan stretched around the northern end of the sitting room, while the fireplace was based on a Persian design with a cone-shaped chimney which Paddy had seen at Băleni. Tall windows with deep embrasures revealed the thickness of the walls, into which bookcases were set. The books in the northern end of the room were largely devoted to English poetry and French literature, while at the southern end were full sets of Kipling, Dickens, Hardy, Henry James, Scott, and any number of biographies and histories. This end of the room also housed a battery of reference books and encyclopaedias, for it was closest to the dining table – so any arguments that arose over a meal could be instantly settled. The coffered wooden ceiling was of pine, but over the years the wood mellowed to a dark gold. French windows opened on to the terrace with the sea beyond, while at the southern end, a pair of whitewashed columns and a step brought one down into a room within a room. With a low roof, windows and a divan on three sides, this was the Turkish *hayati* – a pool of warmth and light in winter, and an oasis of green in summer.

For their dining table Paddy conceived a great circle of red and white marble, inlaid with a design he had copied from a *tondo* in the church of Sant'Anastasia in Verona. This was not the sort of thing that could be made in Greece: the commission was given to a firm of *marmoristas* in Venice, who had worked for Freya Stark.

The cats appeared out of nowhere: wild, half-starved Greek cats with huge ears, wary eyes, pointed jaws and flanks so narrow they looked as if they had been pressed flat. Joan put out food for them, and soon a little troop of her favourites would follow her about the house. She cut a hole in the door to her room, so they could come and go at night. Paddy welcomed them too, and watched tolerantly as they ran their claws down the new divans: 'born down-holsterers', as he put it, the cats moved in and out of open doors and windows as freely as air currents. 'In the early days', recalled their friend Peter Levi, 'the chickens used to roost in the olive trees and one would hear Joan's plaintive individual voice coaxing them down at dusk. "Chick chick chick, come along down. Come along down then. Oh *if* you won't come down I'll break your **** necks." Now she has them in a shed under sterner discipline.'[2] As time went on, more animals arrived. The cat population stabilized somewhere between twenty and twenty-five, with twenty-odd chickens and a cock, two turkeys, a few rabbits, and two pigs that belonged to Petro and Lela.

The pigs rootled about in the olive groves, which was said to be good for the roots.[3]

A few years after they came to Kardamyli, Paddy and Joan decided to put a tap on the water pipe that ran from the village to their house, so that any passer-by might relieve his thirst. But as soon as the hot weather came, the standpipe in the olive grove by the little church began to attract people from remote homesteads and villages for miles around, who found it far easier to draw water from a tap than haul it out of a deep well as they did at home. They brought their children, dogs, transistor radios and washing, put up shelters, and soon the surrounding area began to look like a refugee camp. In a letter to Paddy in the early summer of 1971 Joan wrote to tell him that 'The squatters are here, rather more solid huts than last year and a very noisy first night with barking dog and early radio but I let it be known . . . that if it wasn't quiet I'd take steps (I don't know what!) and there wasn't a sound last night.'[4]

But the peace did not last. As more people came the rubbish spread, while the noise from radios and barking dogs increased. Joan and Paddy felt wretched about removing the standpipe, but in the end it was the only way to reclaim their tranquillity and isolation.

On 21 April 1967, a group of middle-ranking army officers took over Greece in a coup that left the country in a state of shock. Paddy wrote to Joan a week later, from Spain.

> The queer thing about the recent events in Greece is that you prob-
> ably know more about it than I do. All internal papers stopped.
> Athens radio gave out nothing but official bulletins and no foreign
> papers came into the country. I first heard about it at 1 o'clock on
> the day of the putsch, when Lela came from the village . . . like
> Cassandra saying a dictatorship has been declared and that the gendar-
> merie were bringing communists from the mountain villages in
> handcuffs after arresting them in the middle of the night . . .

Paddy had the feeling that the provinces, and certainly the Mani, believed the Junta's claim that they had taken over the country in order to save it from the threat of Communism and the return of civil war:

others say it is balls, and that there is no possible *raison d'état* for the coup whatever. All the leaders are unknown . . . I don't know what to think. All my spontaneous sympathies (in spite of my official views generally*) are against the coup . . . The dotty sumptuary laws about church, dress,† morality in general, strike a chill. It's the quantity of hit and miss arrests and banishment to the islands without trial that fill one with the most horror and disgust.[5]

King Constantine, who had at first given his support to the junta, launched a counter-coup against the Colonels in December with elements in the army that remained loyal to the crown. But since the King refused to permit bloodshed, his counter-coup failed almost before it had begun and Constantine was sent into exile. As time went on the regime's contempt for democracy, its ever-increasing corruption and its blundering cruelty turned almost everyone except the army against it. Yet unlike Maurice Bowra, who denounced the junta at every opportunity and exiled himself from Greece for as long as the regime was in power, Paddy took no political stand. The Cyprus question had involved Britain directly, but who governed Greece was a matter for the Greeks alone. At some point, George Seferis sent a roundabout message to Paddy and Joan, with a question: if he sent someone in secret to Kardamyli, would they be willing to shelter that person? The answer was, of course they would; but the fugitive never appeared.

That summer they invited a great many people to stay. Among their guests were Magouche, Alex and Roxanne Sedgwick, Mark Ogilvie-Grant and Nancy Mitford, Ian Wigham, Barbara and Nico with her daughter Lucy Warner. Later on came Barbara's daughter Miranda Rothschild, who was often at Kardamyli in the coming years. Diana Cooper and Patrick Kinross – now neighbours in Little Venice, where Diana had bought a house when she left Chantilly in 1960 – came in October, followed by Tom Driberg and Joan's sister Diana Casey.

There was still a certain amount of work to do on the house and

---

* Paddy was known to be pro-monarchist, anti-Communist and generally conservative.

† The Colonels announced a crackdown on men with long hair and women in miniskirts.

Paddy had done very little else besides, though he had – after considerable trouble – finished the piece on the Kreipe Operation commissioned by Barrie Pitt. He had had grave misgivings about how to approach the task. Towards Billy he felt a sort of survivor's guilt, and he dreaded writing anything that might cast a shadow on his friend or his book. Then there were the Cretans to consider, for it was more than likely that anything he wrote on the Kreipe Operation would find its way back to Crete. When translated from English into Greek, his account might sound understated and mealy-mouthed; but if he adopted a heroic style closer to theirs, it risked sounding bombastic in English. It was also vital not to leave anyone out. This writing on eggshells meant that the simplest sentence became a quagmire of scruples, while deadline after deadline came and went. Like 'The Pleasures of Walking', the piece grew considerably longer than expected. Paddy had been sending it to the editor as it was written, and when it was complete he gave it the title 'Abducting a General'.

When Barrie Pitt received the final instalment, he unleashed his pent-up feelings:

> I will briefly (and with no trace of bitterness in my heart) recap the events of the last twenty months . . . On 2 April, 1966 I commissioned you to write a 5,000 word article for delivery last November. Nearly eleven months after the deadline I receive the last hand-written instalment, which brought the entire work up to some 36,000 words. I therefore had to hire, with extreme urgency, a professional writer to reduce the work to the size and shape which I could use – a task for which I had to pay him 60gns out of the 75gns budgeted for this article. I am not really very happy in offering you the remaining 15gns for all your labour and hard work, despite the near disaster with which the project was threatened, and the appalling strain on my nervous system and blood pressure.[6]

Paddy did not like the shortened version, but he was in no position to complain.

Joan was keen that he should develop 'Abducting a General' into a proper book, feeling that he owed it both to himself and to his friends in Crete. Paddy raised the possibility of doing so in a letter to Diana Cooper, but only briefly, and he asked her not to mention it; it was as if he knew it would never be written.

'Abducting a General' fills in several gaps in the Kreipe story, and contains some intriguing details such as Paddy's arrival in Anoyeia after the abduction. At that point he was still in German uniform and so was shunned by everyone, and it was only with difficulty that he persuaded the terrified priest's wife of his true identity. He described the General with a compassion that bordered on affection, as a melancholy, solitary man who was in an impossible position. He and Kreipe's love of Horace went a long way towards humanizing their relationship, and Paddy could never have formed such a bond with the hated Müller. It would also have been far harder to stop the Cretans from slitting his throat in the night.

At the same time, this piece is not so much an adventure as a confession, a tribute, a plea for understanding. Pages are devoted to weighing up the various reasons the Germans gave for the reprisals they unleashed in the second half of 1944. And while he argues that Kreipe's abduction was not the prime cause for the destruction, his loyalty to Billy forbids him from mentioning the Damasta raid that led directly to the razing of Anoyeia. 'Abducting a General' is, above all, a paean of praise to Crete and the Cretans. They were all nonpareils of generosity, style, courage and endurance, but he was supposed to be writing history. In the typescript, long passages of nostalgic eulogy for his clandestine life in the mountains are struck out by the editorial pencil, with an occasional agonized 'No! No!' in the margin.

Two public events punctuated the year at Kardamyli. The first was Greek National Day, 25 March, always celebrated in Kalamata and Kardamyli a day earlier than in the rest of Greece, since this was where the flag of freedom was first raised. Paddy and Joan would make their way to the little square in front of the church at the top of the village, and sit with the rest of the village elders while the long service took place inside. When the service was over food and wine were brought, and everyone celebrated.

The second was Paddy's name day. Since he was known as 'Mihali' in Greece, his name day fell on 8 November, the feast of SS. Michael and Gabriel. By chance, a tiny chapel dedicated to the Archangels stood on the path to Kardamyli a few minutes from the house (where the standpipe had once been), and here Paddy's friends from the village would gather. Only the priest and his acolyte could fit inside, so people stood about talking as the chanting went on, until the priest came out to bless Paddy and the great cartwheel loaves that had been brought for the feast. Then it was open house for the whole village. Lela and her helpers would cook mountains of food, everyone would drink a lot, and the dancing spilled out on to the big terrace. 'When they vanish we sink into bed for several hours, surface about ten for a little consommé and Debussy, then back to the depths . . .'[7]

At the same time, Paddy and Joan did not want to become too involved in the life of Kardamyli. Although they never saw themselves as rich and powerful, in the eyes of the village they were. Joan in particular was aware that for their own tranquillity they should not become embroiled in local rivalries, or be seen to be taking sides. The villagers understood and accepted their detachment. In October 1967, Paddy was made an honorary citizen of Kardamyli.

That winter they returned to England as usual, and just before Christmas Barbara gave a dinner party. Among the guests were Balasha's niece Ina and her husband, Michel Catargi, who had left Rumania and were living in Paris; and the now widowed Amy Smart. Amy, whom Paddy described as 'captivating and maddening by turns', began teasing Paddy and Joan about their long and so far unformalized relationship. Paddy countered by saying that they had always meant to get married, but now they were settled in Kardamyli, 'it seemed idiotic not to. *So why not now?*'[8] Suddenly, without any planning, the moment had arrived and Paddy was ready. Joy and excitement broke out round the table, and Amy was so pleased with herself for having pushed him into it that Paddy was almost tempted to call it off.

They had to prove a two-week residence before they could get married in London, and as usual, they separated for Christmas. Joan joined Graham at Dumbleton where they listened to music and ignored the tinsel, while Paddy went to Chatsworth, where the feast was celebrated with Dickensian enthusiasm. They returned to London early in the new year, and the wedding took place on 11 January

1968. In a letter to Balasha, Paddy described it as being 'nearly as easy as getting a dog licence'.[9] Supported by Barbara, Nico and Patrick Kinross, they were married at Caxton Hall and immediately repaired to the pub for a 'recovery swig'. A lunch at Barbara's was followed by an evening party given by Patrick Kinross. Among the guests were Maurice Bowra, Cyril and Deirdre Connolly, Iris Tree and Ivan Moffat, Coote Lygon, Raymond Mortimer, Diana Cooper, John Julius and Anne Norwich, Andrew Devonshire and a triumphant Amy Smart. When Diana asked why they had got married so swiftly, Paddy replied: 'I've never believed in long engagements.'

The next day, they had lunch at the Café Royal with Paddy's mother and Vanessa. They had been dreading the meeting with Æileen, but 'Mummy's spiky eccentricity was in complete abeyance, and she was her old, amusing, intelligent and charming self . . . It wouldn't last through too many contacts: I know Mummy too well.'[10]

There was a great deal of speculation as to why Paddy and Joan had married in such haste. Some people thought it was to smooth out administrative and financial arrangements, while others thought it might be because their traditionally minded Greek neighbours did not approve (though they had been living in Kardamyli for three years with no complaints). Some even thought that Joan had given Paddy an ultimatum. Paddy's explanation to Balasha is still the most likely: they had always planned to marry, and now that they were so well settled in Greece, the time was right. The news flew ahead of them to Kardamyli. On entering the house they were greeted with hugs and congratulations from Petro, Lela and several other friends and neighbours, while Joan was embarrassed and amused to find that her bed had been covered with rose petals and sugared almonds. For days they were visited by a succession of neighbours and villagers 'bringing loads of sticky cakes and bottles of ouzo'.[11]

Paddy was still working on 'Parallax', which had started life as an article on 'The Pleasures of Walking' five years before. In March he had told Jock Murray, 'some bits are dreadfully overwritten, and will have to be bled. But I feel that something respectable will emerge.'[12] Nothing did emerge, and by May the pressure from Jock Murray was mounting. 'Your urgent but kindly worded pleas for haste could not fall on less deaf ears,' wrote Paddy on 10 May.

I'm at it all the time, and have been for weeks . . . The only damnable interruption has been the constant presence of the builders. The trouble is we have no architect (we had one, but he has only been here six times in all), with the result that again and again during the day I'm reft from my table for orders and consultation . . . They work fast and well, so that conundrums are cropping up all the time and one is constantly being summoned.[13]

Ironically, the builders were then at work on Paddy's studio: a large, high-ceilinged room with a bedroom and bathroom attached. Once it was finished Paddy was sure the work would forge ahead, but the industrious workers he had had in May were slacking off by late July. 'About twenty different people are doing to me exactly what I'm doing to you,' he told Jock.

I know it's no consolation, but if I am causing anguish, anger, sorrow and disappointment in Albemarle Street, the same difficulties are being visited on me here twenty-fold . . . The studio for writing in, the power-house for prose about thirty yards from the house in seques-tered silence, was supposed to be finished three months ago. The shell is up, but carpenters, tile makers, plumbers, electricians, glaziers – every single artisan whose combined efforts would make the thing habitable is doing a Leigh Fermor on me . . .[14]

And of course there were guests: Peter Quennell and his wife in April, and the new Ambassador, Sir Michael Stewart, with his wife Damaris in June. George and Maro Seferis came for a few days in August, followed by Freya Stark and Patrick Kinross. George Jellicoe came with Philippa, and they loved the place so much that they took the house every summer from then on. George used to jump into the sea from a great rock that jutted out over the water – it was known ever afterwards as Jellicoe's Leap. One person whom Paddy and Joan would have loved to see at Kardamyli was Iris Tree, but she died of cancer in May.

Later that year, Paddy went to France to meet up with Pomme Donici, who was in France to see her daughter Ina. He took Pomme down to Grasse to see their old friend Costa, who had taken the photographs for *The Traveller's Tree*. From there they went to stay with Xan and Daphne Fielding in Uzès. Paddy was worried about

Xan, who was under tremendous strain. He was embroiled in a court
case of Byzantine complexity, which concerned the palatial villa in
Nice overlooking the sea where he had been brought up. It had
been torn down years before to make way for the Corniche; but
the family felt they had a claim to a considerable sum in compensation, and if it were upheld, Xan stood to make a fortune. He spent
a huge amount of money on the case, which was being handled by
his brother-in-law.

> Xan's brother-in-law is either very crooked or a lunatic [Paddy told
> Joan], and this delay and worry over the case . . . has driven Xan
> nearly mad; terrifically nervy and frowning and anxious. The bugger-
> in-law's false promises have nearly landed them in terrible soup, from
> which Derek Jackson nobly rescued them two months ago . . . Daphne,
> in spite of her several drawbacks and a dash of arrested development,
> is very good and calming and kind . . . [15]

On top of all this, Xan had made an extraordinary discovery. The
woman he had always thought of as his mother turned out to be
his grandmother. Her daughter Mary had married a Captain
Alexander Wallace of the 52nd Sikh Frontier Force in Calcutta, and
had died giving birth to Xan. So he had been adopted into his
grandparents' family, his father had never been mentioned again, and
he had grown up with several brothers and sisters who were in fact
his uncles and aunts. 'He . . . tells the still only half-comprehended
tale with considerable humour and bewilderment.'[16]

Larry Durrell lived not far away from Uzès at Sommières, so
Paddy and Pomme, Xan and Daphne went over to visit him. He
lived 'in one of the ugliest and gloomiest Charles Addams houses
I've ever seen,' wrote Paddy, 'ingeniously uglified still further by all
sorts of recent changes. But Larry was better than ever, not nearly
as circular as they say, ebullient and full of beans and ideas, waiting
when we arrived with a giant magnum.'[17]

They did not go back to England that Christmas, but spent it
at Kardamyli with Barbara and Nico Ghika. Then in the New
Year they set off for the Far East, leaving on 20 January, accompanied by Ian Wigham and Joan's brother Graham. The journey,
which was to take several weeks, began in Formosa, now Taiwan.

Hong Kong was a mere staging post to Cambodia and Angkor Wat, followed by Bangkok, 'which has become a tangle of Edgware Roads from a sort of tropical Venice in ten years'.[18] Bali was all the more beautiful by comparison. They flew to central Java to see the great Buddhist shrine at Borobudur, and then to Madras where they said goodbye to Graham. After visiting any number of temples, they flew north to Bombay where Ian left them. Paddy and Joan then went on to the great painted caves of Ajanta, and the carved ones of Ellora. 'Dealing with us, the Indians have a chip on one shoulder, a bunch of forget-me-nots on the other; and so, we began to notice, have we . . .'[19] From Delhi they flew to Nepal and Katmandu where, in a car belonging to a Nepalese prince with whom Joan had danced barefoot in Bombay three decades before, they drove into the terraced foothills of the Himalayas.

They were back in Greece in March, just in time to hear George Seferis's denunciation of the Colonels' regime. It had been recorded in Athens, smuggled out of the country and broadcast on the Greek language service of the BBC. Over the coming days the statement was reprinted everywhere, even in newspapers loyal to the Colonels. There was much criticism from official sources, but Seferis stood his ground, and no one dared touch Greece's first Nobel prize-winner. In contrast to this triumph came news that left Paddy feeling very shaken: Ricki Huston had been killed in a car accident. 'I feel dreadfully upset,' he wrote to Diana Cooper. 'Nothing but sweetness, kindness and fun, and long years ago in Ireland, dashing protection from massacre by wild fox hunters.'[20]

Among their guests that summer were Paddy's sister Vanessa, and John Betjeman – toothy, crowing with laughter and delighted with everything. In his letter of thanks to Joan he wrote:

Oh, I did enjoy myself at Kardamyli. Of course that big room, as I've written to Paddy, is one of the rooms in the world. It is the thought in everything you look at which delights me about the house . . . I've never seen you so beautiful, not even when with eyes as big as your cheeks and downy soft and straight, you stood in the Ritz. I've written Jock a long letter giving him news of George [Seferis] and telling him also about the house – how it is really a book of Paddy's and more lasting.[21]

The last sentence must have given Jock a wry smile.

'It was marvellous having John B. here,' Paddy told Jock. 'He was funny, absolutely perfect, lots of reading aloud from Dickens and Tennyson. He left us a beautiful rather maiden-auntish watercolour of a bit of the house, entitled "*A Glimpse of Old Mani*: John Betjeman, 1904." I'll get it put into an Oxford frame.'[22] But the main subject of his letter to Jock was not Betjeman but George Psychoundakis, who wondered whether there were any *Cretan Runner* royalties waiting for him at John Murray. George had not made a single drachma in six months, and his credit with the grocer had reached its limit. On top of that, because so many foreigners came to visit him (thanks to the success of *The Cretan Runner*), he was widely suspected of stealing a valuable cross that had disappeared from the village church.

One of the reasons George was so poor was that he had begun a new project that was taking up a great deal of time: he was translating the Odyssey into the Cretan tongue, using the metre of the *Erotokritos*. Paddy was enthusiastic and encouraging, and hoped he could interest George Seferis in it too. 'It would be splendid if something came of it,' he wrote to Seferis. 'He is an angelic chap, and seems to have been dogged by ill-luck while the unjust prosper.'[23] Seferis was unimpressed, and thought Psychoundakis's project overambitious. 'The best solution for your friend's problems is to find for him a good regular job which can allow him to nourish his children', was his blunt conclusion.[24] Paddy sent George some money, and so did Jock; and, undaunted, Psychoundakis carried on with his translation.

Paddy too, after a fashion, was preparing for work. 'Good news – the studio is finished at last,' he told Jock.[25]

With generous shelves and bookcases, a huge desk and plenty of room to pace over the stone floor, by November 1969 the 'powerhouse for prose' at Kardamyli was ready at last. Sunlight streamed in through the windows that overlooked the garden, while in the conical Băleni fireplace set into the corner, the logs were laid ready for the cold weather. 'I'm in it. There are . . . pens, paper, no guests, a winter ahead. I'm keeping my fingers crossed, hoping the veil of sloth and procrastination and distraction may lift and the Muse tiptoe in. Not a word . . .'[26]

The image of luring the Muse into this beautiful space would work only if Paddy was then willing to sit down and pay her some attention, but having a big room of his own gave rise to a new set of delightful distractions. His books and works of reference had to be arranged and revisited. He had subscriptions to most of the literary magazines in English and French, as well as a number of smaller literary journals, all of which suggested more books that he wanted to read. Letters, both reading and writing them, took up a considerable amount of time – particularly those whose replies had been put off too long, and began 'In sackcloth and ashes'.

Above all, there was the creative exercise of playing with words. Looking over his letters and notebooks, it becomes evident that Paddy's most beguiling distraction was always his own mind, filled with poems and songs, puns and riddles, limericks, sonnets, lists of hats and stars, and verses by the yard. All were composed in a mood of kaleidoscopic energy and inventiveness, drawing on the vocabulary of at least eight languages which existed in his head in a state of perpetual acrobatics. The best of his poems and pastiches were polished with care and often given as presents to his friends. In the winter of 1969, he was in the mood for verses. 'Voix d'outretombe' is a Victorian ballad about a friendly old mass-murderer; while 'O Gemme of Joye and Jasper of Jocunditie: Soho Thoughts from Abroad' imitates the alliteration and rhythm of a poem by William Dunbar, 'London thou art the floure of cities all'.

As a dedicated practitioner, Paddy was very interested in the work of other writers in this anarchic branch of letters. In a later review of George Seferis's verses for children, Paddy wrote that while the English were naturally more playful, the real skill seems to have developed in French. In this language, tightly laced into its grammar and controlled by the dictates of the Institut Français, 'genius triumphed over the vetoes into dazzling feats'. He mentions the liberties with rhyme taken by Victor Hugo and Mallarmé; Raymond Queneau's *Exercices de style*, and how he had devoted an entire edition of the journal *Oulipo* to translations of 'Jabberwocky'. Paul Cerdan, Laforgue, Apollinaire, Tristan Derème, Léon-Paul Fargue had all been experimenters. And among an infinite variety of constructions Paddy cites *holorimes*, anagrams, spoonerisms, back formations, artificial malaprops, portmanteau words, and the 'verses in transition' of Eugene Jolas, 'which relied entirely on improvised onomatopoeia'.[27]

Every form of verbal doodling had been a part of his life ever since he could read, and the linguistic inventiveness of Lewis Carroll in the two *Alice* books had bitten deep. Both his parents loved puns, while his mother had translated 'It's a Long Way to Tipperary' into Hindustani, a trick Paddy had followed when translating 'Widdecombe Fair' and 'D'ye ken John Peel' into Italian. To pass the time on his walk across Europe he had recited the poems and songs he knew backwards. These games did not help him meet deadlines, but they did nourish the extraordinary prose that he produced with such agonizing slowness.

In the spring of 1970, Paddy and Joan set off on a journey round western Turkey with Michael and Damaris Stewart. Michael Stewart was a scholarly diplomat who had taken up his position as Ambassador to Greece just as the Colonels took power, and he and his wife had already been to stay twice at Kardamyli. They knew Turkey well since Michael had worked in Ankara for four years, and both spoke Turkish. The party travelled by road in the Stewarts' open-topped Land Rover, an odyssey that Paddy listed using the Hellenistic names: Caria, Lycia, Pisidia, Pamphylia, Cilicia, Karamania, Lycaonia, Iconium, Ephesus and Smyrna. He could not get over the magnificence of the sites they saw, nor their remoteness: 'Vast theatres with cornfields running into the orchestra stalls, huge cities in folds of mountains overlooking mythological rivers, colonnaded Byzantine harbours at the end of small estuaries, as overgrown with jungle as Yucatan or Angkor . . .'[28]

Paddy managed to leave something behind in every place they stopped, and every evening began with a search for *mumlar* – the Turkish word for candles, the singular being *mum*. 'I've got the *mums*,' he would say, melting the ends and sticking them on to saucers in a taverna. 'Can't have dinner without candles.'[29] At some point on the coast road between Kuşadasi and Antalya, they stopped at a village and Paddy went for a walk. He came back very excited, having found some Greek-speaking Muslims who had been expelled from Crete during the forced exchange of populations in the 1920s.

Later that year, another distraction arrived in the shape of an apricot-coloured puppy – a present from Aymer Maxwell – with white paws and floppy ears. Paddy was enchanted by it and called it Troilus (Petruchio in *The Taming of the Shrew* speaks of 'My spaniel Troilus'). Having just picked up the dog he took it to the island of Spetses, where Diana Cooper had been lent a house. Over the next few days all Diana's female guests (including the author, aged seventeen) took it in turns to cuddle Troilus, and over the coming months Paddy wrote pages of affectionate description to his friends about the dog's beauty, friendliness, and sensitivity to music. 'I'm sorry going on so obsessively about him,' he wrote to Diana; 'I've never possessed a dog since I was ten, it's obviously gone to my head.'[30] Tragedy struck in June 1971 when, at the age of seven months, Troilus contracted distemper and had to be shot. Paddy never had a dog again.

He was also very involved with the Greek edition of *Mani*, which had been translated by a new friend, Tzannis Tzannetakis.* At the time of the 1967 coup, Tzannetakis had been a young submarine commander in the Royal Hellenic Navy. Realizing that any colonels who ordered tanks on to the streets of Athens could hardly be freedom-loving democrats, he had immediately resigned his commission. Two years later he was imprisoned, kept for months in solitary confinement, and finally sent into exile on the island of Kythera. While he was there, a friend sent him a copy of *Mani*.

It was an inspired choice. Tzannetakis was a Maniot himself, from Gytheion, and descended from the eighteenth-century Tzanni Bey, who was mounting attacks and raids against the Turks thirty years before the War of Independence. He was captivated by the book, and by the time he was released in 1971, he had translated it into Greek.

Since he had only had a very small English–Greek dictionary while doing the translation, Tzannetakis got in touch with Paddy and invited him to stay, so they could revise it together. Tzannetakis

---

* Tzannis Tzannetakis would serve as Minister of Tourism, Minister of Works, and was briefly prime minister in 1989.

was beginning a career in politics in the New Democracy Party, and had a house in Kifissia, on the northern outskirts of Athens. Paddy pored over the translation all day, and when his host came back from work, they would go over it again. Paddy wrote a new chapter for the Greek edition, on olives and olive trees, which does not appear in the English one. As he put it to Jock, 'it is too specifically designed for a Greek public to be a valuable addition to the English one. It was even written in parts in Greek, as an aid to the translator!'[31]

Jock was more concerned by the fact that Paddy was now having doubts about everything that he had written so far on his walk across Europe. 'It has dawned on me that, thanks to the compression of the first part – Germany and Austria – when I still thought I was writing a 3000 word article on the Pleasures of Walking – some of the most interesting, lively and amusing bits have been entirely left out . . .'[32] Paddy went through so many layers of manuscript and typescript, and so many drafts were chopped up, thrown away or reabsorbed that it is impossible to chart the long gestation of *A Time of Gifts*. But as he did so, he had learnt a great deal about how he wanted to write about his walk, and this was at his fingertips when he went back to the beginning.

Now in his fifties, the older Paddy brought the craft, broad learning and experience of time passing that he could not possibly have had at eighteen; yet he never loses touch with the overflowing joy and curiosity of his younger self. The balance was no easy feat to pull off, and he dramatizes the tension between the two personae in a passage about Cologne. The eighteen-year-old Paddy is 'A', and the older, unusually schoolmasterish Paddy is 'B':

B: What's all this about Carpaccio and the legend of St Ursula, and the 10,000 Virgins of Cologne? . . . You'd never heard of Carpaccio till you went to Venice, on the way back from Rumania in 1939. We're in 1933 now. You seem to forget I was there too.
A: I don't. It was you who told me about it.
B: Don't confuse the issue. Now, what's all this? 'Theophano, married to the Holy Roman Emperor . . . and grand-daughter of Constantine Porphyrogenitus' – oh dear, oh dear – 'one of the Byzantine Emperors of the Macedonian dynasty, was buried in

one of the old churches of Cologne, I can't remember which' – a
nice touch – 'in 991.' You didn't know anything about Byzantium
then!

A: That's your fault! I'd read some Gibbon and *The Station*. I do
remember seeing her tomb, though I admit I couldn't remember
her name till I looked it up just now. Or perhaps you did?

B: One of us must have. [PAUSE] Well it won't do. And there's another
thing . . . If you can't remember, don't apologize. Just forge ahead
until you do.

A: I'll try, Sir.

B: You needn't call me sir, it makes me feel my age.[33]

That September, they set off in different directions. Joan went to
Russia, Georgia and Bokhara with Graham, while Paddy joined an
expedition to Peru organized by Robin and Renée Fedden, whom
he had known in wartime Cairo. After the war Robin had joined
the National Trust, and had written several books of which perhaps
the best known was *Chantemesle*, an autobiographical sketch of his
childhood in France. In the course of their erratic marriage, he and
Renée shared a passion for climbing, and the intensity of life at high
altitude is described in Robin's book *The Enchanted Mountains*.

The group assembled by Robin for this trip to Peru was a mix
of experienced climbers and complete beginners – though the
climbing part would occupy only eleven days of a four-week trip.
The experienced ones were Robin and Renée; André Choremi, a
French lawyer and social anthropologist; and Carl Natar, who had
been the manager of Cartier's in London for thirty years. As a Swiss,
it was no surprise that Natar should be an expert climber and an
ex-skiing champion; but Paddy was delighted to hear that his mother
tongue was Romanche, one of the rarest of the Swiss languages. The
neophytes were Andrew Devonshire, who had serious doubts about
his ability to keep up once the climbing began, and Paddy. Even he
was a little daunted; but he had always trusted his physical strength,
despite being a heavy smoker.

The climbing began 'Somewhere above Moyoc-Moyoc in the
Salkantay-Huanay range, South-Central Peru'[34] – it was hard to be
more precise since the maps for this region were vague and

contradictory. Their gear had been shifted on to the backs of eight little ponies, one of which had a four-month-old foal trotting beside her. These ponies belonged to Antemio and Alejandro: cabinetmakers by trade, now turned into sherpas.

That first day, 5 August, they climbed 4,000 feet in seven hours. Paddy was more exhausted than he had ever been in his life, and at 13,000 feet they were now higher than Cuzco. It was not the season for bad weather; but snow, rain and wind kept everyone in their tents for the next few days, and the mountaineers – who had hoped to scale a peak or two – descended from the glacier feeling crestfallen, beaten by soft waist-high snow that hid every crevasse and ravine. It was bitterly cold. Paddy took charge of the Primus stove, which meant he was usually the first up in the mornings: it took an hour and a half for their kettle to come to the boil at that altitude.

The weather did not clear till the 11th, a day of brilliant clarity. The whole party roped up and, with ice-picks and crampons, they climbed across the glacier till they were standing on the col that formed the skyline from their camp. This was not a very challenging climb for Robin and Renée, but for Paddy and Andrew it was a triumph: 'after all our misgivings, we'd actually *crossed a glacier, roped up, shod with crampons and wielding ice-picks, 600 feet above the summit of Mont Blanc!*'[35]

The following day, Robin, Renée and Carl – having done their duty as instructors on the nursery slopes – climbed the three summits of Huanay unhampered by the beginners. Everyone else spent the day in their tents, where Paddy wrote to Joan and read Prescott's *Conquest of Peru*.

On the 13th they began to make their way down again, through a green world of ravines and waterfalls that opened into a high pasture cradled by mountains. Although Paddy and Andrew had not done as much climbing as the others, they felt the same regret as they made their descent, which was long and arduous. By now the little foal was utterly exhausted, and came to standstill. It was offered some lemon-flavoured glucose tablets, but refused them. So Antemio 'slipped his poncho under its belly, lifted it off the ground, slung it over his shoulder and trotted the remaining five miles with the little pony on his back . . .'[36]

Refreshed by the clear air of the Andes, Paddy went back to the start of his long walk across Europe. 'How on earth can I get hold of calendars for 1933 and 1934?' he asked Jock. 'It is for moons and when Sundays fell. I've got all the days of the months, but don't want to put my foot in it with "the blaze from the shops contended with the effulgence of the full moon", when it was Sunday with no moon at all . . .'[37]

Xan and Daphne Fielding came to stay at Kardamyli, while Paddy was 'back in the thick of snowy Bavaria in January 1934 and enjoying it . . . I read the two opening chapters of Departure – Holland – and some of Germany out loud to Xan and Daphne, and to my delight and surprise, their reaction was encouraging and enthusiastic. Morale has shot up.'[38] Xan was not in such high spirits. Compensation for the family house in Nice seemed as distant as ever while his brother-in-law, who was handling the case, was dying – which was likely to leave Xan saddled with enormous debts.

In the same letter, he also mentioned how worried he and Joan were about George Seferis, who was gravely ill in Athens. In fact he had died that very day, 20 September 1971. Despite the fact that demonstrations were forbidden by the junta, thousands of people followed his coffin through the streets, singing Mikis Theodorakis's setting of his famous Denunciation of the regime.

The Kreipe Operation had taken place almost thirty years before; yet it continued to define Paddy in the Greek imagination, and in early 1971 a Greek film called *Castle of the Immortals* appeared. Paddy thought it was going to be about the Cretan resistance, but it turned out to be largely focused on him. To Michael Stewart he described it as

> literally beyond belief . . . It was a wild fantasy for ten year olds, although the place was packed with a whiskery audience of riper years. Not only are generals abducted, but strong points assaulted and carried, huge petrol and ammunition dumps sent sky-high, armoured columns annihilated and the enemy mown down in scores . . . The General and I are the only characters called by their real names, and this the whole time. I come out of it as an intrepid, humourless Tarzan grasping a smoking Tommy-gun half-dead with metal fatigue, barking curt orders and gazing mysteriously into the *Ewigkeit* against

a background of explosions and sunsets. My sincere disavowals, when questioned about it, were taken for becoming modesty, so what the hell . . .[39]

The following year produced an even more extraordinary commemoration, when Nico Mastorakis, who presented a Greek version of *This Is Your Life*, decided to reunite the surviving members of the Kreipe Operation. Paddy, who was still trying to live down *Castle of the Immortals*, did not want to get involved. But when he heard that none of his Cretan friends would take part unless he did, and that General Kreipe himself had agreed to appear, he could hardly refuse.

The programme went out on 7 April 1972. 'I sat with Mastorakis to tell the tale,' wrote Paddy in a long letter to his mother, 'and the Cretans, as they were mentioned, came in one by one – terrific rejoicings and embraces.'[40] First to come on was Manoli Paterakis, then George Tyrakis who had come all the way from Johannesburg, where he was running a restaurant. Antoni Papaleonidas was next, and soon the set was crowded with grizzled Cretans in their Sunday best. The last figure to emerge, to gasps of surprise and a round of applause from the audience, was General Kreipe himself, looking remarkably unchanged from the photographs of him taken by Billy during the abduction. Paddy greeted him in German, and the General shook hands cordially with all his erstwhile abductors – he seemed particularly pleased to see Manoli again. The presenter, who spoke no German, asked Paddy to ask the General whether he harboured any bitterness against them. Paddy relayed this to the General as tactfully as he could, and the General gave a robust reply. 'If I had any bad feelings,' he said, 'I wouldn't be here, would I?' – '*Wunderbare Antwort!*' breathed Paddy with a sigh of relief.

After the programme, all the participants went off and had 'a huge banquet in a taverna. Lots of Cretan songs and dances, a few German songs sung by the General and me, after much wine had flowed.' A few journalists worked their way into the taverna towards the end, and one of them asked the General how he had been treated during his ordeal. The General replied, '*Ritterlich! Wie ein Ritter*' – chivalrously, like a knight. Paddy was deeply touched. 'I felt a halo beginning to form, and am not quite back to normal yet,' he confided to his mother. 'I stayed two more days,' he went on, 'and had nearly every meal with them. We liked and got on with each other, as we always did, extremely well.'[41]

As spring turned into summer, Paddy once again went walking with Robin and Renée Fedden, Carl Natar, Andrew Devonshire and Peter McCall, an old friend of Robin's who worked in the City. Robin's initial idea had been to climb in the Hakkiari mountains of Turkish Kurdistan, but the night before they were due to leave, permission was refused by the Turkish authorities. Instead, Robin decided that they would climb the Pindus mountains in northern Greece. Their first ascent was a twelve-hour endurance test, climbing almost vertically through woods clinging to the rock; but once this marathon was over, they were in the high meadows of Sarakatsani country. The men were still in their stiff capes, with steel-tipped crooks, but more of them now lived in shacks rather than their traditional wigwams. 'Thank God I saw Sarakatsans when they still *were* Sarakatsans!' Paddy wrote to Debo.[42] Andrew Devonshire recalled how, as the walk progressed, everyone began to dread the familiar sight of a solitary shepherd. Paddy would invariably hail the man and engage him in a long conversation, which left everyone else hanging about, kicking stones, for a good twenty minutes.

20

Shifts in Perspective

Paddy was uncharacteristically quiet and diligent for most of 1973, producing draft after draft of the early chapters of the book he still thought of as 'Parallax', although Jock was not happy with that title. He relied on cigarettes to keep the words flowing, and again in those moments when the flow dried up; but he had a persistent cough, and knew that the time had come to kick the habit. If one is used to high levels of nicotine to maintain concentration, giving up involves much more than suppressing a craving: it means relearning how to work.

In July Paddy told Diana that he had gone three months without a cigarette. 'It *was* a wrench! Considering I'd been smoking from eighty to a hundred a day for the last thirty years, end to end they would have formed a single monster cigarette, stretching all the way from Victoria Station to Brighton. Then came the death-grapple with weight . . .'[1]

One thing Paddy could not give up was what George Seferis had called his 'Penelope-izing', and indeed he spent as much time unpicking his work as he did putting it together. Jock told Paddy that in New York, Cass Canfield of Harper & Row was in despair about the lateness of the latest Leigh Fermor, but he would not, could not be rushed. 'If Mr Canfield is upset by the slowness of all this, we should tell him that sudden haste now can't possibly redeem my appalling unpunctuality in the past; but the extra delay will make it into a *much better book*, and that is the only thing that matters.'[2]

By June the following year Jock was thinking of dividing the book into two volumes, because he felt – as he had with the Greek book – that the author was sinking under the weight of too much material. Paddy was instinctively opposed to the idea, but came round to it. However long the book would take, he was pleased with the early chapters on Germany and Austria, and felt he had found his voice at last. In October he told Jock that 'Raymond Mortimer and Dadie Rylands have just been here for a fortnight, and extracted the . . . typescript from me. I was enormously binged-up by their reaction to it which really was enthusiastic, beyond any demands of guest-to-host civility, and I feel much spurred-on.'[3]

That summer Greece had finally rid itself of the junta, largely thanks to the regime's catastrophic bungling of the latest Cypriot crisis which had brought Greece and Turkey to the brink of war. The government, which had seemed to have such a stranglehold on the country, simply crumbled away. Constantine Karamanlis came back to Athens on 24 July 1974, amid scenes of wild rejoicing, to become prime minister once more.

Joan, on the other hand, was feeling anxious and downcast. She had already lost two of her closest friends, Maurice Bowra and George Seferis; and now, in the early winter of 1974, there seemed little doubt that Cyril Connolly was dying. Leaving Paddy in Greece, she flew to London where Cyril lay in hospital: emaciated, exhausted, but still retaining complete clarity of mind. Quite apart from the anguish of seeing him so close to death, Joan found herself playing the role of umpire between Connolly's devoted wife Deirdre on one side, and his equally devoted mistress Shelagh Levita on the other. 'Everything is really too much agony to write about and I'm going off my head trying to manage things with Deirdre and Sheila [sic],' she wrote to Paddy. 'He's getting weaker and weaker and it can't last long now, though he is still completely lucid at all times.'[4] He died at St Vincent's Hospital in Ladbroke Grove, on 26 November 1974.

In the 1970s, their axis of friends had shifted to Spain. Having seen the collapse of all his hopes in Nice, Xan could no longer face the prospect of living in France, and – to Paddy's regret – he and Daphne had split up. He had fallen in love with Magouche Phillips, and they were building a house in the hills near the cliff-hanging town of Ronda.

An hour to the south of Xan and Magouche was Janetta, who had married the designer Jaime Parladé in April 1971. They lived in the Torre de Tramores in Benahavis, a beautiful Andalusian house in the hills to the west of Marbella. Janetta too had been devoted to Cyril, and Joan found her company consoling after his death. They spent much of January in Spain, where Paddy was polishing and unpicking his work. There was a lunch with Gerald Brenan, expeditions to Trujillo and Madrid, and Paddy went riding with Robin Fedden in the hills around Ronda. Robin was planning a kayak journey down the Achelous river in western Greece, and Paddy was keen to join the party.

Although he had given up cigarettes, there was a persistent soreness in Paddy's mouth and throat. He hoped it was no more than an annoying infection; but in February 1975, it was diagnosed as cancer of the tongue. The kayaking trip was cancelled, but he was determined to finish the book before beginning what would probably be a long course of treatment. On 22 April, he was able to give Jock the good news: 'I finished the last chapter of Vol 1 last night.'

Unless one has seen a manuscript of Paddy's it is impossible to imagine what John Murray was faced with when taking delivery of a book by Leigh Fermor. But Paddy donated the autograph manuscript of *A Time of Gifts* to be sold at auction, in aid of English PEN, in 1988; and a perfect description of it exists in Sotheby's catalogue:

> Lot 171 . . . *c.*450 pages, the majority written on rectos only, some on both sides, the first chapter on lined foolscap sheets, some cartridge paper, others lined, heavily revised and corrected, revised passages frequently written on separate sheets and pasted and clipped over the original, corrections or elucidations often in red ink, foreign or difficult words printed in the margin, many sheets with encouraging notes to the typist, often stapled or stitched with coloured thread into gatherings, generally of ten pages, no date.[5]

A month later, in Kardamyli, Paddy received an unexpected call from Micky Akoumianakis in Crete, shouting for joy: Yorgo Tsangarakis, who had been wanting to avenge his uncle's death at Paddy's hands for so many years, had announced the end of the blood feud. This was all thanks to the efforts of George Psychoundakis, and now Yorgo proposed the traditional happy ending. He invited Paddy to baptize his nineteen-month-old daughter, and choose her name.

Joan had already left for England, so Paddy flew out alone from Athens to Heraklion, armed with all the traditional gifts: ribbon buttonholes, bags of sugared almonds, a gold inscribed cross, a complete baby outfit, and a candle two yards long adorned with a pink tulle bow. He was met at the airport by a crowd of his old brothers-in-arms, including Manoli Paterakis, Micky Akoumianakis, George Psychoundakis, and of course Yorgo Tsangarakis. After wild embraces he was whisked off to a banquet in the mountains, then back to Heraklion for the service. Paddy named the little girl Ioanna, in honour of both Yanni and Joan; and once the ceremony was over, 'we all gathered at a taverna where a table was laid for 300, sucking pigs roasting, wine flowing, lyras, lutes and violins a-playing . . . I had to lead the dances (plenty of foot-slapping!) everyone was very happy as it was the end of a miserable saga; all wartime Crete rejoiced.' As Yorgo and Paddy sat side by side with their arms round each other's shoulders, pretty drunk by this time, Yorgo said, '"Godbrother Mihali, if you've got any enemy, anyone you want to get rid of, just say the word . . . "'[6]

Joan's sister Diana Casey had lent the Leigh Fermors her flat in Ormonde Gate, so they could be near the Royal Marsden Hospital; a month after the christening, Paddy was due in London to begin the cancer treatment. At first he was encouraged by how relatively gentle the process seemed; but as the radiation bit deeper, it became considerably more painful. 'The last part of the treatment', he wrote to Jock in August, 'made me feel rather battered and gloomy: sleepy, headachy, and everything so raw and blistered one could neither eat nor talk – no supper and no song!'[7] Joan had by now gone back to Greece, leaving Paddy to recuperate with a succession of friends on what he called 'Mr Sponge's Reviving Tour'. Among those he stayed with were Ann Fleming at Sevenhampton, the painter Rory McEwen and his wife Romana in Scotland, and Pamela Egremont at Cockermouth Castle in Cumbria.

Supremely elegant, Pamela Egremont was also an intrepid traveller. She had accompanied Wilfred Thesiger in India, and as a nurse in Vietnam during the war, had helped to evacuate an orphanage under fire. Nonetheless, keeping up with Paddy was a challenge. Because he was under doctors' orders to talk as little as possible, they communicated on school slates, which were left about in different rooms for either party to find. His messages were so funny and entertaining that Pamela admitted, 'I laboured for hours over my responses.'[8]

To Paddy's disappointment, his doctors insisted on one more course of radiotherapy on the cancer before they would allow him to return to Greece. He was back home in December, elated and relieved, having been given the all-clear – and then he heard that Balasha was dying of breast cancer. Had she had it treated earlier, she might well have survived; but she had kept the symptoms to herself, refusing to see a doctor until it was too late to operate. It was a decade since Paddy had been to see her in Pucioasa and now he wanted to rush to her bedside, but Balasha forbade him to come: 'nothing would upset me more,' she told Pomme to write on her behalf.[9] Her letters to Paddy, and Joan to whom she wrote separately, reveal that she had made a decision to live in books and her memories and expected nothing more from life. She died in March 1976. Seven months later her niece, Ina Catargi, who had taken him to Pucioasa on the back of a motorcycle, was also dead – of lung cancer. Of that generous family which had been such a part of his life only Pomme Donici remained, now bereft of husband, sister and daughter. She arranged for Balasha and Constantin's remains to be buried in the Cantacuzene family crypt in the cemetery at Băleni, where she eventually joined them in 1983.

Clear of cancer and with his book now finished, Paddy decided to go to India that winter. Robin Fedden was planning a walk in the Himalayas in October and early November, and in January he, Joan and Graham were going to visit Ian Wigham in Malaya. Rather than return home in between, Paddy planned to base himself in Simla: a town which was part of his family's history and which his parents and sister knew intimately, though he had never been there. He also had an idea for a long article, along the lines of the one he had written about the Danube. He would follow the journey of Rudyard Kipling's *Kim* (a boy who is raised in one world, and claimed by another) from Lahore through Amballah, and on to the Grand Trunk Road.

Paddy hoped to work on the proofs of the new book in Simla, but he and Jock were still not agreed on the title. Then Paddy came across a poem by Louis MacNeice called 'Twelfth Night', one line of which reads 'For now the time of gifts is gone'. 'A marvellous solution to the title question has descended on me,' he wrote to Jock, 'viz. *A Time of Gifts*. You will see the relevance in the attached poem of Louis MacNeice's, my old pal. It gets over my growing feeling *against* the down-beat note of *A Winter Journey* [Jock's suggestion] and all your objections to 'Parallax' . . . I think it's just what we were searching for: indefinite, a poetical quotation, susceptible to many interpretations, and all of them lucky and charming ones.'[10]

The Himalayan party consisted of Robin and Renée Fedden, her friend Rosie Peto, Myles Hildyard, Carl Natar and Peter Lloyd, and Paddy. They flew north from Delhi, assembled a team of six Ladakhi porters and began their climb in mid-October. They were following the Beas river upstream, which marks the easternmost point of Alexander's conquests in 326 BC. Their goal was Malana: one of the most isolated villages in the world, which lay to the north-east of the Kulu valley, dominated by the great peaks of Chanderkhani and Deo Tibba.

The people of this village worship an ancient god called Jamlu, and believe that even the sight of a foreigner, let alone his touch, risks pollution and defilement. The travellers spent their first night outside the village, waiting for permission to enter, and this permission was granted only on condition that they touch nothing, not even the walls. They also had to remove their watches, boots and belts, for leather is an abomination to Jamlu. As they entered the village 'Men averted their gaze, children ran off as though ogres were coming down the street and the women at the spring . . . stood transfixed, and after a long disbelieving glance, turned away in a rictus of bewilderment and pain. Nearly all the village was out of bounds . . . and even along the permitted ways a flutter of anxious hands herded us innocuously into the middle.'

The holiest spot in the village was an open space, where a slab of stone lay embedded in the grass. One of the villagers, a kind man called Sangat, had made himself their guide and mentor. Under his direction the party made offerings, joined their hands in prayer and prostrated themselves before the stone. 'Our pious homage to Jamlu had made a good impression, it seemed; and here, bit by bit, linguistic curiosity began to break the ice.' Exchanging words was one of Paddy's favourite games, and as usual his enthusiasm flung bridges over the chasms of fear, shyness and suspicion that separated the strangers and the local people. Soon sherpas, foreigners and villagers were swapping words in Tibetan, the Hindi dialect of Kulu, English, and Kanishta, the language spoken by the Malanis. 'By now we were among friends.'[11]

Malana was every bit as strange and mysterious as the travellers had hoped, but the whole expedition was overshadowed by the fact that Robin was becoming increasingly ill. He was diagnosed with cancer on his return to England, and within three months he was dead. The article that Paddy wrote about his last journey appeared two years later as 'Paradox in the Himalayas', in the *London Magazine*. It was dedicated to Robin's memory, though neither Robin, nor Renée, nor any other member of the group was mentioned by name in the piece.

When the group separated, Paddy headed for Simla, perched in the foothills of the Himalayas. With its half-timbered, turreted villas and baronial hotels strung out across a sharp ridge and the rest of the town tumbling down steep slopes either side, Simla was very much as his mother had described it, and he saw it through her eyes. In the dress circle of the old Gaiety Theatre, he found photographs of his sister in 1930, playing in *The Constant Nymph*; and in an album called *Simla Past and Present*, there were several complimentary mentions of Æileen acting on the same stage. Æileen must have cut quite a dash in the Simla of the period; Vanessa remembered their mother's rickshaw as being 'purple with a grey fur rug, mounted on purple velvet and a purple silk parasol in a wickerwork attachment – the rickshaw drawn by four purple-liveried runners. No one else, as far as I can remember, had such a swish equipage . . .'[12]

From Simla he made his pilgrimage in the footsteps of Kim, and was particularly moved by the English cemetery in Amballah – though he never wrote the article. He joined Joan in Delhi and, after Christmas in Benares, he visited Calcutta, where his parents were married and where his father had spent most of his working life. He made his way 'rather timidly' to the Geological Survey's offices, where to his surprise 'They seem to worship Daddy's memory', as he told Vanessa. The Deputy Director, Dr S. V. P. Iyengar, described their father as 'the most imaginative, helpful and constructive [figure], he contributed more than anyone else, and all his prophecies and conclusions have been proved right.'[13] Both he and Vanessa had absorbed their mother's bitterness towards Lewis, and it was strange for them to find him both loved and admired.

A Time of Gifts was published in September 1977. The finished book, resplendent in a jacket designed by John Craxton, opens with a long introductory letter to Xan Fielding which puts the journey into context. Beginning with his idyllic infancy in Weedon, it charts his failures at school, his expulsion from King's, Canterbury, his unfitness for the army or indeed any other profession, and his descent into despondency before the moment of illumination when he decides to walk across Europe: 'my first independent act and, as it turned out – with a run of luck – the first sensible one'.[14]

There follow eleven chapters of writing that had been built up, layer upon layer, over the years. These levels of writing were so folded over one another, so detailed in some passages and so deliberately blurred in others, uproariously funny one minute and burrowing into the bowels of historical conjecture the next, that the book reads like a journey across a continent that exists somewhere between memory and imagination. Paddy had found a way of writing that could deploy a lifetime's reading and experience, while never losing sight of his ebullient, well-meaning and occasionally clumsy eighteen-year-old self. As one critic pointed out, this was a wonderful way of disarming his readers, who would then be willing to follow him into the wildest fantasies and digressions.[15] Paddy's highly-wrought style did not please everyone; but for those who enjoyed it, it was gloriously exhilarating. 'I began reading straight away,' wrote one young writer who picked up a used copy of *A Time of Gifts*, 'but after a few pages stopped and rubbed my eyes in disbelief. It couldn't be this good.'[16] The book ends with Paddy standing on a bridge over the Danube just short of Esztergom, poised between

Czechoslovakia on the northern bank and Hungary to the south. The last words read, TO BE CONTINUED.

The reviewers were enthusiastic, although they were determined not to get carried away. Jan Morris in the *Spectator*, while full of admiration in some respects, felt that the journey was 'less reportage than romantic impressionism'.[17] Dervla Murphy in the *Irish Times* also had doubts about his recollections of aesthetic experiences but, she continued, his writing was so enjoyable that 'it doesn't matter a damn whether he is describing it as he remembers it in 1934 or in 1964 or simply as he fancies it might have been in 1634.'[18] In the *Sunday Times*, Frederic Raphael noted the deliberation with which Paddy chose what he was going to see, and admired the generosity of his footnotes. 'One feels he could not cross Oxford Street in less than two volumes, but then what volumes they would be!'[19] In the *Observer* Philip Toynbee agreed. Sometimes he felt like shouting, '"Hold it, Paddy! Watch it now!" He is a writer whom it is easy to tease, but I find it much more natural to rejoice with him.'[20]

No one rejoiced more in Paddy's success than his mother Æileen, who was now living out her last days in a nursing home near Brighton. 'She was immensely proud of him,' recalled Mary Wood, a retired schoolteacher who had first met her when they were both living in the same residential hotel. 'He would come down and see her, always on a flying visit, never more than forty-eight hours, and take her to the theatre or a concert.'[21] In the last few years, Paddy had been good about coming to see her; but she had never come to Kardamyli, and he never brought Joan with him on his visits to Brighton. He had sent her an early copy of *A Time of Gifts*, and Vanessa reported that she was delighted with it. But she was now drifting in and out of consciousness, having suffered a series of small heart attacks. She died on 22 October, by which time Paddy had already left for Greece.

Vanessa thought that Æileen had mellowed in her last years, and become less capricious and quarrelsome. But Paddy's feelings for her had for a long time been closer to loyalty than love, and whatever he felt of loss or remorse, her death must have come as a relief. He remained resolutely true to her memory, to the fun of her company, her jokes and songs and her imagination.

★

The idea of putting up a plaque to all the Allied servicemen and Cretans who had died in the Cretan resistance had first been mooted after the war, but nothing had happened and the project gathered dust through the long years of the Cyprus crisis and the Junta. Now Paddy's friend Micky Akoumianakis, one of the prime movers, decided to try again and enlisted Paddy's help. In the spring of 1979, they went to visit the monastery of Arkadi, near Rethymno, as a possible site for the plaque.

The monks and bishop gave them an enthusiastic reception, and seemed very keen. But a few days later, Paddy heard that the police had visited the abbot and advised against the plaque being placed there, as they had been tipped off that the Communists would pull it down. Next they tried the monastery of Preveli. The monks were delighted, but on this occasion permission was denied by the Bishop of Spili. 'If Yerakari – last resort – fails, we will have to chuck it. I must say, I brood a lot . . .'[22] There had always been those who insisted that British wartime support for Crete had been a ruthlessly imperialist attempt to gain control of the island, and as the left gathered strength again in the wake of the Colonels' downfall, the rumours and accusations re-emerged.

Paddy was back in Kardamyli when, about two weeks later, someone planted a bomb under his car: it went off on the Sunday of Orthodox Easter, 22 April. The car had been parked at the top of the hill just off the road, and no one was in it; but it had been blown to bits, and a Communist party flyer was found in the wreckage.

The horror and indignation expressed by the Greek press touched Paddy deeply, as did the letter of support signed by many of his friends in Crete:

Your friends . . . cannot find words to express our anger at this most uncharacteristic act. Thirty-eight years ago you came to Crete to share with us the four darkest years of recent history . . . With your kindness and your dashing spirit you won for ever the hearts of your old brothers in arms and not the passage of time, nor any other factor can diminish in the slightest degree the love we all feel for you.[23]

An attack of a different sort appeared in the wartime memoirs of Manoli Bandouvas, published that spring. His pre-emptive guerrilla raid against the Germans in September 1943 had unleashed terrible reprisals in the Viannos area, in which over five hundred people were killed; and now, thirty years later, his ghosted memoirs were stirring up a hornet's nest of bad feeling. Paddy was upset that Bandouvas should have tried to put all the blame for the Viannos disaster on him, though he never contemplated legal action – unlike several others, who were clamouring for redress.* Paddy's Cretan friends urged him to defend himself, and them, against Bandouvas's slanders – which he did in the Cretan press; but apart from Bandouvas's supporters, few people took the book very seriously.

As for Paddy's own work, it had not been a very productive year. 'Please do not fall into the deadly sin of despair about my appalling slowness,' he wrote to Jock, 'though I can't blame you if you are assaulted by it now and then. I wish I knew what slows things up sometimes, then sometimes sends them shooting forwards at high speed. I'm going through one of the former at the moment, but believe that one of the latter is looming . . . I sometimes regret having settled so definitely in Greece, but don't tell anyone!'[24]

By this, Paddy meant that life in Greece had created time-consuming obligations that he had not foreseen when they were building Kardamyli. One example was the plaque. Another was George Psychoundakis, who was still struggling to make ends meet and was easily swayed by malicious neighbours who told him that he was surely being cheated by John Murray. Paddy spent a lot of time trying to persuade him otherwise, and pressing John Murray to send him any royalties owed promptly. Thanks to Paddy's lobbying, Psychoundakis's translation into Cretan of the *Iliad* and the *Odyssey* was at last being published, and in 1981 he was honoured by the Academy of Athens, who awarded him a prize of a hundred thousand drachmas.

Nico and Barbara Ghika were still at the heart of Paddy and Joan's

---

* Bandouvas's brothers were suing him, for saying that they had killed German prisoners taken in the Viannos raid against his express orders. Kapetan Petrakogeorgis was suing him for calling his father a sheep-rustling black-marketeer, and the family of Colonel Papadakis (briefly the self-styled leader of the Cretan resistance) were outraged by his insinuations that the Colonel's wife had had an affair with Jack Smith-Hughes.

Greek life, particularly since they had now bought a property on Corfu. In the 1970s, a few years after the destruction of their house in Hydra, Nico and Barbara and her son, Jacob Rothschild, bought an abandoned olive press at Kanonas at the northern end of the island. The olive presses were restored, wings added, and two airy courtyards framed views of woodland, coastal villages and the distant Albanian coast.

Yet Paddy's English friends sometimes wondered whether he regretted being so tied to Greece. Andrew Devonshire recalled dining alone with him one night. He seemed very downcast, and confided that he missed London, literary life and his friends more than he cared to admit. Ann Fleming had noticed this feeling in him too, though he was still invited to the great parties of the day – one of which was Diana Phipps' Opera Ball given at Buscot in the summer of 1978. Paddy stayed with Ann for the evening. On discovering he had forgotten the stockings that would complete his outfit as the eighteenth-century French poet André Chénier (subject of an opera by Giordano), he was obliged to borrow a pair of tights from a member of the staff at Sevenhampton. In a letter to Michael Astor, Ann wrote that she had 'tried to prevent Paddy over-tipping the parlour maid, "but look here darling, I went to the ball in her tights, and they're most frightfully laddered, swine that I am." Poor Paddy hates his visits here more and more, no circle of friends in London, and somehow out of things, although still the life and soul of . . .'[25] The circle of friends he did have was diminishing. Michael died of cancer in 1980, and Ann a year later.

In 1982 another book came out in Greece, attacking British involvement in the Cretan resistance. This time it was Xan rather than Paddy who was maligned,* but – as Joan reported to Vanessa – 'he [Paddy] is terribly upset about it.' It helped that they were now seeing a lot more of Xan: as Joan put it, they could 'share the rage and the unhappiness'.[26] At the same time, these new perspectives changed nothing in the villages where they were known and loved.

Feelings towards the heroes of the Cretan resistance seemed equally

---

* Xan was accused of killing a Cretan andarte, although he was in France at the time and his alleged victim was in prison.

warm in the wider Cretan diaspora. In May the following year, 1983, Paddy and Manoli Paterakis were guests of the Cretan Union of America. They were honoured by a tremendous round of lectures and dinners, toasts and ceremonies; but what he remembered best was seeing Manoli with a pensive expression, at the top of the Empire State building in New York. Paddy asked him what he was thinking. '"I'm just thinking that back in Crete it would be just about time to go up the folds and feed the ewes."'[27]

The Mani was no longer as remote as it had been, and even the Leigh Fermors' house was under threat. Their neighbour to the south owned the little ravine leading down to the pebbled beach that Joan could see from her window. Without warning he began to cut a road right through the ravine, to link the main road and the beach. 'A bulldozer with a 5m wide blade. Can you imagine the havoc and desecration?' Paddy wrote to Aymer Maxwell.[28] They were appalled by the prospect of what the road might bring: houses, tavernas, discos, cars, and all the terrors of Greece's burgeoning tourist industry, unshackled by any planning restrictions. Yet they need not have worried. One or two private houses were built overlooking the sea, but the threatened nightclub never progressed beyond a concrete shell.

Tourism was taking root in Kardamyli too. When Paddy and Joan had first travelled in the Mani in the early 1950s, hardly anyone had seen a foreigner. Now foreigners came in a seasonal influx, bringing a prosperity never seen before. Their neighbours to the north, the Ponireas family, built a hotel (partly modelled on the Leigh Fermor house) called the Kalamitsi, a few hundred yards through the olive groves. This proved very useful, for it was far more convenient to have their overflow of guests a five-minute walk away than to lodge them in the village, and in time Paddy came to rely on Nicos and Theano Ponireas for the use of the hotel's fax and photocopier. Then Lela, who had been steadily saving money, opened a taverna in the village overlooking the sea; while the children of Strati Mourzinos, the fisherman whom Paddy had made the last Emperor of Byzantium in *Mani*, set up a supermarket at the other end of Kardamyli.

From about the mid-1980s, Paddy and Joan began to think about what would happen to their house after they were gone. At first, they offered it to friends; but no one wanted the responsibility of so big a house in so remote a spot. The answer came from Paddy's Maniot friend, the politician Tzannis Tzannetakis, who suggested that they leave it to the Benaki Museum. It seemed an ideal solution. The Benaki would keep the house as it was, for use as a conference centre or a writers' retreat. Paddy was particularly taken with the idea, since he had depended so much in his youth on people giving him house-space.

He wrote for the *Spectator* and the *Times Literary Supplement*, and more and more people asked him to write obituaries, contributions and introductions to books. Incapable of saying no (and happy to postpone the real work in hand), he obliged – though friends often had to wait a long time for the work to appear. Among the most successful of his pieces written in the late seventies and early eighties are his portrait memoirs. There is Auberon Herbert (1979), in the uniform of the Carpathian Lancers, instructing the barman at Wilton's how to make the cocktail that he, as a Catholic, refused to call a Bloody Mary; the art historian Roger Hinks (1984), whose scholarly prejudices were expressed with barbed humour; and a happy afternoon at the Guards Depot, drawing heraldic helmets and mantling and shields with Sir Iain Moncreiffe of that Ilk (1986).[29]

Stephen Spender was sent an early copy of a book of Roger Hinks's Journals, to which Paddy had contributed the piece mentioned above. 'I do think you are extraordinarily evocative, vivid and moving about people you know,' wrote Spender, and admitted to being rather surprised by this talent, since Paddy was obviously not 'an empathizing introvert . . . And yet by some opposite process of seeing them from the outside – visually . . . [by] deducing all sorts of things about their inner workings . . . you can bring people to life quite wonderfully. I wish you would do a book of characters: Cyril Connolly, Roger Hinks, Ann Fleming, Greeks, Turks – all sorts of people you have known.'[30]

All this time, Paddy had been working on the second volume of his book on the great walk. One might imagine that the enthusiasm which had greeted the first volume would have made the second one easier to write. He had found his voice and his style, and a devoted readership was eagerly awaiting the next instalment. But this is to forget how many metamorphoses the first volume had undergone, whilst the very success of *A Time of Gifts* had created the one thing he could never cope with: a sense of expectation.

In March 1982, Paddy decided that he needed to refresh his memory about Hungary and Rumania. He flew to Budapest, hired a Volvo, and drove all over the Great Hungarian Plain. 'Most of my halts were at places I had stayed at of old, a series of minor Bridesheads really . . .'³¹ At Körösladány, where Paddy had stayed in the spring of 1934, he met Johann (Hansi) Meran, the son of the house: Hansi had been twelve and Paddy nineteen, at the time of his visit. Count Meran had spent ten years in Siberia after the war, and returned to marry a girl in his home village and to till the communally owned fields. 'With him, visiting from Vienna, was his sister Marcsi . . . "Do you [remember] that table," they said, pointing to a rickety Biedermeier affair. I said no. "You sat writing in a big green book all the morning. We used to peep round the library door" . . . It was all very moving.'³² He slipped over the wall of O'Kígyós, the house bristling with turrets and finials in whose courtyard he had played bicycle polo with the Wenckheims. It was now a school, but the gardens were well kept, and the old Slovak gardeners still remembered the Wenckheims with affection.

From Hungary he flew to Bucharest, hired another car and drove to Pucioasa, where Pomme was still teaching English and French. 'Everyone seems to like and respect her there very much; but she's utterly lonely and lives in books and music. We talked for countless hours on end, laughed a great deal. I took her lots of things, which she wore like a child on Christmas Day.' Again, he did not dare stay with her more than twenty-four hours for fear of attracting official attention. He flew to Transylvania, where he revisited several houses – 'nearly all loony bins now, with wild-eyed figures mopping and mowing among the tree-trunks . . .'³³ Among them were the Palladian house at Borosjenő, the house at Zám where he and Xenia had listened to the nightingales in her moonlit garden, and Elemér's thick-walled manor house at Guraszáda, now an experimental plant nursery. 'In all these places, the locals were thrilled to learn that I had been a friend of the old folks. [At Guraszáda they] said, "Have some *barack* made out of Mr Elemér's plums. Please give him our respects. We feel guilty living in a stolen house, but it's not our fault." '[34]

The oppressive hand of the state was far more stifling in Rumania than it had been in Hungary, as Paddy observed when he gave people lifts. 'I gave lifts to about 15 people a day,' he told Vanessa, 'as transport is very scarce. If there were two people together, and I said, How's everything here? (still fairly fluent!) they would say, "very well!" But if they were alone, they flew off the handle about the regime, the poverty, the cruelty and the tyranny with astonishing violence . . .'[35] He considered going back to Băleni, but thought better of it. He knew the house had been destroyed, and the changes would be too painful.

Paddy was very fit and healthy for a man in his late sixties. When at home he swam every day from his pebbled cove, and went for long walks into the hills. His now iron-grey hair had lost none of its thickness, and despite a prodigious intake of alcohol, his constitution and his memory were the envy of his contemporaries. There would be no more mountaineering; but there was still one physical challenge that he wanted to achieve while he still had strength and energy.

In October 1984, at the age of sixty-nine, he decided to swim the Hellespont: the winding channel that joins the Sea of Marmara to the Aegean, and separates Asia from Europe. Joan, Xan and Magouche had come to cheer him on, and they all booked into a hotel at Çanakkale on the Asian side, overlooking the narrowest point of the Dardanelles. Leander and Lord Byron had both started from ancient Sestos, a mile or so to the north on the European side, but a Turkish military zone had put that site out of bounds. A helpful guide called Sevki Suda found a boat with a boatman to accompany him, and Paddy dived into the Hellespont just north of Çanakkale on the morning of 13 October. With Joan and Sevki in the stern to keep an eye out for shipping and shout encouragement and directions, all went well at first. Lighthouses, minarets and forts on the opposite bank 'changed places with heartening speed, and the current didn't seem very strong'. It only made itself felt when he thought he was about halfway, and 'the water became ruffled, and much harder to push through. Joan and Sevki both kept urging "Ten minutes fast now and you'll be there!" but I could see by the speed of the changing scenery how fast the current was running.'

'So here I was,' he continued, 'floundering across the wake of the *Argo*, a mile north of Xerxes' and Alexander's bridges of boats, only a few leagues from Troy and about a mile south of the point where Leander, Lord Byron and Mr Ekenhead [who accompanied him] swam across; but too concerned with the current to think about them in more than fitful snatches . . .' He was advancing, he felt, with the gait of a Victorian clergyman and at one point, as the channel widened and the European shore slid alarmingly into the distance, he thought he might be swept out to sea.

Paddy had been in the water for over two hours and fifty-five minutes, and had swum about three miles before he felt pebbles under his feet on the European side, and Joan was shouting, 'You've done it!' He was hauled into the boat, utterly exhausted but jubilant. 'We headed full tilt for Çanakkale and Asia, where Xan and Magouche were waiting with champagne; they had followed our course with field-glasses from a balcony, like Zeus and Hera on Tenedos.'

He and Joan were too exhausted to eat on their return. They slept for hours, after which Paddy hobbled off for a Turkish bath and a massage to ease his aching and petrified limbs. They all celebrated that night with a feast and many bottles of wine; after which, feeling light as air, Paddy sat and smoked a narghile in a coffee shop. 'I knew I was only the last in a long line of copy-cats; but I felt sure I had beaten all records for slowness and length of immersion; certain, too, that this was a wreath no future swimmer was likely to snatch at. Serenity was complete.'[36]

That winter the writer Bruce Chatwin came out to Kardamyli, to finish a book he had been struggling with for seventeen years. Originally called *The Nomadic Alternative*, it would finally emerge in 1987 as *The Songlines* (Paddy reviewed the book in the *Spectator*). The Leigh Fermors had first met him in 1970, through Magouche Fielding, and Paddy described him as a 'Very very extraordinary, highly gifted, rare person'.[37] Like Paddy, Chatwin was an omnivorous reader and interested in everything; but there was an intensity about him, a need to find the essential and strip it free of everything else, that made him seem more restless and driven. Over the course of his life Bruce had many mentors, and Paddy was one of the last and most revered. He admired the breadth of his knowledge, and the agility of his mental cross-referencing that enabled him to link divergent subjects in aston- ishing ways. In literary style, however, they were aiming for opposite poles. While Paddy's prose was a rich and elaborate tapestry built up in layers, Chatwin was aiming for an austere simplicity that used as few words as possible to maximum effect.

After staying with Paddy and Joan for a few days in early December, Chatwin moved into the Kalamitsi Hotel. He stayed there for the next seven months. He often strode down the path to eat, drink and talk with the Leigh Fermors, and he and Paddy went for long walks in the hills. *Solvitur ambulando*, said Paddy – it is solved by walking. Bruce, who passionately believed that walking constituted the sovereign remedy for almost every mental travail, was delighted and immediately wrote it down in his Moleskine notebook.[38] Another bond was the anguish of writing. The construc- tion of *The Songlines* gave Chatwin a lot of trouble, and as a fellow perfectionist, Paddy could understand only too well the struggles he was having to pull it together.

They talked incessantly, feeding off each other's knowledge and curiosity, and after Bruce's death Paddy described the scale of his conversational range to his biographer: 'Abstruse art-forms and move- ments of thought, history, geology, anthropology and all their kindred sciences were absorbed like breathing . . . There was always John Donne or Rimbaud to think about, paleontological riddles to brood over, speculation on the influence of Simonides of Ceos on the memory techniques of counter-Reformation Jesuits in China, and the earliest whereabouts of Mankind.'[39] Four years later, in February 1989, Bruce's widow Elizabeth brought his ashes to Kardamyli. He had asked her to bury them near the tenth-century Byzantine chapel of St Nicholas in Chora, built on a promontory among the rocky hills that tumble down to the sea. Paddy, Joan and Elizabeth left his ashes under an olive tree, and made a libation of wine to the gods.

By July 1985, Paddy had almost finished the second volume of his great walk, *Between the Woods and the Water* – a title that echoed what Saki referred to as 'those mysterious regions between the Vienna Woods and the Black Sea'. A month later, he received the cover design by John Craxton.

Their partnership had begun decades before, when Craxton drew the illustrations for *A Time to Keep Silence*. Craxton's style sprang from the English romantic tradition of William Blake and Samuel Palmer. He had been in Greece almost as long as Paddy and had settled in Chania, where he drew its waterfront bars full of cats and sailors, as well as the goats and the stunted, thorny trees of the Cretan mountains. Paddy and Joan had collected several of his paintings, and Paddy had insisted on a Craxton jacket for every one of his books published by John Murray. But he did not like the image John produced for *Between the Woods and the Water*, and was disappointed with the figure on horseback that represented his younger self. Whereas he had been fair-haired on the cover of *A Time of Gifts*, now he had been given 'a cropped dark head like a match-stick's, narrow champagne-bottle shoulders, and arms like sausages . . .'[40] He felt that it should have been the cover to a book called '*Pony-trekking in Cumberland* by Wendy Brown',[41] but his complaints were overruled and the cover remained unchanged.

In October 1985, Paddy and Joan set off on a tour of German Baroque churches with Xan and Magouche, after which they followed the Danube as far as Vienna. Here the party split up, with Paddy carrying on to Hungary. He had with him a typescript of *Between the Woods and the Water*, parts of which he wanted to show to two friends in Budapest. The first was Elemér von Klobusitzky, his Transylvanian host in 1934. Called 'István' in *Between the Woods and the Water*, it was Elemér who had introduced Paddy to Xenia Csernovits. The second was Rudolf Fischer.

An Australian of Transylvanian origin, Fischer was language editor for the *New Hungarian Quarterly*, a broad-ranging journal dealing with history, politics and economics. Paddy had received a fan letter from him after the publication of *A Time of Gifts*, from which he gathered that Fischer's breadth of knowledge was matched by a meticulous attention to fact and detail. Fischer had pointed out several mistakes in *A Time of Gifts*, and Paddy was determined that its sequel should not be published without Fischer's eagle eye having scanned it first. In the Introduction to *Between the Woods and the Water*, he acknowledged a debt to Fischer that was 'beyond reckoning'.[42]

Having left Fischer with a copy of the typescript, Paddy went off to find his friend Elemér. Elemér now lived on the eastern side of Budapest, in a bleak concrete block of flats surrounded by rubbish and graffiti. Paddy had taken him out to lunch on his previous visit in 1982, and hoped to do the same now; but his friend did not answer the telephone, and at the block of flats he was told that Elemér had broken his leg and was in hospital. The following day, with the help of Fischer's wife Dagmar who drove him all over the city, Paddy tracked down Elemér to an old people's home in Pest, where he lay in a room with five other men.

Elemér seemed very tired, and despite explanations and frequent references to mutual friends he could not grasp who Paddy was. 'Greece!' he repeated, after Paddy said he had a house there. 'My old friend Patrick Leigh Fermor lives in Greece.' – 'Yes, Elemér, it's *me*, it's Paddy!' – 'No, no, you are much too young . . . But if you go to Greece tell him I'm here, I hope he remembers me.'[43] Paddy felt wrung out by the visit, and knew he would never see Elemér again. Oppressed by these sad thoughts he set off for Sofia in Bulgaria, where his mood sank even lower. In the half century since he had been there last, 'the cheery little Balkan capital [had changed into] the HQ of a dim and remote Soviet province . . . I had meant to explore the whole of Bulgaria in a hired car as a refresher for vol III, but caught a bus to Salonika instead.'[44]

Between the Woods and the Water came out in October 1986. The glittering gold and silver winter of *A Time of Gifts* has given way to early summer, and this book is suffused with blue skies, and sunlight seen through a canopy of leaves. It begins with a rout of parties and nightclubs with the fast set in Budapest, before Paddy sets off on horseback to cross the Great Hungarian Plain. Then comes the series of friendly castles and manor houses he stayed in that summer, with their eccentric owners – Count Lajos Wenckheim and his bustards, Count Józsi Wenckheim and the game of bicycle polo, and Count Jenö Teleki, the passionate entomologist whose Scottish nanny had left his English peppered with Scottish phrases.

Every house and its inhabitants are affectionately romanticized. As Graham Coster complained in the *Independent*, 'Every girl is pretty, every man dashing. Horses are strong, dogs eager', and the result is 'a quite ruthlessly pleasant journey'.[45] Paddy was aware that the people and places he described seem 'improbably perfect . . . but I can only set it down as it struck me.'[46]

The country-house life reaches its climax with the high summer idyll at Guraszáda with Elemér, and Paddy's affair with Xenia Csernovits, now disguised as 'Angéla'. To soothe the ache of parting, he leaves the road when walking south to lose himself for a while in the forested wilderness of the central Carpathians – one of the most hauntingly beautiful and timeless passages of descriptive prose he ever wrote. The book ends with a meditation on the little Turkish island of Ada Kaleh, now submerged under thousands of cubic metres of water, created by the huge dam across the Iron Gates of the Danube.

Most reviewers agreed that the new volume was a worthy successor to *A Time of Gifts*. John Ure in the *Times Literary Supplement* wrote that 'you never quite know what the next few pages will have in store, but you can be reasonably certain that you will be carried on by the sheer momentum of the whole unstructured performance.'[47] John Gross, reviewing the American edition, agreed, adding that the book should be read 'for its sumptuous colouring, the acuteness of his responses, the loving precision with which he conjures up people and places'.[48] Almost all remarked on how long they had had to wait for this second volume of the trilogy, and expressed the hope that the last volume would follow soon. The stakes for volume III had just been raised.

Between the Woods and the Water won the Thomas Cook Travel Book Award, and the International PEN/Time Life Silver Pen Award. In England at least, Paddy was now at the peak of his fame and success, recognized as one of the great prose stylists of his generation. And since he was now approaching the status of a national treasure, the television arts programme, the South Bank Show, commissioned a documentary film about him presented by Melvyn Bragg.

The programme took several days to make, using different locations in and around Kardamyli. Although Paddy and Joan had dreaded the intrusion and upheaval at first, they liked the crew and kept them well supplied with refreshments. (This was much appreciated: John Updike, a recent subject, had offered them nothing at all.) Melvyn Bragg came out for two days to do the interviews, which always made Paddy nervous. He was perfectly prepared to talk about his experiences, and some – like the Horace Ode shared with General Kreipe – he never tired of. But as soon as the interviewer sought to penetrate deeper and inquire into his writing, his natural tendency was to deflect the question. Bragg, however, was an experienced interviewer who had done his homework. He wanted to know how much Paddy relied on memory, how much on notes, and how much on his well-stocked imagination.

'I go back to the place that memory plays in your writing,' said Melvyn, 'because one is struck again and again by detail remembered from thirty or forty years before. However intensive your notes, you can't have covered everything . . .' – 'Yes,' said Paddy. This was not a helpful answer, so Bragg suggested that in the course of the long walk, books and solitude had built up the 'muscles' of his memory. Gratefully clutching at the straw, Paddy replied, 'Do you know, I've never thought of it – I think perhaps they might have – I hope so.' Then he described the deliberate act of remembering in terms of an old and dusty mosaic, that cannot be seen until water has been poured over it.

> It seems to me that thinking hard about a particular part of one's past is comparable to this pouring, flushing water onto a mosaic until everything is clear in the end. And then one can corroborate it with all sorts of other things, like a few old letters, you know, one's diaries come in handy, a few things scribbled down which one couldn't really put into place . . . [49]

Bragg also asked him how he was getting on with the third volume. Paddy admitted that the success of the last two was making him 'a bit nervy' about the third, but he was masking a deeper malaise. 'Sloth in writers', wrote Cyril Connolly in *Enemies of Promise*, 'is always a symptom of an acute inner conflict . . . Perfectionists are notoriously lazy and all true artistic indolence is deeply neurotic; a pain not a pleasure.'[50]

For reasons that Paddy rarely talked about and seldom confronted, he could not seem to lift volume III off the ground. Perhaps part of the trouble was that most of the final third of the 'Great Trudge' had already been written. 'Parallax', which Jock had renamed 'A Youthful Journey' (1963–4), stopped just short of Constantinople. He also had his original diary (1934–5), which preserved in note form his doings in the city and included the account he had written at the time of his journey to Mount Athos. He wanted to end the book with the Venizelist revolution and the gallop over the Orliako bridge, which had already appeared in *Roumeli* (1966). All three elements were very different in tone, and finding an overarching voice that would pull them together seemed an almost impossible challenge. Moreover, there was another thought; one so dark and bleak that it could scarcely be put into words, except perhaps to Joan. The whole subject was beginning to feel stale, barren, written out, and he feared he no longer had the strength to bring it back to life.

Paddy had been able to wriggle out of writing any more books about Greece after *Roumeli*, but *Between the Woods and the Water* ends with the implacable words, TO BE CONCLUDED. There was no escape.

21

'For now the time of gifts is gone'

ı

A few months after the filming of the South Bank Show, Paddy thought that the logjam he was wrestling with on volume III might be eased by another visit to Rumania and Bulgaria. He wanted to do the Rumanian part of the trip alone, and would then join Joan and Janetta Parladé in Sofia.

Paddy was already well acquainted with the destructiveness of East European Communism. On his previous trips to Transylvania he had seen the roads going nowhere, the hunger and waste brought about by collectivization, and what Dervla Murphy described as the 'ugly, impoverished, dispirited villages . . . their sturdy dwellings replaced by dreary rows of jerry-built farm-workers' blocks'.[1] But in spite of these sad transformations, Paddy's last two visits had reaffirmed his memories and inspired the writing of *Between the Woods and the Water*.

This time, something went very wrong. When Paddy arrived in Sofia, Joan and Janetta were dismayed to see how downcast he looked, with scarcely a word about where he had been or what he had done. As they set off in their hired car to explore Bulgaria, things did not improve. Apart from a fleeting visit to Sofia in 1985, Paddy had not travelled in Bulgaria since before the war; he was 'utterly crushed' by what he saw, so Janetta reported. Rudolf Fischer pointed out that the changes in Bulgaria were very similar to those he had seen in Rumania, yet according to Janetta, he seemed dismayed and disoriented. 'He kept saying "Just around the next corner we'll see such and such", and it never appeared. Most of the best things he remembered were Turkish, but all the Turkish buildings and every vestige of Turkish culture had been demolished.' At one point they came to a place which he said he knew would be untouched – 'and there were four hideous tower blocks in the middle of a wilderness: one could not imagine why they had been built.' Farming was still largely unmechanized, and Paddy was comforted by the sight of so many horses and carts, and people out in the fields with scythes. Joan teased him for being a Rip Van Winkle: 'she said it was as if someone had come to England still expecting to find people in smocks and gaiters, sucking on straws.' Sooner or later, they hoped, something would come along to jog a memory or evoke an image, but the drab concrete horror of it all seemed to do the opposite. 'As if', said Janetta, 'his own memories were being eradicated as we watched . . . The whole thing had been a terrible mistake.'[2]

The opportunity to visit Rumania again came in February 1990, when the *Daily Telegraph* commissioned him to write about the new, post-Ceauşescu republic. The December Revolution had started in Timişoara, when thousands of demonstrators surged on to the streets in the teeth of the Rumanian security forces. The uprising spread to Bucharest, and on Christmas Day 1989, after an abortive attempt to escape by helicopter, the Ceauşescus were sentenced by a hastily convened tribunal, put up against a wall and shot. Paddy arrived on 22 February, to be met by Alec Russell, the *Telegraph*'s correspondent in Bucharest, and Clare Arron, the photographer who was to accompany him. It was only six weeks since the fall of the most brutal regime in Eastern Europe, and with the future so uncertain and the present in a state of flux, Russell described it as a time 'when every moment was spent in the present, not the past'.[3] Russell was struck by what a good listener Paddy was, open to every idea and insight while diffident about putting forward any of his own. Yet Alexis 'Bishi' Catargi, an old Bucharesti friend of Paddy's, remarked a few weeks later that Paddy had seemed very sad and depressed at this time.

Leaving Russell in Bucharest, Paddy and Clare Arron hired a car and began driving around the country. Petrol, food and places to stay were all hard to find, but Paddy had come prepared. He had several bottles of whisky in his suitcase which he decanted into a hip flask kept in his coat pocket, and bars of chocolate for the children. But since huge stale loaves of bread were often all there was to buy in the shops, they ate most of the chocolate with the bread.

They visited Timişoara, and saw Cathedral Square with its forest of crosses and candles. In Cluj he had a long conversation with Doina Cornea, who had stood up to the regime and suffered for it at the hands of the Securitate: 'Her interviews with the public prosecutor', wrote Paddy, 'must have resembled Cauchon's with St Joan.'[4]

As they entered Moldavia, Clare lost control of the car on the icy road and it slewed into a tree. 'Now if I had been driving,' said Paddy reassuringly, 'we'd have done that long ago.'[5] For a while they thought they might have to spend the night in the freezing car, but they were rescued by a teacher of mathematics who took them to Suceava, arranged for the car to be mended, and gave them breakfast next morning. That night they went to a concert, given by Moldavian musicians from north Bukovina, which had been annexed by the Soviet Union in 1944. This was the first time they had been able to cross the frontier, and the audience and musicians wept as they sang their traditional songs together. Paddy knew a good many of the songs as well, and wept too. 'At moments like these,' he wrote later, 'it is hard not to feel that things will get better.'[6]

Among the visitors to Kardamyli that summer was Antony Beevor, who was researching a book on the Battle of Crete and the campaign of resistance that followed. Its publication was scheduled to coincide with the fiftieth anniversary of the battle, in May 1991. Because it was the first to give an overview of the Cretan resistance, both Paddy and Xan went through the proofs with considerable care. And though Joan and Xan both urged him not to over-correct, Paddy could not resist altering any passage that might cast the Cretans in an unfavourable light. Coming across one grisly detail he wrote in the margin, 'Oh dear . . . I *wish* this bit of dirty linen could remain in the basket . . .'[7]*

It was not until two years later that Paddy was at last given a

---

* In a chapter dealing with the aftermath of the German occupation, Antony Beevor described the fate of a Cretan traitor captured by andartes. The man begged for permission to commit suicide. But the andartes 'broke his legs with heavy stones some way from the edge of a cliff so he had to crawl the rest of the way and push himself over'. See Antony Beevor, *Crete: The Battle and the Resistance* (John Murray, 1991), p.336.

glimpse into the German view of their occupation of Crete, and the Kreipe Operation. Billy Moss's daughter Gabriella Bullock was going through some old papers of her father's when she came across a letter in German, dated 27 September 1950. It had been written by a Dr Ludwig Beutin, who had just read *Ill Met by Moonlight*. He pointed out such details as Billy's giveaway puttees, the General's impatience with roadblocks, and his unpopularity – 'many units were jokingly accused of having abducted the General themselves . . . and many a raki was drunk to your health.' Paddy was fascinated by this view from the other side, and bitterly disappointed that he had not known about it forty years earlier. With Dr Beutin's help and contacts, so much more could have been learnt about the last days of the occupation; but Beutin had died in 1956, and now it was too late.

'Paddy is very well,' Joan wrote to Janetta in early 1991, 'tremendously busy with everything except his book. I daren't mention it but I fear he's badly stuck still. It's sad and worrying . . .'[8] There was one glorious moment, when it looked as if the block might have burst. Paddy was working feverishly in his study at all hours of the day and night, and finally emerged clutching a sheaf of paper. 'I knew it could be done!' he told Joan, and just as she was about to congratulate him he added: 'I *knew* P. G. Wodehouse would translate into Greek!'[9] He had just translated 'The Great Sermon Handicap' from *The Inimitable Jeeves*.

Every year now seemed to bring the death of a friend, though 1991 seemed particularly hard. Graham Eyres Monsell was developing Alzheimer's, which plunged Joan into despair when she heard the news. At the same time, Xan Fielding was dying of cancer. He was strong enough to make one more visit to Crete, in time for the fiftieth anniversary of the German invasion, in May 1991. This anniversary was particularly significant, for it would be the first time that both Allied and Axis veterans had attended and commemorated their dead together. On the night before the main service of remembrance in Heraklion, the Greek prime minister Konstantinos Mitsotakis (a Cretan who had served in the resistance, and been imprisoned by the Germans) gave a dinner near Chania, at which the German Chancellor Helmut Kohl was the guest of honour. At one point

Mitsotakis, who was sitting opposite Kohl at one of two long tables, told the Chancellor that the man sitting immediately behind him was Patrick Leigh Fermor, the kidnapper of General Kreipe. The affable Kohl immediately turned round to greet him. Paddy, taken by surprise, exclaimed '*Ah! Herr Reichskanzler!*' Germany had not been a Reich since the fall of Hitler; but the *Bundeskanzler* roared with laughter, and gave Paddy a hearty slap on the back.[10]

After the public ceremonies were over, Paddy and Joan, Xan and Magouche went to visit their friends in the mountains of western Crete. Xan had not been back for many years, and seemed, according to Paddy, 'tremendously fit and well – apart from all hair having vanished – and it was a glorious success'.[11] Yet Xan knew he would not be coming back. He died in Paris on 19 August, and some of his ashes were scattered in the White Mountains. Paddy and Xan had met at the most intense and dangerous moment in their lives, and the bond made in the caves of western Crete had given their friendship an extraordinary complicity. Although they had spent most of the intervening decades in different countries, they had lived their lives in parallel, never losing sight of each other.

In July, Paddy was awarded an honorary doctorate by the University of Kent, the investiture taking place in Canterbury Cathedral. He revelled in the scarlet robes and black Holbein hat he was given to wear for the occasion, and basked in the eulogy of his achievements – 'I must get a copy to read when feeling depressed,' he wrote to Debo.[12] He was also offered an even greater honour. George Jellicoe had spearheaded a campaign to award him a knighthood, and Paddy was asked whether he would be willing to accept the title of Knight Bachelor for his services to Anglo-Greek relations. With many misgivings and considerable regret, he declined. Joan had always scoffed at titles, and he knew how much she would loathe being addressed as Lady Fermor.

The following month saw the publication of *Three Letters from the Andes*, a slim volume consisting of the letters he had written to Joan on the journey to Peru in 1978 with Robin Fedden. Jock Murray hoped that the act of seeing another book – albeit a short one – through to publication might inspire him to take up volume III again, but it failed to have the desired effect. *Three Letters* was greeted with a polite round of applause, but it was not the book his public had been waiting for.

In interviews, Paddy always declared his firm intention to apply himself to finishing volume III just as soon as he could clear his desk. But since he accepted every journalistic commission and every request to write an introduction or an obituary, the task was forever postponed for more pressing commitments. 'Paddy is 77 today,' wrote Joan to Michael Stewart on 11 February the following year, 'but, unlike me, has no intimations of mortality and still thinks he is going to write at least three more books,* each taking, I suppose, about ten years.'[13]

The following summer, Jock Murray died. Paddy gave the address at his memorial service, knowing he had lost not only the most loyal and painstaking publisher any author could have wished for, but also his literary midwife. Jock had coaxed every book out of him, using a combination of encouragement, cajoling, threats, and even sleight of hand. Paddy was left with a bitter regret that he had failed to present his old friend with the promised third volume, and with Jock's death, the book seemed to sink still deeper into the shadows.

When Graham Eyres Monsell died in November 1993, he left Joan the bulk of his estate, and the Mill House at Dumbleton. All would eventually be returned to Graham and Joan's nieces and nephews; but for the rest of their lives Paddy and Joan had a house in England, with a wonderful cook called Rita Walker to look after them. The rooms at Dumbleton were large and airy, with huge windows that looked out on to the garden and the Malvern hills. Over the years Graham had built up a magnificent music library, and collected a great many books and contemporary paintings, particularly by Robin Ironside. Joan undertook basic repairs and some modernization and admitted that the rooms needed cheering up, but then found she could not bear to change anything.

Two years later, when Colin Thubron came to stay at Kardamyli, Joan confided to him that she never asked about volume III any more, 'it makes him so miserable.'[14] Colin and Paddy went for a long swim together, in the course of which Paddy admitted how wretched he felt about not being able to complete the book. He was so

---

* These being volume III, a book on Crete and another on Rumania.

desperate that he had even consulted a psychiatrist, although he did not think the consultation had done much good.

He fretted too about Joan's health. Her eyes had always been very sensitive, and now she had to have a patch over one eye to read. She would lie full length on a sofa in the evenings, reading under the lamp, with at least two cats purring beside her. She was also beginning to have trouble with her balance, and he begged her to be careful as she crossed the stone floors.

After Lela had left to devote herself to her taverna in the village, Paddy and Joan found another couple with whom things had run smoothly for several years. The woman was a good cook, and her husband tended the garden. But then, almost from one moment to the next, the woman seemed to undergo a personality change – brought on, it was said, by the shock of hearing that her son was going to become a monk on Mount Athos.

After the couple's departure, it proved difficult for Joan to find help. Drawing from a pool of part-timers, she managed; but the one who grew into being a proper housekeeper was Elpida Beloyannis. Elpida's grandmother, Eleftheria Beloyannis, had run the little inn in Kardamyli when Paddy and Joan had first arrived in the 1960s, and her father had been the mayor and a friend of Paddy's. Elpida had two young children, and little experience of cooking. But she learnt quickly, absorbed the principles of good cookery from Joan, and taught herself the rest from Joan's English recipe books.

Janetta and Jaime seldom came to Kardamyli, although Paddy and Joan often went to see them in Spain; and with Nico and Barbara dead (Nico had died in September 1994), Magouche Fielding was almost the last of the old friends who came out regularly to Kardamyli. The names of new, younger friends began to appear in the guestbook: Joachim Voigt, originally a friend of Graham's, with whom they talked about translation and music; the poet Hamish Robinson, with whom the conversation was often on French literature; William Blacker, with whom Paddy talked endlessly about Rumania; and Olivia Stewart, then a film producer, who was the younger daughter of their friends Michael and Damaris. Olivia was particularly close to Joan, and was at Kardamyli on the morning of 4 June 2003, which began like many another.

'I went to see [Joan] just as she was finishing breakfast,' wrote Paddy to Lyndall, 'with nine kittens scattered about the bed . . . occasionally bumping into the pieces on the chessboard where she was grappling with a problem, occsionally pushing them off. We made plans for lunch, with Olivia . . .' Paddy retired to his studio; but an hour later, 'Elpida dashed in in floods saying *Kyria Ioanna* . . . so I ran across and there was Joan dead on the bed. She had fallen in the bathroom, banged her head and death was immediate. The following days were a sort of trance of shock and disbelief.'

Olivia and Paddy accompanied Joan's body back to England, where she was buried at Dumbleton on 12 June next to Graham. It was only when Paddy returned to Kardamyli in early September that he began to absorb the shock of his loss. He would spend hours lying on her bed, gazing at the white arch that framed the window and the olive tree beyond, and it took a long time to get used to the loneliness. 'I constantly find myself saying "I must write – or tell – that to Joan"; then suddenly remember that one can't, and nothing seems to have any point. Then I remember all those happy years and what undeserved luck one had had, and the tears shift a bit . . .'[15]

A collection of Paddy's writing appeared towards the end of this sad year. Paddy dedicated it to Joan, and called it *Words of Mercury*, from the last lines of *Love's Labour's Lost*: 'The words of Mercury are harsh after the songs of Apollo.'

Joan was irreplaceable, but Paddy's friends now stepped in to ease his life. Although she lived in Rome, Olivia was often at Kardamyli: keeping Paddy company, maintaining the household, and 'struggling with the constant correction of various articles, introductions and obituaries that he had persuaded me to put on computer for him'.[16] Magouche had him to stay while he was in London, as did his doctor, Christian Carritt. She had looked after both Paddy and Joan for years, and devoted days to chauffeuring him round the various specialists whom she had arranged for him to see. In later years Joachim Voigt, or Olivia, or Hamish Robinson would accompany him on the long flights between Athens and London.

Paddy was once again offered a knighthood, and this time he did not turn it down. When his name appeared in the 2004 New Year Honours list, Mr Mark Edwards of Whitney, Oxon., wrote to the *Daily Telegraph* to say that while he had no objection in principle to Paddy's knighthood, it should have been made conditional on his 'completing the masterpiece he began with *A Time of Gifts* and *Between the Woods and the Water*'.[17] Paddy was knighted on 11 February, his eighty-ninth birthday, and was particularly touched that the Queen wished him many happy returns.

In May 2007, at the age of ninety-two, Paddy embarked on what was to be his last expedition, to western Macedonia and Albania. The party consisted of Pamela Egremont, Paddy, Patrick Fairweather who had been Director of the Butrint Foundation for eight years, and his wife Maria. They all noticed how the long drives tired Paddy. It took real determination for him to pull himself together and walk round the tomb of Philip of Macedon at Vergina, or round the recently restored acropolis of Butrint, or clamber into a boat to see Ali Pasha's fort close by. But on every occasion he made the effort, and it never failed to ignite his curiosity and enthusiasm. At Metsovo, 'he engaged the waiter in the taverna in Vlach. The waiter seemed a bit tongue-tied – it may have been shyness or that Paddy's Vlach was rusty . . .'[18] And in another taverna, a middle-aged Greek came over to ask if he really was *the* Patrick Leigh Fermor, whom he had admired all his life and who had done so much for Greece.

In fact Paddy was still doing a lot for many people, whether it was sending money to old friends who were ill or hard-up, or encouraging young writers. When Imogen Grundon wrote a biography of John Pendlebury, who had set up the resistance networks in Crete just before the invasion and died in the battle for Heraklion, Paddy much admired the book and agreed to write a foreword. It was a long time coming but since the subject was not widely known, Paddy's support attracted attention. Another he encouraged was William Blacker, urging him to write a book about his experiences of living in the depths of rural Rumania in the early 1990s. When *Along the Enchanted Way* was finished, Paddy gave it passionate, whole-hearted praise in the *Sunday Telegraph*. 'The review definitely had a huge impact,' wrote Blacker. 'It seems that many people saw the review, and all sorts of wonderful things sprang from it.'[19]

The idea for his last book, *In Tearing Haste*, came as Debo Devonshire was setting up the Mitford Archive to house the family's correspondence. Since Andrew's death in May 2004, a month before Joan's, she had moved out of Chatsworth and into the nearby village of Edensor, where Paddy spent New Year 2007 with his old friends Robert Kee and Sir Nicholas Henderson. Nico Henderson noted that he seemed 'very down in the dumps', though he rallied considerably when Debo brought out her old letters and the party began reading them. Henderson suggested that her correspondence with Paddy might be turned into a book, especially since it would give Paddy a cheerful task to work on.[20]

Debo asked Charlotte Mosley, who had edited the letters of the Mitford sisters, to edit the correspondence; and in July 2007, she went out to Kardamyli with the typescript. Charlotte wrote to Debo after the visit, to say that 'I think the book has given him a new lease of life – he feels appreciated, and it takes his mind off Vol III which is clearly never going to appear. He reads out passages from his own letters (& sometimes yours) and roars with laughter . . .'[21] When the book came out in 2008, the reviews were highly appreciative of this cheerful correspondence, and the world of lost glamour it evoked. The *Observer* went so far as to say that 'the result is surely one of the great twentieth-century correspondences.'[22] Paddy enjoyed the parties and the events surrounding publication, at which he and Debo read aloud from the book, but above all he enjoyed the book itself. He would ring up Debo and say, 'Do you know, I'm reading our book and it's *jolly, jolly* good.'[23]

Paddy had been noticing for some time that his voice was very croaky. By late March 2011, it had become almost inaudible and he was having trouble breathing. He was referred to the Genimastas Hospital in Athens where, on 4 May, a large cancerous tumour was removed from his throat. Olivia flew out from Rome, and for the eight days he was in hospital, Elpida barely left his room.

The doctors agreed with his decision to refuse any treatment for the cancer, which would have been an appalling ordeal for a man of ninety-six. When he returned to Kardamyli the doctors thought he still had a few months to live. In fact it was only weeks, but they were good ones. After his spell in hospital, he was delighted to be back in the beauty of the house he and Joan had created. Philippa Jellicoe drove him out to visit the surrounding villages, and when William Blacker arrived, he rediscovered the energy to tackle volume III – Olivia wrote that 'he rang me two nights before he went back into hospital, full of excitement and optimism.'[24]

But the tumour had grown back with aggressive speed. On 1 June he was once more in the Genimastas, where the surgeon performed a tracheotomy to ease his breathing. From then on he could no longer talk, and there was little else to be done. Now his only thought was to get back to England in order to see Debo and Magouche again. On 9 June, he left Greece for the last time. With Olivia coordinating the efforts of several friends, and Elpida who never left him, the flight and the long drive back to Dumbleton were made as smooth as possible. Rita lit a fire in the sitting room, and he was happy to be home at last; but the journey had taken all his remaining strength. Calm and fully conscious, he died the following morning.

At one point Olivia had asked him to think about the service he would like, and he decided that he would like the same readings that he had chosen for Joan. One was from the apocryphal Book of James, describing a moment when time stands still; another, a mysteriously beautiful and arcane passage from Sir Thomas Browne's *The Garden of Cyrus*: 'But the Quincunx of Heaven runs low,' it begins, 'and 'tis time to close the five ports of knowledge.'

Paddy had endured his last illness and the inevitable shrinking of his world with a kind of bewildered sadness. 'It's very odd,' he said to one friend at Kardamyli after the operation to remove the tumour. 'My life has suddenly gone out of kilter, familiar and yet utterly strange, like before and after the war.'[25] He never talked about death, though of course he thought about it. In a short biography of Proust which was found in his room in Kardamyli, he had written a message in the middle of the night, at a moment when he felt the end was close. Yet whatever sorrow he felt at leaving this world, what he wanted to express was a sense of profound gratitude.

'Love to all and kindness to all friends,' he wrote, 'and thank you all for a life of great happiness.'[26]

A Note on the Green Diary and 'A Youthful Journey'

The various written versions of Paddy's great walk are going to keep graduate students busy for decades, and I do not want to spoil their fun. Yet two documents keep cropping up in this book, and it might help to have some idea of what they are. The first is Paddy's only surviving diary, which he called the Green Diary; the second a typescript of his trans-European odyssey called 'A Youthful Journey', though Paddy preferred the title 'Parallax' – see p.325. The page numbers referring to the Diary and 'A Youthful Journey' come from the typescripts, not the originals.

In *A Time of Gifts*, Paddy describes how his first diary was stolen, along with his rucksack, in Munich in January 1934. 'I started a fresh lot immediately,' he tells us in 'A Youthful Journey', 'in thick German stiff-covered notebooks and drawing pads, and kept them up, at least the notebooks, until the end of the journey . . . The sketches, rightly, as they were never much good, became scarcer and died out.' But conflicting evidence comes from the Green Diary itself. Paddy notes on 11 September that a friend is going to Budapest, 'where she promised to collect my *second* volume of diary and post it to Mummy when she arrived in England'. To complicate things further, Paddy also states elsewhere that he had left all the surviving notebooks and papers in Rumania at the beginning of the war. The only thing one can say with any certainty is that the Green Diary is the only original document that still exists.

Paddy bought this thick green notebook with lined pages in Bratislava, in March 1934. The first long entry is about his visit to Baron Philip Schey at Kövecses in Slovakia. After Esztergom he wrote nothing for four months, as he progressed through the schlosses and country houses of eastern Hungary and Transylvania. The entries pick up again as he enters Bulgaria, and in Constantinople he writes only in note form. He starts writing properly again in Mount Athos, and continues his Athonite journey on foolscap pages folded into the back of the book.

Although there are moments of reflection, the prevailing tone is brisk, immediate and uncontemplative. In Sofia, he plays cricket with the British Consul. In Bucharest he lists the names of almost everyone he meets, and is dazzled by the beauty and sophistication of the women. He is often snobbish, sometimes patronizing – but he is only nineteen, and when he gives himself the time to write things up in full, it is evident that this is the diary of an acute observer. The back of the notebook is almost more revealing than the entries. Here are pages of vocabulary and phrases in Hungarian, Rumanian, Bulgarian and Greek; a recipe for Turkish coffee; sketches of musical instruments, peasant costumes, an Orthodox church, Bulgarian songs and the occasional portrait. He has copied out the Cyrillic, Greek and Arabic alphabets, plus a translation of the Call to Prayer; and, at the very back, are the names and addresses of almost everyone he met or stayed with.

When Paddy left Rumania to join up in September 1939, he left the Green Diary with Balasha Cantacuzene, with whom he had been living for the past four and a half years. Despite the upheavals of the war and exile from her home under the Communists, Balasha held on to the book; and when he came to visit her in Rumania in 1965, she gave it back to him.

'A Youthful Journey' is an incomplete typescript of some sixty thousand words. From the Hook of Holland to Orşova the writing is very compressed, but the last third of his walk, from Orşova to the Black Sea coast, is covered in detail. It is this unpublished document that will form the bulk of the posthumous conclusion of Paddy's great walk, begun with *A Time of Gifts* and *Between the Woods and the Water*. It was written on the island of Euboea in 1963, at which point Paddy had not yet been reunited with the Green Diary. The full story of how 'A Youthful Journey' was commissioned as an article, and almost grew into a book, can be found in Chapter 18.

Paddy never tried to reconcile 'A Youthful Journey' with the

Green Diary – and because they cover the same period, it is interesting to compare the two side by side. At the heart of 'A Youthful Journey' is his time in Bulgaria, where he became friends with two young people. The first was a beautiful student of French he calls Nadejda, and the other – also a student – was called Georgi Gatschev: a wild and moody character, whom he met in Tirnovo and looked up again in Varna. In 'A Youthful Journey' Paddy's time with both of them, and what they did together, is expanded, embroidered and elaborated a long way beyond the short entries of the diary, although the diary supports the bare bones of each story.

It is also worth looking at how he used the Green Diary in his two published works. On page 248 of *A Time of Gifts* he writes: 'I can't resist using a few passages of this old diary here and there. I have not interfered with the text except for cutting and condensing and clearing up obscurities.' Needless to say, he did more than that. His tidies up the raw style of his youth, and removes some uncharitable remarks about the brutal-looking faces of the Czech cavalry. Two incidents where his hand was kissed by old female servants have been inserted, as has the passage with the Slovak schoolmaster. The order of events is rearranged, and two informal quotations (Elijah fed by ravens, the gold bar of heaven) are introduced. The line from Tennyson's 'Locksley Hall' is quoted correctly in *A Time of Gifts*, while used rather more loosely in the diary: admiring two gypsy girls he writes, 'I must say, I understand those chaps who take some swarthy bride to rear their dusky race.' He is fascinated by the gypsies, and the diary contains a long passage on the effect their music has on the Hungarians. He certainly felt the de-barbarizing influence of Pips Schey, as the passage quoted about their long walks in Chapter 4 shows; but the significance of his stay at Kövecses is given more depth and richness in *A Time of Gifts*, no doubt as a result of the passing of time. Schey's parting gift of the volume of Hölderlin is not mentioned in the diary, though the cigars and the tobacco are.

Between the time he went to bed in Esztergom on the night of 31 March 1934 (Easter Saturday) and 14 August, when the diary resumes (at Lom in Bulgaria), Paddy wrote nothing. So the diary was of no use to him in recreating the long summer of 1934, which is the subject of *Between the Woods and the Water*.

But although his use of the Green Diary is relatively slight, Paddy attached enormous importance to it. When the diary was misplaced, which happened quite often, he was not happy until it turned up again: it was a talisman, a holy relic, like his second passport, which he kept all his life. The diary's great importance is that it survived. It is proof that that extraordinary walk did take place; it all really happened.

APPENDIX II

Patrick Leigh Fermor's Walk across Europe,
1933–5

This table does not include every place mentioned in the published and unpublished accounts that Paddy wrote about his walk. It is merely a way of expressing the chronology, and highlights the gaps and the overlaps.

– mentioned
★ described

	The Green Diary, 1934–5	(vol. III) 'A Youthful Journey' 1963–4	(vol. I) A Time of Gifts 1977	(vol. II) Between the Woods and the Water, 1986
London			★	
Holland				
Rotterdam		–	★	
Germany				
Heidelberg		–	★	
Munich		–	★	
Austria				
Pottenbrunn			★	
Vienna		–	★	
Czechoslovakia				
Bratislava	★	–	★	
Prague		–	★	
Kövecses	★	★	★	
Hungary				
Esztergom	★	★	★	★
Budapest		★		★
Szolnok		–		★
Körösladány		–		★

Vesztö		–	★
Doboz		–	★
Békéscsaba		–	★
O'Kígyós		–	★
Lökösháza			★
Rumania			
Zám		★	★
Guraszáda		★	★
Alba Iulia			★
Cluj			★
Sighişoara			★
Caransebeş		★	★
Iron Gates		★	★
Giurgiu	★	★	
Bucharest	★	★	
Bulgaria			
Lom	★	★	
Sofia	★	★	
Rila	★	★	
Plovdiv	★	★	
Karlovo	★	★	
Shipka	★	★	
Kazanlik	★	★	
Tirnovo	★	★	
Ruse	★	★	
Varna	★	★	
Nesebur	★	★	
Black Sea Cave	★	★	
Burgas	★	★	
Turkey			
Edirne	★		
Constantinople	★		
Greece			
Salonika	★		
Mount Athos	★		

Horace's Ode 1.9, 'To Thaliarchus'

The following is Paddy's youthful translation of Horace's Ode 1.9, 'To Thaliarchus', to which was owed the extraordinary moment of recognition in his encounter with General Kreipe on Crete (see page 184, above). It appeared in the December 1930 issue of his school magazine, *The Cantuarian* (Vol. XII, No. 6).

See Soracte's mighty peak stands deep in virgin snow
And soon the heavy-laden trees their white load will not know,
When the swiftly rushing rivers with the ice have ceased to flow.
Pile, O Thaliarchus, pile the good logs on the fire!
Fetch up some crusty four-year wine in cobwebbed Sabine jar!
Thus we'll drive away Jack Frost, with his biting cold so dire!
Care-free, all other matters among the gods we'll keep
They when they've checked the battling wind upon the boiling
    deep
Untossed about the cypress and the old ash tree may sleep.
Seek not to know what changes to-morrow may be found
But count as gain whatever lot the change of days brings round;
Spurn not, young friend, sweet love-making, nor yet the dances
    round,
While withered age is distant from thy youth frequent the plain,
The thronged lawns, each fashionable haunt, a crowded lane,
And at the trysting hour, e'en night-fall, softly whispered love's
    refrain.
Now doth a roguish laugh our hiding girl betray
From her dark cover, where love's token, perforce, is snatched away,
And her ill-withstanding finger but feebly bids him nay.

Acknowledgements

Paddy did not like the idea of someone writing his biography, so my first thanks must go to the late Joan Leigh Fermor, and Paddy's literary agent Anthony Sheil, for persuading him to change his mind. Originally, I was going to write this book jointly with my husband Antony Beevor; but his career as a historian took him into the great battles of the Second World War, while I had the joy of spending days on end in the company of one of the kindest, funniest and most interesting people on earth.

Many gaps in Paddy's life were filled in by Joan, although she hated talking about herself; and for the story of his parents and grandparents, I am much indebted to Paddy's nephew and niece, Miles Fenton and Francesca Willoughby, the children of his sister, the late Vanessa Fenton. I also had invaluable assistance from Francis Fermor, Rosalind Ambler, and Sheila Fermor-Clarkson. On Joan's side of the family, I would like to thank Michael and Joey Casey, and Robert and Bridget Kenward.

This book could not have been written without Paddy's closest friends, particularly Magouche Fielding, the late Andrew Devonshire and Deborah Devonshire, Janetta and Jaime Parladé, the late George Jellicoe and Philippa Jellicoe, and Olivia Stewart; also John Craxton, who did the jacket illustrations for all Paddy's most important books, and Paddy's publisher, the late Jock Murray. I would also like to thank Angela Allen, Sarah Anderson, Clare Arron, Alan Baker, Elpida Beloyannis, Freda Berkeley, William Blacker, Melvyn Bragg, the late John Campbell, Sheila Campbell, Pamela Cantacuzene, Sherban Cantacuzino, Mark Carleton-Smith, the late Maurice Cardiff, Dr Christian Carritt, Elizabeth Chatwin, Peter Chenery, Anne Chisholm, Cressida Connolly, Hayward Cutting, William Dalrymple, the late

Michael Davie, William Davies, Ben Downing, Pamela Egremont, Jason Elliott, Patrick Fairweather, Rudolf Fischer, Reg Gadney, Frank and the late Kitty Giles, Jason Goodwin, Imogen Grundon, Alexandra Hadjimichalis, the late Billa Harrod, Max Hastings, the late Dorothy Heber-Percy, the late Priscilla Hedley, the late Canon Ingram Hill, Christopher Hourmouzios, Christopher Hudson, Louisa Lane Fox, Robin Lane Fox, Xara Kiosse, Leda Kostakis, the late Jon van Leuwen, Deirdre Levi, Michael Llewellyn Smith, Professor Peter Mackridge, Helen Marchant, Rosanna Marston, David Mason, Nadia and Jean-Marc Mitterer, Caroline Moorehead, Fionn Morgan, Charlotte Mosley, the late Sophie Moss, the late William Mostyn-Owen, Diane Naylor, Anne Norwich, Chloe Obolensky, Frances Osborne, Mrs Barrie Pitt, Heulyn Rayner, Rob Rayner, Dr Patrick Reade, Hamish Robinson, Miranda Rothschild, Marie-Lyse Ruhemann, the late Steven Runciman, Alec Russell, Tom Sawford, Nicholas Shakespeare, the late David Smiley, Xan Smiley, John Stathatos, Charlotte Szapary, Santiago de Tamaron, Damaris Stewart, Colin Thubron, Ioanna Tsangarakis, Peter Tzanetakis and Tonia Tzanetaki-Yanidi, Miklos Vajda, Joachim Voigt, Rita Walker, Sara Wheeler, Joan Winterkorn, Mary Wood and Kyril Zinovieff.

I am particularly grateful to Biddy Hubbard, Allegra and Tony Huston, Lyndall Passerini-Hopkinson and David Pryce-Jones for allowing me to use letters and diaries that provided unique insights into Paddy's life; to Robert Harding, for allowing me to study, and quote from, the first autograph manuscript of *A Time of Gifts*; to Rudolf Fischer, who gave me such invaluable assistance on the chapters dealing with Hungary and Rumania; and to Tim Todd, who answered so many questions about the Kreipe Operation. Gabriella Bullock and Isabelle Cole not only gave me access to the unpublished diary of their father, William Stanley Moss, but also kindly allowed me to use several of his photographs. Paul Pollak and Peter Henderson have guided me through the Archive of the King's School, Canterbury. Simon Fenwick, who made the initial catalogue of Paddy's archive, found the last lines of the book, as well as many other treasures that I had overlooked; and I am grateful to Professor Roderick Beaton for correcting my brief descriptions of twentieth-century Greek politics.

It would have been impossible to chart the gestation of Paddy's books without his letters to his publisher, Jock Murray; and for giving me access to these and all Paddy-related papers at Albemarle Street, I owe a huge debt of thanks to John and Virginia Murray. Thanks to their Charitable Trust, the papers of Patrick Leigh Fermor have now found a permanent home in the John Murray Archive, held in the National Library of Scotland, which also has the photographs of Joan Leigh Fermor. I am grateful to David McClay, the archivist, for giving me a new perspective on her work, and to the Trustees of the National Library of Scotland for allowing me to reproduce her photographs in this book. I would also like to thank the Department of Special Collections and Archives of the McFarlin Library, the University of Tulsa, for permission to quote from the papers of Cyril Connolly; and the Special Collections Research Center of the Morris Library, University of Southern Illinois, for permission to quote from the papers of Lawrence Durrell. Thanks too to the librarians and archivists of the Travellers Club, the Northamptonshire Record Office, the Geological Society of London, the National Archives at Kew, the Gennadius Library in Athens, and the London Library.

In 2008 I joined an expedition to Crete, organized by Chris Paul and Alun Davies. Their aim was to retrace the route taken by the kidnappers of General Kreipe. Thanks to the good offices of Colonel Theodore Kitsos of the Greek Embassy in London, we were accompanied by Nicos Frankioudakis of the Greek Armed Forces who acted as guide and interpreter; and with his help, we were able to talk to people who still had vivid memories of the Kreipe Operation. I was only with them for a few days, and failed to climb Mount Ida, but the experience was unforgettable. I would also like to mention the late Ralph Stockbridge. He and Paddy were both in occupied Crete, and their correspondence reveals how perceptions of the Kreipe Operation changed over the years.

Felicity Bryan, my agent, and my editor Roland Philipps, have given me unfailing support and encouragement, and the book is more readable thanks to the work of Howard Davies. I would also like to thank Douglas Matthews who compiled the index, Rodney Paull who drew the maps, Caroline Westmore and Rosie Gailer at John Murray, and Sara Marafini, who designed the stunningly beautiful jacket.

Paddy used to say that when writing a book, it is very important to keep an ideal reader in mind. I have two. One is my father, John Julius Norwich, and the other is Antony Beevor. I owe them both more than I can say.

Illustration Acknowledgements

Courtesy of Patrick Fairweather: 16 above. Courtesy of Miles Fenton: 1 below left and right. Patrick Leigh Fermor Archive, reproduced by permission of the Trustees of the National Library of Scotland: 1 above right, 2, 3, 4 below left and right, 5 above left and right, 7 below left, 8, 9 above left and right, 10 above, 11 above right and below, 12, 15 above and below left, 16 centre and below. Courtesy of Bridget Flemming: 15 below right. By permission of the Geological Society of London: 1 above left. Harry Gillard: 13 above. Courtesy of Mrs Biddy Hubbard: 4 above left. Courtesy of Allegra Huston: 13 below right. Courtesy of Philippa Jellicoe: 14 below right. © the Estate of William Stanley Moss, reproduced by permission: 6, 7 above and below right. Courtesy of John Murray Collection: 4 above right, 9 below (photograph by Joan Leigh Fermor), 14 below left. Reproduced by permission of the Trustees of the National Library of Scotland (photographs by Joan Leigh Fermor): 5 below left and right, 10 below left and right, 11 above left, 14 above. Courtesy of Lyndall Passerini-Hopkinson (photograph by Josephine Powell): 13 below left.

Notes

The following abbreviations are used in the ensuing notes:

AC   Artemis Cooper
AF   Ann Fleming
BC   Balasha Cantacuzene
DC   Diana Cooper
DD   Deborah Devonshire
FP   Family papers held by Miles Fenton, PLF's nephew
JGM   John Grey Murray
JMC   John Murray Collection
JR   Joan Rayner, until 1968 when she becomes . . .
JLF   . . . Joan Leigh Fermor
LPH   Lyndall Passerini-Hopkinson
PLF   Patrick Leigh Fermor
PLFA   Patrick Leigh Fermor Archive
WSM   William Stanley Moss

Unless otherwise stated, all the papers, notebooks, manuscripts, typescripts and letters cited are in the Patrick Leigh Fermor Archive. In 2012, with a grant from the John Murray Charitable Trust, this was bought by the National Library of Scotland.

The letters of John Grey Murray, his memos, and all the papers concerning the editing and publication of PLF's books form part of the John Murray Collection. This will eventually join the John Murray Archive in the National Library of Scotland, but is currently housed in the John Murray premises in Albemarle Street.

Chapter 1: Neverland
Sources consulted on PLF's family include interviews with PLF, the late Francesca Willoughby (PLF's niece), Miles Fenton (PLF's nephew), Mrs Priscilla Hedley, Mrs Rosanna Marston; papers of Lewis Leigh Fermor held

in the Royal Geological Society, London; papers in the Northamptonshire Record Office; Ambler family papers belonging to Rosalind Ambler; and papers held by Miles Fenton.

1. PLF, *A Time of Gifts*, p.36.
2. Ibid., pp. 36–7.
3. Letter from Mrs Charles Ambler, 17 February 1909 (FP).
4. Lewis Leigh Fermor to Mrs Charles Ambler, 1 July 1910 (FP).
5. PLF, *A Time of Gifts*, pp. 2–3.
6. *The Pleasure of Reading*, ed. Antonia Fraser (Bloomsbury, 1992), pp. 35–6.
7. PLF to AC.
8. PLF, *A Time of Gifts*, p.3.
9. PLF to AC.
10. PLF, 'A Youthful Journey', p.382.
11. PLF to AC.
12. PLF, *A Time of Gifts*, p.4.
13. Letter to PLF from Deryck Winbolt-Lewis, 12 September 1987.
14. Æileen LF to Mrs Charles Ambler, 1 February 1923, from 3 Primrose Hill Studios (FP).
15. PLF to Æileen LF.

Chapter 2: The Plan
Sources consulted include interviews with the late Canon Ingram Hill, Paul Pollak, then Archivist of the King's School, Canterbury, and with Mr A. C. Baker.

1. Interview with the late Canon Ingram Hill, 2002.
2. PLF, autograph MS of *A Time of Gifts*, Ch. V, 38–9.
3. PLF, *A Time of Gifts*, p.8.
4. Alan Watts, *In My Own Way* (Jonathan Cape, 1973), p.73.
5. Ibid., p.118.
6. PLF, 'A Youthful Journey', p.375.
7. PLF, *Mani*, p.195.
8. PLF, *A Time of Gifts*, p.8.
9. PLF to AC.
10. PLF, 'All Saints' (short story), *The Cantuarian* (December 1929), Vol. XII, No. 3, p.151.
11. PLF, 'Phoebe' (poem), *The Cantuarian* (March 1930), Vol. XII, No. 4, pp.196–7.
12. PLF, 'To Thea' (poem), *The Cantuarian* (July 1930), Vol. XII, No. 5, p.253.
13. PLF to AC.

14. PLF, 'Raiding Song of the Vandals' (poem), *The Cantuarian* (July 1932), Vol. XII, No. 11.
15–16. PLF, *A Time of Gifts*, pp. 8–9.
17. PLF to AC.
18. PLF, *A Time of Gifts*, p.10.
19. PLF, 'A Youthful Journey', p.380.
20. PLF, *A Time of Gifts*, p.11.
21. Ibid., p.110.
22. PLF to AC.
23. PLF, *A Time of Gifts*, p.113.
24. PLF, autograph MS of *A Time of Gifts*, Ch. V, 40.
25. Ibid., Ch. V, 39.
26. PLF, *A Time of Gifts*, p.113.
27. Ibid., p.11.
28. Ibid., p.12.
29. PLF to AC; see Esmond Romilly, *Boadilla* (London, 1937; Macdonald, 1971), pp. 21–3.
30. PLF, autograph MS of *A Time of Gifts*, Ch. V, 41.
31. PLF notebook, salami-patterned cover, *c.* 1963.
32. PLF, *A Time of Gifts*, p.14.
33. PLF to AC.
34. PLF to AC.
35. PLF, 'A Youthful Journey', p.384.

Chapter 3: 'Zu Fuss nach Konstantinopel'
Nick Hunt's *After the Woods and the Water* (http://afterthewoodsandthewater. wordpress.com) proves that PLF's walk across Europe can still be done, and includes photographs of the landscapes he passed through and houses that he stayed in. To be published by Arcadia in 2013.

1. PLF, *A Time of Gifts*, p.20.
2. Ibid., p.24.
3. Gareth Jones, 'Hitler's Policy Towards the East', *Western Mail*, 8 June 1933.
4. PLF, *A Time of Gifts*, p.32.
5. Ibid., p.34.
6. PLF, autograph MS of *A Time of Gifts*, Ch. II, 3.
7–8. PLF, *A Time of Gifts*, pp. 116–17.
9. PLF, 'A Youthful Journey', p.4.
10. Ibid., p.8.

11–12. PLF, *A Time of Gifts*, p.60.

13. PLF, Katounia notebook, *c.* 1963, cream crocodile cover.

14. PLF, autograph MS of *A Time of Gifts*, Ch. V, 50, 51.

15. Daniel Guérin, *The Brown Plague* (*La Peste brune*) (Duke University Press, 1994), p.91.

16. PLF, *A Time of Gifts*, pp. 86–7.

17. Ibid., p.97.

18. Ibid., pp. 72–5.

19. PLF, 'A Youthful Journey', p.12.

20. PLF, *A Time of Gifts*, p.121.

21. Stefan Zweig, *The World of Yesterday* (London, 1943; University of Nebraska Press, 1964), p.281.

22. See Tim Kirk, *Nazism and the Working Class in Austria* (Cambridge University Press, 2002), p.43.

23. PLF, Morocco notebook, 1963.

24. Stefan Zweig, op. cit., pp. 290–91.

25. PLF, *A Time of Gifts*, p.185; PLF to AC.

26. PLF, autograph MS of *A Time of Gifts*, Ch. VIII, (b)4.

27. PLF, *A Time of Gifts*, pp. 197–8.

28. Ibid., p.207.

Chapter 4: An Enchanted Summer

1. PLF, *A Time of Gifts*, p.213.

2. Ibid., p.216.

3. Ibid., p.223.

4. Ibid., p.229.

5. Ibid., p.245.

6. Ibid., p.255.

7. PLF, Green Diary TS, p.9.

8. Ibid., p.12.

9. PLF, *A Time of Gifts*, p.281.

10. PLF, Green Diary TS, p.26.

11. PLF, *Between the Woods and the Water*, pp. 22–3.

12. Ibid., p.30.

13. PLF, 'A Youthful Journey', p.23.

14. PLF, *Between the Woods and the Water*, p.58.

15. Ibid., p.44.

16. PLF to AC.

17. PLF, *Between the Woods and the Water*, p.75.

18. Ibid., p.77.

19. Dervla Murphy, *To Transylvania and Beyond* (John Murray, 1992), p.iii.
20. PLF, 'Travels in a Land before Darkness Fell', *Weekend Telegraph*, 12 May 1990.
21. Ibid.
22. PLF, *Between the Woods and the Water*, p.111.
23. Ibid., p.95.
24. PLF, 'A Youthful Journey', p.222.
25. Daphne Fielding to DC.
26. PLF, 'A Youthful Journey', pp. 54–5.
27. PLF to JGM, undated, from Katounia, *c.* November 1963 (JMC).
28. PLF, *Between the Woods and the Water*, p.130.
29. Rudolf Fischer to AC, February 2012.
30. Ibid.
31. Xenia Csernovits to PLF, undated, ?June 2000; Xenia arraigned for murder: conversation with Miklós Vajda; Rudolf Fischer to AC, 1 March 2007.
32. PLF, 'A Youthful Journey', p.63; *Between the Woods and the Water*, p.197.

Chapter 5: Bulgaria to Mount Athos
1. PLF, 'A Youthful Journey', p.71.
2. PLF, Green Diary TS, p.31.
3. Ibid., pp. 33–4.
4. Ibid., p.35.
5. PLF, Bulgarian notebook, 1988.
6. PLF, Green Diary TS, p.41.
7. PLF, 'Roger Hinks: A Portrait Memoir': see *The Gymnasium of the Mind: The Journals of Roger Hinks 1933–1963*, ed. John Goldsmith (Michael Russell, 1984).
8. Conversation with Sir Steven Runciman, May 2000.
9. PLF, 'A Youthful Journey', p.97.
10. PLF, Notebook 1962, Rome.
11. PLF, Green Diary TS, 22 September, p.49.
12. PLF, 1963 notebook, Katounia.
13. PLF, Green Diary TS, p.50.
14. PLF, 'A Youthful Journey', p.127; quotation from 'Nous n'irons plus au bois', by Théodore de Banville.
15. PLF, Green Diary TS, pp. 51–2.
16. Ibid., p.54.
17. Ibid., p.56.
18. Ibid., pp. 20–22.

19. Ibid., p.57.
20. Ibid., p.60.
21. PLF, 'A Youthful Journey', p.162.
22. Ibid., p.186.
23. PLF, Green Diary TS, p.69.
24. Ibid., p.73.
25. PLF to AC.
26. PLF, Green Diary TS, p.77.
27. Ibid., p.85.
28. Ibid., p.88.
29. Ibid., p.91.
30. Ben Downing, 'A Visit with Patrick Leigh Fermor', *Paris Review*, No. 65 (Spring 2003), p.192.
31. PLF, Green Diary TS, p.92.
32. Ibid., p.96.
33. Ibid., p.97.
34. Ben Downing, op. cit., p.193.
35. PLF, Green Diary TS, p.104.
36. Ibid., p.45.
37. PLF to AC.
38. PLF, Green Diary TS, pp. 109–10.
39. Ibid., p.123.
40. Ibid., p.124.
41. Ibid., p.127.
42. Ibid., p.135.
43. Ibid., p.137.
44. Ibid., pp. 137–8.
45. Ibid., p.140.
46. Ibid., p.141.
47. Ibid., p.172.
48. Ibid., p.174.
49. PLF, 'First Journey in Greece', p.5.
50. PLF, Green Diary TS, p.182.
51. Ibid., pp. 180–81.
52. Ibid., p.183.
53. Ibid., p.189.
54. Ibid., p.222. '*Fellers*' appears in the diary, although PLF did say that Father Belisarios had used a stronger word at the time.

Chapter 6: Balasha
1. PLF to AC.
2. Email to AC from John Stathatos, July 2011.
3. PLF to JGM, 29 August 1988 (JMC).
4. PLF, *Roumeli*, p.49.
5. Ibid., p.30.
6. Ibid., pp. 51, 53.
7. Ibid., p.49 footnote.
8. Email from John Stathatos to AC, February 2012.
9. PLF to AC.
10. BC to PLF, 17 April 1970.
11. PLF, 'The Aftermath of Travel', informal talk given at the Gennadion Library, Athens, 18 March 1997.
12. PLF to AC.
13. 'Biddy's Băleni': Mrs Biddy Hubbard's diary of her time at Băleni, summer 1938.
14. PLF, 'Travels in a Land before Darkness Fell', *Weekend Telegraph*, 12 May 1990.
15. Ibid.
16. PLF to AC.
17. PLF to AC.
18. PLF, 'Travels in a Land before Darkness Fell'.
19–20. PLF, unpublished fragment, 'Westwards from the City', pp. 4–8.
21. PLF to AC.
22. *Authors take sides on the Spanish Civil War*, Left Review pamphlet, November 1937.
23. BC to PLF, 16 March 1968.
24–25. PLF to DD, 31 January 1992, *In Tearing Haste*, p.283; also Frances Osborne, *The Bolter* (Virago Books, 2008), pp. 230–31.
26. PLF to AC.
27. BC to Serge Cantacuzene-Speransky, 1938.
28. Biddy Hubbard, 'Biddy's Băleni', TS, pp. 11, 8.
29. BC to Serge Cantacuzene-Speransky, 1938, p.21.
30. PLF to JGM, 20 February 1993 (JMC).
31. Roger Hudson to JGM, 23 April 1991 (JMC).
32. *The World Mine Oyster: The Memoirs of Matyla Ghyka KCVO, MC* (Heinemann, 1961), introduction by PLF.

Chapter 7: An Intelligence Officer
1. BC to PLF, 27 January 1946.

2. PLF to AC.

3. PLF's Service Record, 1939–46, Caterham Military Hospital, 16 December 1939.

4. PLF to AC.

5. WSM, MS diary, p.17 (memories of Corporal Hibberd).

6. Biddy Hubbard, diary, 12 January 1940.

7. PLF to Adrian Pryce-Jones, 1 February 1940.

8. The Frank Delaney Show, 27 November 1982.

9. PLF's Service Record, 1939–46.

10. PLF notebook, SO book 129.

11. PLF, Tribute to Deborah Devonshire on her eightieth birthday, *Daily Telegraph*, 31 March 2000.

12–15. PLF notebook, SO book 129.

16. PLF, Tribute to Deborah Devonshire on her eightieth birthday, *Daily Telegraph*, 31 March 2000.

17. PLF notebook, SO book 129.

18. PLF to AC.

19. PLF to AC.

20. C. M. Woodhouse, *Something Ventured* (Granada, 1982), pp. 9–10.

21. PLF notebook, SO book 129.

22. PLF to AC.

23. Antony Beevor, *Crete: The Battle and the Resistance* (London, 1991), p.10.

24–25. PLF, *Remembering George Katsimbalis*, New Griffon Series No. 3 (Athens: Gennadius Library, 1998).

26–30. PLF to AC.

31–32. Lt Col. P. L. Smith-Dorrien, 'Account of the Evacuation of Lt Col. P. L. Smith-Dorrien and Party from Greece, 5 May 1941' (PLFA).

33–35. PLF to AC.

36. Antony Beevor, op. cit., pp. 207–8.

37. Ibid., p.243.

38. Charles Johnston, wartime notebook, undated; quoted Artemis Cooper, *Cairo in the War 1939–1945* (Hamish Hamilton, 1989), p.222.

39. PLF to AC.

40. PLF, Narkover notebook, 29 January 1942.

41. Ibid., 6 February 1942.

42. PLF, personal memoir of Costa Achillopoulos, undated.

Chapter 8: Crete and General Carta
For the most acurate chronology of events in occupied Crete, PLF always cited N. A. Kokonas MD, *The Cretan Resistance 1941–1945* (Rethymnon,

1992), with prologue by Jack Smith-Hughes and forewords by R. H. Stockbridge and PLF. This is based on Lieutenant Colonel T. J. Dunbabin's Final Report on SOE Missions in Crete, NA HS5/724. PLF's personal reports from Crete, between 5 January 1943 and 30 March 1944, are in NA HS5/728. The one on the capture of General Kreipe is NA HS5/418.

1. Antony Beevor, *Crete: The Battle and the Resistance* (London, 1991), p.239.
2. Xan Fielding, *Hide and Seek* (first published 1954; George Mann, 1973), p.23.
3. Ibid., p.55.
4. Ibid., p.75.
5. N. A. Kokonas, *The Cretan Resistance 1941–1945* (Rethymnon, 1992), p.46; Joint Planning Staff paper No. 99, dated 22 June 1942.
6. PLF, Report I, 5 January 1943, p.9.
7. Xan Fielding, op. cit., p.87.
8. George Psychoundakis, *The Cretan Runner: His Story of the German Occupation*, translation and introduction by PLF (John Murray, 1955; paperback edition, 1988), p.2.
9. PLF to AC.
10. PLF, Report I, 5 January 1943, p.23.
11. Letter from Major General Mark Carleton-Smith to AC, 5 July 2011.
12. George Psychoundakis, op. cit., p.85, PLF's note.
13. PLF, Report I, 5 January 1943, p.25.
14. PLF to AC.
15. PLF, Report I, 5 January 1943, pp. 9–10.
16. Xan Fielding, op. cit., p.127.
17. Ibid., p.126.
18. Ibid., p.87.
19. PLF, Report I, 5 January 1943, p.26.
20. Xan Fielding, op. cit., p.133.
21. George Psychoundakis, op. cit., p.103.
22. For PLF's description of Oak Apple Day: see his Report I, 5 January 1943, p.27.
23. Ibid., p.28.
24. PLF, Report II, 27 April 1943, p.39.
25. Ibid., p.40.
26. Ibid., p.41.
27. PLF, Report III, May–June 1943, pp. 9–10.
28. Ibid., p.12.
29. Ibid., p.13.

30. N. A. Kokonas, op. cit., p.62.
31. PLF, 'The Spiriting Away of General Carta', unpublished and unfinished account, TS, p.2.
32. PLF, Afterword to the Folio edition of W. S. Moss's *Ill Met by Moonlight* (2001), p.198.
33. PLF, Report V, 3 September 1943, p.3.
34. PLF, 'The Spiriting Away of General Carta', op. cit., p.11.
35. Ibid., p.14.
36. Ibid., p.15.
37. Antony Beevor, op. cit., p.290.
38. PLF, Afterword to the Folio edition of W. S. Moss's *Ill Met by Moonlight* (2001), p.200.
39. Ibid.
40. Ibid., p.202.

Chapter 9: Setting the Trap
This chapter and the one that follows relies on William Stanley Moss's *Ill Met by Moonlight* (Folio edition, 2001), William Stanley Moss's complete MS diary, and PLF's own account of the Kreipe Operation, written in 1966–7. Entitled 'Abducting a General', it has not yet been published in full. (How it came to be written is described in Chapter 19.)

1. Mark Mazower, *Inside Hitler's Greece* (Yale, 2001), p.108.
2. John S. Koliopoulos and Thanos M. Veremis, *Modern Greece: A History since 1821* (Wiley–Blackwell, 2010), p.112.
3. C. M. Woodhouse, *The Apple of Discord* (Hutchinson, 1948), p.150.
4. Richard Clogg, *A Concise History of Modern Greece* (Cambridge University Press, 2002), p.146.
5. PLF, 'The First Ball at Tara', unpublished TS, p.3; also WSM, MS diary, p.9.
6. David Smiley to AC, 2007.
7. Bickham Sweet-Escott, *Baker Street Irregular* (London, 1965), pp. 197–8.
8. A. M. Rendel, *Appointment in Crete* (London, 1953), pp. 133–4.
9. PLF, 'Abducting a General', p.8.
10. WSM, MS diary, p.32.
11. PLF, 'Abducting a General', pp. 14–15.
12. Ibid., p.15.
13. Ibid.
14. Ibid., p.25.

Chapter 10: The Hussar Stunt
Much work has been done on retracing, as closely as possible, the route taken by General Kreipe and his kidnappers. For this, and a great deal more information on the Kreipe Operation, see www.illmetbymoonlight.info.

1–2. PLF, 'Abducting a General', p.27.

3. Ibid., p.29.

4. Ibid., p.30.

5–6. Ibid., p.32.

7. Ibid., p.33.

8. Ibid., p.37.

9. Ibid.

10. PLF, *A Time of Gifts*, pp. 73–4; see also Appendix III, p.396.

11. PLF, 'Abducting a General', p.46.

12. Excerpt from PLF's translation of Giorgios Phrangoulitakis, *Eagles of Mount Ida*, p.8 (unpublished TS: PLFA).

13. PLF, 'Abducting a General', pp. 46–7.

14–15. Ibid., pp. 48–51.

16. Ibid., p.55.

17. WSM, *Ill Met by Moonlight*, op. cit., p.158.

18. PLF, 'Abducting a General', p.82.

19. WSM, *Ill Met by Moonlight*, op. cit., p.165.

20. PLF, 'Abducting a General', p.84.

21. Ibid., p.87.

22. WSM, *Ill Met by Moonlight*, op. cit., p.170.

23. PLF, 'Abducting a General', p.95.

24. WSM, *Ill Met by Moonlight*, op. cit., p.183.

25. PLF's Service Record, Proceedings of a Medical Board of the 15th (Scottish) General Hospital, Cairo, 14 August 1944.

26. PLF to Iain Moncreiffe, 17 November 1944, quoted in Moncreiffe's Epilogue to *Ill Met by Moonlight*, op. cit., p.191.

27. PLF to Ralph Stockbridge, 27 October 1989.

28. Final Report on SOE Missions in Crete, by Lt Col. T. J. Dunbabin, NA HS5/724; also N. A. Kokonas, *The Cretan Resistance 1941–1945* (Rethymnon, 1992), p.94.

29. PLF to Ralph Stockbridge, 2 September 1991.

30. PLF, Report VIII, 31 January 1945, p.6.

31. PLF to AC.

Chapter 11: The British Institute, Athens

1. Alan Pryce-Jones, quoted in John Craxton's obituary of Joan Leigh Fermor, *Independent*, 10 June 2003.
2. William Stanley Moss to PLF, 5 December 1944, from Tara.
3. JLF to AC.
4. PLF, 'Where Eagles Nearly Dared', *Observer*, 22 November 1981.
5–6. PLF's SOE file: TNA HS9/507/4.
7. PLF to AC.
8. PLF to AC.
9. Maurice Cardiff, *Friends Abroad* (Radcliffe Press, 1997), p.12.
10. Sir Steven Runciman to AC, May 2000.
11. Maurice Cardiff to AC, May 2001.
12. Sir Steven Runciman to AC.
13. *Remembering George Katsimbalis*, New Griffon Series No. 3 (Athens: Gennadius Library, 1998).
14. C. M. Woodhouse, *The Struggle for Greece: 1941–1949* (Hart-Davis, 1976; Hurst & Co., 2002), p.173.
15. Cyril Connolly, 'Sir Maurice Bowra: A Memoir', *Sunday Times* magazine, 17 December 1971.
16. Maurice Bowra, Report on the British Council in Greece, undated: NA BW83/1.
17. Maurice Cardiff, op. cit., pp. 15–16.
18. Maurice Cardiff to AC, May 2001.
19. PLF, *Mani*, p.31.
20. JLF to BC, 27 November 1968.
21. PLF to BC, 28 June 1975.
22–23. PLF, 'Reflections on a Marine Vulcan', memoir of Lawrence Durrell, *Twentieth Century Literature*, Vol. 33, No. 3 (Fall 1987).
24. Lawrence Durrell to Henry Miller, *c.* October 1946, *The Durrell–Miller Letters: 1935–1980*, ed. Ian S. MacNiven (Faber, 1988), pp. 199–200.
25. PLF to AC.
26. PLF to Lawrence Durrell, 18 December 1946 (Special Collections Research Center, Morris Library, Southern Illinois University, Carbondale).

Chapter 12: The Caribbean

1. PLF, letter to Jessica Mitford, 29 October 1982, from Kardamyli; for Jessica Mitford's biography, see *Faces of Philip* (Heinemann, 1984).
2. PLF, 'Travels in a Land Before Darkness Fell', *Weekend Telegraph*, 12 May 1990.
3. BC to PLF, 1 July 1947.

4. PLF to Alexander Mourouzi, 6–9 December 1948.

5. JGM, personal memos, 27 August 1947 and 30 September 1947 (JMC).

6. PLF to Manager of Harrods, 22 November 1988.

7. House Committee Minutes of the Travellers Club, April 1950.

8. PLF to AC.

9–10. PLF, Caribbean notebook.

11. PLF, *The Traveller's Tree*, p.51.

12. Ibid., p.88.

13. Ibid., p.174.

14. PLF, Caribbean notebook.

15. PLF, *The Traveller's Tree*, p.100.

16. Ibid., p.183.

17. Ibid., p.294.

18. Ibid., p.293.

19. Ibid., p.84.

20. Ibid., p.152.

21. PLF, red and blue Caribbean notebook.

22. Ibid., p.350.

23. PLF, red and blue Caribbean notebook.

24–28. PLF, British Honduras to El Salvador notebook.

29. PLF, red and blue Caribbean notebook.

30. PLF to JGM, 4 May 1948, from El Vale, Panama (JMC).

Chapter 13: Writing The Traveller's Tree

1. PLF to JGM, 4 May 1948.

2. Cyril Connolly to Mollie Connolly (his mother), 11 January 1949, quoted Jeremy Lewis, *Cyril Connolly* (Random House, 1997), p.417.

3. 'Happy Deathbeds', unpublished novel by Cyril Connolly, Cyril Vernon Connolly Papers, coll. no. 1976.002, Department of Special Collections and University Archives, McFarlin Library, University of Tulsa, Oklahoma, USA.

4. JR to PLF, undated, from Château de Curemonde.

5. Jeremy Lewis, op. cit., p.419.

6. PLF to JR, *c*. August 1948.

7. PLF, *A Time to Keep Silence* (Queen Anne Press, 1953), p.19.

8. JR to PLF, undated letter to St-Wandrille, October 1948.

9. PLF to JR, ?October–November 1948, from St-Jean de Solesmes.

10. PLF, *A Time to Keep Silence*, p.46.

11. PLF to JR, ?October–November 1948, from St-Jean de Solesmes.

12. JR to PLF, undated, addressed to PLF at Solesmes.

13. PLF, *A Time to Keep Silence*, p.60.
14. Ibid., p.70.
15. Ibid., p.66.
16. Ibid., pp. 68–9.
17. PLF to JR, March 1949.
18. 'The Wounded Gigolo' and 'On the Shores of Terra Fermor' were not published in the posthumous collection of Bowra's poems, *New Bats in Old Belfries: or some Loose Tiles*, ed. Henry Hardy and Jennifer Holmes (Oxford, 2005).
19. Alan Pryce-Jones, *The Bonus of Laughter* (Hamish Hamilton, 1987), p.29.
20. JR to PLF, from Bel Soggiorno, Taormina, Monday.
21–22. PLF, 'The Aftermath of Travel', an informal talk given at the Gennadion Library in Athens, 18 March 1997.
23. PLF to Ann Fleming, 22 February 1979.
24–25. JR to PLF, 14 July 1949, from Dumbleton.
26. Peter Quennell, *The Wanton Chase* (Collins, 1980), p.64.
27. JGM, personal memo, 9 September 1949 (JMC).
28. PLF to Edward Shackleton MP, 28 November 1949.
29. PLF to JGM, 10 February 1950, c/o Mrs Batt, Britcher Farm, Egerton, Kent (JMC).
30. Letter to JGM from T. D. Walker of Layton-Bennett, Billingham & Co., Chartered Accountants, 29 March 1950 (JMC).
31. Harold Nicolson, *Observer*, 19 March 1950.
32. PLF to AC.
33. JR to PLF, postmark 28 May 1950.

Chapter 14: Travels in Greece
1. PLF to JGM, 26 September 1950 (JMC).
2. Freya Stark to Stewart Perowne, 27 August 1950, Freya Stark Letters, Volume 6: *The Broken Road, 1947–1952*, ed. Lucy Moorehead (Michael Russell, 1981), p.188.
3. PLF, *A Time to Keep Silence*, p.81.
4. PLF to DC, 15 March 1952.
5–6. Notebook with no cover, September 1950.
7–8. Notebook: Macedonia, Thessaly, October 1950.
9. PLF, *Roumeli*, p.94.
10–11. PLF to JGM, 1 December 1950 (JMC).
12. *Times Literary Supplement*, 29 December 1950.
13. *Evening Standard*, 19 December 1950; *Scottish Daily Mail*, 16 December 1950.

14. JR to PLF, 8 January 1951.

15. PLF, Obituary of Kevin Andrews, *Independent*, 9 September 1989.

16–17. PLF on Louis MacNeice, for his biographer Jon Stallworthy, 26 September 1983.

18. PLF to JGM, undated, *c.* February–March 1951, from the island of Salamis (JMC).

19. Michael Powell, *Million-Dollar Movie* (Heinemann, 1992), pp. 123–4.

20–21. PLF to JR, 24 February 1951, from Salamis.

22. PLF to JGM, undated, *c.* February–March 1951, from Salamis (JMC).

23. Cass Canfield to JGM, 9 August 1950 (JMC).

24. JR to PLF, 6 January 1951.

25–27. PLF, grey crocodile notebook, 1951.

28–29. PLF to JGM, 12 April 1951 (JMC).

30. PLF, *Roumeli*, p.190.

31. PLF to JGM, 12 April 1951, from Astros (JMC).

32. Joan Leigh Fermor's photographs were given to the National Library of Scotland by PLF in 2010.

33–34. PLF, grey crocodile notebook, 1951.

35–36. PLF's Introduction to George Psychoundakis, *The Cretan Runner* (1988 edn), pp. 14–15.

37–38. PLF to BC, 28 June 1975.

39. Ruth Page, quoted in Meredith Daneman, *Margot Fonteyn* (Viking Books, 2004), p.270.

40. PLF to AC.

41. PLF, *Mani*, p.3.

42. Ibid., pp. 8–9.

43. Ibid., p.13.

44. PLF, black notebook, Crete–Mani 1951.

45. PLF, *Mani*, p.112.

46. PLF to JGM, 5 August 1951, from Skopelos (JMC).

Chapter 15: Byron's Slippers

1. PLF to JR, undated, *c.* February 1952, from Paris.

2. PLF to JGM, 19 March 1952 (JMC).

3. PLF to DC, 14 March 1952.

4. PLF to DC, 3 May 1952.

5. Letter from Professor Richard Dawkins to PLF, 28 April 1952 (JMC).

6. See Evelyn Waugh to DC, 10 April 1948, *Mr Wu and Mrs Stitch: The Letters of Evelyn Waugh and Diana Cooper*, ed. Artemis Cooper (Hodder & Stoughton, 1991), p.102.

7. PLF to DC, 17 July 1952.

8. PLF to AC.

9. PLF to JR, *c.* September 1952, from Chantilly.

10. PLF, *The Traveller's Tree*, p.71.

11. PLF, *Between the Woods and the Water*, p.105.

12. JGM to PLF, 8 December 1952.

13. PLF to DC, 13 December 1952.

14. PLF to DC, 2 February 1953.

15. James Pope-Hennessy, *Times Literary Supplement*, 24 July 1953.

16. Dom Joseph Coome-Tennant to PLF, 13 February 1982.

17. PLF to DC, 1 March 1953.

18. Mary Dilke to JGM, March 1953 (JMC).

19. Lawrence Durrell to PLF, undated, ?1955, from Bellapaix.

20. PLF to DC, 26 March 1953.

21. PLF to JR, 10 April 1953.

22. PLF to JR, 27 March 1953.

23–24. Peter Quennell, *The Wanton Chase* (Collins, 1980), pp. 166–70.

25. PLF to DC, June 1953.

26. *Spectator*, 5 June 1953.

27. PLF to JR, undated, *c.* June 1953.

28. PLF to DC, June 1953.

29. PLF to Vanessa Fenton, 6 July 1953.

30. Letter to JGM, *c.* July 1953, c/o British Consul, Rome (JMC).

31. PLF to JGM, 30 July 1953 (JMC).

32. PLF, *Roumeli*, p.159.

33. PLF to DC, *c.* July 1953.

34. John Cam Hobhouse, quoted in Leslie A. Marchand, *Byron: A Portrait* (John Murray, 1971), p.467.

35. PLF to DC, *c.* July 1953.

36. PLF to JGM, 30 July 1953 (JMC).

37–38. PLF to Jessica Mitford, 29 October 1982, from Kardamyli; for Mitford's biography, see *Faces of Philip* (Heinemann, 1984).

39. PLF to Lawrence Durrell, remembering an evening 'two years ago', 21 May 1955 (Special Collections Research Center, Morris Library, Southern Illinois University, Carbondale).

40. Maurice Cardiff to AC, May 2001.

41. Janetta Parladé to AC, November 2004.

42. Maurice Cardiff to AC, May 2001.

43. Lawrence Durrell, *Bitter Lemons* (London, 1957), p.105.

44. PLF to DC, 11 January 1954.

45. PLF to JR, 9 January 1954.
46. PLF to DC, 30 January 1954.
47. PLF to AC.
48. PLF to DC, 'Sunday, [c/o John Betjeman]', *c.* January/February 1954.
49. PLF to DC, 22 March 1954.
50. PLF to DC, 22 May 1954.
51–52. PLF to DC, 22 May 1954.
53. PLF to Vanessa Fenton, undated, 1954.
54. PLF to DC, 29 June 1954.
55. PLF, 'The Background of Ghika: Thoughts on a Greek Landscape', *Encounter*, February 1957.
56. PLF to JGM, 19 July 1954 (JMC).
57. Leslie Mitchell, *Maurice Bowra* (Oxford University Press, 2009), p.90.
58. PLF to JGM, 19 July 1954.
59. JR to PLF, 24 August 1954, from Amalfi.

Chapter 16: Cyprus
1. Robert Holland, *Britain and the Revolt in Cyprus 1954–1959* (Clarendon Press, 1998), p.35.
2. David Roessel, *In Byron's Shadow* (Oxford University Press, 2002), p.45.
3. PLF to Lawrence Durrell, 24 November 1954 (Special Collections Research Center, Morris Library, Southern Illinois University, Carbondale).
4. George Seferis to JR, 24 December 1954, from Beirut; see *The Correspondence of George Seferis, P. Leigh Fermor and J. Rayner (1948–1971)*, ed. Photios Ar. Demetrakopoulos and Vasiliki D. Lambropolou (Nicosia: Publications of the Centre for Academic Research, 2007). The original correspondence is held by the Gennadius Library, Athens.
5. George Seferis to PLF, 23 January 1955.
6. PLF to George Seferis, 25 May 1955, from Hydra.
7. PLF to JR, 2 January 1955, from Hydra.
8. JR to PLF, January 1955.
9. PLF to DC, 2 April 1955.
10. Ian S. McNiven, *Lawrence Durrell: A Biography* (Faber & Faber, 1998), p.421.
11–12. PLF to DC, 1 June 1955.
13. Rodis Roufos, 'Philhellenism and Primitivism', republished in *Oi metamorphoseis tou Alachriou* (Athens: Ikaros, 1971).
14. PLF to DC, 22 June 1955.
15. PLF to DC, undated, late summer 1955.

16. PLF to JGM, 17 July 1955 (JMC).
17. Ibid.
18. John Julius Norwich, address for PLF's memorial service, 15 December 2011.
19. Roderick Beaton, *George Seferis: Waiting for the Angel* (Yale, 2003), p.320.
20. Letter in Greek from George Katsimbalis to PLF, 20 March 1956.
21. George Seferis, pencilled into a letter from JR of 1 May 1956.
22. PLF to JR, 28 October 1955.
23. JR to George Seferis, 1 November 1955, from Dumbleton.
24. George Seferis to JR, 1 December 1955, from Athens.
25. PLF to JGM, undated, *c.* November 1955, from Normandy (JMC).
26. *Spectator*, 9 December 1955.
27. PLF to Vanessa Fenton, 26 February 1956.
28. PLF to DC, 26 October 1966.
29. Paul Conway, Seventieth birthday tribute to Malcolm Williamson, *Daily Mail*, 30 November 1966.
30. PLF to Xan and Daphne Fielding, quoted in *In Tearing Haste: Letters between Deborah Devonshire and Patrick Leigh Fermor*, ed. Charlotte Mosley (John Murray, 2008), p.9.
31. PLF, 'The Background of Ghika: Thoughts on a Greek Landscape', *Encounter*, February 1957.
32. PLF, 'Sounds of the Greek World', *Encounter*, Vol. VI, No. 6, June 1965, pp. 55–8.

Chapter 17: In Africa and Italy
1. PLF to DD, 18 April 1997.
2. PLF to DD, 26 August 1956.
3. PLF to JR, undated, August 1956.
4. AF to Evelyn Waugh, 27 August 1956; see *The Letters of Ann Fleming*, ed. Mark Amory (Collins Harvill, 1985), pp. 184–5.
5. PLF to DD, 26 August 1956: see *In Tearing Haste: Letters between Deborah Devonshire and Patrick Leigh Fermor*, ed. Charlotte Mosley (John Murray, 2008), pp. 19–22.
6. AF to Evelyn Waugh, 27 August 1956.
7. PLF to DD, 26 August 1956.
8. PLF, *Mani*, p.111 footnote.
9. PLF to DC, 12 November 1956.
10. Ibid.
11. PLF to WSM, 26 November 1956.

12. Michael Powell, *Million-Dollar Movie* (Heinemann, 1992), pp. 358–9.
13. PLF to DC, 28 September 1956.
14. PLF to Vanessa Fenton, 24 February 1955.
15. PLF to DC, 27 January 1957.
16. PLF to DD, 5 July 1957: see *In Tearing Haste*, op. cit., p.32.
17. PLF to DC, *c*. January 1958.
18. PLF to Xan Fielding, 1 April 1958.
19. PLF to DC, *c*. January 1958.
20. PLF to JR, 25 April 1958.
21. PLF to Xan Fielding, 1 April 1958.
22. Juliette Gréco, *Jujube* (Stock, 1982), p.201.
23. PLF to DC, March 1958.
24. John Huston, quoted in Lawrence Grobel, *The Hustons* (Bloomsbury, 1990), p.455.
25. DD to AC.
26. PLF to DD, 12 August 1958: see *In Tearing Haste*, op. cit., pp. 49–51.
27. Compton Mackenzie, *Greece in My Life* (Chatto & Windus, 1960), p.185.
28. Judy Montagu to DC, 24 October 1958.
29. PLF to LPH, 23 November 1958; LPH to AC.
30. PLF to DC, undated postcard of Pope John XXIII.
31. *Times Literary Supplement*, 19 December 1958.
32. *The Times*, 4 December 1958.
33. Lawrence Durrell to PLF, undated letter, from Faber & Faber, London.
34. PLF, *Mani*, p.241.
35. Ibid., p.207.
36. PLF to JR, undated, spring 1959.
37. PLF to LPH, 30 April 1959.
38. PLF to JR, April 1959.
39. PLF to DC, 8 June 1959; also PLF to DD, 27 July 1959: see *In Tearing Haste*, op. cit., pp. 54–5.
40. PLF to DC, 8 June 1959.
41. PLF to JR, 1 June 1959.
42. PLF to Vanessa Fenton, 29 October 1959, from Ischia.
43. PLF to JR, 1 June 1959.
44. PLF to DC, 20 August 1959.
45. PLF to DC, November 1959, from Ischia.
46. PLF to LPH, 28 October 1959.

Chapter 18: A Visit to Rumania

1. PLF to JR, undated letter, January/February 1960.
2. PLF to JGM, undated, *c.* February 1960, from Chagford (JMC).
3. Magouche Fielding to AC.
4. PLF to LPH, 8 July 1960.
5. PLF to DC, 9 September 1960.
6. PLF to DD, 23 or 24 October 1960.
7. PLF to DC, 9 September 1960.
8. PLF to DD, 23 or 24 October 1960.
9. PLF to DC, The Nones of December 1960.
10. PLF to DD, 16 February 1961.
11. PLF to Ricki Huston, 18 January 1961.
12. PLF to AC; see *In Tearing Haste: Letters between Deborah Devonshire and Patrick Leigh Fermor* (John Murray, 2008), p.108, note 3.
13. PLF to Ricki Huston, 28 April 1961.
14. George Hayim to AC, October 2010.
15. PLF to Ricki Huston, 22 June 1961, from Dinas, Pembrokeshire.
16. PLF to Ricki Huston, 17 July 1961.
17. Ricki Huston to PLF, undated.
18. PLF to Ricki Huston, 11 August 1961.
19. PLF to Lawrence Durrell, 30 October 1961 (Special Collections Research Center, Morris Library, Southern Illinois University, Carbondale).
20. PLF to DD, November 1961; see *In Tearing Haste*, op. cit., p.88.
21. Undated memo from JGM, *c.* January 1962 (JMC).
22. PLF to JGM, 4 February 1962 (JMC).
23. PLF to JGM, 9 March 1962 (JMC).
24. PLF to JR, 4 June 1962.
25. PLF to AC.
26. PLF to JR; the date '30 June 1962' has been inscribed later, the only contemporary dating being 'Tuesday'.
27–28. PLF to JR, undated letter, 'Monday 9am', ?summer/autumn 1962, from Athens.
29. JR to PLF, undated.
30. PLF to JGM, undated, *c.* January 1963, from Chester Row (JMC).
31. PLF, autograph MS of *A Time of Gifts*, Ch. XI, 10.
32. PLF to JGM, January 1963, from Chester Row (JMC).
33. PLF to JGM, 8 February 1964, from Katounia (JMC).
34. PLF to DC, 5 September 1965.
35. PLF, 'The Aftermath of Travel', an informal talk given at the Gennadion Library, Athens, 18 March 1997.

36. PLF to Aymer Maxwell, 8 November 1964.
37. PLF to JR, undated, March/April 1965, from Chester Row.
38. PLF, 'Travels in a Land before Darkness Fell', *Weekend Telegraph*, 12 May 1990.
39. Balasha's eviction from Băleni: Dorin Pintile and Mariana Pintile, *Comuna Baleni: Studiu monografic complex* (Cluj-Napoca: Editura Eurodidact, 2003).
40–41. PLF, 'Travels in a Land before Darkness Fell', *Weekend Telegraph*, 12 May 1990.
42. PLF to JR, 3 September 1965.
43. PLF to JGM, 6 July 1965 (JMC).
44–47. PLF to DC, November 1965.
48. PLF to Aymer Maxwell, undated, 1965.
49. PLF to JR, 3 September 1965.
50. PLF, *Roumeli*, p.97.
51. Ibid., p.99.
52. Ibid., p.123.
53. *The Times*, 21 April 1966.
54. Dilys Powell, *Sunday Times*, 17 April 1966.
55. 'Londoner's Diary', *Evening Standard*, 20 April 1966.
56. PLF, 'Londoner's Diary', *Evening Standard*, 25 April 1966.
57. PLF to JGM, 24 September 1966 (JMC).

Chapter 19: A Monastery Built for Two
1. PLF to AC.
2. Peter Levi, *A Bottle in the Shade* (Sinclair Stevenson, 1966), p.54.
3. PLF to DC, 30 October 1973.
4. JLF to PLF, 1971.
5. PLF to JLF, 27 April 1967, from La Tartan, Spain.
6. Barrie Pitt to PLF, 31 October 1967; PLF's article appears in *The Purnell History of the Second World War* (n.d.), Vol. 5 (of 20), No. 7, p.1984.
7. PLF to Vanessa Fenton, 8 November 1981.
8–11. PLF to BC, 26 February 1968.
12. PLF to JGM, 10 March 1968 (JMC).
13–14. PLF to JGM, 10 May 1968 (JMC).
15–17. PLF to JLF, 1 October 1968.
18–19. PLF to DC, 28 February–20 March 1969.
20. PLF to DC, undated, spring 1969.
21. John Betjeman to JLF, 29 September 1969; see John Betjeman, *Letters 1926–1984* (Methuen, 1994–5), Vol. II, pp. 389–90.

22. PLF to JGM, 17 November 1969 (JMC).

23. PLF to George Seferis, 10 December 1969.

24. George Seferis to PLF, 26 December 1969.

25–26. PLF to JGM, 17 November 1969 (JMC).

27. For PLF's review of George Seferis's *Poiémata me Zographies se Mikra Paidia*, see *Times Literary Supplement*, 28 January 1977.

28. PLF to AF, 1 July 1970.

29. Damaris Stewart to AC.

30. PLF to DC, 'Late-ish Feb', 1971.

31. PLF to JGM, mid-August 1973 (JMC).

32. PLF to JGM, 23 March 1971 (JMC).

33. PLF, autograph MS of *A Time of Gifts*, Ch. III, 14.

34. PLF, *Three Letters from the Andes* (John Murray, 1991; Penguin edition, 1992), p.21.

35. Ibid., p.36.

36. Ibid., p.50.

37. PLF to JGM, 5 or 6 September 1971 (JMC).

38. PLF to JGM, 20 September 1971 (JMC).

39. PLF to Michael Stewart, undated, early 1971.

40–41. PLF to Æileen LF, 11 May 1972.

42. PLF to DD, account of the walk in the Pindus, 28 June 1972: see *In Tearing Haste: Letters between Deborah Devonshire and Patrick Leigh Fermor* (John Murray, 2008), p.138.

Chapter 20: *Shifts in Perspective*

1. PLF to DC, 17 July 1973.

2. PLF to JGM, 29 August 1973 (JMC).

3. PLF to JGM, 18 October 1974.

4. JLF to PLF, undated, from Dumbleton.

5. Sale of English Literature and History, Sotheby's, 21 July 1988.

6. PLF to BC, 28 June 1975.

7. PLF to JGM, 4 August 1975, from Cockermouth.

8. Pamela Egremont to AC.

9. Hélène Donici to PLF, 6 December 1975.

10. PLF to JGM, August–early September 1976 (JMC).

11. PLF, 'Paradox in the Himalayas', *London Magazine*, December 1979–January 1980.

12. Vanessa Fenton to PLF, 21 December 1976.

13. PLF to Vanessa Fenton, *c.* January 1977.

14. PLF, *A Time of Gifts*, p.16.

15. See David Roessel, *Anglo-Hellenic Review*, No. 44 (Autumn 2011), p.23.
16. Ben Downing, 'A Visit with Patrick Leigh Fermor', *Paris Review*, No. 165 (Spring 2003), p.186.
17. Jan Morris, *Spectator*, 24 September 1977.
18. Dervla Murphy, *Irish Times*, 15 October 1977.
19. Frederic Raphael, *Sunday Times*, 25 September 1977.
20. Philip Toynbee, *Observer*, 25 September 1977.
21. Mary Wood to AC.
22. PLF to JLF, 3 April 1979, from Kardamyli; the plaque was eventually put up in Heraklion.
23. From a letter in Greek from PLF's Cretan friends, quoted by PLF to JGM, late June 1979.
24. PLF to JGM, 16 October 1980.
25. AF to Michael Astor, 10 July 1978; see *The Letters of Ann Fleming*, ed. Mark Amory (Collins Harvill, 1985), p.418.
26. JLF to Vanessa Fenton, 17 September 1982.
27. PLF to DD, 7 December 1985.
28. PLF to Aymer Maxwell, 22 April 1980.
29. PLF on Auberon Herbert, *Auberon Herbert: A Composite Memoir*, ed. John Jolliffe (privately published, 1976); PLF on Roger Hinks, *The Gymnasium of the Mind: The Journals of Roger Hinks 1933–1963*, ed. John Goldsmith, (Michael Russell, 1984); PLF on Iain Moncreiffe, from *Sir Iain Moncreiffe of that Ilk: An Informal Portrait*, ed. John Jolliffe (privately published, 1986). All can be found in PLF, *Words of Mercury*, ed. Artemis Cooper (John Murray, 2004).
30. Stephen Spender to PLF, 1 December 1983, from Mas St Jerome.
31. PLF to Vanessa Fenton, spring 1982.
32. PLF to DD, 16 July 1982.
33. PLF to Vanessa Fenton, spring 1982.
34. PLF to DD, 16 July 1982.
35. PLF to Vanessa Fenton, spring 1982.
36. PLF, 'A Slow Change of Continents', 13 October 1984.
37. Nicholas Shakespeare, *Bruce Chatwin* (Harvill Press, 1999), p.445.
38. Ibid., pp. 447–8.
39. Ibid., p.446.
40. PLF to JGM, 23 August 1985 (JMC).
41. PLF to JGM, undated (JMC).
42. PLF, *Between the Woods and the Water*, p.13.
43. PLF to AC.
44. PLF to DD, 7 December 1985.

45. Graham Coster, *Independent*, 16 October 1986.

46. PLF, *Between the Woods and the Water*, p.69.

47. John Ure, *Times Literary Supplement*, 7 October 1986.

48. John Gross *Arizona Republic*, 14 December 1986.

49. TS of the South Bank Show on Patrick Leigh Fermor, a Willow Films Production for London Weekend Television, transcript of interview with Melvyn Bragg, pp. 55–7.

50. Cyril Connolly, *Enemies of Promise* (Routledge & Kegan Paul, 1949), p.III.

Chapter 21: 'For now the time of gifts is gone'
New information on PLF, plus photographs, tributes, articles and recollections are emerging all the time. Most of these find their way on to http://patrickleighfermor.wordpress.com, a blog written and coordinated by Tom Sawford.

1. Dervla Murphy, *Transylvania and Beyond* (John Murray, 1992), p.28.

2. Janetta Parladé to AC, November 2004.

3. Alec Russell to AC, December 2011.

4. PLF, 'Ghosts that Haunt the New Dawn', *Weekend Telegraph*, 19 May 1990.

5. Clare Arron to AC, January 2012.

6. PLF, 'Ghosts that Haunt the New Dawn', *Weekend Telegraph*, 19 May 1990.

7. TS of Antony Beevor's *Crete: The Battle and the Resistance*, with corrections by PLF, p.394.

8. JLF to Janetta Parladé, 22 February 1991.

9. JLF to AC, November 2002.

10. Antony Beevor (fellow guest at the dinner) to AC.

11. PLF to DD, 18 June 1991.

12. PLF to DD, 27 July 1991.

13. JLF to Michael Stewart, 11 February 1992.

14. Colin Thubron to AC.

15. PLF to LPH, 9 August 2003, from Dumbleton.

16. Olivia Stewart to AC, 19 February 2012.

17. Mark Edwards, Letters section, *Daily Telegraph*, 2 January 2004.

18. Patrick Fairweather to AC, 8 September 2011.

19. William Blacker to AC, 16 January 2012; for PLF's review of Blacker's *Along the Enchanted Way* see *Sunday Telegraph*, 30 August 2009.

20. Charlotte Mosley to AC, 20 January 2012.

21. Charlotte Mosley to DD, summer 2007.
22. James Purdon, *Observer*, 26 July 2009.
23. Charlotte Mosley to AC.
24. Olivia Stewart to AC, 19 February 2012.
25. PLF to AC, 11 May 2011.
26. Found in PLF's bedroom in Greece, written on the title page of a short life of Marcel Proust; dated August 2010.

Select Bibliography

Almond, Mark, *The Rise and Fall of Nicolae and Elena Ceauşescu* (Chapmans, 1992)

Almonds Windmill, Lorna, *A British Achilles: The Story of George, 2nd Earl Jellicoe* (Pen & Sword, 2005)

Andrews, Kevin, *The Flight of Ikaros: Travels in Greece during the Civil War* (Weidenfeld & Nicolson, 1959)

Bailey, Roderick, *The Wildest Province: SOE in the Land of the Eagle* (Jonathan Cape, 2008)

Beaton, Roderick, *George Seferis: Waiting for the Angel* (Yale University Press, 2003)

Beevor, Antony, *Crete: The Battle and the Resistance* (John Murray, 1991)

Betjeman, John, *Letters 1926–1984*, 2 volumes, ed. Candida Lycett Green (Methuen, 1994–5)

Blacker, William, *Along the Enchanted Way: A Romanian Story* (John Murray, 2009)

Bradford, Sarah, *Sacheverell Sitwell: Splendours and Miseries* (Sinclair-Stevenson, 1993)

Byron, Robert, *The Station, Athos: Treasures and Men* (Duckworth, 1928)

——*The Byzantine Achievement: An Historical Perspective, AD 330–1453* (Routledge, 1929)

Callimachi, Princess Anne-Marie, *Yesterday Was Mine* (Falcon Press, 1952)

Campbell, John K., *Honour, Family and Patronage: A Study of Institutions and Moral Values in a Greek Mountain Community* (Oxford University Press, 1964)

Cardiff, Maurice, *Friends Abroad* (The Radcliffe Press, 1997)

Chisholm, Anne, *Frances Partridge: The Biography* (Weidenfeld & Nicolson, 2009)

Clark, Bruce, *Twice a Stranger: How Mass Expulsion Forged Modern Greece and Turkey* (Granta, 2006)

Clogg, Richard, *A Short History of Modern Greece* (Cambridge University Press, 1979)

Cocker, Mark, *Loneliness and Time: The Story of British Travel Writing* (New York: Pantheon Books, 1992)

Collins, Ian, *John Craxton* (Lund Humphries, 2011)

Connolly, Cyril, *Enemies of Promise* (Routledge, 1938)

Cooper, Artemis, *Cairo in the War: 1939–1945* (Hamish Hamilton, 1989)

Cooper, Artemis (ed.), *Mr Wu and Mrs Stitch: The Letters of Evelyn Waugh and Diana Cooper* (Hodder & Stoughton, 1991)

Dalrymple, William, *From the Holy Mountain: A Journey in the Shadow of Byzantium* (HarperCollins, 1997)

Devonshire, Deborah, and Fermor, Patrick Leigh, *In Tearing Haste: Letters between Deborah Devonshire and Patrick Leigh Fermor*, ed. Charlotte Mosley (John Murray, 2008)

Douglas, Norman, *Old Calabria* (M. Secker, 1915; M. Secker, 1930)

Du Boulay, Juliet, *Portrait of a Greek Mountain Village* (Oxford University Press, 1974)

Durrell, Lawrence, *Reflections on a Marine Venus: A Companion to the Landscape of Rhodes* (Faber & Faber, 1953)

—— *Bitter Lemons* (Faber & Faber, 1957)

Durrell, Lawrence, and Miller, Henry, *The Durrell–Miller Letters 1935–1980*, ed. Ian S. MacNiven (Faber & Faber, 1988)

Eames, Andrew, *Blue River, Black Sea: A Journey Along the Danube to the Heart of the New Europe* (Bantam Press, 2009)

Fermor, Patrick Leigh, *The Traveller's Tree* (John Murray, 1950)

—— *A Time to Keep Silence* (Queen Anne Press, 1953)

—— *The Violins of Saint-Jacques* (John Murray, 1953)

—— *Mani* (John Murray, 1958)

—— *Roumeli* (John Murray, 1966)

—— *A Time of Gifts* (John Murray, 1977)

—— *Between the Woods and the Water* (John Murray, 1986)

—— *Three Letters from the Andes* (John Murray, 1991)

—— *Words of Mercury*, ed. Artemis Cooper (John Murray, 2003)

Fielding, Xan, *Hide and Seek: The Story of a War-Time Agent* (Secker & Warburg, 1954)

—— *The Stronghold: An Account of Four Seasons in the White Mountains* (Secker & Warburg, 1953)

Fleming, Ann, *The Letters of Ann Fleming,* ed. Mark Amory (Collins Harvill, 1985)

Fussell, Paul, *Abroad: British Literary Travelling Between the Wars* (Oxford University Press, 1980)

Ghyka, Matyla, *The World Mine Oyster: The Memoirs of Matyla Ghyka,*

KCVO, MC, with an introduction by Patrick Leigh Fermor (Heinemann, 1961)

Goodwin, Jason, *On Foot to the Golden Horn* (Chatto & Windus, 1993)

Gréco, Juliette, *Jujube* (Paris: Stock, 1982)

Grobel, Lawrence, *The Hustons* (Bloomsbury, 1990)

Grundon, Imogen, *The Rash Adventurer: A Life of John Pendlebury* (Libri, 2007)

Guérin, Daniel, *The Brown Plague* (*La Peste brune*, 1936), translated and with an introduction by Robert Schwartzwald (Duke University Press, 1994)

Hale, Julian, *Ceauşescu's Romania: A Political Documentary* (Harrap, 1971)

Harokopos, George, *The Abduction of General Kreipe* (Crete: Kouvidis-Manouras, 2003)

—— *The Fortress Crete: 1941–1944* (Athens: B. Giannikos & Co., 1993)

Henderson, Mary, *Xenia – A Memoir: Greece 1919–1949* (Weidenfeld & Nicolson, 1988)

Holland, Robert, *Britain and the Revolt in Cyprus 1954–1959* (Clarendon Press, 1998)

Hynes, Samuel, *The Auden Generation: Literature and Politics in England in the 1930s* (Bodley Head, 1976)

Judt, Tony, *Postwar: A History of Europe since 1945* (Heinemann, 2005)

Keeley, Edmund, *Inventing Paradise: The Greek Journey 1937–1947* (New York: Farrar Strauss, 1999)

Knox, James, *Robert Byron: A Biography* (John Murray, 2003)

Kokonas, N. A., *The Cretan Resistance 1941–1945* (Rethymnon, 1992)

Kolyopoulos, John S., and Veremis, Thanos M., *Modern Greece: A History since 1821* (Wiley-Blackwell, 2010)

Lancaster, Osbert, *Classical Landscape with Figures* (John Murray, 1947)

Levi, Peter, *A Bottle in the Shade* (Sinclair-Stevenson, 1996)

Lewis, Jeremy, *Cyril Connolly: A Life* (Jonathan Cape, 1997)

Macmillan, Margaret, *Peacemakers: The Paris Peace Conference of 1919 and Its Attempt to End War* (John Murray, 2001)

MacNiven, Ian, *Lawrence Durrell: A Biography* (Faber & Faber, 1998)

Mansel, Philip, *Levant: Splendour and Catastrophe on the Mediterranean* (John Murray, 2010)

Marchand, Leslie, *Byron: A Portrait* (John Murray, 1971)

Marnham, Patrick, *Wild Mary: A Life of Mary Wesley* (Chatto & Windus, 2006)

Mason, David, *News from the Village: Aegean Friends* (California: Red Hen Press, 2010)

Mazower, Mark, *Inside Hitler's Greece: The Experience of Occupation, 1941–1944* (Yale University Press, 2001)

Mazower, Mark (ed.), *After the War Was Over: Reconstructing the Family, Nation and State in Greece, 1943–1960* (Princeton University Press, 2000)

Miller, Henry, *The Colossus of Maroussi* (San Francisco: Colt Press, 1941; Heinemann, 1960)

Mitford, Jessica, *Faces of Philip: A Biography of Philip Toynbee* (Heinemann, 1984)

Moss, William Stanley, *Ill Met by Moonlight*, with Introduction by M. R. D. Foot, Prologue and Epilogue by Iain Moncreiffe, and Afterword by Patrick Leigh Fermor (Folio Society, 2001)

—— *A War of Shadows* (T. V. Boardman & Co., 1952)

Murphy, Dervla, *Transylvania and Beyond* (John Murray, 1992)

Powell, Dilys, *The Villa Ariadne* (Hodder & Stoughton, 1973)

Powell, Michael, *Million-Dollar Movie* (Heinemann, 1992)

Psychoundakis, George, *The Cretan Runner: His Story of the German Occupation*, ed. and trans. Patrick Leigh Fermor (John Murray, 1955)

Quennell, Peter, *The Wanton Chase* (Collins, 1980)

Raban, Jonathan, *For Love and Money: Writing, Reading, Travelling 1969–1987* (Collins Harvill, 1987)

Rendel, A. M., *Appointment in Crete* (London, 1953)

Rodocanachi, C. P., *Forever Ulysses*, trans. Patrick Leigh Fermor (New York: Viking Press, 1938)

Roessel, David, *In Byron's Shadow: Modern Greece in the English and American Imagination* (Oxford University Press, 2002)

Russell, Alec, *Prejudice and Plum Brandy: Tales of a Balkan Stringer* (Michael Joseph, 1993)

Seferis, George, Fermor, Patrick Leigh, and Rayner, Joan: *Correspondence*, ed. Photios Ar. Demetrakopoulos and Vasiliki D. Lambropolou (Nicosia: Publications of the Centre for Academic Research, 2007)

Shakespeare, Nicholas, *Bruce Chatwin* (Harvill Press, 1999)

Smiley, David, *Albanian Assignment* (Chatto & Windus, 1984)

Sweet-Escott, Bickham, *Baker Street Irregular* (London, 1965)

Veremis, Thanos, *The Military in Greek Politics from Independence to Democracy* (Montreal: Black Rose Books, 1997)

Waal, Edmund de, *The Hare with Amber Eyes* (Chatto & Windus, 2010)

Woodhouse, C. M., *The Apple of Discord* (Hutchinson, 1948)

—— *The Struggle for Greece, 1941–1949* (Hart-Davis, 1976)

—— *Something Ventured* (Granada, 1982)

Zweig, Stefan, *The World of Yesterday* (Cassell, 1943)

Index

NOTE: Works by Patrick Leigh Fermor (PLF) appear under title; works by others under author's name